THE SENSES IN RELIGIOUS COMMUNITIES, 1600–1800

Women and Gender in the Early Modern World

Series Editors:
Allyson Poska, The University of Mary Washington, USA
Abby Zanger

The study of women and gender offers some of the most vital and innovative challenges to current scholarship on the early modern period. For more than a decade now, "Women and Gender in the Early Modern World" has served as a forum for presenting fresh ideas and original approaches to the field. Interdisciplinary and multidisciplinary in scope, this Ashgate book series strives to reach beyond geographical limitations to explore the experiences of early modern women and the nature of gender in Europe, the Americas, Asia, and Africa. We welcome proposals for both single-author volumes and edited collections which expand and develop this continually evolving field of study.

Titles in the series include

Imagining Women's Conventual Spaces in France, 1600–1800
Barbara R. Woshinsky

English Women, Religion, and Textual Production, 1500–1625
Edited by Micheline White

Dominican Women and Renaissance Art
Ann Roberts

Wives, Widows, Mistresses, and Nuns in Early Modern Italy
Edited by Katherine A. McIver

Women, Reading, and the Cultural Politics of Early Modern England
Edith Snook

The Senses in Religious Communities, 1600–1800

Early Modern 'Convents of Pleasure'

NICKY HALLETT

University of Sheffield, UK

ASHGATE

Published by
Ashgate Publishing Limited
Wey Court East
Union Road
Farnham
Surrey, GU9 7PT
England

Ashgate Publishing Company
110 Cherry Street
Suite 3-1
Burlington, VT 05401-3818
USA

www.ashgate.com

British Library Cataloguing in Publication Data
Hallett, Nicky.
    The senses in religious communities, 1600–1800 : early modern 'convents of pleasure'.
    – (Women and gender in the early modern world)
    1. Monastic and religious life of women – Belgium – History – 17th century – Sources.
    2. Monastic and religious life of women – Belgium – History – 18th century – Sources.
    3. Senses and sensation – Religious aspects – Christianity. I. Title II. Series
    271.9'00493'09032-dc23

Library of Congress Cataloging-in-Publication Data
Hallett, Nicky.
    The senses in religious communities, 1600-1800 : early modern 'convents of pleasure' / by Nicky Hallett.
        p. cm. – (Women and gender in the early modern world)
    Includes bibliographical references and index.
        ISBN 978-1-4094-4946-1 (hardcover : alk. paper) – ISBN 978-1-4094-4947-8 (ebook) – ISBN 978-1-4724-0137-3 (epub) 1. Monastic and religious life of women – Europe – History – 17th century. 2. Monastic and religious life of women – Europe – History – 18th century. 3. Senses and sensation – Religious aspects – Christianity – History – 17th century. 4. Senses and sensation – Religious aspects – Christianity – History – 18th century. 5. Europe – Church history – 17th century. 6. Europe – Church history – 18th century. I. Title.
    BX4205.H35 2013
    271'.90094–dc23

2012045927

ISBN 9781409449461 (hbk)
ISBN 9781409449478 (ebk – PDF)
ISBN 9781472401373 (ebk – ePUB)

MIX
Paper from responsible sources
FSC
www.fsc.org
FSC® C018575

Printed and bound in Great Britain by the
MPG Books Group, UK.

For my Maiden aunts

Contents

Acknowledgements

My primary debt is to members of the current and early modern religious communities whose rare and wonderful insights have made this work possible. I express especially affectionate gratitude to the English Carmelite convents formerly at Lanherne in Cornwall and at Darlington in County Durham, for their support and generosity and for permission to produce studies of material from their archives, and to those in the community at St Helens, Merseyside. As I have previously noted, the warmth of their welcome has made this an inspiring journey. In particular I thank Reverend Mother Margaret Mary from Lanherne and Sister Frances Thérèse from Darlington. The late Sister Margaret at Darlington was equally kind and permissive in her encouragement.

In addition, I am very grateful to Caroline Bowden and Laurence Lux-Sterritt for their advice and support in parallel projects on the history of women's religious communities, especially that arising from Caroline's 'Who Were the Nuns?' AHRC-funded project at Queen Mary, University of London, which has laid firm and lasting foundations for future research. Together with other members of the History of Women Religious of Britain and Ireland network, most particularly Carmen Mangion, they form a richly rewarding group with whom to travel.

I also wish to thank Jaime Goodrich and Claire Walker, co-panellists in a session on nuns' writing kindly chaired by Arthur Marotti at the Renaissance Society of America Conference at Venice in April 2010, aptly delivered in a splendid Renaissance chapel. I am grateful to them and to other participants for continuing insightful discussion of some of the ideas in this book. Thanks too to those at the RSA Chicago panel on diet and disease in 2008; University of Paris Nanterre colloquium *Les Lieux de Femmes dans La Littérature Féminine de Langue Anglaise* in 2009, especially Emily Eells for her invitation to consider convents as creative spaces; and the University of York's Renaissance Studies Conference in 2010. The following have been extremely helpful with suggestions about particular elements in my study: Marie-Louise Coolahan, Jim Fitzmaurice, Mark Greengrass, Helen Hackett, Frances Harris; members of the University of Sheffield Death Group, especially Julie Ellis and Jenny Hockey; the University's Early Modern Group, particularly Marcus Nevitt, Emma Rhatigan, Cathy Shrank, Victoria Van Hyning and Gillian Woods; from English Heritage at Bolsover Castle, Crosby Stevens; from the National Portrait Gallery, London, Erika Ingham and Elizabeth Taylor. Jan Montefiore from the University of Kent has been a friend throughout and I have greatly benefited from her views. Long-standing admiration goes to Peter Brown at Kent and Derek Pearsall at York who steered my early medieval way with guidance on the perils and pleasures of interdisciplinary research.

Some arguments and sections in this book appeared in earlier studies for which I thank editors and publishers for their permission to reprint material. Ideas on authorship and its relationship to exile featured in 'Paradise postponed the nationhood of nuns in the 1670s' in *Religion, Culture and the National Community in the 1670s*, ed. Tony Claydon and Thomas N. Corns (Cardiff: University of Wales Press, 2011), 10–34. Sections of Chapter 2 can be found in 'Philip Sidney in the cloister: the reading habits of English nuns in seventeenth-century Antwerp', *Journal of Early Modern Cultural Studies*, 12:3, Summer 2012, 88–116; and discussion of 'alteration' and of temporal structure in '"So short a space of time": Early Modern Convent Chronology and Carmelite Spirituality', *Journal of Medieval and Early Modern Studies*, 42:3 (Fall 2012), 539–66.

I am greatly indebted to this book's anonymous reader for generously supportive insights and suggestions for improvement, and to Ann Allen for her editorial care at final stages. Ashgate readers will have noted that authors frequently mention Erika Gaffney's wisdom as a commissioning editor. Her enduringly creative mark on early modern studies is appreciatively felt here as elsewhere.

My final thanks are as ever to Rosie Valerio, without whom none of this is even thinkable: la que en el corazón ardía.

A Note on Sources, Style and Abbreviations

This book draws primarily on papers compiled in two Carmelite convents of English women living in exile in Antwerp and the nearby town of Lierre during the period from around 1600 to 1800. The communities returned to England at the time of the French Revolution bringing with them some of their documents, leaving other material behind. They settled first in accommodation provided by Catholic families, afterwards in newly-established convents in England, at Lanherne in Cornwall, and Darlington in County Durham respectively. There they remained for over 200 years until falling numbers meant that the nuns needed to join with other communities. Their documents therefore bear testimony to both Catholic diaspora and to 400 years of continuous female experience, remarkable writing that has mostly remained undisclosed and unpublished.

The references in this book are to the latest archive system in operation at the various locations of documents. In order to link them to their convent of likely origin or long-term archive position, I prefix references with *A* for Antwerp and *L* for Lierre. One of the challenges of dealing with such material is its state of bibliographical flux, in the early modern period when nuns or papers moved between convents and more recently when communities relocated. Since the archives have until very recently been relatively fixed, if only sometimes partly catalogued, this system gives the best route to the main locations of manuscript material; a summary of source references is provided at the beginning of the Bibliography.

I retain original spelling for both manuscript and early printed material, glossing obscure words where necessary; original punctuation is also kept even if this sometimes gives an odd rhythm to the prose. This retention reproduces as far as possible the style of the original writers, a wide range of individuals, not all of them known by name. Part of the pleasure in reading this material is the individual stylistic idiosyncrasies it reveals. I provide where possible the dates of sources, largely based on reconstructing internal cross-references, by knowledge of events or of the people concerned. Because nuns have been so long obscured by historical process, I identify them where I can at least by name and dates, giving personal and professional information where available or appropriate.

Since much of this material is unpublished, I have needed to provide more quotation than might be usual in a study of this kind. In order not to unduly encumber the narrative flow, longer references are occasionally placed in footnotes. Excerpts of material appeared in my two earlier books, *Lives of Spirit* (2007a) featuring selected material composed by around 60 women, and *Witchcraft, Exorcism and the Politics of Possession* (2007b) which presented a previously unknown case of exorcism featuring two of the nuns. This book is an independent analytical study; readers who may wish to see longer and different extracts of original material are referred to those previous texts where relevant.

When I mention early modern printed material, again I provide full references to the edition consulted which is as far as possible the version that the Carmelite nuns themselves used, identified through evidence within existing archive copies (such as nuns' names written there), from book lists, or because they were recommended specifically by the Carmelite constitutions. Many nuns mention particular books they studied before and after profession. Other texts are known to have been read in Catholic households. In some of the nuns' writings, the traces of such materials are evident (by quotation, synthesis or theme) if sometimes obscured, and I seek to identify their sources in order to expose the nuns' authorial methods.

The work of Teresa de Jesus of Avila (1515–82), founder-reformer of the female Carmelite Order, naturally features strongly here. Again I have tried where possible to use versions of her work that were known to the Antwerp and Lierre communities. For example, I quote from *The Flaming Hart* (1642), the translation of Teresa's Life by Tobie Matthew (1577–1655) known to the Antwerp nuns for whom he prepared it. When I refer to the collected works of Teresa de Jesus, edited in three volumes by E Allison Peers, I simply give the title and volume number, though if drawing on editorial matter in those volumes, I cite Peers' name. Biblical quotations are generally from the Vulgate or the English translation prepared at the English Catholic College at Douai: the Douay-Rheims New Testament was published in 1582, the Old Testament in two volumes in 1609 and 1610. If I draw on a secondary source, I retain its author's original scriptural quotation.

In this book I use the term 'Life' to indicate both longer, single-subject volumes of life-writing and shorter personal accounts within annals, whether written in the first- or third-person (or a combination of both). This avoids using 'autobiography' with its later modern assumptions of single authorship (many of the nuns' Lives are multi-authored, embracing a range of sources), and driven by an urge to self-present (many nuns express rhetorical reluctance to compose). Although 'Life' has hagiographic connotations that are sometimes but not always applicable to the nuns' writing, this usage seems at least to draw attention to the generic category as problematic, fluid and sometimes derivative.

Details of texts and individuals are provided as they arise in the book. On the first mention of names in the main discussion (even if they have previously been referred to in a footnote) I give full references (such as the birth and professional name of a nun, provided by the Carmelite papers, glossed where necessary to clarify), and thereafter generally refer to the nun by her religious name if her papers were written in the convent, and by her birth name for work written before that. If two nuns bear the same name in religion (a common enough occurrence), then I differentiate as necessary. The index draws together all references by name, and also seeks to weave a route through the material via alternative themes.

Introduction
Touching Nuns

What did it mean to be sensate in an early modern convent? How did it *feel* to be alive – or dead – in a contemplative community?

In an attempt to answer these questions, and others that they in turn raise, this book draws on the papers of English Catholic nuns in exile in northern Europe at a time of Protestant persecution in their homeland. It is primarily based on material from Carmelite convents in and around Antwerp in the Spanish Netherlands. The Antwerp community was specifically created for English women in 1619, established with support from Spanish Carmelites who were direct successors of Teresa de Jesus of Avila (1515–82; canonised in 1622), reformer of the female Discalced Order.[1] In 1648 nuns from the English Carmel formed an additional community in the nearby town of Lierre.

Successive generations of women joined these groups in a period of sustained Catholic renewal, travelling from England, Wales, Ireland and in some cases from America, often undertaking hazardous journeys. They remained in the region through a turbulent period of political and religious change until July 1794 when communities returned to England in the face of advancing French revolutionary troops.

Discussion in this book is based largely on material from the Antwerp and Lierre communities, whose papers are now relatively dispersed.[2] This encompasses several genres, including chronicles (referred to by the nuns as annals), necrologies, obituaries, letters, personal notes and devotional 'confession', as well as more sustained 'autobiographical' and biographical (sometimes multi-authored) life-writing. Since Teresa's 'mystical theology' (by which I mean knowledge of God that is said to be intellectually obscure or concealed)[3] presupposed a personal

---

[1] 'Discalced' literally means 'unshod' (*descalzo*); the nuns wore sandals referred to generally as 'spargatts' (*alpargatas*). By the time of Teresa de Jesus' death there were 17 Carmelite convents in Spain. Teresa's nuns travelled to Paris in 1604, then across northern Europe via Mons to Antwerp where in 1611 they founded what has become known as the 'Spanish Carmel'. In this book, the English Carmelite community, based in the Hopland area of the city, is referred to simply as the Antwerp Carmel; when it is being differentiated from the Spanish community, 'Hopland' will be added for clarity. The lay founder of the English Carmel was Mary, Lady Lovel; for an account of her activity in the foundation movement, see Guilday, 1914, 360–63.

[2] See Note on Sources, p. x.

[3] 'I thinke they call it Mysticall Theologie; and it suspends the Soule in such sort, that she seems to be wholly out of her self' (*Flaming Hart*, 1642, 108). Teresa found the phrase

transformation (before, during and after spiritual union), forms of self-writing compiled by her followers are particularly revealing of states of spiritual flux. A nun's personal documentation is purposeful, to help herself and, if she shares her writing, to help others in their spiritual progress. The devotional self is an especially elusive (and effusive) one, subject to perceived vicissitudes of faith and understanding, aridity and satisfaction. In this life-writing the author is secondary, her goal personal annihilation.

Teresian reform emphasised a life of intense prayer within strictly enclosed convents, with women contributing to a wider evangelising mission. Teresa had designed for her nuns a system of relative administrative autonomy and some devotional independence within established systems of meditation. Female Discalced convents were able to appoint their own confessors and doggedly campaigned to retain this right, often facing hostility from male ecclesiastical opponents who remained suspicious of women's spiritual endeavours.[4] The nuns' papers show the marks of this struggle. In recent years I have had privileged access to Carmelite archives, uncovering the nuns' testimony to – among other matters – their sensory experiences. It is on this testimony that this book will focus.

Despite the temporal specifics of their situation when Protestant discourse construed nuns as intrinsically deviant, and despite the geographic complication of their lives in exile, evidence suggests it was not so peculiar to *be* a nun.

Here is one example of ordinariness. Margaret of Jesus (Margaret Mostyn: 1625–79), born in north Wales and living in turn at Antwerp and Lierre, 'had so great contrary in wearing wollen yt euen ye only touching of it wth her hand would alter her all ouer' (*L13.7*, 63). The reflex urgency of this response – hers and vicariously our own – appears to collapse both time and space. The agrising shudder, after all, makes us most human, humane, real: this is a literature that makes 'one's flesh creep with sincerity' (Kermode, 2010, 13).[5]

Some sensations indeed cut through. We know, as early modern people say they knew 'The grateing of a Saw when it is sharpned … setteth the Teath on edge' (Bacon, 1626, 275). We know as if we bit it 'That bitter Apple which edged all mens teeth'; 'In like manner we perceiue by the little tickling of our sides, or the soles of our feet, how wee are moued to laughter'; 'scraping of trenchers' [plates] does not only offend the ear but also 'punisheth and fretteth the heart' (Wright, 1630, 170). Modern and early modern people may offer different explanations for

---

in *Tercer Abecedario Espiritual: Third Spiritual Alphabet* by Francisco de Osuna (*c.*1492–1540) who distinguished between 'speculative' theology, relating to understanding, and hidden (*escondida*) and mystical (*mistica*) theology, relating to the will (Williams, 1991, 72). On 'theologia mystica' in John of the Cross, and on the influence of Osuna and Fray Bernardino de Laredo on Teresa's thinking see Tyler, 2010, 64–76; 2011, 111–12, 117–24, respectively.

    4   For an account of the female Carmelite mission see Bilinkoff, 1994; Weber, 2002, 3.

    5   Kermode is writing about T.S. Eliot's views of Tennyson's *Maud*, where 'he finds much to dislike'; it fails 'to make one's flesh creep with sincerity' (2010, 10).

these effects, but at such moments impulse itself seems historically unbounded. Thomas Wright's *Passions of the Mind in General* appears just that.

Here a book on early modern perception might well end with a claim for sensory essentialism, and with Lyndal Roper's observation that 'the supposed gap between ourselves and the past world is less complete than we sometimes suppose, and that assumption of difference is not always a useful heuristic tool' (1994, 190, 3).[6] This book might then turn with clear conscience to celebrate the continuous 'shudder that seizes the human being .. as far as there is life in it' (Kant, 2006, 45–6). Indeed, in these convents, excitation continues when the living come into contact with the seemingly still-sentient corpse.

And it is here, of course, that we reach areas of peculiarity, of ideology, anthropology.[7] This is where a natural history of the senses is abandoned in favour (there could be no doubt) of a social history; where we explore 'the relationship between biological constants and historical variables' (Benjamin, 1973, 237).[8]

Mine, I might say, is a history of contingency: things (most of all humans) touching.[9]

Sensory transfer within and between bodies, and between minds recalling absent bodies, is closely bound up with matter, with physics and with physiologies of mind, body and soul. The nuns' writing, like other early modern texts, shows the influence of ancient philosophies of self. It is clear for example they where exposed, directly or indirectly, to Aristotle's ideas of sensory disturbance, famously his claim that 'a sense is that which is able to receive perceptible forms of things apart from their matter, as wax receives the imprint of the signet ring' (*De Anima*, Book II, 424a.17; Durrant, 1993, 47).

I am interested in what the nuns did with such ideas, and how they combined them with their own notions of the sensory spiritual in a history of somatic expressiveness that is itself entangled with conceptions of the imagination and of mystic, extra-sensory revelation. As Teresa's primary spiritual objective was to facilitate an inward and immaterial union of the soul with God, we might expect Carmelite writers to offer particular explanations of the role of the senses in their devotions, if only to explain how they dampen their dependence on physical stimuli. They adopt a sustained system of sensory mortification. I am interested in

---

[6]   Roper refers to the 'sheer agony' of a woman accused of the murder of her own child, of a grief that is beyond its own temporal moment. See also ideas on the 'hermeneutics of empathy': Simpson, 2006; Watson, 1999.

[7]   The history of the senses 'in its fullest development is not only evocative ... it is also interpretative: it makes sense of the past ... through the analysis of sensory practices and ideologies' (Howes, 2005, 400).

[8]   See Jütte, 2005, 9. Crucially, as Mark Smith notes 'the senses are historical ... not universal but, rather, a product of place and, especially, time, so that how people perceived and understood smell, sound, touch, taste and sight changed historically' (2007b, 3).

[9]   See Dinshaw's (very different) 'history of things touching: contingent < L. *com-* + *tangere* >, to touch' (1999, 39).

the effects that this had on their perception of their physical environment, and the ways that this experience was translated into literature.

Because they were so occupied with direct communion with God, we might also expect Teresians to pay special attention to those moments in which 'perceptible forms' are outwardly and inwardly received. Indeed, Teresa herself considered the physical senses to be 'handmaidens' of the intellect which relayed information to the mind so that it could interpret divine operations. In *Las Moradas*, an 'itinerary toward union with God' (Ahlgren, 2005, 121) typically translated as *Interior Castle* (*c*.1577), the senses occupy the first of seven mansions in the last of which the soul eventually achieves spiritual union. The physical senses are temporarily useful. In more advanced contemplative stages they are withdrawn in a process of recollection (*un recogimiento interior*). It requires much training to achieve this stilled or numbed withdrawal of the physical senses, and the Carmelite nuns' descriptions of their sensory process over several generations is especially illuminating for an understanding of early modern sensory perception more widely. As so often, meditative systems that insist on eradication of individualised self-hood initially rely on acute self-scrutiny; for historians seeking to understand the role of the senses in personal cognition, texts which detail a process of systematic sensory abnegation are therefore helpfully informing.

At times the nuns ponder on what is received when direct knowledge of God is acquired in and through the body as well as within the soul. If, as Aristotle claimed, 'actual knowledge is identical with the thing known' (*De Anima*, 7.431a1; Durrant, 1993, 63), then how does this 'thing' transfer from immaterial to material realms (and sometimes back again), and thence into language? And how might the nuns' own words convey ontological truth?

Words in Aristotle's terms are themselves contingent. Language 'hardly leaves the things from which it arises'; spoken sounds

> are signs of *impressions* [my emphasis] on the soul (*passiones*) which, in turn, are the images of things (*res*). Speech is thus tied, in two steps, to the world of things: its sounds point, as symbols, to psychic imprints that, for their part, attest to the beings with which the soul is already familiar. ... Even at its end, language ... thus hardly leaves the things from which it arises. (Heller-Roazen, 2003, 11)

Behind this, of course, is Aristotle's idea of *species*. 'The process of movement involved in the act of perception stamps in, as it were, a sort of impression of the precept ...'; here again in *De Memoria* he uses the analogy of the seal in wax or a picture lodged in the memory (450a, 25–32). 'Sensible' qualities were said to transmit likenesses, in the case of vision for example, from seen object to eye, importantly 'without any of the associated matter' (Clark, 2007, 15).

This proposal is problematic enough in terms of representation theory alone; in a visionary context nuns often struggle to describe the transition between bodily and mind's eye. In a contemplative situation that has its own evangelising imperative, integrity of words and meaning is naturally vital. It is also, in both spiritual and philosophical terms, apparently impossible.

I will return to the detail of Teresa de Jesus' spiritual system in later chapters. For now it is enough to note that she combines several meditative modes, one primarily based on exercises centring on imaging (such as Ignatian practices focused on scenes from Christ's passion) and another centring on imageless states within which the senses necessarily played at most a very minor role.[10] The ideally recollected soul excludes sensory stimuli and can find no words to express her happiness, or indeed afterwards even to describe her experience of divine union. 'And now let us come to the interiour of that which the Soule is wont to feele, at these times' wrote Teresa de Jesus of her ecstatic experiences in which the senses fail, 'it cannot be well vunderstood, and much lesse expressed'; 'The Vunderstanding, if it vunderstand, it is not yet vunderstood, how it vunderstands; and, at least, it can comprehend nothing of that, which it vunderstands. To me it doth not seem, that it vunderstands; because (as I was saying) it is not vunderstood; and for my part, I attaine not, to vunderstand all this' (*Flaming Hart*, 1642, 227, 228–9).

Luckily for us, in their writing her Carmelite successors often think aloud about sensations (of body, mind and soul) and about the language they might use to describe them; they account in various ways for perception itself. To be sentient is not only to feel; it is also to be aware of having felt, and to reflect upon sensitive effects. 'I did not see with my eyes ... I think my eyes were shutt. I think it was a Lively representation' wrote Anne of the Ascension (Anne Worsley: 1588–1644), the first Prioress at Antwerp whose extensive personal writings will feature strongly here.

Given the ideologies of gender operating in the early modern period, the nuns' writing exposes particularly nuanced facets of spiritual materialism. Assertions about women's alleged vulnerability that linked humoural physiology and reasoning, and medically-discursive assertions about the susceptibility of 'virgins' to melancholia and 'hysteria', were used by church authorities to justify scrutiny of women's spiritual states.[11] The ways in which nuns initiated and interacted with theories of the female self accordingly inform their interpretations of personal experience. Like Teresa de Jesus, and newly influenced by later sixteenth and seventeenth century concerns, the Carmelite women adopted literary as well as theological strategies to avoid restrictions that were significantly less acute for

---

[10] Barbara Mujica provides a succinct summary of Teresa's two spiritual approaches, outlined by the Pseudo-Dionysius as 'kataphatic' which uses images and 'apophatic' which 'obliterates all anthropomorphic notions of God' including sensory analogy, 'in order to confront the unknowable' (2001, 741).

[11] 'In humoralism, the coldness and springiness of female flesh, relative to the flesh of men, become traits of great ethical consequence by explaining the sex's limited capacity for productive agency, individuality, and higher reasoning' (Paster, 2004, 78–9). See Burton, 1621, I, 429; Jorden, 1603 for early modern quasi-medical claims about women's physiology.

male Carmelites and writers. So, while some aspects of the English nuns' writing drew on a shared intellectual vernacular (European) tradition, other aspects of their experience were shaped by gendered reception and by concerns to present a female 'civil' self-hood.

Even when Teresa de Jesus claims to be unable to explain the precise mechanics of spiritual revelation, in part because of her declared inadequacies as a woman,[12] she nonetheless shows acute awareness of philosophical thought on the matter. She makes distinctions between the outer senses and the inner interpretative faculty. The latter was accounted for by Aristotle as 'koina aistheta': 'common sensible qualities' (*De Anima*, 2.6.418a, 17–18), denoting the capacity to discern that 'exceeds the bounds of the five senses': 'It is the sense of sensing, the mere feeling that something at all is felt' (Heller-Roazen, 2007, 32, 34). Again, Teresa de Jesus whose *Vida* so shaped subsequent Carmelite self-writing, helpfully thinks aloud about this:

> … But that, which I would faine relate now, is the manner, how our Blessed Lord is pleased to shew himself, by these Visions. I say not, that I will declare, in what sort, this so strong a light may be able to conuey itself, into the inward sense, and to imprint so exact, and cleare an Image, vpon the Vunderstanding, as to make it directly seem, to be very there … (*Flaming Hart*, 1642, 392)

This at least is how Tobie Matthew (1577–1655) translates the passage in his version of Teresa's Life prepared for the Antwerp nuns.[13]

---

[12]   Teresa often claimed, for example, 'I am so very ignorant, and of so grosse an Vunderstanding' (*Flaming Hart*, 1642, 392). Alison Weber has persuasively argued that Teresa de Jesus adopted a 'rhetoric of femininity': 'a strategy which exploited certain stereotypes about women's character and language' in order to circumvent scrutinising church authority (1990, 11). Teresa's stylistic apparent 'Disorder, digression and imprecision … disguise a charismatic text as women's chatter' (109). On Teresa's careful self-censorship in order to sidestep suspicion of her mysticism in the face of the Inquisition, see Ahlgren, 1996.

[13]   In Spanish this reads: 'No digo que declararé de qué manera puede ser poner este luz tan fuerte en el sentido interior, y en el entendimiento imagen tan clara, que parece verdaderamente está allí, porque esto es de letrados …' On differences between Teresa's use of the term and that of John of the Cross, see Howells, 2002, 75. Matthew's *Flaming Hart* is the primary early modern version of Teresa's *Vida* to which I will refer. Copies were owned by both the Antwerp and Lierre Carmel whose successors retain manuscript copies of Matthew's text. In an *EEBO* copy (Wing CD ROM 1996 T753) writing within the printed title page states: 'Belonging to the English Teresians Antwerp'. Matthew had a close relationship with the Carmelites who often refer to him in their papers; indeed, he had strong links with many religious communities in northern Europe and translated several key devotional texts for them and for lay English Catholics. Some of these texts are discussed here. The strength of Matthew's relationship with the Antwerp women is attested by his 1647 will which makes it clear he had formerly intended to be buried within the

It is worth considering the use of the phrase 'inward sense' within other early modern English texts, to give a context to Matthew's translation. In *Arte of Rhetorique* (1553), Thomas Wilson explained this as 'so called because it geueth iudgement, of al the fiue outwarde senses' (112; *OED*). In the 1639 version of George Chapman's *Ouid's Banquet of the Sence* 'inward taste' is glossed: 'He intends the common sense which is *centrum sensibus et speciebus*' (34).[14] John Davies (1569–1626) neatly summarises such views in his long poem *Nosce Teipsum*, accounting for the role of memory in sensory retention: 'And yet these Porters which all things admit, / The selues perceiue not, nor discern the thing: / One *Common* power doth in the forehead fit, / Which all their proper forms together brings'; 'Those outward Organs present things receiue, / This inward *Sense* doth absent things retaine; / Yet straight transmits all forms she doth perceiue; / Vnto a higher region of the *braine*' (1653, 46). In a devotional context, St Gregory's *Moralia in Job* which was known to Teresa from 1539 (Carrera, 2005, 164) and to seventeenth-century Carmelites at least indirectly, explains that sensory understanding (apart from touch of which the body alone is cognisant) is located in 'the head of the body [which] has use of all the five senses at once' (1844 ed., Book I, 129).

One way or another, then, the nuns were aware of Aristotelian and other classical precepts of sensory perception. They were also exposed to Descartes' ideas, through Jesuit and other influences within the convents. Their writing shows understanding of Cartesian and other challenges to long-standing conceptions of the senses found within philosophical and theological discourse that was so central to both Catholic and Protestant reformist debate on the relationship between the mind and the body, and of these to the soul.

René Descartes (1596–1650) explained the mechanism for the route of sensation from object to understanding in his *Rules for the Direction of the Mind* (completed in *c.*1628 and published in Holland in 1684): 'when an external sense organ is stimulated by an object, the figure which it receives is conveyed at one

---

convent by permission of the Prioress (he now wished to be taken to the English College at Ghent). Among other gifts to the nuns, he bequeathed £600 to the convent, paying an especially affectionate tribute to the then-Prioress (Mathew and Calthrop, 1907, 339). One of his executors was Lionel Wake, father of a nun who features in this book; see Hardman, 1939, 126–9. On Matthew's links with the Antwerp community, see also Vander Motten and Daemen-De Gelder, 2011, an essay which appeared after my book was written.

[14]   The quotation continues: 'and calls it [taste] because it doth, *sapere in effectione sensuum*'. (In the original the italics and normal fonts are reversed.) On Chapman's text, 'one of the most difficult poems in the language' see Kermode, 1971. See Edward Herbert (1583–1648), *De Veritate ...* (Paris, 1624; London, 1633) who also refers to inner senses. In general in this period '*internal sense* (*sensus internus*) referred to the conscious activities that the mind developed in and of itself (reason, memory and imagination) on the basis of information provided by the *external senses* (sight, hearing, taste, touch and smell' (Starobinski, 1989, 354); Mazzio, 1998. On Aquinas, Thomas Wright and *sensus communis*, see Craik, 2007, 14, part of her excellent discussion of Wright's ideas on emotions (11–21).

and the same moment to another part of the body known as the "common" sense, without any entity really passing from one to the other' (1985 ed., I, 41). The delicate question of the nature of transfer between human and holy figures will be returned to later. As one might imagine, this was an issue that occupied the nuns when they tried to understand and to explain their own spiritual experiences whilst remaining orthodox.

Most crucially, *sensus internus* is the point where the body meets the mind: 'A representation through sense of which one is conscious as such is called *sensation*, especially when the sensation at the same time arouses the subject's attention to his [sic] own state' (Kant, 2006, 45).[15]

In such terms the nuns self-consciously discuss sensory capacity and those areas that language, like bodies, cannot apprehend: the extra-sensory that so structures their approach to meaning. As one Carmelite text stated, enacting the paradox of its own apophatic spirituality, Teresa was 'struck and wounded at the very heart with a fearfull noyse in the most inward of her substance … though this noyse is not heard, with corporall eares, for it is inward and a very silent noyse …' (*The Soul's Delight*, 1654, 67–8).[16]

Any study of theology is also a study of words, and of theories about their capacity to describe the ineffable. This book will pursue, then, another approach to contingency which Boethius, to whose ideas the nuns were also exposed,[17] renders as *contigens*: 'the term by which Aristotle refers to that of which language speaks when, at the limit of its canonical operation, it refers to what is not a thing and what, in a certain sense, is not at all' (Heller-Roazen, 2003, 12).

I am also interested, then, in those areas where words and the senses meet, where both apparently fail or sit in satisfying paradox.[18] Here, as elsewhere, the material and immaterial frequently abut. 'There are' noted John of the Cross (1542–91), a Carmelite friar and collaborator of Teresa de Jesus, drawing on Thomas Aquinas' views of the senses, 'two ways by which these notions and

---

[15]　Famously, Descartes wrote: 'it was not unreasonable for me to think that the items which I was perceiving through the senses were things quite distinct from my thought, namely bodies which produced the ideas' (*Meditations on First Philosophy*, 1641: Sixth Meditation, 1984 ed., II, 52). On 'interior sense' by which 'we perceive everything we know, and through it distinctions knowable by reason are grasped' see Summers, 1987, 95.

[16]　*The Soul's Delight*, a treatise to which I will refer several times in this book, was written by Paul of St Ubald (Paul Brown: 1598–1671), a Carmelite originally from Dublin. He probably began writing it in around 1650 in Italy, and completed it in Louvain; it was published in Antwerp in 1654 (see Mansfield, 1984, 54). The Lierre nuns owned a copy: Darlington Book 78.

[17]　For example in *The Practise How to Find Ease* … by Thomas Doughty (discussed below, pp. 200–1) which quotes Boethius (1619, 340, 377), and draws on his ideas of natural social order (165ff).

[18]　'The apophatic-kataphatic dialect creates an exquisite tension in [Teresa's] work' (Mujica, 2001, 741).

intelligent acts enter into the understanding; one is natural, the other supernatural' (*Subida del Monte Carmelo*: *The Ascent of Mount Carmel*, 1906 ed., 102).[19] These two interconnected facets will shape the divisions of this book.

So too will notions of 'coming to'; I will explore most particularly those 'moments when the senses rise, for one reason or another, to points of particular precision' (Heller-Roazen, 2007, 65).[20] When the nuns write most vividly about their sensory states it is often because they have been, in their word, 'out' of them. My discussion will, then, examine how the nuns account for their senses at moments of literal awakening – from sleep, from and into states of rapture – and at moments of sensory excitement when they are aware of their own responsiveness to stimuli. I will focus in separate chapters on the seeing, hearing, smelling, tasting nun; because touch is so central to the Carmelite sensorium I will start by discussing that sense individually. In Chapter 1, I outline more fully ideas about the senses that have been adumbrated in this general introduction for which Chapter 2 presents illustrative case studies. Chapter 3 considers the role of Touch in the convents, leading to a discussion of the other 'proximate' sense which is said to have the body (the tongue) as its medium, namely Taste (Chapter 4). Chapters 5 (on Sound) and 6 (on Smell) consider senses which allegedly share the medium of air. Finally, perhaps perversely, Chapter 7 discusses Sight, frequently claimed to be the primary 'mediator of pleasure'. Clearly there is some intermingling of the senses, in life and in this book; I cross-reference connections between chapters. The conclusion outlines implications arising from this Carmelite study and suggests areas for further research.

* * *

'It is indeed a good moment to be a sensory historian' (Mark Smith, 2007a, 841). It is even a good moment to be interested in the role of the senses in religion.[21] In recent years much has been written about early modern passions and the humoural

---

[19]   The two met in Medina in 1567 where Teresa was preparing her second foundation. On their spiritual rapport and John's biography, see Tyler, 2010, 9–37. On differences in their theology, see Howells, 2002, 129–37.

[20]   Heller-Roazen presents a compelling literary analysis of moments of awakening from sleep (2007, 73–7). His powerful insights have greatly influenced my thinking for this study of Carmelite expressiveness. He cites Proust: 'J'avais seulement dans sa simplicité première, le sentiment de l'existence comme il peut frémir au fond d'un animal': 'the feeling of existence as it may quiver in the depths on an animal' (75).

[21]   We might look no further for evidence of a burgeoning interest in this field than the Renaissance Society of America 2010 Conference; there were no fewer than seven dedicated panel sessions on 'Religion and the Senses' as well as several other individual papers where this and related topics also featured. Even so, there was scant reference to convents.

body; the history of senses has also been extensively explored.[22] Nuns' literature has not so far been examined in this light.

This book will discuss the nuns' own writing about sensitivity. It adopts an ecumenical approach, 'considering not only the history of a given sense but its social and cultural construction and its role in texturing the past' (Smith, 2007a, 842). It seeks to understand the role the senses played in the way the nuns structured their lives, considering particular early modern moments that seem to shape a Catholic conception of 'ensouled flesh'.[23] Since the women I write about lived in exile, to some extent I will consider the possible effects of physical transition across different kinds of nation, and from domestic to religious environments.

It is often assumed that women who profess as nuns assume an entirely fresh identity when they take a new name and separate themselves from family and friends. Certainly the Antwerp and Lierre women frequently describe their struggle to divest themselves of affectionate ties; the devotional discipline to which they committed themselves seeks to complete their separation from both old self and others. However it is also clear that nuns retained aspects of personal behaviour, indeed elements of their domestic training stood them in good stead for convent regimes. The links between secular conduct books and devotional manuals is discussed in Chapter 1. It is evident that some personal effects endure in the way that Pierre Bourdieu accounts for *habitus*: 'The structures constitutive of a particular type of environment (eg the material conditions of existence characteristic of a class condition) produce *habitus*, systems of durable, transposable *dispositions*' (1977, 72). Convent records attest to the fact that some nuns retained their 'natural' propensities, struggling to break their humoural 'temper'.[24] In exploring the nuns' writing about sensory subjectivity and their efforts to adapt personally as well as to change their environment in order to create conducive conditions for their pious purposes, I investigate the material traces of their embodied activity. I am also able to test precepts of spatial and social conditioning. Of all groups, given their transfer from one regime to another and their determined documentation of endeavour, early modern nuns might serve as an exemplary test-bed for Bourdieu's theories.

It is clear, for example, that some nuns before and after profession display attitudes outlined in both domestic and contemplative conduct manuals. Their

---

[22]   On the humours, senses and literature see: Cahill, 2009; Caldwell, 1979; Craik, 2007; Dugan, 2008; 2009; 2011; Hillman and Mazzio, 1997; Paster, 2004; Paster, Rowe and Floyd-Wilson, 2004; Vinge, 1975. For an overview of sensory history, see: Classen, 1993; Howes, ed., 2005; Mark Smith, 2007a and b.

[23]   'the ensouled body ... must be something solid ... the body must be the naturally cohering medium for the faculty of touch, through which the plurality of perceptions is communicated' (Aristotle, *De Anima*, 423.a.22; Durrant, 1993, 45).

[24]   Bourdieu defines disposition as 'a *way of being*, a *habitual state* (especially of the body) ... a *predisposition, tendency, propensity* or *inclination* (1977, 214, note 1). For discussion of reconceptualising identity and feminist responses to Bourdieu see Adkins, 2004.

sense of civility is shaped by these books and shows deeply embedded notions of national as well as devotional decorum. On encountering the habits of other ethnic heritages on their arrival in Antwerp, for example, some lament the 'rudeness of Spanish natures' (*A1*, 5, 7). Their sensory reaction to foreign food also suggests that not only personal taste buds are affected but notions of civilisation *per se* (see Chapter 4 on Taste).[25] Sensory analysis can reveal much about class and racial attitudes, of course, especially when early modern writers reflect on the ways in which passions govern somatic behaviour. In these papers, being in control of one's senses signals a form of (bourgeois) civility.[26]

I will ask from time to time whether there is anything particularly English in the way that the women conduct or describe their sensory responsiveness. If some of their attitudes enforce ideas of difference, others appear to transcend geographic boundaries. We can as we might expect detect pan-European Catholic influence in their writing; here their emphatically patriotic views are nuanced by the influence of Latin, Spanish and French texts, many of them translated or produced in the printing power-house of Antwerp.

I am interested in Antwerp itself as a sensory space, although that is not the principal focus of this volume except insofar as it impinges on the nuns' experience. During this period the city was a busy commercial centre, by the mid-sixteenth century comprising around 85,000 citizens including many English expatriates with whom the nuns had intermittent contact.[27] Although Antwerp offered English Catholics a haven of relative security, protected by Spanish governance, the region as a whole suffered turmoil throughout this period as a result of religious and political upheaval. Displaced groups migrated internally according to sequential shifts of relative allegiance. In the years after 1585, only 30 or so years before the English Carmel was founded in the city, Protestants (until then forming an estimated half of the population) left for northern Netherlandish towns (Israel, 1995, 219).

---

[25] Mark Smith considers that 'sensory histories will increasingly go beyond the analytical and geographic borders of the nation-state ... that historians will apply the senses in an effort to understand the process by which nation-states were created' (2007a, 852). It has long been recognised that Protestants produced an emphatic nationalism based on antagonism to the Catholic Other (see Claydon, 2007; Marotti, 1999; Tumbleson, 1998). Sensory evidence complicates the picture of how both Catholic and Protestant English patriots shaped their sense of nation around sensory response – real or rhetorical – to somatic foreignness.

[26] Thomas Wright considers those 'whom Nature monstrously hath signed, what affections rule Rustickes, possesse Citizens, tyrannize ouer Gentlemen': 'I might discourse ouer Flemings, Frenchmen, Spaniards, Italians, Polans, Germans, Scotishmen, Irishmen, Welshmen, and Englishmen, explicating their nationall inclinations good or bad ... (1630, 44). For our purposes we might regret that he side-steps the issue since 'euery one of these exacteth a whole Chapter'.

[27] From mid-1656 Antwerp, Bruges and Brussels were increasingly popular places for émigré royalists to live (see Smith, 2003, 80).

The area was intellectually and culturally vibrant. Among others, Descartes lived for some time in the region, based in Holland from 1628–49. His *Discourse on Method* was published in Leiden in 1637. His ideas were received and debated among Jesuit circles in northern Europe, circles which naturally overlapped with Carmelite convents for whom Jesuit priests often acted as confessors. I am interested in the proximity of ideas as well as people, and the effects of interchange between different and ostensibly separate spheres.

Among other texts, Antwerp presses published key works of religious and philosophical polemic, many for English markets: several will be discussed in this book.[28] Some texts indeed were given to the nuns by pious donors who visited the convents. Although the cloisters were strictly enclosed under post-Tridentine strictures, it is evident from the papers that the nuns received news from elsewhere; among the many letters exchanged, one originally contained a map showing the location of various battles.[29] The nuns' sense of geography was a complicated one; conception of individual and community spaces was combined with national and regional knowledge and aspiration for return to a restored Catholic homeland (Hallett, 2011).

Antwerp was a garrison town with all the sensory disturbances that this entailed; one woman whose father was stationed there expressed her fear of the sound of gunshots. Soldiers from the 'citadel' protected the nuns at times of civil disturbance (see p. 109). Occasionally the nuns gave hospitality to exiled 'cavaliers', providing them with food and medical necessities (see p. 16). Members of the royal family and Stuart court in exile regularly visited. Charles II and his brother, James, Duke of York, came inside the convent enclosure; one account describes them in the kitchen, talking to nuns there.[30] Some nuns arrived with news from these courts; one entertained the community by mimicking, giving 'a pretty account of ye King, Queen, Princes & Passages of court during her residence there' (*L13.7*, 297).[31] Nuns also received into the enclosure young women whom they hoped might enter the Order. When the convent buildings were extended or altered, the enclosure

---

[28]   For example, the Antwerp based Richard Verstegan (Richard Rowlands: *c.*1550-1640) published a range of books for the English mission including translations of works by Antony of Molina and Peter of Alcantara (see pp. 56, 57 n. 79, 58, 65, 133). His former bookbinder, Henry Jaye, published the English edition of Teresa de Jesus' Life in 1611. On Verstegan and the English merchant community in Antwerp, see Arblaster, 2004.

[29]   On the role of nuns in contemporary politics see Walker, 2000; 2001; 2004.

[30]   In this context, there is a strikingly unusual reference in the Antwerp annals to the personal appearance of Tecla of St Paul (Catherine Clifton: 1624–71): 'She had a most Angellicall Innocence, and an agreeable sweet temper, and her Person so lovely and beautiful that when King Charles the second and his Brother came in our Monastery, the Duke of Yo[r]k came to the King and told him, if he had a mind to see a Pritty Woman he must go to the Infirmary which he did where Dear Sr Tecla was' (*A1*, 386–7; Hallett, 2007a, 86).

[31]   Mary Constantia of the Assumption of the Blessed Virgin (Laura Bulstrode: 1680–1752).

was breached, and the nuns describe the disruption this involved. They were also clearly aware of the population outside, presenting them in terms of both class and nation. At Lierre the Prioress struggled to raise funds to erect a boundary wall in order to hide 'the rabble' on the river boats (*L13.7*, 143); an Antwerp source refers to the 'vulgar sort' who gathered outside the convent to watch the nuns process for an enclosure ceremony (*A1*, 67).

Otherwise nuns received visitors in the convent speak-house, the parlour where they were separated by iron grilles. Conversation was strictly controlled under the terms of the Carmelite constitutions, confined to pious matters and always conducted within earshot of two other nuns. Sight of the religious was also generally restricted by walls and by use at the main entrance of the turn – a rotating barrel-shaped contrivance, separated vertically so that items could be conveyed in and out of the enclosure without giving a glimpse of the nuns within. When the public did gain sight of the religious it was in well-managed ways, during processions, clothing services and professions, and in liturgically-orchestrated ceremony such as when a dead nun was 'exposed' in the choir, visible through peep-holes or grilles. Such physical restrictions underline concepts of enclosure and naturally affected the sensory experience of and by the nuns, heightening or dampening intensities accordingly.

Convent servants acted as intermediaries in daily life, visiting the markets and wash houses. One oblate had previously been employed in the Antwerp coffee house; her arrival in the convent is emblem enough of the meeting of 'public' and 'private' spheres.[32]

My book takes its sub-title by reference to a play by Margaret Cavendish, Duchess of Newcastle (1623–73): *The Convent of Pleasure* was published in 1668 soon after Cavendish herself had returned to England from Antwerp where she and her husband had been royalist refugees from 1648–60, based at Rubenshuis, only a garden away from the English Carmelite convent. The boundary walls of the two properties abut (something that so far seems so to have gone unnoticed by Cavendish historians).[33]

---

[32] Convents, with their own spaces of debate, in this way may be felt to complicate Habermas' theories of 'spheres of public authority' which use the coffee-house as a prime example (see Habermas, 1962, trans. 1989).

[33] Erin Lang Bonin (2000) refers to the nunnery in *Convent of Pleasure* as 'a space historically and geographically distant from Cavendish and her contemporaries' (347), concentrating on the 'symbolic potential' of her utopianism: 'The convent's walled exclusivity facilitates Cavendish's representation of a space aggressively separate from the heterosexual economy' (347). Scholars have tended to rely on fictional representations of convents for a sense of Cavendish's and other writers' understandings of devotional milieu, taking these often fantasised accounts at face-value. None to my knowledge has explored Cavendish's experience of the 'reality' of Antwerp convent life. On Aphra Behn's *Love Letters Between a Nobleman and His Sister* set in monastic Brussels presenting convents as 'early modern luxury resorts' see Mendelson, 2004 who, while she identifies the importance of Antwerp's ambience on Cavendish's imagination ('Influence also invades the mind

The play's lead character, Lady Happy, declares: 'I intend to incloister my self from the World, to enjoy pleasure … for ever Sense shall pleasure take'; 'My Cloister shall not be a Cloister of restraint, but a place for freedom, not to vex the Senses but to please them …':

> *Wee'l Cloth our selves with softest Silk,*
> *And Linnen fine as white as milk.*
> *Wee'l please our Sight with Pictures rare;*
> *Our Nostrils with perfumed Air.*
> *Our Ears with sweet melodious Sound,*
> *Whose Substance can be no where found;*
> *Our Tast with sweet delicious Meat,*
> *And savory Sauces we will eat:*
> *Variety each Sense shall feed …*
> (2000 ed., 101; italics in the original)

'What profit or pleasure,' she asks 'can it be to the gods to have Men or Women wear coarse Linnen or rough Woollen, or to flea their skin with Hair-cloth, or to eat or sawe thorow their flesh with Cords?' (99).

Meanwhile, over the wall, Margaret of Jesus with her own aversion to wool, pursuing penances just like those Lady Happy describes, might ask the same question, but answer differently; her sensory mortifications were aimed at pious profit.[34]

Cavendish had direct experience of at least one aspect of convent life and herself played a part in the ritualised sensory practices it contained when she led Mary Cotton (later Mary of the Blessed Trinity: 1629–94) to her clothing ceremony.[35] This is strikingly described in the Antwerp annals: 'When she came to

---

through the pathways of the five senses, the writers physical, cultural and psychological milieu … The sights and sounds and even the smells she took in – in fact the very air she breathed – affected the way she thought and wrote': 5), still draws on literary descriptions rather than actual events to illustrate the 'cult of religious aestheticism' featuring in Cavendish's work. On Cavendish's interest in Catholicism, and Catholic circles of Antwerp see Kelly 2004; on her intellectual circles and the city as a brain, see Siegfried, 2004. James Fitzmaurice describes how Antwerp featured in Margaret Cavendish's own writing which 'alternates between depicting the city itself and describing it as it is found transformed in her mind' (2000, 30). See also the catalogue of the exhibition *Royalist Refugees, William and Margaret Cavendish in Rubens House*, 1648–60, ed. Beneden and Poorter, 2006 for detailed discussion of the wide range of the couple's cultural activities while in the city.

[34]   'To conquer oneself for one's own good is to make use of the senses in the service of the interior life' (Teresa de Jesus, *Way of Perfection*, II, 122).

[35]   According to the Antwerp annals, Mary Cotton was the daughter of Edward Cotton and Mary, the daughter of Alexander Brett (*A1*, 475). Other nuns with the surname Cotton (daughters of Richard Cotton of Gloucestershire) were also in the convent. I have so far been unable to establish familial connection between them and Charles Cotton (1630–87),

be Religious the Dutchess of Newcastle being then here was much taken with her as being extreamly pritty entertained her at her own house dress'd her with her own hands for her entering like a nimph and led her in her self' (*A1*, 482).[36] Clothing and profession ceremonies were elaborate services that marked the women's transition from secular to convent life, often accompanied by sumptuous food, music and entertainment, akin to their secular equivalent in marriage festivals.[37] During these celebrations they changed from often very elaborate clothing to religious vestments. This particular ceremony, with Cavendish's support of the young woman in her home and her sponsorship of the occasion, indicates how closely two spheres temporarily cohered, and how their subsequent divergence marked the sensory and other dissonances of the nun's experience.

We have, then, two adjacent, sometimes overlapping, social and sensory spaces, separated only by the formally designed garden of Rubenshuis: the Cavendishes in 'one of the most architecturally distinguished houses in the whole of Antwerp' (Jardine, 2009, 193) entertained aristocratic visitors in showy style, surrounded by the cultural trappings of the house itself, even emptied of its previous interior luxury. In February 1658 they hosted 'a soiree of glamour and revelry' for Charles II and his entourage including a song by 'Lady Moore, dressed in feathers' who sang one of Margaret Cavendish's songs arranged to music by Nicholas Lanier. 'The occasion itself' notes Lisa Jardine, 'was resolutely English' (198).

Some of the nearby nuns, a number of them accompanied by servants who professed as Lay Sisters, had come originally from similar, if less ostentatious households. Some indeed were, or had consorted with, 'members of international high society' that comprised the Cavendish's circle (Harting, 2006, 63). Some came from the English court in exile in France, or that of the Spanish Infanta. They discuss their difficulties in adapting to the austerities of Carmelite profession.

We might imagine how much sensory stimulation these abutting environments shared (the sounds of bells, the smells of smoke that penetrated both environments), and how much their experiences differed. Cavendish's 'Recreations for every Season of the Year' (*Sociable Letters*, 191) had little in common with the nuns'

---

the likely translator of Hobbes' *De Cive*; he was part of the network of the Newcastle-Cavendishes in Derbyshire and Nottinghamshire, including Sir Gervase Clifton who employed Hobbes as tutor for his son, 1629–30 (see Malcolm, 1999/2000, 234–58). On Hobbes' *De Mirabilibus Pecci* (1636) and Charles Cotton's *Wonders of the Peake* (1681), see Edwards, 2012.

[36] 'Nymph' was used from the fourteenth century onwards to refer to a semi-divine spirit or a beautiful young woman. The word was also used euphemistically for prostitute, and anti-convent writers linked it to Catholic women in this context (see *OED*). Puccini's *Life of Mary Magdalene of Pazzi* refers to fantasies of the celestial marriage which has saints and 'Paranymphs' as witnesses (1687, 5).

[37] Caroline Bowden presented a paper on clothing ceremonies at the Renaissance Society Conference, with examples from various religious Orders (York, July 2010). See also *Manner of Receiving the Poor Clares* (1795); Hallett, 2007a, 18; 2012a, 249–58; Kuhna, 2003.

entertainment when 'att sertine times when it was the Priorisse Feasts ore the lik, accordinge to our custum the Religious makes for Recreation some little actions ore representation of deuotion' (*L13.7*, 19). We assume that no one here was dressed in feathers.

In her letters Cavendish describes the feel of cold during the freezing winters. She mentions people 'in Sleds by Torchlight',[38] while the nuns in their papers do not. Instead they recall

> when king charles ye second was in banishment in these countries, there was a regiment of his quarter'd in this towne [Lierre], all persones of good quality, that had neither money nor bread to eat, and most of them sicke and euen ready to drope downe as they walked in ye streets for want ... [The Prioress, Margaret of Jesus Mostyn] commanded the Portresse not to deney relief to any that came and for some months there dined aboue twenty persones a day in the seruants quarter where they had fier alsoe to warme 'em and none of ye common soldiers were refused Bread and Bier tho' they came in crouds dayly, it being a uery sharpe wintour ... our provisions of corne wood Butter bier extli held out ye same as other years (*L3.30G*; Hallett, 2007a, 85)

In England the Cavendish couple showed a compelling interest in the fashionable trope of the senses, encapsulating their fascination in the decorative scheme of their Bolsover home. Painted images in the Ante-room represent the four humours; the 'Pillar Parlour' displays Oderatus, a woman smelling flowers; Tactus, her hand to the wind, holding a red bird; Auditus, with instruments, next to a stag; Gustus, accompanied by an ape, steals fruit. This was the likely scene for the 1634 feast at Bolsover when Charles I and Henrietta Maria as guests witnessed the 'banquet of sense' from Ben Jonson's *Love's Welcome* with its song 'When were the senses in such order plac'd? The Sight, the Hearing, Smelling, Touching, Taste, All at one Banquet' (see Raylor, 1999). Outside, William Cavendish's Riding House exemplifies reason and mastery, enacting in extended, playful architectural juxtaposition a topical debate on the tension between passionate impulse and rational control, one played out rather differently within the convent.[39]

The Cavendish circle embraced several philosophers. Descartes, whom the family finally met in Paris in 1647 and to whose dualistic theories Margaret

---

[38]   'Although I am as Unwilling to stir from the Fire-side this Cold weather ... yet my Husbands Perswasion ... Forced me out of the City, as without the Walls, to see Men Slide upon the Frozen Moat', Cavendish wrote, in her *Sociable Letters* (Number 192).

[39]   On Reason and horsemanship, see pp. 63, 64 n. 94; on William Cavendish's art of manège and connections between Antwerp and Bolsover, see Worsley and Addyman, 2002; on visual representation of the senses in other aristocratic homes, see Mulherron and Wyld, 2012. Thanks to Crosby Stevens of English Heritage for her insights on Bolsover's decorative schemes and allowing the University of Sheffield Early Modern Group special access there in May 2012.

Cavendish later objected, wrote to Newcastle in 1645 'I am convinced that hunger and thirst are felt in the same manner as colours, sounds, smells and in general all the objects of the external senses, that is by means of nerves stretched like fine threads from the brain to all other parts of the body' (*Descartes: Philosophical Letters*, 182). He proposed that the main seat of the soul was in the pineal, a 'small gland located in the middle of the brain' (*Passions of the Soul*, 1985 ed., I, 341). In her own *Philosophical Letters* (1664) Margaret Cavendish doubted the brain was the location of this 'Spider in a Cobweb' (111). Such thinking is in dialogue with contemplative ideas (and *vice versa*) about the location of locution and the nature of its relationship with the senses.[40] Descartes considered 'it is the soul which has sensory perception, and not the body. For when the soul is distracted by an ecstasy or deep contemplation, we see that the whole body remains without sensation, even though it is has various objects touching it'; it follows that sensory perception is located in the brain where it 'exercises the faculty called the "common sense"' (*Optics, Discourse Four*, 1985 ed., I, 164). Cavendish conceived 'some of the sensitive Parts are so sociable' that they cohere with the rational; 'in deep Contemplations, some of the Sensitive Parts do not take notice of Forrein Objects, but of the Rational Actions' (*Grounds of Natural Philosophy*, 1668, 160). Disturbance – of the kind the nuns describe (pp. 29–33) – creates personal commotion of constituent parts, causing a person to feel fearful or insane, experiencing the 'strange or unusual' (127).[41]

Another of the Cavendish circle was Thomas Hobbes (1588–1679), tutor to the Devonshire family and close friend of Cavendish's husband and his brother.[42] He

---

[40]   On intertextuality between Cavendish's work, Descartes and Hobbes, see Semler, 2012, 327, 337; on Cavendish's challenges to Cartesian dualism, see Sarasohn, 2010, 129–41.

[41]   See Webster, 2011, for discussion of the relationship between rational and sensitive parts in Cavendish's writing and the suggestion that she revises Descartes' analogies to promote a 'vitalist' mind-body system modelled on ideas of 'commonwealth' and reflecting her own displaced exilic situation.

[42]   Hobbes was appointed in 1608 as tutor to William Cavendish (1590–1628), later second Earl of Devonshire, cousin to William Cavendish (1593–1674), first Duke of Newcastle, who married Margaret née Lucas in 1645. He was also tutor to the third Earl, another William (1617–84). Margaret Cavendish claimed that she did not have personal exchanges with Hobbes on philosophical matters, though she was part of his social *milieu* and clearly knew his work, systematically reading it and other philosophic and scientific works during the 1660s (*Philosophical and Physical Opinions*, 1655). In her *Life* of her husband, Cavendish records his conversations with Hobbes on men who could fly and on witchcraft (1667, 143–5). On Cavendish's disingenuous naiveté as a gendered strategy, see Semler, 2012, 328, and below, p. 202. In 1634 Hobbes was commissioned by Newcastle to find a copy of Galileo's *Dialogue*; Hobbes' treatise the *Elements of Law* was dedicated to him and he read *Leviathan* as early as 1650 (Malcolm, 1996, 23, 27). In 1636 he invited Hobbes to join his household. On the 'mutuality of patronage' between the two men, see Sarasohn, 1999a, who notes that as early as 1635 Hobbes expressed to Newcastle his hope '"to be the first" to speak sensibly about the faculties and passions of the soul' (726).

published *Leviathan* in 1651, the same year in which Margaret of Jesus, by then living in nearby Lierre, underwent an anguishing exorcism, the sensory cause-and-effects of which will be discussed in Chapter 2. 'For there is no conception in a mans mind' Hobbes states in the second paragraph of his study, 'which hath not at first, totally, or by parts, been begotten upon the organs of Senses' (1973 ed., 3).[43] These sorts of ideas informed Margaret of Jesus' understandings of her condition, exacerbating her anguish if failure to guard the senses potentially contributed to her unfortunate condition.

Hobbes, had he been available to be called over the wall,[44] might also have explained the mechanism for Margaret's aversion to wool (p. 2): 'Sense, is Motion in the organs and interiour parts of mans body, caused by the action of the things we See, Heare, &c; and that fancy is but the Reliques of the same Motion, remaining after Sense … ' (23); 'so when the action of the same object is continued from the Eyes, Eares, and other organs to the Heart; the real effect there is nothing but Motion, or Endevour; which consisteth in Appetite, or Aversion, to, or from the object moving. (25).

Hobbes' views were, of course, commentaries on earlier theories. His *Elements of Law* (1640) presented the passions as 'pre-social, morally indifferent urges', dissenting from Aristotle's and Augustine's views of them as 'expressions of good or bad will' (Tilmouth, 2007, 222). Hobbes' treatise on optics (completed in 1645) challenges ideas of *species*, 'and other innumerable such trash' (1839–45 ed., VII, 470; James, 1997, 127).

Margaret Cavendish was herself interested in optics.[45] Her *Blazing World* (1666) discusses the use of microscopes to reveal the structure of eyes, exposing their cornea and 'glassie humor'. Charcoal examined through a lens opens up 'as an infinite multitude of pores' with 'very little space betwixt them to be filled with a solid body'. The credulous onlooker, Cavendish's figure of the Empress, is shown a flea and a louse through the microscope which 'appear'd so terrible to her sight, that they almost put her into a swoon' (2000 ed., 173). Cavendish's witty take on women's intellect, in its gambol through contemporary views on 'rational and sensitive perception' (183), also lays out ideas about the relationship between form and matter, asking whether 'spirits give motion to natural bodies?'; 'Whether they could speak without a body, or bodily organs?' (197). Her lengthy discussion

---

[43]   This phrase appears frequently in the works of other writers, see pp. 49 n. 61, 65. For discussion of Hobbes' 'refugee' status and his ideas of exile and subjection, see Loxley, 2010.

[44]   Hobbes was in London when he refused a dinner invitation from Margaret Cavendish, visiting the city in 1651–52 (*Philosophical and Physical Opinions*, 1655, sig. B3v; see Battigelli, 1998, 41).

[45]   See Sarasohn, 2010, 160 on Cavendish's study of Hooke's *Micrographia* and her response in *Observations Upon Experimental Philosophy* (1666, 12–13). For her visit to the Royal Society and the sarcasm of *Blazing World*, see ibid., 25–33, 161; Dear, 2007.

thus encompasses many topics that also occupied the nuns and others concerned with the relationship between 'sensitive and rational self-moving Matter' (215).

I am interested in how these two spatially connected, at times radically divergent, sensory and intellectual worlds developed their readings of what we might imagine to be the same physical effect. Proximity of sensory spaces does not, after all, mean proximity of experience or of explanation, even for English women in exile in the same city.[46]

Differences are apparent too in the ways that physiological and medical frameworks impinge on the nuns' explanations of physical effect. Although their understanding was underlined by essential tenets of somatic theory and by medical authorities with whom they came in contact, their own theories were shaped by belief in miracles and divine alteration of natural cause and effect. They finesse medical explanations. For example, like Hobbes and others they express views on the central role of the heart in receiving impulse from the senses leading to physical reaction.[47] The nuns supplement such knowledge: when they go pale or flush, for example, they often provide a pious explanation (see Chapter 3). Physical and metaphysical explanations are not, of course, mutually incompatible; the Carmelites synthesise ideas in ways that are sympathetic to their creed no less than other 'physitians of the soul'.[48]

It is clear, then, that the convent is (and in many ways is not), a 'distinct sensory realm' (Dugan, 2009, 729). To the advantage of this study it is an enclosed (if sometimes porous), time-framed, lived-in space. As well as exploring intellectual structures that shape the nuns' understanding of the senses, I also try to understand the ecological effect of cloisters as 'cognitive and social spaces' where 'bodies and souls ... prove permeable to their past as well as their environment' (Floyd-Wilson and Sullivan, 2007, 7, 8). It is partly because of their memories of previous domestic habitation that some nuns when they arrive at the convent are 'extreamly opprest & grieved', 'immortified that ye littleness of ye house did oppress me' (*A1,* 13*)*, or in the close quarters of the infirmary 'opress'd by to[o] many in ye room' (*A2*, 51). Anticipation of enclosure also affects sensory responsiveness: another wrote that she had 'strange notions of religious life beleiving that when she enter'd the Monastery she should never more see the sun and such like' (*A2*, 82).

---

[46]   Leibniz noted: 'one and the same town viewed from different sides looks altogether different and is, as it were, *perceptively* multiplied' (in Shuger, 1999, 35).

[47]   'Bloud in danger gathers to the hart' wrote John Davies in his long poetic excursion 'of humane knowledge', *Nosce Teipsum* (1599, 7) in which he muses on the location of the soul in the sensitive body. 'All Physitians commonly agree ... as also naturall Philosophers ... how an operation that lodgeth in the soule can alter the body, and move the humours from one place to another (as for example, recall most of the blood in the face, or other parts, to the heart, as we see by daily experience to chance in feare and anger)' (Wright, 1630, 4). For a discussion of 'alteration', see pp. 29–33.

[48]   This is Wright's term (1630, 4). Alison Weber observes of Teresa de Jesus' Carmelite reform was marked by her quest to harmonise 'charismata with Galenic medicine' (2000, 124).

One of the great advantages of discussing sensory experience in a convent is that we have such a clear idea of its architecture, in general monastic terms and in particular for Antwerp and Lierre. We also have many vivid accounts of the nuns' direct experience of those spaces; their papers describe excursions to the garret and the 'dead cellar' (the convent crypt), their fearfulness of dark corners. They log coincidence (a nun dies in the same bed, the same chair, the same room as her predecessors), and they log the unexpected, as when a nun dies suddenly in the chapel, another whilst whitewashing a wall, or taken ill after working in the crypt. The women describe how they intimately interact in and with such spaces in the course of a community life lived cheek-by-jowl in small groups (roughly 20 at one time), in confined enclosures. This is the space in which they have extra-sensory encounters, seeing spirits on the stairs or in their cells. In their natural and supernatural lives, proximity was strictly regulated by constitutions that mediated sensory behaviour as well as any other.

Space, after all, produces specific sensory effects; 'the way people experienced space and imposed their meanings upon it' (Flather, 2007, 1) is a key component of sensory – as well as gendered or other ideological – identity.[49] We might ask how far the nuns' sense of interiority related to their awareness of the outer world, within and without the convent walls; and how far they 'reimagined the body as separate from its environment' in ways that Cartesian and other philosophies of self might suggest (Paster, Rowe and Floyd-Wilson, 2004, 15).

In Bordieu's terms, 'the lessons of architecture are embedded in the body itself' and in convents we might most particularly expect that 'social hierarchy [is] spatially performed' (Hills, 2003, 9).[50] If 'The built environment of monasteries and convents created a sacred space that enshrined and celebrated ... virtuous behaviour' (Lehfeldt, 2003, 133) then what of the sensory bodies that also tried to encapsulate this ideal? What about resistant nuns, not complicit with enclosures' metaphors? What means of expressiveness are open to those whose sensory specifics (for personal or health reasons, perhaps) deviated from the cloistered ideal of a 'paradise on earth' (see p. 112)?

This book will consider various theories of early modern space and examine how the nuns weighed up apparently competing versions of their own reality. It will become clear that the nuns were by no means passive. Teresa de Jesus' energetic mission to create environments for women to engage in undisturbed meditation informed the Carmelite's arrangement of space. They could not have succeeded in their sensory subjection had they not adapted both themselves and it to their purpose.

---

[49]   The self is 'created in the active relationship between human bodies and their material environment' (Burkitt, 1991, 190; see Bound, 2000, 206).

[50]   On convent architecture see Gilchrist, 1994; Hills, 2004. On how 'buildings reshape those who inhabit them' see Hills, 2005, 95. See also Dunn, 2003; Lindquist, 2003; Weddle, 2003.

Overall, I am interested in what is historically general and what is extraordinary in the ways that early modern Carmelites described their senses. When Margaret of Jesus expressed aversion to a particular sensory stimulus (p. 2), we might ask whether hers is simply an account of biological reflex? Might her reaction be in part social, signalling the distaste of one more used to sumptuous textures (Chapter 3)? Are nuns' sensory reactions cultural manifestations, overlaid (or not) by devotional? Might they (also or instead) be giving a response based on gendered reception; idealising their expressiveness to fit the expectations of a (particular kind of) woman, of a nun, of a Carmelite? Which came first in their self-perception, and does this perception coincide with their self-presentation? All we have, of course, is what they said they felt. We can go behind those statements to see how far they were likely to be structured by surrounding conditions: expectations, aspirations, devotional desire.

Certainly we might expect that distribution of power affects both meaning and expressiveness. In a provocative aside during his paper on the psychology of music at a University of Sheffield Arts-Science encounter,[51] Paul Robertson, leader and violinist of the Medici String Quartet, suggested that sensory experience is dependent on prevailing ideas of order. Those living in rigid hierarchies might actually hear sound differently from those who do not. He was alluding to composers and audiences in Stalinist Russia. Convents, of course, are intrinsically hierarchical. Nuns pledge to obey their superiors and subsume their wills to divine control.

In exploring power structures in such communities we invariably encounter moral ecologies as well as gendered ideologies. Attitudes *to* nuns might be expected to shape their attitudes to themselves. Part of their defiance of sensory 'norms' appears to be a rejection of Protestant material modes. Their sensory metaphors reveal conceptual frameworks as well as levels of appreciation: when the nuns write about the 'sweet scent' of saintly bodies, they betray not only 'cognitive patterns of sensation' but also an understanding of language as a bridge, 'as much a part of our functioning as our sense of touch, and as precious' (Lakoff and Johnson, 1980, 239):[52] contingency in yet another sense.

I will be asking how the practice of writing itself shaped the nuns' sensitivities. Did they rework their experience and in turn their understanding under pressure of textualisation, introducing thereby another dimension to their self-consciousness and another hiatus in their expression of 'inner sense'?[53] Some nuns claim to write swiftly and spontaneously, under holy inspiration. Sensory-spiritual effects are visible on their skin (Chapter 3). Others claim to be more inhibited and slow in

---

[51] 4 May 2010. This fruitfully imaginative series, originated and organised by Rachel Falconer of the University of Sheffield's School of English, ran over several semesters from 2009–10, bringing together in conversation academics, practitioners and the general public from diverse fields.

[52] Dugan relates 'the sweet smell of an actual rose' and cultural representation of it (2009, 728). See also her 2008 essay on *Twelfth Night*.

[53] On the time-delay between experience and narrative see Heller-Roazen, 2007, 27, 38.

their writing; some papers were ostensibly prepared reluctantly 'under obedience' to confessors or superiors, and notwithstanding the nuns' familiar use of modesty *topoi* in this respect, their work does bear the marks of spiritual licence and reworking. Sometimes spiritual directors correct the nuns so that they revisit their previous sensory experience to explain themselves, or to be seen so to do. These are multi-layered narratives compiled by women who, after all, are experts in strategic self-scrutiny.

In writing about rhetoric that describes feeling, Robert Cockcroft asks 'Can it preserve the candour and clarity, or the conflicts of emotion and perception, in our spontaneous responses to texts, or to other people's readings? How much of this can survive transplantation into a persuasive argument? Can the *affective* quality of spontaneity be mirrored in that of deliberate utterance?' (2003, 2). This might infer that there is an originating 'pure' sensation behind words, struggling to get out. Certainly the nuns often write with a sense of urgency, as if divinely-inspired truths pour forth through them as imperfect ciphers, their language causing them to stumble. I am interested in the relationship between literary positioning and the sensory life behind.[54] This study will show that expressiveness and experience were interactive.

Notwithstanding the general consensus of spiritual approach that informs the nuns' writings, they express a diversity of self-perception. Their writing style (if we can equate eloquence and education) reveals a range of training (in composition, letter-writing and general self-expression). Lay Sisters from different social levels as well as Latinate choir nuns are included here. Although clearly this material is not representative of early modern culture at large, shaped as it is by circumstance, that is in many ways its strength. I am not assuming (or denying) that the nuns were necessarily influenced by intellectual rather than 'proverbial' understandings of the senses (nor are these necessarily separate). Nor am I assuming that 'theory' inevitably informs experience (or *vice versa*). If they are governed by canonicity, nuns are by no means canonical characters.[55]

---

[54]   Cockcroft asks 'can emotion, viewed primarily as a subjective experience rather than as a phenomenon to be studied and interpreted, possess some kind of truth-value?' (2003, 3). In her DPhil thesis Fay Bound notes an absence of research into 'affect displays', noting that distinctions between 'expression' and 'gesture' are unhelpful: 'the term 'expression' implies something 'real' waiting to be expressed, and reinforces the notion of affect as a pre-cultural or innate world of experience' (2000, 133). Her own subsequent work has gone some way to filling this gap. This book considers how gestures are themselves part of sensory expressiveness (Chapter 3).

[55]   The material allows for an exploration of a (not unlimited) 'diversity of self-perception', avoiding an exclusively 'intellectualist history of selfhood' of the sort that bothered Mark Jenner (1999, 144). He is also critical of assumptions that early modern understandings of the body were necessarily learned (149). The nuns' references to illness and anatomy suggest they were exposed to contemporary medical views (several served as convent Infirmarians, and one woman trained as an apothecary: see p. 94) and they

It might be thought that because some of the sources I refer to are institutional (chronicles or accounts compiled to demonstrate an exemplary individual history, for example) that nuns are merely *displaying* the senses in terms that would show them in the best possible light. In fact, such 'semi-public' documents were very rarely actually 'published' or read beyond the convent itself, so the nuns performance affirmed modes of sensory behaviour to a captive, complicit audience. These 'idealised' sources are also offset by more raw and personal material compiled by the nuns for their own individual purposes or confessionally for spiritual directors. It will be clear that writing and performance are mutually reinforcing; often we cannot tell them very much apart. When Anne of the Ascension, for instance, writes a meditation for another nun, she not only expresses a sensory ideal, she also enacts it; she 'inhabits' her own text and it 'becomes' by performative process the nun who reads it (see Chapter 2).

Writing inevitably reshapes experience; all autobiography is retrospective. And reading has an effect on the senses as well as the intellect. This is what makes it so potentially dangerous (Chapter 2). Teresa de Jesus tells us that when she read in Augustine's *Confessions* that he was converted by hearing God's voice in a garden,[56] it seemed to her that God was also speaking to her with just the same immediacy, so she dissolved in tears (*Vida*, Chapter 9). Seventeenth-century Carmelites seek to induce a similar effect; they say that they wrote their histories so that those who follow 'may be animated' to follow the example of their predecessors (*A1*, ix). This is a key precept of Teresian spirituality, and that of other Orders, in which saintly souls and Prioresses inspire other members of their community by process of positive promulgation in practice and text, based on concepts of *suavedad*: cheerful contagion (Weber, 2002, 15).

Convent chronicles chart collective remembrance. They are 'a powerful source of material memories'; in them, as in other shared documentation, 'sense experiences are registered and continued from generation to generation' (Stewart, 2005, 59).[57] The nuns accordingly seek to present themselves as models of earlier, saintly religious, in sensory behaviour as in other matters. In doing this they are not simply advertising their desirable discipline, but enacting it; after all, their predecessors claimed to have achieved devotional results so it was useful to copy

---

mention convent physicians, if only to lament the suffering they caused. Their knowledge is augmented (sometimes compromised) by their belief in miracles.

56   Teresa read Augustine's *Confessions* in 1554, the year in which it was translated into Spanish (Carrera, 2005, 27, 164). Several Carmelites echo in their Lives this detail of receiving their vocation in a garden, reflecting presumably their own experience and also a literary history of epiphany; life-writing by textual proximity.

57   Stewart is writing about Marx's *Economic and Philosophic Manuscripts of 1844* in which he argues that the senses are not merely organs but are themselves a source of material memory registering physical experience such as repression or oppression (Stewart, 2005, 59). On Marx and the social history of sense perception see Jütte, 2005, 9; on obituary writing and the development of collective memory in convents, see Bowden, 2010.

them. More pragmatically, and Teresa de Jesus was ever tactical, by modelling their life-writing on the pattern of women whose behaviour was endorsed by the established church as saintly, early modern nuns could avoid suspicion in a period of acute post-Tridentine scrutiny.

There are, then, many strands to what might seem to be sensory subterfuge. This book will try to unpick some of the component threads.

In seeking to create an over-arching history of the female Order, the Antwerp Carmelites wrote a narrative that attended to sensory re-generation, to the spiritual powers that reside in somatic permanence in particular. I discuss the role played by the intact and sentient corpse (Chapter 3), and the descriptions of nuns who are especially sensually receptive in its presence (Chapter 6). It will be clear that the incorrupt, sweet-smelling body has a key role in Carmelite imaginative frameworks that influence their sensory as well as spiritual fantasies. Sensorial historicising, too, has its own history.

Teresa de Jesus was naturally enough an important source of inspiration for Carmelite women, who shaped their own writing around her works. After 1622 when she was canonised she represented a relatively unproblematic role model; mirroring her exemplary behaviour in all aspects of their lives enabled the Carmelite nuns to avoid some, by no means all, of the criticism that so disabled women's devotional progress in the early modern period. I am interested in available models of expressiveness, in sensory and other orthodoxy. After all, 'An individual's sensory perception is always social perception. The individual perceives what is socially permitted to be expressed in language' (Rindisbacher, 1992, 5).

I consider the effect of religious homogeneity on sensory heterodoxy, insofar as this is manifested in the nuns' writing. When they appear to rewrite accounts of their own sensory (as other) experience to reflect a saintly model, are they thereby falsifying their memories of past events? 'One of the main problems with sensate certainty and sensory experience lies in their purely momentous nature, without past, without future' (Rindisbacher, 1992, 4). The nuns, though, give the sensual-ephemeral longevity beyond personal life-span. If individual experience of the past is ostensibly less important to the nuns than collective commemoration, then we might expect that the nuns' personal sensory histories were rewritten along with their other accounts.

It is clear from their documents that the nuns had a complicated relationship to temporality. They aspire to immediate-future spiritual union, and insist on the pious importance of historical narrative, reclaiming their own history of the female Order at key moments of Carmelite crisis, in the face of opposition from the Carmelite friars. For this and for other reasons, at times there appears to be little distinction between individual and corporate sensory recollection.

This, then, is also a book about memory. Hobbes considered it to be a 'decaying sense', 'like that which happens in looking upon things at a great distance' (*Elements of Philosophy*, I, 398; James, 1997, 167).[58] Teresa de Jesus, on the other hand, claimed an immediacy of recall and affect; the voice that spoke to Augustine through his text is conveyed to her readers via her own. She seems to challenge the view that successive process, whether in memory or report, is necessarily diluted. Much of her writing is indeed concerned to re-enact sensory urgency. This book will consider the effects of the sequential conduits she describes, and of the intrusion of mnemonic systems practised in the convents, when nuns were trained to forget their own past lives in order to concentrate on the meditative emphatic present.

Hobbes, in doubting memory, further complicates our initial response to Margaret of Jesus' reaction to wool described in this introduction. She is, says a later biographer, 'euen yet very sensible of it' (*L3.27*, 15).[59] Her sensibility to the memory of her shudder (for that is partly what I assume her 'alteration' to be) appears to be as sharp in the narrative present as it was at the original moment of sensation. This suggests that (to some not very serious extent) she failed to divorce herself from sensory feeling and to forget past memory. A sensitive nun is, we might think, also a negligent nun.

Ideas of memory and forgetfulness occupied Carmelite writers as they had Augustine in his *Confessions*.[60] Other early modern writers without such meditative

---

[58]   'And any object being removed from our eyes, though the impression it made in us remain ... the Imagination of the past is obscured, and made weak; as the voice of a man is in the noyse of the day' (*Leviathan*, 1651, 5).

[59]   In fact when this account was written Margaret of Jesus had been dead for over a year, so we might assume – though in Carmelite narratives this is never self-evident – that by then she was not 'sensible' at all. (It is likely that her biographer simply transcribed from a previous text; see Hallett, 2007b, 118–27.)

[60]   Augustine wrote extensively on memory and its sensory store. 'Memory preserves in distinct particulars and general categories all the perceptions which have penetrated, each by its own route of entry. Thus light and all colours and bodily shapes enter by the eyes; by the ears all kinds of sounds ... Memory's huge cavern, with its mysterious, secret, and indescribable nooks and crannies, receives all these perceptions, to be recalled when needed and reconsidered ... But who can say how images are created, even though it may be clear by which senses they are grasped and stored within. For even when I am in darkness and silence, in my memory I can produce colours at will ... On demand, if wish, they can be immediately present' (*Confessions*, X.viii.13; 1992 ed., 186); 'Great is the power of memory, an awe-inspiring mystery ... As I rise above memory, where am I to find you?' (xvii.26; 194–5). Teresa de Jesus wrote that in rapture 'all the Powers of the soule fall short of operation'; 'If she were thinking of some Mysterie, it is instantly so forgotten as if there had neuer bee anie such thought. If she were reading, there is no remembrance of it; nor yet of pawsing ... So that now, this importune little Gnatt of the Memorie, hath her wings burnt heer, and can no longer spring-vp, nor stirre ...' (*Flaming Hart*, 1642, 238). Tobie Matthew's translation of *The Confessions* was first published in 1620.

priorities also discussed mnemonic process; like Teresa de Jesus they seem to contradict Hobbes' claims on memory's diminution of sensation. Giovanni Della Casa, for example, in a frequently reprinted text translated from Spanish from the sixteenth century onwards, asserts as 'an undoubted Rule' '*That Whatsoever thing, word, or action,* offends *any* of the senses, *or* annoys *the* stomack, *or is apt to imprint on the mind the* resemblance *of that which is* odious *and* filthy … *not only the* doing *or the* remembring *such Things, but even the* representing *of them by any mode or gesture to the Imagination of another, is wont to be exceeding* irksome *and* unpleasant' (1663, 9).[61]

Across the 'distance of time and space', in the immediacy of her recall, Margaret of Jesus appears to defy both Hobbes and her own devotional discipline. The early modern Carmelites sit amidst an array of sometimes contradictory injunctions about their own sensory experience, the unravelling of which is the purpose of this book.

---

[61]   *The Refin'd Courtier* is shaped around ideas of sensory assault and the role of the senses in well-mannered society. Chapter 1 begins with 'several things which annoy the senses' considering them '*indecent*' (1663, 10–11).

Chapter 1

In Which Mrs Eyre Protects the Impressionable Souls of her Tender Daughters

In around 1681 Mary Bedingfield, wife of Thomas Eyre, left her family home at Eastwell in Leicestershire accompanied by her three youngest daughters, 'exposing her owne person to the trouble of a tedieus journy' to Flanders. They eventually arrived at the Carmelite convent in Lierre where Mary's sister Margaret was Subprioress, and her uncle, Edmund Bedingfield, had for a long time been Confessor. In fact, several members of the family were nuns at the convent.[1] Visits of this sort were not uncommon for business, education, for pleasure, or to escape persecution in England.[2] This occasion, however, had a specific sensory-censorious reason.

Mrs Eyre's eldest son had lately married 'a young Catholique Lady of Birth and fortune' and the newly-weds went to live with his parents at Eastwell. Extended family life was not always easy.[3] The arrival of the young couple brought with it inconvenience: 'they must bring their seruants along with them, friends, and much Gentry of all thos parts must nessarily pay their visits to the young Bride and her spous, Neither one nor the other, could happen without some distractions in the Family'. Mrs Eyre took action 'not to let them take any impressions in the tender soules of her three youngest daughters':

---

[1]   Margaret Bedingfield (1646–1714); Edmund Bedingfield (1615–80). See Hallett, 2007a, 197–209 for excerpts from the Lives of several Bedingfield nuns and of Edmund Bedingfield.

[2]   For example, the so-called 'Popish' plot is mentioned in the Life of Mary Anne of St Wenefrid (Anne Mostyn: 1663–1715), a niece of Margaret Mostyn, who came to Lierre after her family had travelled to Paris 'till such time as the pretended plot of Oates and Bedlow against Roman Cathholliques broke out. Then [they were] forced to go ouer to Paris, as many others did to decline the cruel persecution that raged all ouer England' (*L13.7*, 257).

[3]   Margaret Mostyn was commended for her management of her grandmother's extended family home from the age of around 12: 'her great discression in maneging ye house, was ye admeration of ye whole cuntrie, wth so much order and prudince, yt she gaue a genarall sattisfaction to all, tho it consisted of 2 or 3 seuerall famelys, difernt in youmers' (*L13.7*, 42). Her spirit of 'peace and concord' in this endeavour (which informed her work as a Prioress) was also noted in another source (*L3.31*, 7–8).

... no thing was to be done in their sight, nor a word spoken within their hearing, but what should relish of Pietie, Godliness and deuotion, the whole course of their future liues did much depend upon those first impressions of Good and Euill which in those tender years they receaued from exteriour sensations entering into their minds, by the Litle gates of their curious eyes and eares when once got in, they were not easily to be remoued from thence but were usualy layd up in their memories, and from whence readily brought out as often as any occasion of good or euill presented it self during the whole course of their succeeding Liues ... (*L13.7*, 224–8)

Their mother therefore 'resolued to remoue them to a nursey of piety abroad, where they should neither see nor hear any thing but what should be good or perfect'. And there two of her daughters stayed: Martha Eyre (*c.*1672–1706) professed at Lierre in 1689 as Mary Martha of Jesus; her sister Catherine (1674–*c.*1729) professed as Mary Catherine of the Blessed Sacrament in 1691.[4]

This account of their arrival, most probably written just after Martha Eyre's death in 1706, reflects views of the senses outlined in my general introduction.[5] It is important now to examine these in more detail to see just why Mrs Eyre was so cautious about the influences to which her daughters were exposed.

The image of the senses as gates was commonplace enough. It derives from Jeremiah 9:21 and Job 38:17[6] familiarly picked up by Jerome and later commentators to refer to the senses as the gates of death.[7] Thomas Wright, explained that 'All senses no doubt are the first gate wherby passe and repasse all messages sent to passions' (1630, 150).[8] Passions are 'prouoked', stirred 'by humors arising in our bodies, by externall senses and secret passage of sensuall obiects'. Where the senses lead, passions follow; they in turn inform cognitive processes of memory and reason.

---

[4] Catherine Eyre was initially admitted on trial as a novice because she suffered from a range of physical ailments and, like several others in the family, was 'short of stature' (*L13.7*, 271–3).

[5] In normal practice at Lierre, the accounts were written soon after a nun's death by the then Prioress, at this time Margaret Teresa of the Immaculate Conception (Margaret Mostyn: 1657/9–1745) who succeeded her aunt, Ursula of All Saints in 1700.

[6] Jeremiah 9:21: 'For death is come up through our windows'; 'Quia ascendit mors per fenestras nostras'. Job 38:17: 'Have the gates of death been opened to thee, and hast thou seen the darksome doors?'; 'Numquid apertae tibi sunt portae mortis, et ostia tenebrosa vidisti?'

[7] For discussion of Gregory's *Moralia in Job*, see pp. 57, 64–5, 141, 151 n. 13.

[8] Wright cites Old Testament scriptural authority, using the warning example of David who once 'glanced awry and let goe the reines of his eyes' when he saw Bathsheba. He claims that 'of all senses, sight was the surest and certainest of his obiect and sensation' (1630, 151) – a claim to which we will return in Chapter 7. On the iconography of the senses as gates, see Ripa, 1603 in Kermode, 1971, 87.

In a text that was known to at least some of the nuns before and after arrival at the convent, Jerome Plautus' *The Happiness of a Religious State*,[9] there are warnings about the ways in which passions can be 'inflamed by the presence of the sensible object'; 'because while our soule is enclosed within our bodie, and so linked vnto it that they make one man, the things which our Senses as messengers do bring vnto it, must needs make great impression in it' (1632, 91). Like other writers of devotional manuals, Plautus proceeds to set out various means to overcome the senses in order to temper the passions.

The sensory sequence is also comprehensively outlined by the Carmelite Paul of St Ubald. He states all passions 'doe follow the knowledge that preceede's from the senses' (1654, Part III, 98). Importantly, the senses agitate: 'The passion is a motion of the sensitive part, which is moued by the apprehension of some good, or euil, as conuenient, or disconuenient, pleasing or displeasing to it' (Part III, 95); 'the passions allwayes come's with some alteration of the body, chiefly of the heart, where all of them doe end' (97).[10]

The speed and unexpectedness of these 'strong motions' is felt to be a mark of their authenticity in this and many similar accounts by other writers: 'when one doth heare a good sermon, of God well spoaken of, or praised, or musick, or at the sight of some sweet, and deuout picture; and this cometh with an impulse in the depth or most inward of the soul so vehement, sudden, and swift, that she cannot resist it ... but away she is taken'. In awe of divine revelation 'she is much terrified, and doth conceiue a reuerentiall feare, which causeth the very haires on her head to stand' (Part III, 69–70). Other Carmelite sources describe similar sensation, sometimes resulting in pallor.[11]

'And in his herte he sodeynly agroos, And pale he wex':[12] an interlude on alteration

Ambroise Paré explained sudden pallor in his *Introduction to Surgery* (1585). He suggested that agitations in the soul, like those in the body, 'cause the movement

---

[9]   Margaret of Jesus Mostyn among others referred to reading this text before she joined the convent (*L3.27*, 7). It was said to have inspired many religious vocations (Hardman, 1937, 9).

[10]   On the relationship between emotion ('emoveo', to move out or away) and 'affetto' (movements of mind or soul), see Gouk and Hills, 2005, 17.

[11]   See Chapter 3 for discussion of passionate effects. The description of similar physical response to extra-sensory impulse is found in a ghost story copied out by Margaret of Jesus. In this a young maid in an English Catholic household was terrorised by a restless spirit: 'it seemed to her that she heard a most heuenly musick in [the] passage neare by her, which caused such an alteration in her that her mistris discouered something by the paleness of her countenance' (*L3.34*, 5). See Hampton, 2004 on pallor in Cervantes.

[12]   Chaucer, *Legend of Good Women*, 830 (*OED*: 'agrise'). See Hallett 2012c for a discussion of alteration and time.

of spirits and of natural heat, which in turn dilate or compress the heart, thereby releasing or restricting the movement of spirits which change the color of the face' (1585, 36; trans. Hampton, 2004, 277). Descartes, as ever, located such changes in the brain.[13] He suggests that it is not the objects themselves that stimulate the senses but human perception of the ways in which they may harm or benefit the recipient.

Writers of Catholic devotional manuals suggest that pious pallor (and its opposite, the blessed blush: see p. 120) results from holy action on or beyond the senses. According to the Spanish Dominican Luis of Granada (1505–88) whose works were widely published in this period, these effects reveal the origin of alteration, making visible the final cause through sequential unfolding: 'the power and force of the cause is knowne by the effects and work, and by the power & force the Essence is knowne' (*The Sinner's Guide*, 1598, 17). For Teresa de Jesus cause *is* effect: 'the Soule now and then, spring-vp euen out of her self, as it were a kind of fire, which is burning vp, in a flame; and sometimes the fire encreases, with a kind of impetuositie … it is no distinct thing, from the verie fire; but it is the flame it self, which still is in the fire' (*Flaming Hart*, 1642, 217).[14] In her comparison, things move from being 'kind of' to being 'verie'. 'Alteration' therefore advertises its own cause even in the sudden moment it arrives.[15] It is worth considering for a moment the nuns' use of this word.

Margaret of Jesus, for example, reported that she heard 'in a loud sweet voice this word *Adsum* which all changed mee into a great deal of peace & ioy' (*L3.31*, 39). The devil, too, advertised his presence through the senses, experienced by Margaret and her sister Ursula of All Saints (Elizabeth Mostyn: 1626–1700) as altogether less joyful alterations that were 'impressed' on long-term memory.[16]

---

[13]   Descartes gave 'the proximate cause of the passions of the soul' as 'simply the agitation [of] the little gland in the middle of the brain', that is the pineal gland (*Passions of the Soul*, 1649, Part II, 51; 1985 ed., I, 349). Importantly, 'sense perception occurs in the same way in which wax takes on an impression from a seal. It should not be thought that I have mere analogy in mind here: we must think of the external shape of the sentient body as being really changed by the object in exactly the same way as the shape of the surface of the wax is altered by the seal' (*Rules for the Direction of the Mind*, c.1628, published 1684; 1985 ed., I, 40).

[14]   See Craik, 2007, 5 on 'The inseparability of affect from its display'. John of the Cross gave six different sources for happy agitation: temporal, natural, sensual, moral, supernatural and spiritual good (*Ascent of Mount Carmel*, 1906 ed., 285).

[15]   Ecstasy: ek + stasis; 'to be put out of place': the state of being beside oneself, thrown into a frenzy or stupor, with anxiety, astonishment, fear or passion' (*OED*). See Tyler, 2010, 68 on spiritual union and erotic alteration.

[16]   For Margaret, 'if it chanced she was alone, all ye dores would be made fast one a sudan, and ye place filled wth a black cloud, wch did cause so great fiere and alteration in her, yt she could not so much as moue a finger, or make ye singe of ye crosse' (*L13.7*, 53). During the same events which led to exorcism in 1651 (see Chapter 2), Ursula described 'finding my selfe altered & transported with ugly desires & fancyes'. She heard the words '*thou shall be damned*' and not surprisingly they had a profound long-term effect on her:

Anne of the Ascension, when she heard of Protestant abuses 'was stroken with so deep a sence as her whole body seemd to be altered' (*L3.35*). Like others, she employs the language of unwelcome recall as a sudden, physical, painful experience; striking, indelible, disruptive of devotional calm.[17]

All in all, for better or worse, the senses were thought to create a direct and vulnerable line to the passions, initiating rippling somatic effect with impact on memory. Whether it was moral purpose or more fundamental psychic health that needed to be safeguarded, Mrs Eyre, it seems, was wise to protect her daughters.

It is clear, then, that the nuns use 'alteration' to describe their deep-seated reaction at moments of acute, unwonted awareness of the impact of 'other' on self. Some nuns indeed appear to draw on Galenic medicine to explain the process, implying that in alteration matter actually changes from one form to another. Certainly, it signals dramatic change.[18]

Often it is marked by astonishment ('estonnement')[19] which Descartes again characteristically locates in the brain. Like Teresa de Jesus, and the nuns who describe themselves as unable to move during episodes of sensory-passionate drama, he describes paralysis, but in mechanical rather than spiritual terms. It 'causes the spirits in the cavities of the brain to make their way to the place where the impression of the object of wonder is located. It has so much power to do this that sometimes it drives all the spirits there, and makes them wholly occupied with the preservation of this impression that none of them pass into the muscles … the whole body remains as immobile as a statue'; 'Astonishment is an excess of wonder, and it can never be other than bad' (*The Passions of the Soul*, 1649; 1985 ed., I, 354).

Teresa de Jesus, on the other hand, describes the positive and vivid after-effects of such shock. In her youth she was warned away from 'particular friendship' by a vision of Christ seen, she insists, 'with the eys of my Soule', 'and he remained so deeply imprinted there, that although it hapned to me aboue six and twentie yeares agoe, me thinkes he is stille as present to me now, as he was then; But I am sure,

---

'I find these words haue left a very deep inpression in mee, & it is impossible for mee to forgett them or take any content in whatsoeuer I doe' (*L3.31*, 36). See Chapter 5 on violent alteration caused by hearing bad news.

[17] 'I was upon A sudon stroukin wt ye remembernce of what had pased wth me at 11 years a goe and could not put it forth of my mind' wrote Anne of St Augustine (Anne Wright: 1619–47), Anne of the Ascension's successor as Prioress at Antwerp (*L.1.6A*).

[18] Teresa of Jesus Maria Joseph (Mary Poole: 1696–1793) was said to have been born prematurely because of the pressures of persecution in England 'her mother falling suddenly into labour from the alteration she was seized with on seeing her husband hurry'd off in the night to prison' (*L13.8*, 18). The editor of the 1639 version of George Chapman's *Ovid's Banquet of the Sence* glosses 'alterationem pati est sentire' as 'change then, and suffer for the use of sence'.

[19] See Mary Thomas Crane (2007) for a discussion of 'amazement' in Marvell's 'The Garden'.

I remained so altered, yea and so astonished, that I intended to see that person no more' (*Flaming Hart*, 1642, 62–3).[20]

This kind of alteration is, then, marked and attended by transformation or epiphany of one sort or another. Paul of St Ubald refers to *Instructions for Novices* (a book in the Lierre library) which characterises alteration as a state in which the soul is with 'great swiftness carried away from the senses'. Then the body becomes light and agile, and the joyfully infused subject 'doth tremble and shake with strang fits, and they do leap, runne and cry out by reason of the excesse of inward ioy' (*The Soul's Delight*, 1654, 107–10).

Such signs arrived with text-book precision in the account of the pre-profession cure of Mary Xaveria of the Angels (Catherine Burton: 1668–1714). During her youth she suffered prolonged and perplexing illness, manifesting a bewildering array of symptoms that doctors and priests failed to alleviate over several years. She attributed her sudden return to health to the intercession of St Francis Xavier to whom she prayed using 'the devotion of ten Fridays' in his honour. The first time she did this she experienced a temporary remission; the second time: 'so great a joy seazed my soul that it diffused it self all over my body, finding my self as if new life and blood were infused into me and such an alteration all over me gave me extraordinary agility … [my joints] became on a suddain plyable' (*A3*; 93; Hallett, 2007a, 147).

Burton's account, which is contained in a book-length version of her Life prepared in around 1723 by her confessor, Thomas Hunter (1666–1725),[21] echoes many features of the 'ten Fridays' prayers and of Francis Xavier's own Life,[22] both of which were readily available. His Life was 'Englished' several times by Jesuits including Louis Sabran (1652–1732) who visited the ailing Catherine Burton in 1691.[23] Abridgements of Francis Xavier's Life include a number of cases of

---

[20]   For other examples of 'astonishment' resulting in paralysis, see Hallett, 2007a, 27, 168, 182; Hallett, 2007b, 114, 134. Literal 'estonement' seems to have been exemplified by Ursula of All Saints in her grief at the death of her sister Margaret when she 'remained kneeling like a statuary' at Margaret's bedside until she gave up the ghost (*L3.30C*).

[21]   Hunter studied at the English College at St Omers, became a Jesuit in 1684 and was appointed Professor of logic and philosophy at Liège. He professed in 1702, and acted as spiritual advisor to the nuns at Antwerp for several years (Coleridge, 1876, viii; *ODNB*).

[22]   Francis Xavier (1506–52) was canonised in 1622, the same year as Teresa de Jesus and Ignatius Loyola. His body was said to have been miraculously preserved, like that of Teresa de Jesus.

[23]   'Father Louis Sabran of ye Society was lately arrived in England and being in our neighbourhood my father out of civility went to meet him and invited him to our house, he heard of my long sickness and desired to see me … he advised my Confessor to make me begin [the ten Fridays devotion] anew' (*A3*, 83–4). Sabran preached a sermon outlining the miracles of Francis Xavier in the chapel of the Spanish Ambassador, solemnising the Saint's feast in December 1687. In this he attributed Margaret of Austria's conception of a child to the saint's intercession (1687, 39). Sabran, the son of the French ambassador to England, was chaplain to James II, fleeing to the continent in 1688. He held a number of

'sudden change' in which, typically, an ill person 'rises up amazed, and leaps for joy' (1667, 26).

Among other details, instructions for performing the novena specify the devout person should offer up to the saint some forms of mortification: 'They are to curb their senses, their Eyes, and ears, and their Tongue, endeavouring to avoid even the least of Sins' (1690, 7). According to her later account, Burton followed such a course in her youth. In the chronology of her *Life*, Burton's mortifications are mentioned before her cure and the reading of the Fridays devotion. It is as if she was instinctively exemplary even before she had the inspiration to be so. As so often in this life-writing, narrative structures belie the sequence of events: accounts are, as it were, rewritten, to stress correspondence between behaviour and the mimetic model that preceded the actual moment of fixation. The 'alteration' that results from the Saint's alleged intercession marks the point at which Burton most perfectly imitates him; she is 'infused' with new blood, as it were a transfusion from the saint himself and, textually, from devotional manuals surrounding such accounts. This is a literary as well as somatic intermingling.

Burton's Bookish Behaviour

It is also possible to trace close correlation between Mary Xaveria's *Life* and details in John of the Cross' *Ascent of Mount Carmel*, mentioned by Hunter in his preface.[24] Hunter indeed follows John's advice, making his spiritual charge retrace her past sinful life, 'putting her on the rack anew' (1906 ed., 6).[25] This is part of

---

senior ecclesiastical offices, and died at the English College in Rome in 1732 (Hardman, 1939, 17). Dryden's 1688 translation of Francis Xavier's *Life* is dedicated to Mary of Modena; it too mentions the saint's role in curing 'barrenness', and like other Catholic texts of the period, it reassures the Queen that she will bear an heir and 'God will restore his Church in *England*' (1688, dedication; pages unnumbered). See Chapter 3 for Carmelite contribution to this cause.

[24]   '*Blessed John of ye Cross* a most spirituall man and Director of St Teresa, in his 2d book of *ye Ascent to Mount Carmel* esp. 11th discoursing of exterior visions & satisfaction a soul feels in them declares yt a soul desireous of perfection ought absolutely to reject them all as in themselves most dangerous' (*A3*, viii). John's Book discusses the souls' progress through various nights: of the senses, the faith and the spirit (1906 ed., 66–7). See also the Carmelite treatise from the English community at Hoogstraeten (now in the Baltimore Carmelite archive) on 'the night or active mortification of the senses', edited by Laurence Lux-Sterritt (2012, 193–202). It includes sections on imaginative reflection on 'objects, whos species entered in by the sense', and on memory as 'a magazin of objects laid up by passions, corporal senses etc' (200, 201).

[25]   Paul of St Ubald similarly suggests that devout persons should mentally run through their past life in order to remember precisely how chaotic it was: 'Then consider how vnmortified your passions and senses, your inclinations and affections ... were and are' (1654, Part II, 60). This process, which he compares to turning over the soil and weeding

John's famous discussion of 'dark night, the necessity of passing through it in order to attain divine union' (9): 'the privation of, and purgation from, all sensual desires in all outward things of this world' (10):

> Philosophers say that the soul is a blank when God first infuses it into the body, without knowledge of any kind whatever, and incapable of receiving knowledge, in the course of nature, in any other way than through the senses. Thus, while in the body, the soul is like a man in a dark prison, who has no knowledge of what passes without beyond what he can learn by looking through the window of his cell ... we cannot help hearing, seeing, smelling, tasting, and touching, but this is of no moment, and does not trouble the soul, when the objects of sense are repelled, any more than if we neither heard not saw ... I call this detachment the night of the soul ... that detachment which consists in suppressing desire and avoiding pleasure ... (14–15)

He concludes that the soul needs to persist 'until we have so habituated our senses to this purgation from sensible joy' (319).

Hunter maps Mary Xaveria's *Life* onto this purgative pattern, stressing her accomplished detachment. Again, he does so in an editorial process that moves back and forth chronologically in order that we witness for ourselves the ways in which she systematically disengages from worldly ties and the prison of her own passions. She is already exemplary, even as we encounter her youthful self: 'From 10 or 11 til 16 I lived a more sensual life, following too much ye bent of my own passions; tow or three times on occasion of some words of humiliation said to me by servants, I found my blood to rise, and my self tremble with passion ...' (*A3*, 16).

The narrative begins as if the nun herself is just beginning, aged 30, told by Hunter to write down her experience, reluctant until St Xavier 'told me he would help me, that he would indite it for me, and yt there should be nothing in

---

a garden, should only be done on the instruction of superiors or spiritual directors. There follows a lengthy discussion of sensory vigilance, calling the five senses to account in turn in order to obtain 'mastery and dominion' (77) over them. 'Thus the soul begins to put her inward house or common wealth in good order ... [to] make his body, senses, powers, and passions subiect to the spirit' (95). It is impossible, he claims, to advance to the next stage of prayer until the senses have been purged by examination of the self through time. He suggests linking mental prayer to sensory stimuli, such as touching the rosary or praying 'when the cock doth crowe or any bell doth ring'. His spatial mnemonic system is very like others: 'to giue a denomination to the rooms of the house, of the passages of our Sauiours life and death ... that when you goe into any of these rooms you may call to mynd the mistery of that place' (137–8). The Dominican Johannes Romberch, for example, whose influential treatise *Congestorium Artificiose Memorie* was published in 1520, structured memory around an abbey. Similar plans of memory rooms are widely found in manuscript and printed treatises (Yates, 1966, 116–17). Some texts assign different parts of Christ's Passion to different rooms, so the devout person mentally follows and experiences in sensory-affective ways the Stations of the Cross.

it but what was true' (*A3*, 2). John of the Cross noted: 'This knowledge of pure truths requires ... that God should hold the hand and wield the pen of the writer' (1906 ed., 205). The Saint proceeds figuratively (we assume) to do just this: Mary Xaveria is 'amazed', she says, 'when I read over what I have write, it seems as if I had not done it but as if some other had done it for me'; 'if I go on writeing he must be by me, and dictate to me as he has already done; as to myself I remember little or nothing when I take my pen' (*A3*, 8; 207).

On being told by Hunter to write about her early illness, 'as soon as I had set pen to paper, I found no more dificulity then if it had been all writen before me & yt I had transcribed it' (4). Hunter then tests her obedience and the authenticity of her claims by telling her in scathing terms to destroy all that she has written.[26] A few days later, Hunter told her to start writing again as if for the first time. And so it goes on; St Xavier himself joins in, telling her to write no more at which she says 'I remained for above half an hour in rapt, without being able to stir my right hand or make a letter; tho I endeavour'd never so much' (6). Hunter commends her exemplary detachment: 'she was so farr disingaged from any tye to her self or her own performance, yt she was perfectly indifferent whether her writings were kept or burnt, liked or not liked' (9).

The narrative then moves back to Burton's earlier life. In a series of editorial manoeuvres, Hunter shows the nun's progress through dark nights of sensory detachment. Her early penitential behaviour brings her to the state in which her cure (which precedes the narrative that contains it) is possible. She is exemplary before she knows how to be. 'I would' she says, 'lace my self so straight, that my stayes were more painful then any chain I have wore since I came to religion' (25); 'I had now a vocation to be religious, tho' I knew not well what religion was' (26). We see before our own readerly eyes this spirited young woman metamorphose into the ideal nun: whereas before she had 'tremble[d] with passion' now in the same paragraph, in the presence of Christ, she felt 'great remorse of conscience, and an alteration over my whole Body' (16). Finally, Hunter quotes a letter from a nun present at Mary Xaveria's death-bed, watching a surgeon lancing her wounds: 'she did not make ye least sign or shew yt she had any feeling of it, so yt ye Doctor supposed ye flesh so much mortifyed yt she had not felt it, wch made him order ye surgeon to cutt in deeper til she came to have some feeling; she hearing this, replyed calmly, he need not do so, for that she had felt ye same very sensibly' (433).[27]

---

[26]   Mary Xaveria records Hunter's words of deliberately provocative contempt: 'if every Nun were to write her fancyes we should have pleasant volumes; he allso put some very slight expressions in regard of ye papers I had given him to transcribe' (*A3*, 6). On Hunter's method to ensure authenticity, see p. 37, note 29. See also Bilinkoff, 2005, on the life-writing collaboration of women and their confessors.

[27]   Hunter authenticates his source by giving a precise date for the letter (17 January 1714).

Mary Xaveria is living, dying proof of the efficacy of sensory denial and mnemonic redirection. When she receives knowledge of God, and the cure as part of this, it is because she is ready to receive it: 'when the senses are in some measure prepared, God is wont to perfect them still more by granting them certain supernatural favours and consolations' (*Ascent*, 145). In fact, she is said to experience the range of locutions that John of the Cross, among others, describes: 'through the exterior senses, as voices and words in the ear, visible visions of the saints and beautiful lights, odours to the smell, sweetness to the palate, and other delectations of the touch which are wont to proceed from the Spirit; or through the exterior senses as the interior imaginary visions' (149–50). In the end, we witness that she is 'self-recollected and forgetful of all things' (*A3*, 257).[28]

There appears to be a remarkable degree of correlation between authoritative, licensed accounts of alteration and the nuns' own descriptions. Notwithstanding the 'reality' of such agreement of detail, for reasons of coherence (explaining themselves to themselves and to others) and because they sought to advertise their orthodoxy, such coincidence is not surprising. As ever, the women draw on and extend available literature. If this is textually neat, it is not always personally comfortable. Nuns often express bewilderment in the face of events which is in some part assuaged by placing their experience within existing narrative frameworks. Naturally enough, such correlation is also evident in descriptions of spiritual revelation.

While Catherine Burton claimed to be emphatically replenished and recognised herself as someone new, Anne of the Ascension reported herself dramatically depleted and self-alienated when, she says, 'I saw our Blessed Saviour standing some distance from me ... I did not see with my eyes ... I think it was a lively representation wch suddainly passed away but made such alterations in me, that I was like a nother' (*A1*, 5).

---

[28]   Typically, Anne of the Ascension was esteemed as 'wholy forgettfull of her selfe' (the phrase echoes through these papers); 'that if she had not ben put in mind she would many tymes haue forgotten her nessesary sustenance and in all her sicknesses especially in her last she showed great neclect of her selfe' (*L1.5.C*). Teresa de Jesus wrote extensively on the role and function of memory about which, wrongly employed, she had many concerns. It is clear from their papers that the nuns took seriously her advice to erase their past lives, their forgetfulness relating to sensory matters enmeshed within their general recollecting. On occasion this takes poignant form: so habitual was her practice, or at least the rhetoric of obedience that surrounds it, that for the celebration of her professional golden jubilee the 79-year-old Anne of St Bartholomew (Ann Downs: 1593–1674), confined to the Infirmary 'desired leave of ye Superiour to call to mind some passages of her former life to recreate the Community when they came to see her' (*A1*, 186).

'neither with the Eyes of the Bodie nor of the Minde'

Understandably, given the scrutinising context in which they lived, visions or phenomena that were described as being seen or otherwise apprehended through the senses, are a source of much discussion in the nuns' papers. They question whether they literally see or hear them, or whether they are aware of them in a sensory but non-physical manner.

Again the extent of correlation between life-writing and instructional manuals (and *vice versa*) is striking. What appear to be spontaneous incursions from the spiritual world into their personal lives are in the end seen to be anything but individual or unexpected. Chorality of both narrative form and of the incidents themselves is crucial. Spiritual directors who seek to authenticate accounts of 'marvellous' happenings express themselves satisfied when the nuns' stories correspond, either with what they have already told them or with accounts separately provided by other witnesses.[29] It is of course impossible to distinguish whether, in telling the story, the nuns' singular mysticism took the shape of an authorised script, or whether they actually 'experienced' the script itself. In epistemological terms it hardly matters. After all it does not undermine the 'reality' of dreams, say (if we can equate visions with these for a moment), if what happens in the sleeping-imaginary states coincides with reading-waking moments. It is feasible therefore that the nuns experienced, or thought they experienced, what they read was possible; that reading enabled interior 'happenings' to occur, and that sensory responsiveness was attuned to narrative content as well as mode of expression. In many ways this underlines the successfulness of their imitative method, in devotional and in compositional terms; their texts activate as well as describe experience.

Given the nuns' need to interpret the meaning of their revelations in order to progress devotionally, it is to be expected that much of their meditative writing is occupied with unravelling the conundrum of spiritual knowledge. This arrived (they are at pains to tell us) without any direct action of the senses yet it is experienced in sensual ways, or in ways for which only a language of the senses will suffice. Such moments often cause a form of happy crisis for the women

---

[29]   This is Thomas Hunter's method in his Life of Mary Xaveria: 'I have several times, on set purpose, put her upon recounting some particular passage wch had happened many years before and allways found her as exactly precise to every minute circumstance, as if she had seen it then translaited before her eyes, a convinceing proof to me, yt it was not a fiction of her own head, made at random by ye force of imagination and fancy, this would have alter'd sometimes, and by this have discouer'd it self' (*A3*, 11); 'ye Superior of ye monastery in wch she lived, was desired some years after her death, to order all her Religious who had been her cotemporaries to mark down wt they have observed in her, and that this might be performed with great sincerity, each one was order'd to write apart, without consulting each other, and to send what they had writt to ye person who was transcribeing her writeings' (312).

who struggle to express themselves in the face of what appears like sensory overload yet which devotional manuals instruct them is not to be accounted for by sensual experience, except by simile that relies on accounts of the motion they wish to deny.

Teresa de Jesus explains this paradox in her *Vida* in precisely these terms. Knowledge of God arrives, she says, 'in the most interior part of the Soule … without either anie image of his person, or anie forme of words': 'Now, this kind of Vision, and language, is so inwardly a thing of Spirit, that heer, there is no kind of spring, or euen stirring in anie of the Powers of the Minde, nor yet in anie of the senses of the Bodie …' (*Flaming Hart*, 1642, 371, 372).

The senses are not necessarily 'disabled' at this point; along with the understanding 'they are all at home and in vse'. They are as it were watching the soul not watching itself. Teresa uses the analogy of food being conveyed to the stomach ('though yet, how it got thither, I cannot tell') and of sound (heard with 'some other kind of eares'); 'as if one, who could heare well were not suffered to stop his eares; and that they cryed out alowd to him, who would therefore be faine to heare them …' (373). Teresa is an adept teacher and theologian, cannily circumventing concerns about spiritual materialism especially as it related to female ecstatic experience.[30] She enacts the *process* of the senses even as she denies their effects, giving the wrong impression of their action in order to convey the right idea. Her image remains with us because it effects the same motion as the sight or hearing itself. Her comparisons are (at least temporarily) literal as well as figurative, looked at one way as actual, the other way as the hypothetical.[31] In referring to spiritual cognition as digestion whilst denying material transfer, Teresa literally has her cake and eats it.

She enacts in her similes the very process of spiritual union itself, in which 'two seuerall things become one' (217). Although she eschews comparisons,[32] she cannot but resort to them:

---

[30]   Teresa herself had been subject to extensive scrutiny by Inquisitorial authorities investigating her ecstatic experiences and censoring her works: see Ahlgren, 1996; Slade, 1995, 67–9; Williams, 1991, 20–21; 34–5.

[31]   'We may therefore regard the metaphorical sentence as a "Duck-Rabbit"' (that is, like one of those images which appears like a duck when looked at one way, and like a rabbit in another): 'it is a sentence that may simultaneously be regarded as presenting two different situations; looked at one way it describes the actual situation, and looked at the other way, an hypothetical situation with which that situation is being compared' (Roger White, quoted in Cohen, 2008, Chapter 1; see also White, 2010). Peter Tyler, whose 2011 study was published after I had written this book, uses the same analogy: '*nothing*, and yet *everything*, has changed' (2011, xiii). He suggests that Teresa de Jesus employs a 'Wittgensteinian' performative technique, 'using linguistic strategies of unknowing and affectivity to lead the reader to affective transformation' (169).

[32]   She compares a vision to 'an Image, or distinct representation … yet still, not like those designes and draughts or Pictures of things'; '… Comparisons neuer agree so perfectly, and entirely, as these two things did' (*Flaming Hart*, 1642, 393–4).

For when I say, that I neither saw this with the eyes of the Bodie nor of the Minde (because it was no Imaginarie Vision) how come I to vundertake and affirme more clearly & certainly that Christ our Lord was standing neer me, then if I had seen him with my verie eyes. For it seems, indeed to be, as if a person were in the darke who sees not another, that stands by him; or as if the same person were blind ... a man may come to know it, by way of seuerall Senses; because he may heare the other speake or stirre; or he may touch him. But heer there is nothing of all this; nor is there heer anie darkness at all; but only the thing is represented to the soule by a certaine notice, which is more cleare then the Sunne. I say not that anie Sunne is seen, nor anie clearness, or brightnes at all; but only a certain light, which illuminates and informes the Vnderstanding (though yet without seing anie light) ... (*Flaming Hart*, 1642, 369)[33]

The *effects* of union are all that is needed as evidence of what has happened; knowledge of God is thus directly 'imprinted' or 'engrauen' on understanding without need of image or words (371). This underlines her emphasis on mental prayer in which wordless contemplation leading to de-worded experience is paramount. She enacts, then, the paradox of language's end as a place where language must begin: proximate approximation.

Speaking, as we will find in later chapters, like language and like sound, is always about thresholds; it bridges the hiatus of silence – or silence, ever crucial in a convent, fills the spaces that language cannot reach. Breaking silence marks the crisis point, and the affirmation, of language. In heaven, writes Teresa, 'Soules doe there vnderstand one another, really, without speaking ... euen without so much as signes' (*Flaming Hart*, 1642, 375). God and the soul show 'the mutuall loue, which two deare friends carrie to one another': 'these two Louers looke earnestly vpon one another, in the face; as the Spouse saith to his Beloued, in the Canticles ...'. Her excitement at this pronouncement leads her to apostrophise: 'O admirable benignitie of thee, O Lord ... O my deare Lord ... O great ingratitude of mortall Creatures ... O Soules...' (376). In full poetic flow she flounders: 'this, which I am saying now, is not so much as a little Cipher of that which were to be sayd ...' (377). Here as elsewhere when she bursts into seemingly unstoppable effusion, it is as if her knowingness is summed up by onomatopoeias: the O as the source of the sound it describes.[34] At its most minuscule moment of precision Teresa's language all but ceases, springs then to meaning:

---

[33]   According to Aristotle there were two different ways to compare things: 'a direct comparison where one notes common properties of the two things, and an indirect comparison where, whether or not the two objects have significant common properties, one effects the comparison by introducing a third or fourth term' (White, 2010, 51).

[34]   We might equate this to the lines in *The Spiritual Canticle* of John of the Cross, the 'ah, I don't-know-what behind their stammering' (stanza 7).

> Nowhere is a language more 'itself' than at the moment it seems to leave the terrain of its sound and sense, assuming the sound shape of what does not – or cannot – have a language of its own … It is here that one language, gesturing beyond itself to a speech that is none, opens itself to the nonlanguage that precedes it and that follows it. It is here, in the utterance of the strange sounds that the speakers of a tongue thought themselves incapable of making, that a language shows itself as an 'exclamation' in the literal senses of the term: a 'calling out' … beyond or before itself … (Heller-Roazen, 2005, 18)

'There came vpon me', Teresa writes later, 'so great impetuosities, or impulses of this loue … as if my Soule had been directly torne out of my Bodie'; 'O most admirable kind of artifice of our Lord! … For thou didst hide thy self from me; and yet withal didst euen then presse vpon me, so very close … a delightfull, and sauourie kind of death.' She offers, says the marginal note, 'a rare comparison'; God calms the soul as a nurse does children who 'sobb sometimes, so thick, as that they are euen readie to choake' (*Flaming Hart*, 1642, 415).[35] She marks moments of loss of the senses and of meaning, coming via moments of 'little death' of understanding itself. Expressiveness is always retrospective and signals 'the moment a self recovers itself: the instant in which I come, after sleep, shock, or stupor, to myself'; I turn, then, to such 'startling solicitations of a sensitive nature' (Heller-Roazen, 2007, 211).

Coming To in the Convent: Those States 'Betwixt'

There is a lot of coming to in convents; that is to say there is much self-consciousness about states of awareness and the role of the senses when coming in and out of them. That much we might expect of a devotional discipline concerned to dampen dependence on sensory stimuli whilst maintaining a close hold on the senses themselves. As so often in life-writing, descriptions of thresholds shed light on the occupants' understanding of the structure of the house as a whole. In fact, nuns frequently employ spatial analogy to describe their sensory transport, in and out of themselves.

Importantly, because they live in pious expectation of death and salvation, the nuns are vigilant over themselves and of each other; all waking and declining stages are overseen for signs of change so that the nun can die confessed and shriven. Helpfully for us, they mark the states of each others' consciousness in detail, recording in obituaries that nuns when they died were or were not 'present

---

35   Heller-Roazen notes, 'children at first do not speak' (2005, 9); 'the sounds children forget how to make never leave them' (13). See Chapter 5 for discussion of (in)human sound at moments of extreme crisis. See also Peter Tyler's exposition of language in which he proposes that 'verbal jumblings' are part of a 'mystical strategy' (2011, 125–6). His comments on the role of 'astonishment' in Wittgenstein's philosophy bear out my own analysis.

to themselves', 'in' (or out) of their senses (somatic and intellectual). They wish others to be alert to receive last sacraments and remark on this when they are not.

There are several vital thresholds that warrant their particular attention: sleep (with its own internal liminalities: dreams, hallucinations and semi-waking states); the moments before death; cures considered to be miraculous that return the nun from the brink; and spiritual states, of rapture and ecstasy. The nuns also claim to encounter supernatural forms – ghosts, apparitions, visions – which take them to the edge of another consciousness from which they emerge renewed or changed. The language used in descriptions of these experiences naturally overlaps, suggesting the fluidity of understanding of sensory and semi-sensory states. Paul of St Ubald accounts for 'quiet prayer' in this way when the devout 'are beginning to loose them selues by degrees; as one slumbering, and falling a sleepe': 'this soul is like to one that lyeth a diing ... until he grow so weake, and feeble, that he has scarce any sense, or feeling of anything, knoweth no body, nor where he is, nor what he doth, or is done to him; yet is not dead, but betwixt both' (*Soul's Delight*, 1654, Part III, 13).[36]

Sleep is the main natural and everyday threshold. As Mary Margaret of the Angels (Penelope Chapman: 1693–1739) noted, well ahead of Immanuel Kant, 'if I should live 60 years 20 would be intirely gone in sleep' (*A2*, 62).[37] Nuns, like most thinking subjects, reflect extensively on the stages of passing in and out of sleep. Some of their discussion is metaphorical, some of it literal; all of it is designed to further their understanding of pious perception.

Sleep they seem to understand (uncontroversially) as the condition in which one 'is unable to become conscious of representation through the external senses' (Kant, 2006, 58). Thomas Wright explained that 'even if a man sleepe with open eyes, although his sight be maruelous excellent, yet he seeth nothing, because in sleepe, the purer spirits are recalled into the inner parts of the body, leuing the eyes destitute of spirits, and abandoned of force, which presently in waking return againe' (1630, 35).[38] If thinking relates to things we are aware of – 'with sensory

---

[36] Paul of St Ubald continues by citing Teresa de Jesus' analogy (the edition containing a marginal reference to Chapter 16 of her *Vida*) of a soul wading into deep water who 'begins to sink and fall a diing', losing at this point the power of her senses and understanding and progressing towards union when she is 'voyde of sense, and in a manner dead' (1654, Part III, 14).

[37] Kant noted 'probably a third of our lifetime passes away unconscious and unregretted' (2006, 58).

[38] Descartes considered 'sleep occurs only in the brain, yet every day it deprives us of a great part of our sensory faculties, though these are afterwards restored on waking' (*Principles of Philosophy*, paragraph 196; 1985 ed., I, 283). Thomas Browne (1605–82) devoted a section of *Religio Medici* to sleep: 'Aristotle, who hath written a singular tract of sleep, hath not, methinks, thoroughly refined it; nor yet Galen ... for those *noctambulos* and night-walkers, though in their sleep, do yet enjoy the action of their senses. ... those abstracted and ecstatick souls do walk about in their own corpses, as spirits with the bodies

awareness' (Descartes, 1985 ed., I, 195) – then it follows that thought happens when we are awake.[39] Thinking beings, after all, are post-sleep, just as dream literature is only possible once the dream is done.

On waking, the nuns account for what they think happened during sleep. Some describe interim stages in their coming to, with impassive sensation set amidst semi-alert states. Helen of the Cross (Helen Eddisford: 1672–1755), for example, mentions a vision (perhaps within a dream) that strained her eyes, suggesting her senses were involved (or that she dreamt they were). The idea of either possibility does not appear to shake her delight or conception of orthodoxy:

> [She was] wak'd one night out of her sleep by a great light in her cell and being frighted that she was call'd to some one a dying[40] was going to rise, but harkening and not hearing any thing she look'd about her to find from whence the light could come and perceived the little wooden cross on which is painted a Christ invision'd with a bright glory like to the sun at midday and which continued so long that her eyes was weaken'd ... and shutting them to relieve them and looking again she sees the same as before and also a religious in her habit ... and all this remain'd so long a time she was even spent with looking sitting up all the time in her bed, and shutting her eyes a second time, and when she look'd again all was vanish'd leaving her in admiration and devotion ... (*A2*, 13)[41]

Nuns frequently describe themselves as *altered* by their experiences in sleep, much as they do by wakeful wonders in their daily lives. Often they claim to record matters only after another incident makes them look back to realise the significance of what had happened. Coincidence of the sentient supernatural

---

they assume, wherein they seem to hear, see, and feel, though indeed the organs are destitute of sense, and their natures of those faculties that should inform them' (1642, section 11).

[39]   For Descartes on doubt and being tricked while sleeping, see *Meditations of First Philosophy,* 19; 1985 ed., I, 13; 306.

[40]   Typically two nuns watch over sick and dying sisters, and call other members of the community to the bedside if they perceive her to be fading.

[41]   This incident is credited to Helen of the Cross by a later nun who wrote 'Sister Hellen' in the margin of the Life of Clare Joseph of Jesus Maria (Clare Gerard: 1694–1730), the nun appearing in Helen's vision. On Sister Clare's own dream, see p. 46. Descartes wrote of such moments 'You are dreaming that you are conscious of it, that you do not doubt it, that it is evident to you. There is a wide difference between on the one hand, something's *seeming* certain and evident to someone who is dreaming (or even awake) and, on the other hand, something's *being* certain snd evident to one dreaming or awake' (*Objections and Replies*, Seventh Set; 1984 ed., II, 338). Macrobius' influential *Commentary on the Dream of Scipio* accounts for such apparitions (*phantasma* or *visio*) which appear between waking and slumber, in the 'first cloud of sleep': 'In this drowsy condition he thinks he is still fully awake and imagines he sees spectres rushing at him or wandering vaguely about, differing from natural creatures in size and shape, and hosts of diverse things, either delightful or disturbing' (1952 ed., 89; see Clark, 2007, 323).

and the 'actual' is frequently noted. Then the nuns describe a continuum of the extraordinary between sensate wakeful and sleeping states; these are rendered ordinary by the sheer number of examples in their papers.

The obituary of Anne of the Ascension, the second of that professional name (Catherine Keynes: 1619–78)[42] includes a section taken from the papers of Mary Xaveria of the Angels whom Anne had agreed to recommend when she arrived in heaven. '[A]bout six weeks after [her death]', wrote Mary Xaveria,

> as I remember she appeared to me in my sleep and I cannot doubt of it by what followed, otherwise I am not apt to beleive in dreams,[43] I think it was about one in the morning, that I thought this religious was represented before me in my Cell, att first I was affrighted, knowing she was a Spirit, but att length I resolved to take so much courage, as to speak to her … she said Purgatory was a sad place and that one of the greatest torments was the sight of the devils ... Its impossible to express the change I found in myself … with that I thought I saw St Xavier there … I cannot express the excess of joy I felt in my soul at that time … I awaked and found my self much depleted but in great deuotion and methinks like one come out of another world. (*A1*, 375)

Accounts of this sort do indeed offer a view of alternative interiors, unfolding scenes within scenes, between wakeful perception, memory, dream, vision and, at several removes, reported sights of heaven or elsewhere. As when the nuns describe the appearance of ghosts, it enables them to discuss events that happen as it were off-stage, out of sight of waking eyes. This relieves them of the need to explain or deny the sensory components of their experiences, and also enables them to reflect on enigmatic meaning. Although in sleep they appear to have no sensory reception as such, cognition is explained in terms of the senses and events from dreams are generally lodged in their memory as if they had been physically perceived. As in waking, there is nothing in the dreaming mind that has not apparently first been in the senses.

Often they remember waking up only when the cause of coming to is unexpected or unordinary, agitating their senses outside the sleeping state. This was the case when thieves broke into the convent in the early hours of 7 January 1770 when, because of 'the wrenks & noises they made 3 of ye Religious alarmed got up & calling out of ye window disturbd them'.[44]

---

42 Anne of the Ascension Worsley who appears frequently in this book, is simply cited by her professional name; others are differentiated.

43 Rational distrust of 'paranormal' phenomena is a frequent motif in the papers, underlining for witnesses the power of the revelation's truths.

44 From uncatalogued material, previously in the convent at Lanherne, Cornwall, now at St Helens in Merseyside. The document conjures up a marvellous scene; the brave nuns 'armd with hand brooms' confronted the thieves: 'one of the Rogues hid himself under ye shade of ye Lamps at our Dore wh ye men appeard [the confessor and two others who came

In the normal course of events, the nuns were roused by a bell at five in the morning in summer, six in winter. Bells continued to ring during the day to alert them to services or other activities. These sound with such regularity that they are rarely mentioned.[45] On one occasion it is remarkable only that an old and ailing Lay Sister (one to whom we will return) was not woken by them when she slumbered in the kitchen: Winefrid of St Teresa (Elizabeth Lingen: 1662–1740)

> fell asleep by the fire side very quietly … observing she did not stir when a Mass [bell] tole'd the sister said to one another it is a sign yt Sister Winifride is very fast indeed … others said doe not wake her perhaps she has had a bad night infine the double bells rung for the musick mass and she minded them not which frighted us and we calld her and shaked her but still she remain'd as in a profound sleep and quite insenseble … we placed her upon a quilt on the ground where she received the Holy Oyles, and afterwards was blooded but still she did not come to her self … (*A2*, 90)

Several stimuli are thus used in an attempt to revive the nun.

Sister Winefrid's Life contains several instances of in-between states and consciousness about them (see Chapter 3). As a child of a few months old 'she was subject to violent convolutions and in one fit she was loked upon as dead and as such laid out upon a table in order to be buryed'. After several hours in this state, an old woman 'took ye child before the fire rub'd it with spirits & c till in effect the child began to stir' (81–2).

Other forms of tactile revival are mentioned in the papers. As she approached death, Mary Frances of St Teresa (Mary Birbeck: 1674–1733), when told by her Superior she was to communicate (that is, receive the Eucharist) 'tho very much inclined to be heavey and sleepy, she immediately brisked her self and thanked her using a forceable violence to prepare herself for that happiness, beging others to assist her and keep her awake' (*A2*, 10).

Another nun, committed to perform devotions on every hour for several days is said to be woken 'wth the Clook' by an angel. Margaret of Jesus Mostyn used her own initiative, 'obliging her selfe to wake euery time ye clock stroke, to doe some deuotion, some times she lay wth a bord under her, att other times, to ley ye in an uneasy poustour, for 4 or 5 howers together' (*L13.7*, 62). Sleep or sleep-

---

to help], with his face & handss blackt over the disguise him, & left ye marks of his hands upon ye Durlgate on several places'. Afterwards, 'we got ye smith to examine & repare ye Dore, he put on new hinges & a great iron hook & fixt up a Bell'.

[45]   According to Leibniz, habit renders 'the perceptible imperceptible'. For discussion of his ideas of 'cachées', hidden and minute moments of perception within larger consciousness, see Heller-Roazen, 2007, 189–901.

deprivation, forms of persistent coming to, after all offered opportunity for sensory mortification.[46]

Devotional manuals provide advice on how best to sleep and also to avoid over-sleeping by eating only a light meal before retiring.[47] Carmelite constitutions contain several rules about beds and proper conduct in cells.[48] Such instructions, along with accounts of events that happen in or beside beds, show sleeping to be a state of particular vulnerability in proximity to which disturbing sensory incidents were often said to have taken place, such as bedclothes being turned by demons, and nuns being woken by angelic choirs.[49]

Nuns at such moments come via sensory surprise to a realisation of the remarkable, the miraculous. They also revive from dreams to ponder on the meaning of what they have encountered there. Their dreams fall into several categories, along the lines of Macrobius' influential scheme outlined in *Commentary on the Dream of Scipio*, several editions of which were printed before 1700.[50] Many of

---

[46]   'Euen on her great weaknes' one nun 'sometimes was forgotten to be bidden sleep, or the like, she would express so much joy that it seemed her content was in being neclected' (*L13.7*, 24).

[47]   'A short supper and a hard bed are good meanes for early rising' according to Luis of Granada (*Sinner's Guide*, 1598, 122). In his *Treatise on Mental Prayer*, Alfonso Rodriguez (1526–1616) devotes a whole chapter 'Of the Temptation of Sleepe, and from whence it come, and the remedies thereof'. Some causes of sleepiness are natural: 'as by want of sleepe, much werynes, ill weather, excesse of age, excesse of eating or of drinking'; some causes are influenced by devils who 'put certain fingers into [monks'] mouths and make them yawne'. He recommends 'a good remedy to stand on foote, without leaning; and to wash our eyes with cold water', 'to carry a wet napkin'. 'Others, whilst they are *Praying* giue themseulues some kinde of little payne, wherby they keepe themselues awake ... some say *Vocall Prayers*, whereby a man may be stirred vp and much reuiued' (1627, 204–5).

[48]   'The beddes shall be without mattresses and only canuesse filled wth strawe'; 'That euery one haue her bedd apart; 'Noe religious may enter into ye cell of another without leaue of the Mother Pryoresse' (*L3.34*, Chapters 8, 10). Mary Frances, the nun who 'brisked herself up' from sleepiness (p. 44) persisted in spending the night in her cell 'upon her straw bed and woollen sheets' (*A2*, 3).

[49]   When the Lierre convent was said to be haunted, for example, the nuns were sent to bed wearing rosaries, and devils turned the Mostyn sisters bodily in their beds (*L13.7*, 48; *L3.31*, 25). Eugenia of Jesus (Elizabeth Levesson: 1618–52), later one of the witnesses to the Mostyn exorcism (Chapter 2), 'had often times synes [signs] befor the death of persons ... as for excample heering of Musike; and singing; she oftentimes hard knooking att her beds head; and sometimes her name called ...' (*L13.7*, 5). Indeed, it was not unusual (at least not conceptually disturbing) for nuns to be woken by mysterious signs, as when 'a full quire of angels' presaged the death of Anne of the Ascension over several nights in 1644; one nun, absent from the Prioress' bedside at the instant of her death, 'was awaked by a full quire of musick and being very much affrighted, ran that moment to the Infirmary' (*A1*, 56): see Chapter 5 on miraculous sound.

[50]   Macrobius' *Commentary* identifies 'five main types' of dream: 'there is the enigmatic dream, as in Greek *oneiros*, in Latin *somnium*; second, there is the prophetic vision, in

the nuns' dreams were said to be prophetic, with figures announcing the imminent death of another religious, or a deceased nun or holy figure appearing to offer comfort or warnings. Some dreams are enigmatic, containing elusive images;[51] some are nightmares or arrive in semi-wakeful moments, as when Anne of the Ascension records 'I Doe not know wether I was half asleep or not, but of a suddan a monstrous great head seem'd near unto me, gaping to devour me at wch I ws much frighted, and call'd to our Blessed Lady promising to be Religious' (*A1*, 1). As a child Clare Joseph of Jesus Maria (see note 41) 'was frequently troubled with very frightfull dreames, in which she always found herself assisted by Saint Apolinarius waking her self by calling upon him by his name' (*A2*, 47).

This experience of sensory disturbance within dreams and of being aware of oneself dreaming, suggests an element of consciousness remaining.[52] Dreams naturally offer continuity of a kind with waking states, in a material as well as emotional-aesthetic extension, in Aristotle's terms images in dreams being 'a presentation based on the movement of sense impressions, when such presentation occurs in sleep'.[53]

Dreams, then, and coming to from them by whatever means, mark a moment of perception of oneself as a thinking subject as well as a sensing, or temporarily senseless one: 'If someone is dreaming, then he is thinking' (Descartes, *Objections and Replies*, Seventh Set; 1984 ed., II, 334).

Fainting, another state from which to come to, is rather different. It 'is not far removed from dying' wrote Descartes, 'for when we die then the fire in our heart is completely extinguished, and we merely fall into a faint when it is smothered in such a way that there remain some traces of heat which may afterwards rekindle it' (*The Passions of the Soul*, 122; 1985 ed., I, 371).[54]

Greek *horama*, in Latin *visio*; third, there is the oracular dream, in Greek *chrematismos*, in Latin *oraculum*; fourth, there is the nightmare, in Greek *eypnion*, in Latin *insomnium*; and last, the apparition, in Greek, *phantasma*, which Cicero, when he has occasion to use the word, calls *visum*.'(1952 ed., 88-9).

[51] Lucy of St Ignatius (Catherine Bedingfield:1614–50) 'once recounted as a dream in recreation [the time in which the nuns gathered together] that she saw a most white Orientall perlle in an earthen vassell, and our Lord seeming to take great delight in it, she ask'd how she shoul render her soule like that pearle' (*A1*, 285). This nun was one of the witnesses to dramatic events at the Lierre convent, culminating in the exorcism of the Mostyn sisters (see Hallett, 2007b, 1).

[52] Augustine reported 'seeing an object in sleep I was aware that I was dreaming ... Hence, my soul, which in some mysterious way was awake while I slept, was necessarily affected by the images of bodies, just as if they were real bodies' (see Clark, 2007, 305).

[53] 'Dream sensations were caused by traces of the *species* left behind in the internal senses by the waking perceptions of the external ones, once the latter were no longer active' (Clark, 2007, 301).

[54] He provides a physiological explanation, considering that fainting comes about through extreme joy or, more rarely, through grief. 'Here is the way in which I believe it causes this effect. It opens the orifices of the heart unusually wide, so that the blood from

The papers describe various ways of reviving people who faint, accounting for their sensory or passionate state during the process. At Antwerp in 1744 Ignastia of Jesus (Dorothy Barnaby: 1672–1744), known affectionately as 'old Grany', was being helped to eat chicken by the Infirmarian who 'perceived her head to hang down ... calld upon her, and found she was in a fainting fitt'. She 'came to her self' as she was anointed with oils 'and said what is the matter have I fainted', dying in her chair later that day (*A2*, 184).[55]

There are many other instances of swooning.[56] Some swooning is exemplary. Teresa de Jesus describes the state of approaching spiritual union by comparison to '[n]eare fainting' (*Flaming Hart*, 1642, 224–5).[57] She frequently reflects on sleep-like states in which she claims to experience direct knowledge of God which circumvents the senses. She describes states of deep recollection when the devout

---

the veins enters the heart so suddenly and so copiously that it cannot be rarefied by the heat in the heart quickly enough to raise all the little membranes which close the entrances to these veins. In this way the blood smothers the fire which it usually maintains when it enters the heart in moderate amounts' (*Passions of the Soul*, paragraphs 122, 123; 1985 ed., I, 371).

[55]   Meat was exceptional in the convent diet. The Constitutions state: 'They ought neuer to eate flesh, unlesse it be for necissity ... one ye fast dayes ... ye ordinary meate of Refectory shall neither be eggs, nor whitt meates ... ye Pryoresse may dispence wth this ... wth ye sicke and those wch haue neede and wth whom fish doth not agree ' (*L3.34*, Chapter 8). See Chapters 3 and 4 for further discussion of this scene.

[56]   Anne of the Ascension 'sounded [swooned] divers times ... wth extremity of grief' when she was parted from her beloved Superior and made to move to another convent (*A1*, 9; see Chapter 2). The maid in the ghost story transcribed by Margaret of Jesus Mostyn (see p. 29 n. 11), terrified in the dark and physically molested by the haunting spirit, also, unsurprisingly, faints (*L3.34B*; Hallett, 2007b, 162), as does Mary Terease of Jesus (Mary Warren: 1642–96) who, as a child at Lierre was said to have seen her dead mother being transported to heaven during Mass: 'of a sooden ... she sounded away being very much frighted, comeing to her selfe, she called out to ye deuots ... ye little one was as one transported ye whole day' (*L13.7*, 173). As a young woman Catherine Burton herself caused a fainting fit: just after she had recovered from illness to which she had been given up for dead, she visited a local woman who was so startled and 'so frighten'd yt she was obliged to call for cordials to recover herself'. Burton also records that she herself 'had such a loathing of flesh, broath and eggs, yt ye very naming of meat was almost enough to cast me into a swoon' (*A3*, 36; see Chapter 4).

[57]   'The Soule ... doth find her self, as it were, euen sinke, vunder a sweet, and most excessiue delight; as being all in a certain way of deare [near?] faynting; so that the breath is euen beginning to faile, and so also doth all corporall strength ... The eyes are also closed, though without anie purpose to shut them; and when by accident they chance to be open, she, in effect, sees nothing distinctly'; 'She heares, but yet vnderstands not, what she heares; so that she recceaues no other benefit at all, by her Senses' (*Flaming Hart*, 1642, 224–5). Teresa warns her nuns about the perils of 'excessive rejoicing and delight, which can be carried to such an extreme that it really seems as if the soul is swooning, and as if the very slightest thing would be enough to drive it out of the body' (*Interior Castle*, II, 328).

'are unconscious of anything external, and all their senses are in a state of slumber that they are like a person asleep ... he [sic] thinks that the locutions come to him in a kind of dream'; indeed 'the effects of these locutions resemble those of a dream' (*Interior Castle*, II, 283).

This leads her to fundamental quandary about certainty beyond sensory experience since, although she uses the comparison of fainting and sleep, 'there is no question here of dreaming' (249). An individual in rapture is still aware of activity within the intellectual and physical senses, even in their abeyance: 'All the Senses are taken vp, vpon the finding, and feeling of this ioy, in such sort, as no one of them is so dis-employed, as that it can possibly attend to anie thing els, either in the exteriour, or interiour way'. This joy is beyond description, at least temporarily; afterwards only comparison will do: 'if she is able to communicate it, I say, there is no absolute Vnion' (*Flaming Hart*, 1642, 216, 217).

Teresa writes of spiritual union and of coming to – into and out of rapture – in just such terms, using images from the Song of Songs in which the Bride is 'suspended in those Divine arms' of her Spouse, taking divine sustenance from his breasts; 'Awakening from that sleep and heavenly inebriation, she is like one amazed and stupefied' (*Conceptions of the Love of God*, II, 384).

Re-emerging from such heightened states, not all of them immediately spiritually uplifting, nuns often express dissatisfaction with the waking world. They describe feeling bereft of their lover, or feeling bewildered by their return to wakefulness whereas they have been lucid in sleep-like rapture. Sometimes it takes several days for them to come round fully. In Kant's terms, they appear 'drunk with sleep'; 'disconcerted, beside [themselves] (with joy or fear), *perplexed, bewildered, astonished*' (2006, 59; emphasis in the original).

'I am amazed now that I am writteing this to think that I am still ye same creature' wrote Mary Xaveria of her childhood recovery from delirium. 'I had not force to stir my eyes, thus my soul seem'd forced out of my Body by a strong agony and they say my senses failed me; I cannot express in what light all things of this world appeared at that time, how contemptible in themselves ...' During that time she dreamt she was in a churchyard looking for a place for her own grave (a similar incident is also found in Teresa's *Vida*),[58] then heard it said that she was indeed dead which gave her, she reports, 'joy in my soul' (*A3*, 56).[59]

---

[58]   'That night, I fell into such a Trance, as continued to keepe me, neer foure days, without the vse, almost, of anie of my senses; and shortly, they came to giue me the Sacrament of Extreame Vnction ... yea sometimes they held me for so certainly to be dead, that afterwards, I found the drops of holie Wax-candles, about mine eyes ... the Graue remaining open, in the Church of my Monasterie, a day and a half, where my bodie was expected to be interred ...' (*Flaming Hart*, 1642, 44–5).

[59]   'I thought I saw our Bd Saviour stand like one considering whether he should take my Soul out of my Body then or no ... this disappeared and I return'd to my self again to the admiration of all that saw me' (*A3*, 56–7).

The Life of Mary Xaveria indeed offers many insights into various stages of semi-consciousness from which she returns to write about them, pondering their meaning. This is most helpful for those studying sensory states. In one remarkable passage she describes a period of spiritual surrogacy in which she exchanged conditions with a troubled nun. At the elevation during Mass, the point at which they had agreed to exchange states, 'then on a suddain like one awakeing out of slumber she [the other nun] found an unusual peace of mind ... on a suddain [I] wonder'd to see my self in anguish, desolation and dryness'. On returning to their personal conditions, 'this peace and calm continued as she told me her self for ten days after'; 'As to my self I was all this time in ye greatest darkness' (239–40).[60]

Mary Xaveria, like Teresa de Jesus before her, frequently questions the material nature of her extra-sensory perception. On another occasion, she corrected an account she had previously written: 'What I said concerning my seeing these Angels is not meant to be meant yt I saw them with eyes of my Body, for I never saw any thing of this kind in that manner' (66). Her whole Life is buttressed by phrases like this, underlined by the editorial preface to the book which reassures the reader that the Nun is orthodox. Like other early modern visionaries, Carmelite nuns emphasise the integrity of their experience in the face of scepticism from within the Catholic and Protestant churches, and from male ecclesiastical authorities in their own and other religious Orders anxious about women's devotional charisma. Their writing accordingly shows awareness of wider debates about the contested material nature of revelations.

Sensing something internally – even using the language of sensation, given the delicacy of matters – had its own issues. John of the Cross discussed how such ideas informed notions of 'proximate union'. The senses, he states, fashion forms that have been represented to them physically. All such imaginations are to be emptied from the soul 'which must remain in darkness so far as it concerns the senses, in order that we may attain to the divine union, because they bear no proportion to the proximate means of union with God; as neither do bodily things, the objects of the five exterior senses':

> The reason is, that nothing enters the imagination but through the exterior senses.[61] The eye must have seen, or the ear have heard, or the other senses must

---

[60]   Mary Xaveria also describes a young novice who 'on a suddain fell out of her self ... and within a day or two she fell raveing mad' (*A3*, 245–6). Her account draws on spatial imagery to describe both the novice's mental state and its containment: 'one time she broke out from us' and left the convent, making the nuns fearful of a scandal in the neighbourhood: 'I went where she could see and hear me, and immediately she return'd again of herself' (249–51).

[61]   This oft-repeated phrase, turned here in relation to Pauline teaching, was used by Thomas Aquinas; by Descartes (*Meditations on First Philosophy*, and *Discourse on Method*; Alfonso Rodriguez, p. 65; Thomas Hobbes, p. 18. See Cranefield, 1970, for discussion on the origin of the phrase.

have first become cognisant of all that is in it. Or at the utmost, we can only form pictures of what we have seen, heard, or felt; and these forms are not more excellent than what the imagination has received through the senses.

John implicitly references I Corinthians 2: 9–10 ('But, as it is written: That eye hath not seen, nor ear heard: neither hath it entered into the heart of man, what things God hath prepared for them that love him.')[62] Profound mystery, 'the deep things of God' are revealed by the spirit.[63] He turns the quotation to address contemporary preoccupations with material mysticism, like Teresa de Jesus steering a delicate path and engaging in turn with her own pronouncements on the subject. Crucially, since those created 'cannot have any proportion with the being of God, it follows that all conceptions of the imagination, which must resemble them, cannot serve as proximate means of union with Him' (*Ascent of Mount Carmel*, 1906 ed., 114). Accordingly, spiritual people cannot draw close to God by means of imagery: pure knowledge is wordless, imageless.[64] He goes on, in a series of complicated linguistic manoeuvres, to delineate several kinds of locution, distinguished by their relative materiality. He is most concerned with 'supernatural locutions', 'which are effect without the instrumentality of the bodily senses' (220); 'interior locutions are formal words, uttered in the mind sometimes supernaturally, without the intervention of the senses' (229). 'Interior substantial locutions' 'are formally impressed on the soul' producing there 'a vivid and substantial effect' (233).

Teresa de Jesus also distinguished different kinds of spiritual rapture.[65] She asks of a vision, for instance, 'How did the soul see it and understand it if it can neither see nor understand? I am not saying that it saw it at the time, but that it sees it clearly afterwards ...' Sensory perception thus supersedes sensory near-absence. She counsels 'Do not make the mistake of thinking that this certainty has anything to do with bodily form'; God instead does not 'desire the door of the faculties and

---

[62]   I Corinthians 2: 9–10: 'Sed sicut scriptum est quod oculus non vidit nec auris audivit nec in cor hominis ascendit quae praeparavit Deus iis qui diligunt illum' (Vulgate version). I am very grateful to Helen Hackett for this insight and for discussion of other aspects of this study.

[63]   'The root meaning of "mystical" has to do with hiddenness, closed doors ... deriving from the Greek *muo*, "to close up or conceal"' (Williams, 1991, 184; on Teresa de Jesus' mystical theology).

[64]   *Meditations Collected and Orderd for the Vse of the English Colledge of Lisbon*, a copy of which was in the Lierre library (Darlington Book 5) states that 'a feeling experience' of God tell us more 'then by all the metaphysicall & quaint conceits' (1649, 323).

[65]   In *Spiritual Relations*, written between 1560 to around 1582, she differentiates between rapture (when the soul dies to outward things and is deprived of its senses and understanding) and transport (which happens very rapidly 'in the very depth of the soul', separating the soul from the body, for which she uses the comparison of a 'little bird of the spirit [which] has escaped from the misery of the flesh, and from the prison of the body'; I, 329).

senses, which are all asleep, to be opened to Him; He will come into the centre of the soul without using a door ...' (*Interior Castle*, II, 251–2).

'The litle gates of their curious eyes and eares': The Role of Conduct Books and Devotional Manuals in Sensory Discipline

This brings us back to the central similitude in the account of Mrs Eyre's migration to Lierre. It also brings us to early training of young women and the role played by conduct books and devotional manuals that sought to discipline the senses, texts to which the nuns were variously exposed during their pre- and post-profession careers.

Such books specifically sought to train the senses. 'I beseech you, call your fiue senses to an account; which are the doors by which all vice for the most part, entred into your soul' wrote Paul of St Ubald in *The Soul's Delight* (1654), aimed at both domestic and religious groups. It is clear that books of this kind informed early domestic training for middle and upper class women, seeking to establish styles of decorous female behaviour. Modes of 'civil' behaviour aimed primarily at boys, drawing on Erasmus' enormously influential *De Civilitate Morum Puerilium* (*Civilitie of Childhood*, translated into English in 1560), were drawn together in conduct books and devotional manuals written for the domestic market. Some were specifically designed for Catholic women; several of these underline their advice with a nationalistic polemic that associates Protestantism with 'incivility'. Although we might question the reception and impact of such texts on actual behaviour, and though we might also query Elias' generalisation that the sixteenth and seventeenth centuries were marked by 'stronger restraint on emotions' (1939, rep. 2000, 61), it is clear that rhetorically at least the Carmelite nuns (as those in other Orders) took the advice of such books to heart; that they aspired to behave in culturally approved ways in relation to control of their senses as of their general demeanour.[66]

Nuns who came to the convent from the court or from aristocratic households evidently had been exposed to protocols of behaviour that were in some ways (and not others) eminently suited to the cloister. Of course religious Orders were of their time, and reformers like Teresa de Jesus framed their constitutions around contemporary modes of civil as well as contemplative aspiration. Religious constitutions are themselves extreme forms of conduct book, shaping community

---

[66]   See Armstrong and Tennehouse on conduct literature that sought 'to reproduce, if not always to revise, the culturally approved forms of desire' (1987, 1); and Jones on public self-display, literary performance and conduct (1987). Walter rightly points out that courtesy-books provide only a partial code, for gestures at least; many texts were translated from other European languages and represented codes of societies with more (or less) formal hierarchy. It is clear that such books 'appealed to a readership for whom self-fashioning in the assertion and achievement of status was particularly important' (2009, 103).

behaviour around assumptions of politeness. If on one hand we imagine hiatus, a break in *habitus* for the women transferring from home to convent life, on the other we can recognise continuity in forms of (increasingly exaggerated) vigilance over the body, first instilled via domestic training.

Both aspects (of break and of continuity) are illustrated by *The Accomplished Ladies Rich Closet* (1687) which contains 'directions for the guidance of a young gentle-woman as to her behaviour & seemly deportment'. Aimed at girls from around six onwards, it is based at least in part on advice in texts by Hannah Woolley.[67] Some instructions for 'beautifying' appear anathema to ideals of behaviour in the convent: details of the sensory pleasures in how 'To make the Hair fair and beautifull' are not at all relevant, we might imagine, when hair is no longer 'that comely Ornament' of the female sex.[68] Alternatively, the *Closet*'s admonitions to young women to observe their duty towards God are more pertinent to the nuns' later life. The manual sets out systems for daily prayer at home, as well as general 'directions for behaviour' on all occasions: 'When you are in Church, let not your eyes by any means wander, nor your Body move in an unseemly gesture; but in all things behave yourself' (181). Chapter V outlines the ways in which gentlewomen should behave 'in all Societies', instructing them how to control their senses, 'for the Eyes being the windows of the Soul lets in Good or Evil' (202).[69]

If we are in any doubt about the impact of such texts and the ideas they promulgated on daily practice, we need look no further than a Life of Margaret of Jesus Mostyn which describes the routine that she followed in her childhood under her grandmother's instruction:

> ... from her infancy unto 12 years of age she made her obserue a perfect
> distribution of time, which was in the morning to rise at 7 a cloke & be drist
> in her sight & then to wait in a posteur until 8. some times with a Holly bush
> under her chin, & ribans pinned on ye one side of her head & the other soe yt
> she could not thrust it but upward, her arms pignied [pinioned] & all this to

---

[67]   Woolley produced four cookery-books during the period 1661 to 1675. *Rich Closet* may first have been published in the early 1680s, with a second edition in 1687 prefaced by John Shirley but lifting Woolley's work (see Jenkins, 2009, 77; Lehmann, 2003). See also Antonio de Guevara, *The Government of a Wife* (1697) for correlation between domestic and convent decorum (in relation to nuns' speech, see Chapter 5).

[68]   Under the Carmelite Rules, the nuns 'shall haue their haire cutt yt they may not loose time in koming it: they ought neuer to haue looking glasses nor any curious thinge, but all contempt of themselues' (*L3.34*; Hallett, 2007a, 249). On mirrors, see Chapter 7.

[69]   Married women were instructed: 'Suffer, by no means, your Ears to be penetrated with idle and detracting Stories' of your husband (1687, 220). *Closet* refers to the 'inner senses' in this context (see above, p. 7); in its 'Discourse of the Honourable State of Matrimony' it states that God made Man 'an *Internus sensus*, a second self, to be the sweet Co-partner of his pleasure'; 'the *Husband is the Head of the Wife as Christ is the Head of the Church* (220–21).

learne her a good posteur & garb. At 8 the grandMother would rise alsoe, and spent with her in prayers till 10, afterward cause her to hear Masse, learne her Catichisme & work till diner, where she was to shew her posteur by standing at her grandame elboe untill all the compagny was satt. After diner she was to entertaine the strangers & from them to learne to wright & worke, untill three a clocke, the next hour was spent in practizing how to speake unto all sorts of people, to euery one according to their quality from the king to the beggar, then an houre of prayer afterward catachisme, suppar reading of spirituall bookes & soe to bed. (*L3.31*, 7)

The child's extraordinary physical contortions described here give insight into the likely posture of the older nun. Similarly, if less extreme in its deportment discipline, Richard West's verse manual *The Schoole of Vertue* (1619, 7) gives instruction of the still and moving body: 'Stand straight upright, both thy feet / together closely standing / Be sure on't, euer let thine eye / be still at thy commanding'. Such advice would stand a religious woman in good stead.[70]

West also provides advice on the demeanour in serving at table, how to carve and become 'most expert in that dexterity' of cutting up all manner of small birds including 'Thighing them' (45), the kind of advice that presumably informed Margaret Mostyn's behaviour at a childhood St Luke's day festivity, eating 'the liver & a pignion [the wing] of a chicken' (*L3.31*, 6).[71]

Two books by Richard Brathwaite (1587/8–1673) also suggest the ways in which young women were trained in courtesy and deportment. Dedicatees of Brathwaite's work include prominent patrons such as Henry Somerset, earl of Worcester, a daughter of whom entered the Antwerp Carmel in 1643.[72] *The*

---

[70]   Mary Magdalen of Jesus (Magdalen Leveston: 1619–92) was commended in her Life in the Lierre annals for staying 'uppon her knees upright wth out leaning against any thing for 3th or 4 howers in ye same possture' (*L13.7*, 156). On leaning and becoming behaviour, see Chapter 2.

[71]   This chicken wing was allegedly used to bewitch Margaret Mostyn: see p. 80. Some advice on behaviour is clearly common to manuals intended for boys and for girls, so we cannot claim that modes of idealised behaviour were altogether gendered. It is clear, however, 'that children assimilated gender differences in deportment at an early age' (Mendelson, 2000, 115), and that there are distinctively gendered dimensions to concepts of behaviour outlined in the manuals. See Antoine de Courtin's *The Rules of Civility* (1671) which also describes how to carve fowl; Francis Hawkins' *Youths Behaviour, or, Decency in Conversation Amongst Men* (1651) also outlines civil behaviour. On such books, see Becker, 1988; Bryson, 1998; Elias, 1939, rep. 2000; Erasmus, 1560.

[72]   Anne Somerset (1613–51) professed as Anne of the Angels on 8 October 1643, entering with an entourage of other women (*A1*, 395–400); Tobie Matthew stayed with the family in Raglan castle in 1641 during a period of Catholic exclusion from court (Smith, 2003, 11). Brathwaite published collections of poetry and pastorals, prose romances, plays, and translations as well as conduct books: *The English Gentleman* appeared in 1630, the year before *The English Gentlewoman* (*ODNB*), on which text and other books

English Gentlewoman (1631) parodies women 'saluting the morning with a sacrifice to their Glasse'. They should make devotional meditation 'the perfume of the memory': 'Let it bee your *key* to open the *Morning*, your *locke* to close the *Euening*' (48). Sensory temptation is redirected and stylistically answered sense by sense in 'fragrant' contemplation; readers are urged to 'relish' and 'taste' the state of prayer.

Brathwaite's *Essaies Vpon the Fiue Senses* (1620) sets out the thesis on sensory behaviour that informs his advice book. The eye, he claims, is 'the principall organ of error to the affections' (2). 'Hearing is the organ of vunderstanding': 'A discreet *eare* seasons the vunderstanding, marshals the rest of the sences wandring, renewes the mind ... fortifying them against all oppositions ...' (9). He concludes this section of the book with an illustrative verse:

> The heuenly Exercise of the *fiue Sences* couched in a diuine Poem
> Let *eye*, *eare*, *touch*, *tast*, *smell*, let euery *Sence*,
> Employ it selfe to praise *his* prouidence,
> Who gaue en *eye* to see; but why was't giuen?
> To guide our feet on earth, our soules to heauen.
> An *Eare* to heare; but what? Not iests o'th' time,
> Vaine or prophane, but melodie diuine.
> A *touch* to feele; but what? griefes of our brother,
> And t'haue a *Fellow feeling* one of other.
> A *tast* to relish; what? mans soueraigne blisse,
> *Come taste and see the Lord how sweet he is!*
> A *smell* to breath; and what? flowers that afford
> All choice content the *odours* of *his* word.
> If our *fiue Sences* thus employed be,
> We may our Sauiour *smell, tast, touch, heare, see* (116)

The editor glosses 'five senses' in the penultimate line with a marginal note: 'Alluding to that sacred secret mysterie of his fiue wounds, curing and crowing our fiue Sences' (1620, 116). As we will see, such a manoeuvre of replacing like-for-like in redirecting sensory impulse is typical of devotional manuals.

Habits of thoughts and demeanour instilled in a young woman like Margaret Mostyn in order that she could consort with people of all ranks, stood her in good stead in practical terms (to manage the convent and communicate effectively with external authorities) and to instil ideals of polite behaviour, relevant in whatever community she eventually lived.[73] When the nuns mention 'civility' in their papers

---

of aristocratic self-government for men, see Craik, 2007, 115–34; 118. On Brathwaite's *English Gentlewoman* as 'the first conduct book directed specifically at the female sex' and on secular gender ideology, see Fletcher, 1995, 380; Luckyj, 2002, 56.

[73] Antoine de Courtin's *Rules of Civility* (1671) defines civility as '*A science in instructing how to dispose all our words and actions in their proper and true places*' (6).

they do so in relation to specific contexts connoting modesty and appropriateness (of status and respect) that might pertain inside or outside the cloister; 'incivility' infers sexual impropriety as well as suggesting general impoliteness.[74]

The recommendations of devotional manuals in many ways continued the process of domestic conduct books (or *vice versa*; certainly there is a symbiotic relationship between them). Some such texts had an especially Carmelite design: Paul of St Ubald's *Soul's Delight*, which refers to both a secular and religious audience[75] modelling action wherever it takes place around monastic systems, maps advice directly onto the writing of Teresa de Jesus to whom he frequently refers. Litanies are to take place at designated times; 'sensuality' in eating should be directed to spiritual 'gust', and all daily activities are made sacramental: undressing, for example, serves to remind the reader 'to desire God, to strip you, of all sinne' (1654, Part I, 31). In morning prayers the devout person praises God with 'all my bowels, powers and senses of body and soul' (35). The book sets out a routine that is designed to keep the senses thoroughly composed and directed throughout the day, to ensure 'spirituall obiects will allure them farre more forcibly then any outward things' (Part II, 51). It contains advice for spiritual edification at all stages of training from beginners to those who are more adept to make 'bodies, senses, powers, and passions, subiect to the spirit'; the 'sword of mortification' should be taken 'to cut off the least motion, of any appetite, passion, or sense, inward or outward, that shall apeere to moue or stirre disorderly' (Part II, 95).

The writer uses a spatial mnemonic to chart the soul's progress through various stages of sensory subjection: 'purged soules, may goe forward in, and get downe the stayres to the antecamera, or drawing chamber; for they are not busied nor detained with worldly imaginations', eventually coming 'into the roome, where [their Lord] is resident that face to face they may speake' (Part II, 183). Invoking the spatial and devotional poetic of the Song of Songs, he suggests a mind/body

---

Prioresses were often commended in the Carmelite papers for their ability to write clearly and relate to figures of authority outside the convents.

[74]   Sara Mendelson (2000) suggests similar connotations in her analysis of 'civil' and 'civility' in social contexts affecting early modern women. Margaret Mostyn uses 'uncivil' in relation to Protestant servants engaging in her presence in what appears to be sexually related speech and activity: 'goeing unto a gentlewomans house to learne to work who was an Heritick besides other ill example, she remembreth yt being a bed the men & mayd seruants in her chamber by the fire side 3 or 4 times used very unciuill words & actions, amongst them selfs, all wh wrought not the least ill effect uppon her, wh now she clearly seeth to haue proceeded from ye diuin protection of our Bd Lady' (*L3.31*, 3). The devil was said to have tempted the Mostyn sisters to commit 'uncivil acts' (*L3.31*, 29). In general, the nuns use 'civil' to describe ways in which they 'carry' themselves with persons of quality (*A1*, 123); how they show respect for others (*A2*, 50; 69); how they address servants and superiors (*L13.7*, 3, 5, 10, 101); and to describe generally edifying conversation (variously 'well-bred', 'discreet', 'polite'; *L13.7*, 80).

[75]   For example, he refers to eating in a Catholic household, and to 'Catholick custome' (1654, 28).

separation ('the vunderstanding is parted from his owne house') that culminates in resolution ('the other senses doe follow, and all doors are commonly so shut that no stranger or worldly thought, can get in') accounted for in language resonant of divine union: 'all the senses, well employed, and contented; in so much that they easily forget their outward functions and operations', the soul being in 'the secret roome, farre within her selfe, attended with her powers, and senses, where her beloued spouse is' (184–5).

All aspects of behaviour, from posture to prayer itself, are directed towards overcoming the effects of sensory stimulation. Like so many other books, this serves to entice a would-be nun by stylistic allure. The author structures his argument to reach a crescendo of intimacy based on 'sweet retyrement' (189) and a peak of admonishment (236) designed to suggest that only a religious life, devoid of all sensory satisfactions, can save the soul.[76]

Such books emphatically direct sensory responsiveness to reverential ends. They encourage the pious person (of either gender) to commit themselves to severe self-scrutiny as the first step to sensory mortification: 'Let vs begin to sound and dig deepe into our selves', as Alfonso Rodriguez (1526–1616) whose works were well know to the Antwerp Carmelites, urged in *The Stoope Gallant, Or Treatise of Humilitie* (1631, 54).[77] Manuals of mental prayer included in the libraries at Antwerp and Lierre supported such self-examination. They gave instructions on how to occupy the senses; personal passions should be redirected to Christ's, incarnating sensitivity.[78] Readers are told by Antonio de Molina, a writer recommended by Teresa de Jesus, 'to procure to conforme our life with his' (1617, 90). His *Spiritual*

---

[76]   *Soul's Delight* contains several phrases echoed in Margaret of Jesus' writing, not necessarily meaning she had read the text as such but suggestive of the influence of its kind. For example, the book mentions those who 'diuert their mynds for being religious' (1645, Part II, 229), a phrase used by Margaret of her grandmother; its account of the way 'houres are distributed' (18) recalls her own 'distribution of time' (a common enough phrase in religious papers). Certainly, with this and other similar books, we can envisage the effect it might have in drawing a susceptible young woman to religion.

[77]   Rodriguez's work was frequently reprinted and translated into several languages. It was popular in many of the religious communities. His *Practice of Perfection and Christian Virtues*, first published in Seville in 1609, has an English translation dedicated to Anne of the Ascension. The Antwerp and Lierre Carmels owned copies of his *Treatise on Mentall Prayer* (1627), the Antwerp copy being inscribed on the flyleaf 'For Mother Anne of the Ascension. Remember in your pryares, your to command, John More' (Hardman, 1936, 75). Rodriguez's *Short and Sure Way to Heaven* (1630) has a dedicatory epistle addressed 'To the Reverend and Religious Mother Anna of the Ascension, Prioress of the English Teresians in Antwerpe'. The influence of his writing on the work of this nun is discussed below p. 74. Tobie Matthew, closely associated with the Antwerp nuns, translated several of Rodriguez's works into English.

[78]   See for example Henry More, *The Life and Doctrine of Ovr Savior Iesvs Christ* (1656), in the Lierre library, an *EEBO* copy of which has the name 'Teresa Francisca de Jesu' written on the title page (Wing M2665).

Exercises, translated into English in 1623, contains a series of devotions that 'serueth the chastising of the body, the keeping of the sences, the mortifying of our appetites, and the recollection of our imagination' (271).[79]

The Carmelite women were encouraged to pursue systems of mental prayer in which objects of sensual pleasure were replaced by meditations that stimulated devotion. Vocal prayer also had its place, to prepare the nuns for metal engagement or to be used if a nun felt too distracted or 'dry' to follow intense mental exercises. *Meditations for Use of the English College at Lisbon*, a copy of which was in the Lierre library,[80] is typical of many such manuals which encourage the devout to form 'a liuely and present image' of Christ, to conform their will to his. Meditations show the 'Purgatiue way'. They draw on a long tradition of devotional abjection that commonly cites the example of Job sitting on a dunghill carrying 'back the eye of the mind in a spirit of repentance' (Gregory, *Morals on the Book of Job*, 1884 ed., I, 170). Rodriguez distils such ideas with reference to St Gregory and St Bernard in a system of extreme self-abnegation leading to personal nothingness: 'If you put your selues to consider what you want by your eyes, your eares, your mouth, your nostrills, and the other sincks of the body, there is not in the whole world, any other soe filthy dunghill ...' (*Stoope Gallant*, 1631, 56).[81] Similarly, the Lisbon *Meditations* invite the prayerful to pass through several stages of 'annihilation', considering first 'what man is according to his body' (loathsome),[82] then the pains of hell in which 'euery sense shall haue its particular torment and paine':

> the eye shall see nothing but the shapes of Deuills ... The eare shall euer resound with cryes, groanes, howlings, gnashing of teeth, cursing of one an other, and blaspheming of their Creatour. The tast shall be tormented with an vnspeakable

---

[79]　Molina wrote several influential manuals of advice that were read in the convents. His *Treatise on Mental Prayer* (1617) is dedicated to Mary Wiseman, Prioress of the Augustinian monastery at Louvain.

[80]　Darlington Book 5 (the 1663 edition of the text).

[81]　This text was translated by Tobie Matthew. It culminates in a meditation on nothingness itself: 'O thou who are nothing, which is lesse then dust and ashes? What occasion, or euen colour, can a thing of nothing take, for lookeing bigge, and growing proud, and houlding it self to some account? Infallibly none at all.'; 'O what a deep pitt is this? It is much deeper then Nothing' (1631, 60–61). On Teresa's knowledge of Gregory see p. 65 n. 97.

[82]　'I cannot imagine any prison so darke, so straight, so loathsome as the wombe of a woman in which the child is enclosed, and enwrapped in most foule, blody and matterous skinnes or membranes ... his food, the filthy monstrous bloud of his mother, a thing so nasty, and poisonous, as that what soeuer it toucheth it infecteth, like the plague or lepry' (1649, 11). The text is structured to contrast such human habitation with the immaculateness of the incarnation. The *EEBO* copy of the book has written on the title page 'Str Mary Winefride wth leave' and 'Sister Ann with leave', suggesting the copy was lent to these nuns who had permission to remove them from the convent library for personal use (Wing, 2nd edition, D200aΛ). On reading and borrowing books in the convents, see Wolfe, 2004.

hunger & thirst ... bitternesse of wormewood & the gall of dragons. The smell shall be always filled with most noisome stenches & pestilent smells. But the touch that last and generall sense, shall be continually tossed betwixt two extremes of heat and cold, fire and yce. (87)

Peter de Alcantara (1499–1562), the Franciscan who gave Teresa de Jesus spiritual direction in the 1560s and whose works were recommended by the Carmelite constitutions and mentioned in Teresa's writing (*Flaming Hart*, 1642, 368), follows a similarly purgative route in *A Golden Treatise of Mentall Prayer* (1632). One meditation (for Friday) also features the torments of hell, *poena sensus* and *poena damni*; according to divine justice every sense is punished according to its defect: wanton and lascivious eyes will be tortured by sights of devils; ears 'open to lyes ... shall ring with vnwonted clamours, out-cries and blasphemies'; noses once 'delighted with sweet odours, shalbe poysned with an intolerable stinck'; taste, 'glutted with dainty fare', and touch accustomed to comfort, will be tormented by their opposites. The 'interior sences' of imagination, memory and understanding will also be made to suffer (35). In order to re-educate the senses Alcantara proposes a series of readings and prayers following a 'distribution of dayes' (100). In common with many similar manuals, each part of the day is thus accounted for and the senses are directed to focus on the immediate moment rather than allowed to wander. Alcantara's own behaviour is itself set up as a model, again with reference to Teresa de Jesus' endorsement; his treatise is prefaced with details from his life in which he 'made his senses subordinate to the rule of reason'.[83]

The works of Augustine Baker (1575–1641), for many years a spiritual director of the Cambrai Benedictine nuns, were also available in the Carmelite communities from at least the 1630s (McCann and Connolly, 1933, 139). Baker's *Sancta Sophia*, edited and digested by the Benedictine Hugh Serenus Cressy (*c.*1605–74) in 1657,[84] adopts familiar language to describe this process: the devout person is urged to neglect the 'impression' made on her imagination by sensory stimuli and to signify her renunciation by words and gestures (385). Misleading meditation is

---

[83]   The translator's dedication is signed Giles Willoughby (STC, 2nd edition, 19794). Alcantara's matching of the senses with their uncomfortable opposite is typical of many such texts which seek to mortify the senses and remove reliance on their pleasures. Gertrude More, a Benedictine at Cambrai whose devotions were promoted by Augustine Baker, her one-time spiritual advisor, encompassed similar 'acts of resignation' in her work: 'to vndergoe these ensuing Paines, or Difficulties in my Bodie', for example 'to loose all pleasure, delight, and Gust in the sense of Tast soe that I may noe more tast in the pleasantest meate, then I should doe in eating a chipp, or a stone: or in drinkinge of a thinge that hath noe tast, or is of a very vngratfull Tast' (*Confessiones Amantis*, 1658, 163). On More see Latz, 1989; Marotti, 2009; Merton, 1967; Norman, 1975/6; Travitsky and Precott, 2000; Wekking, 2002; Weld-Blundell, 1910.

[84]   This edition is addressed to the abbess at Cambrai. Baker's works were widely read in the English religious communities. On controversy surrounding Baker's ideas see Walker, 2003, 143–9.

similarly to be erased, 'to wipe out, as it were, the vaine Images contracted abroad, by superinducing, or painting ouer them new and holy Images' (103).[85]

A similar process is induced by Luis de la Puente (1554–1624), a Spanish Jesuit. His *Meditations Vpon the Mysteries of Our Holie Faith With the Practice of Mental Prayer* in the Lierre library, proposes overlaying exterior sensations 'by application of the interior sences of the soule concerning eache mystery' of the Passion. Hence, 'to behould with thei eies of the soule the exterior figure of Christ'; 'to heare interiorlie those affable, and so amorous words of this B. Lord ... the noise of the buffets, blowes, whippes and hammers: feeling in my hart which IESVS Christ felt in his'; 'to smell with the interior smelling as well the stinke and obscenitie of sinne'; 'to tast the bitternesses and gaul of Christ or Lord, and soe to feele bitternes and sorrow of them; as if I tasted them corporally'; 'to touch with the interior touch of the soule, those dreadfull instruments of the passion ...' (1619, 14–15). It is desirable, he writes, to 'discourse thoroughout the fiue sences of Christ our Lord, pondering how much he suffered in euerie one of them': 'His eies were afflicted', his ears, smell, taste and touch each suffered, so that we might pray '*O Sences of my sweet and beloued IESVS ... O that my senses might conforme themselues to those of my Lord, suffering the same paines, sith the fault proceeded from them*' (18).

In more advanced stages of meditation he suggests additional forms of sensory imagining; with 'the interior smell, smell the fragrancy and most sweet odour of this bloud ... tast with the interior pallat of thy soule, how sauory this bloud is ... to touch this bloud, to kisse it, and to bathe my selfe therein'; '*Let me touch, handle and imbrace thee, incorporating and vniting my selfe vnto thee ...*' (160–61). He draws on Bonaventure's system 'denying the fiue sences of the body, and reuiuing those of the soule' during Mass: 'although I see the color of bread, and perceaue the smell, and sauor of bread, yet the substance of bread is not there ...'; '*O my beloued, who remainest in this visible Sacrament, after an inuisible manner ...*' (872–3).

His exercises include systems of sensory deprivation, such as 'shutting of the dores and windows, except when I am to read, or take my refection' (1624, preface). One meditation, in familiar mode, is 'To consider the great hurts, that our soule hath receyued by our senses: for they are the gates, and windows, by which death findeth entrance for the ruyning of our soule ... By them there enter into our mind the images, representations and figures of visible things, that molest and trouble the imagination and memory ... stirring vp and causing disquiet & a disorder of the appetites & passions of the mind' (65). He continues this extended and familiar metaphor. Mortified senses, he says, are models of the *hortus conclusus* (familiarly a figure of the cloister and the immaculate body) 'enclosed as pleasant gardens [which] giue entrance to that only, which may excite and stirre vp the soule' (66).

---

[85]   See Chapter 7 for discussion of visual erasure; Chapter 3 for the role of gesture in replacing sensory impression.

Many devotional manuals provide activity for each waking moment. Luis de Granada (1504–88) who also includes systems of purgation based on envisaging the torture of the senses in hell,[86] offers prayers for different moments of 'coming to': 'As often as thou awakes in the night, say, Glory be to the Father' (*Granados Spirituall and Heauenlie Exercises*, 1598, 9). 'In the morning, when wee awake, as soone as wee open our eyes, let our heartes be powred foorth in the remembraunce of God, before any cogitation doth possesse them'; this is a time of especial vulnerability, as the nuns themselves noted, 'for then the soule is so tender, and so well disposed, that it presently assumeth the first thought, which is offered: and apprehendeth it so firmly that it can hardly be remooued from it, or receuie any other' (*Granados Deuotion*, 1598, 125).[87] Like Mrs Eyre he is, then, most anxious about impressions that lodge in the memory and he seeks to divert them before they can gain entry, replacing them with pious words or action.

Francis de Sales (1567–1622), another very popular writer, himself familiar with Teresa de Jesus' writing[88] likewise offered daily exercises for when 'thou openest the windows of thy soule to the sunne of justice: and by these of the

---

[86]   *The Flowers of Lodowicke of Granado*, translated by Thomas Lodge 1601, 30. The *EEBO* copy of this text (from the British Library: STC 16901) has the name 'Mary Basson' written several times on the final page, as if the signature were being tried out. A nun of this name professed as Agnes Maria of St Joseph at Lierre in 1651; she was a 'native of Holland' the daughter of a merchant, said to be fearful after almost drowning as a child (*L13.7*, 152–67); see p. 93 for other references to this nun. On English interest in Luis de Granada see Cummings, 2009, 613.

[87]   *A Spiritual Doctrine* (1599) sets out meditations 'for al daies of the weeke, one for night, and the other for morning' (7); it has instructions for novices in the mortification of passions. *A Paradise of Prayers*, translated in 1614 by Thomas Lodge has prayers for each hour: 'When the clock striketh' (30). The work of Luis of Granada was extremely popular, widely translated, reprinted and reworked during this period for the intended use of English secular and religious groups. *Of Prayer and Meditation* (1582), translated by Richard Hopkins went to eleven editions between 1582 and 1634; 'of all the Spanish devotional writers whose works were translated into English, none enjoyed a popularity' like his, according to Helen White (1931, 104) who discuses translations of texts for English recusant and exiled groups. His *Sinners Guide*, digested into English by Francis Meres, sets out thinking about 'the fiue coporall sences', claiming that touch and taste are the most ignoble, being shared by all creatures and offering only short-term pleasure, 'as we see in the pleasure of tast which doth no longer endure then the meate touchesth the pallate' (1598, 443–4). He advises abstinence. 'Of the keeping of the sences' urges the devout to be watchful, 'lest theyr eyes, which are as wide gates, by which all vanities enter into vs ... are the windows of our perdition'; we should guard our ears to 'flying brutes & rumors'; smelling brings 'strange and outlandish smels, and fumigations ... the property of lasciuiousness & sensuall men' (1598, 447–8).

[88]   On the influence of Teresa de Jesus, see Chorpenning, 2006. De Sales' work was adapted for Protestant use as well as Catholic. Several of the Antwerp and Lierre Carmelites refer to his work, especially his *Introduction to a Devout Life*. On the influence of de Sales on devotional writing see Helen White, 1931, 111–13.

euening, thou shutteth them warily against infernall darknesse' (*An Introduction to a Deuout Life*, 1616, 216). Mary Frances of St Teresa (Mary Birkbeck: 1674–1733) under whose instruction the Antwerp annals came to be written (see Chapter 3), records that she was drawn to religion after reading this text. In it she will have found the means to assuage the passions. Matters 'presented to our senses' are only temporary pleasures, de Sales insists (243). 'I call those pleasures sensuall which principally and immediately are receiued by the operations and actions of the exterior senses of the body, as is the beholding of faire beautie, the hearing of sweete voices, touching dainties, and the like' (495). He lists various frivolous pastimes including dancing, the effects of which he ingeniously compares to mushrooms, 'spongie, and full of wide pores' that draw in infection, citing Pliny as his authority: 'and as these exercises doe open the pores of the bodie ... they open the pores of the soule ... if any serpentine companion breth into their eares some wanton or lasciuious word ... or some Cockatrice cast an amorous eie, an unchaste looke, the heart is thus opened' (652).[89]

Like so many other writers, he offers like-for-like riposte to sensual pleasure. May-games and the like should be replaced by holy pursuits; 'inflamed alteration which passions produce in our heart' should, predictably enough, be redirected to the passion of Christ (158). Instead of love letters and love poems he proposes that the devout person addresses their delight towards their creator, closing the heart to any but 'the Bride-groome [who] calleth knocking at the gate, and speaking to the heart of his Spouse, to awake her when she sleepeth; to cry and call her, when she absenteth her selfe: to inuite her to his hony, and to gather Apples in his Orchard and flowers in his garden, to sing and cause to sound her sweete voice, to delight his eares' (251). Such passages, echoing so evidently the voice of the beloved in the garden from the Song of Songs, move gradually to their expected conclusion, the union of souls when 'the delicious balm of deuotion distilleth from one hart to the other' (513). Holy friendship thus displaces particular human friendship (514); 'a chaste woman should stop her eares' to the 'ill-sauoured noyse' of suitors who are compared to decked and trimmed peacocks. Devotional communion 'doe passe vnseene and vnfelt from one heart to another, by a mutuall infusion and enterchange of affections, inclinations, impressions' (541):

> The diuine spouse wooing (as it were) the soule; *Place me* (saith he) *euen as a Seale vpon thy heart* ... For whosoeuer hath Christ ingraued and sealed in his heart will quickly haue him in al his exterior actions ... I haue desired aboue all things, to engraue and imprint in thy heart this sacred word, *Liue Iesus* ... (550–51)

---

[89]   Mary Joseph of St Teresa (Mary Howard: 1688–1756) who received her vocation (recalling St Augustine) 'in ye midst of a Country dance', clearly had not read of such dangers (42, 242).

Familiar as such language is in devotional texts, it is nonetheless highly-charged prose, drawing on traditions of mystical theology using libidinal or affective initiation.[90] And this same erotic energy can be found in de Sales' *Treatise on the Loue of God* which another Antwerp religious, Teresa of the Holy Ghost (Teresa Wakeman: 1641–1702) said had enticed her to become a nun (*A1*, 499).[91] There he describes the ways in which the senses are excited (1630, 28), then once more redirects such excitation towards a divine spouse: 'let him kisse me, saith she, with a kisse of his mouth, as if she had cryed out, so may sighes and inflamed grones as my heart incessantly sobs out' (34). Ecstasy, 'a going out of ones selfe' (39) into rapture, a state of melting when 'things doe easily receiue the impressions and limits' (365); 'by this sacred liquifaction, and saintly flowing, [she] forsakes her selfe ... to be entirely mingled and moistened with him' (368). There follows, amidst this richly sexualised poetic, an excursion on Aristotle's ideas, the soul taking the form of the rapture into its imagination and memory as eyes take the impression of a picture: 'The Vnderstanding receiueth from the Imagination infinitly liuelie Species' (384).

It is interesting to envisage the intellectual and imaginative impact of texts such as these on a young woman, already half-desirous of a religious life. Although the book's nuptial language is conventional, it is still arousing in its effect – indeed, given de Sales' warnings that books can inflame passions, he is highly aware of the potential for his own book to give textual delight. He appears to want it both ways, offering in his books a means to overcome sensory passions and an enticement by provoking them.

In *Delicious Entertainments of the Soule*, said to have been translated into English by a Cambrai Bendictine nun, he suggests various means by which modesty can 'bridle the will' (1632, 126). He directs the religious to spiritual reading, the work of Teresa de Jesus among others, specifying exactly the correct demeanour they should adopt in order to avoid just the kind of responses he evokes in his own writing.

For de Sales convents are the apogee of sensory training. In *The Spiritual Directer* he describes a cloister as a 'hospital'[92] (1704, 49): 'It is an academy, or house of exact correction, where every soul must learn to suffer herself to be handled, smoothed and polished; that being at length well framed and planed, she may the better be fitted, joined and fixed more exactly to the will of God' (50–51).

De Sales proposed a process of kinetic memorising, couched in the sensory terms it seeks to displace: 'thou shouldst gather a little nose-gay of deuotion':

---

[90]   See Tyler, 2010, 64–91, on Dionysian pathos and sympathetic (erotic) initiation in the work of John of the Cross.

[91]   She was one of several sisters who became a Carmelite; for her vision of the library in Antwerp see p. 123.

[92]   In convents the spiritually sick can be cured by 'bleeding, launcing, cutting, searing and the bitterest sorts of medicines' (de Sales, 1704, 49).

> Such as haue delighted themselues, walking in a pleasant Garden, goe not ordinarily from thence without taking in their hands four or fiue flowers to smell on, and keepe in their handes all the day after. Euen so ... by affectiue discousing and meditation of some sacred mystery ... (as it were) mentally smell theron all the rest of the day. And this must bee done immediately in the selfe-same place, where wee made our Meditation, walking alone a turne or two, and binding those points in our memorie, as we would doe flowers in a little nose-gay. (1616, 193–4)

Every effort should be made, he continues, not to 'spill the delicious balme of good thoughts'; 'Any man that had receiued some precious liquor in a faire porcellan, or *China* Platter, to carry home to his house, would goe with it faire and softly, neuer almost looking aside, but always eyther before him ... or else vpon his vessell' (197). He warned too of the dangers of 'wanton loues [that] thrust out of doors the heuenly loue of God' (510), devoting several chapters to 'true friendship' as opposed to the 'shadowes of amitie', in similar ways to Teresa de Jesus' own admonitions against 'particular' friendship in the convents against which Sister Ursula was herself warned as the devil's work.[93]

Wills, indeed, need to be broken: 'To chang the forme of stones, Iron, or woode: the axe, hammer and fire is required' (*Treatise*, 1630, 366). Here de Sales' images echo those of other writers who claim that mortification of the senses is the means 'to breake our selues of our owne will', this according to Alfonso Rodriguez: 'Iron is made softe, between the *Anuile* and the *fire* ... we had need to come to the anuile of *Prayer*, and there with the heat and fire of deuotion ... our heart goes softening it selfe ...' (*Treatise of Mentall Prayer*, 1627; translated by Tobie Matthew). Like de Sales, Rodriguez is mindful of the effects of reading and he provides precise instructions to ensure that inflammation, when it occurs, is directed to pious purpose. He recommends steady absorption, using the memorable image that spiritual reading 'must be like the drinking of a Hen, which drinkes by little and little and so lifteth vp the head agayne' (245). That way what is read 'may go imbruing and bathing the very rootes of the hart', not simply passing through like sensory effects (250). This advice draws on a long tradition of reading practice advocated by Teresa de Jesus among others: *lectio divina*, marked by slow and careful absorption that involves the heart as well as (or more than) the intellect, during which the reader is transformed (Carrera, 2005, 21).

Alongside this, Rodriguez advocates systems of mortification, to subdue reliance on the senses and the passions they enkindle. We should behave towards our body 'as a good Cavalier do's, who being mounted on a mettlesome Horse that is hard-Mouth'd, do's not fail notwithstanding to Master him' (*Practice of*

---

[93]   Ursula, 'passinge thorogh the Pant[ry], she heard herself called in a shrill voyce, and turning to see who it was that called, she saw our Blessed Lady, who reprehended her for what she had done, and told her the Divell was very busy' (*L13.7*, 192).

Christian & Religious Perfection, 1697, 47).[94] Accordingly, the humours should be broken in a process of 'habituation'.

We can see the effects of such advice on the nuns' lives. They frequently write of their struggle to overcome natural propensity and to subdue their senses.[95] Mary Joseph of St Teresa (Mary Howard: 1688–1756), for many years the compiler of the Antwerp annals, recorded her own struggle to subdue her senses. Like Margaret of Jesus 'what [she] found hardest was wearing woolen' (*A2*, 250); her 'shy & silent disposition' made community life a huge struggle, especially when she had to read aloud in choir or the refectory 'on account of a great imperfection in [her] speech': 'I beelive my nature was inclined to malancholy but I was bid to be chearfull which I endeavourd at till at last it became pretty habitual at least in my exteriour' (253).

'Habituation' was indeed the key to sensory subjugation. Rodriguez advocates the use of Ignatian exercises 'to the end that a man may be habituated' (*Mental Prayer*, 1627, 223).[96] His *Treatise of Modesty and Silence* aims to distil a demeanour that will inform all action through complete 'custody of our senses' (1632, 1). One copy of this translation in Cambridge University library (STC 2nd ed. 21150) is marked 'nouiship' in writing on the first page; it is indeed a likely source for newcomers to begin their assimilation to religious life. In fact, Rodriguez presents an extended exegesis on Gregory's *Moralia* which itself is a commentary

---

[94]   On governance and equestrian imagery, see Spenser, *Faerie Queene*, 'First learne your outward sences to refraine' (VI.vi.7, 6); 'Abstaine from pleasure, and restraine your will, / Subdue desire, and bridle loose delight' (14.6); James, 1997, 2; Tilmouth, 2007, discusses Robert Boyle's *Aretology* (1645–47) on 'laudable Habitudes' of horsemanship, 29; 72–3.

[95]   For example, Eugenia of Jesus (Elizabeth Levesson: 1618–52), the first nun to die in the Lierre convent and therefore the first to be recorded in the annals, was held up 'as a person of excellent excsmpell in all religious perfection'; 'euer ready and well disposed to comply wth any of the religious and euen the seruants ore most inferior pepelle wth out the Closster when occations ded requier' (*L13.7*, 1). This had not come easy to her; she had been forever 'daying to nature by continuall interior mortification and exterior penances', fervently 'excercissed in the denyall of her owne will' (10). Anne Marie Joseph of St Xaveria (Ann Woolmer: 1662–1740), the widowed sister of Catherine Burton, 'was naturally of a hot hasty temper but by her constant endeavours and continually victorys over her self was all sweetness and mildness' (*A2*, 158).

[96]   Ignatius' *Spiritual Exercises* were not translated into English until 1736, although Henry More (1586–1661) translated adaptations of Ignatius' work: *A Manual of Devout Meditations and Exercises* (1618), and *The Life of Doctrine of Our Savior Iesvs Christ* (1656) which was in the Lierre library (Darlington Book 27). The *EEBO* copy of the latter (from the Huntington Library: Wing M2665) has the name 'Teresa Francisca de Jesu' written on the title page. On Ignatian translation see Dijkhuizen, 2009, 195. John of the Cross similarly advises the devout to 'wean [their] soul from the life of sense' (*The Ascent of Mount Carmel*, 1906 ed., 319).

on the role of the senses in religious life.[97] He quotes Jerome's axiom about Job 38:17, 'Numquid apertae tibi sunt portae mortis' and the 'common doctrine' of philosophy 'Nihil est in intellectu quod prius no fuerit in sensu: That nothing is in the vunderstanding which hath not first passed by the senses' (12, 13).[98] Gregory employs a metaphor of a house robbed because the portress (significantly female) fell asleep: 'a strong and manly activity should be set over the doors of the heart' (Book 1, paragraph 49; 1844 ed., 59). Rodriguez glosses this: 'when the dores & gates of a house are well shut and guarded, all the family is in security' (1632, 13). The idea of 'manly' guard over the gates is also taken up in his *Treatise* (25); at other times this is exemplified by an 'honest Matrone looking out of the windowes' in contrast to the impudent woman who gazes here and there, chatting to this one and the other, 'at euery turne staring out of the windowes' (22).

For Gregory and for Rodriguez the posture of the body reveals inner demeanour and signifies the sensory hold an individual has attained: 'we go forth as though through the door of the tongue, that we may shew what kind of persons we are within' (Gregory, Book II, paragraph 8; 1844 ed., 73). Modest behaviour (and this is their central message) 'excites' other people to devotion (1632, 9). Religious should 'hold their eyes continually fixed on the ground, without so much as casting a looke aside' (9). All aspects of behaviour are covered. One should avoid offending the senses of others by modifying actions, 'gouerning of our voyce', for example, to keep it low, avoiding undue gestures (65).[99] Forget all your 'old childish tricks' Rodriguez urges, that 'giuing way and satisfying your senses, by sending your eyes with regarding euery vaine and curious thing, your eares with desire of hearing euery nouelty, your tongue with talking of idle and impertinent matters ...' (27).[100]

Many writers of devotional manuals are likewise preoccupied with curiosity, 'our senses neuer ceasing to wander curiously, and to draw our interior faculties after them' (de Sales, 1632, 127). Curbing curiosity is closely linked with devotional decorum in general.[101] John of Avila (*c.*1499–1569), favoured by Teresa de Jesus, directs curiosity to God alone who 'opened your eares, and eyes' (*The Cure of Discomfort*, 1623, 103). *The Audi Filia, or a Rich Cabinet of Spirituall Iewells,*

---

[97]   Gregory's *Moralia* was translated into Spanish in 1514 (Carrera, 2005, 27, 164, 177); Teresa de Jesus mentions reading it in her *Vida* (Chapter V). The Discalced Carmelites at the convent of St Joseph's, Avila, were said to have a two-volume edition of the text, apparently read and marked by Teresa (a claim now refuted; see Peers ed., *Life*, I, 30, note 1).

[98]   See p. 49 n. 61 for further reference to this phrase.

[99]   This advice is related to both male and female religious.

[100]   On guarding the senses: see Alcantara, *Mental Prayer*, 1632, 16; Molina, 1623; Rodriguez, *Christian & Religious Perfection*, 1697, 423.

[101]   Augustine Baker, digested by Cressy, writes of 'the mortifying of the curiosity of knowing or hearing strange or new things not pertinent to our Profession: the tempering of tongues from vaine vnprofittable conuersations' (*Sancta Sophia or Directions for the Prayer of Contemplation*, 1657, 103).

translated by Tobie Matthew, instructs the devout 'Do not busy thy selfe to know curious things; but turne in thy sight vpon thy soule: and continue in examining thy selfe' (1620, 292).

Anne of St Teresa Leveson (b. 1607) did just that:

> ... she seemd wonderfully lead by the way of mortification particularly of her senses in so much that she denyd them all innocent recreations, as for example when there was any thing curious to be seen or heard, she would shutt her eyes and give no attention to it ... but so as not to be perceived by others ... [even in] places [which] had most charming prospects of the Sea Ships &c [when] the Religious used sometimes devert themselves at the winddows and would say O Dear Ma Mere here is such or such a fine thing, she would goe amongst the rest not to be Singular, pretending to look as they did but never opend her eyes to see any thing, the same when she walked in the Garden as to flowers fruits &c by this Heroicall practice of turning her self from all created things she had her heart and affections constantly fixd upon God and this in the midest of the most distracting imployments ... (*A1*, 217)

The foundations of such disciplinary injunctions can be seen in a text in the Antwerp Carmel attributed to Anne of the Ascension, headed 'A Gennerall Practies how the Prioriss is to excercisse the religious in mortyfycations, euery one according to ye spirittuall proffet they make of it, wth zeall & charrity': 'Mortyfication being the grownde & presse of all virtue'. Under Teresian reform, powers were given to Prioresses in order that they fulfil an obligation to educate the religious under their authority.[102] In the Antwerp text the Prioress is advised to instil obedience in the nuns by various means such as giving contradictory instructions. To mortify their senses she should 'lay things upon downe ye housse, to see whether any one will be so curious as to locke upon them; & for yt curiosity of ye ey[e]s, giue some lettle reprehention in ye Community or to weer a bynder ouer theer ey[e]s' (*L3.5*, 1–2; Hallett, 2007a, 261–2).

Although the punishment appears extreme, the text only extends the logic of conduct manuals: 'Keep your Eyes ... with compass; that is, let them not be too much fixed upon idle and vain objects, nor drawn away by unseemly sights'; 'for the Eyes being the Windows of the Soul lets in Good or Evil, according as it fixes' (*Closet of Rarities*, 1687, 201–2).

---

[102]   Alison Weber considers that 'Teresa's social egalitarianism should not blind us to the fact that in important respects Discalced prioresses were granted considerable power' (2000, 128). She discusses the ways in which they were able 'to shape the spiritual climate of the convent' by selecting confessors and preachers, and by monitoring her nuns' progress in mental prayer, taking 'considerable responsibility for spiritual discernment ... the act of determining the authenticity of visions and other supernatural graces' (129). Prioresses were also given scope in deciding on punishment under the Rule (133).

That the nuns took such discipline to heart is evident from the many examples in their papers of sensory mortification, the dangers of which in extreme Teresa de Jesus frequently warns.[103] Some of this takes the form of complete obedience to the kinds of fruitless excursions that the Prioress' instructions include: 'To send a religious [on senseless errands]'; 'To cause them to sweept a gaine what hath ben sweept' (*L3.5*, 2).[104]

It is clear, then, that in general and in particular terms the nuns were well aware of contemporary debate about the role and dangers of the senses, and that they sought to discipline their own to devotional ends. In this the Carmelites are not unique; such practice underlay modes of behaviour in other religious Orders. The form it took at Antwerp and Lierre was shaped however by the insights of Teresa de Jesus and specific texts to which the nuns were especially exposed. Mrs Eyre chose wisely in trusting her daughters to the care of the Carmelite women, as will be seen again in the ensuing examples of their sensory steadfastness.

---

[103] Teresa repeatedly advised against extreme mortification, for example in *Way of Perfection*, having cited the instance of a hermit who threw himself down a well: 'we must shorten our time of prayer, however much joy it gives us, if we see our bodily strength waning or find that our head aches: discretion is most necessary in everything' (II, 84).

[104] Monica of St Laurence (Anne James: 1606–78) 'being sent into a Garret with a spoon to emty a Wash Tub sett there to receive the rain comeing tho, she continued some hours to fling out the water with the spoon att the Window ... in like manner she sought for a needle she had lost in the ashes' (*A1*, 389). Mary of St Albert (Mary Trentam: 1607–29), told by her Superior 'stay & I will come to you again' was then forgotten and remained several hours 'tho it was in such an incommodious place, where she was wett with the snow yet would have stay'd there all night if she had not been missed & call'd away' (*A1*, 213). This nun's 'Mortification was such that it seemeth she had no body nor feeling, putting her self to the hardest in all she could conveniently, as for example not to come to the fire tell she was for biden to Suffer so much cold ... in washing the pots in the hardest frost she would put her hands to the Elboes in cold water and many such like inventions she would find to mortify her self ... she had a continuall mortification of her eyes insomuch that alltho some new thing were brought into the room where she was, she did not look up unless it were necessary ...' (*A1*, 211). Mary of the Angels (Mary Chichester who professed 1630), 'would often be inyenting thinges which she found most contrarie to her nature and kept her sences so ordered yt hir mortification in this was perticlerly obserued' (*L1.6M*).

Chapter 2
Becoming Behaviour:
Two Cases of Sensational Reading[1]

> as nothing gets into our Souls but by the Ministry of our Senses, so nothing can well get out but by that way whereby they got in.[2]

So it was written in the Life of the Brussels Benedictine Lucy Knatchbull (1584–1629), compiled between 1642 and 1652 by her spiritual advisor Tobie Matthew. He gives a Teresian gloss to this familiar assertion:

> When therefore Almighty God ... is pleased to infuse certain Verities and Feelings into the Soul, by the only immediate way of his own unlimited power and good pleasure, without any service at all from the Senses, what wonder can it be that such Souls can be no way exact in the delivering of all such interior feelings of theirs by the way of Sense and Speech? One may go offering to express in some sort that fragrant Scent or Odour which hath irradiated her Soul; but she will never be able to satisfy even herself, and much less others, in the full utterance and unfolding thereof. Which truth we shall find recorded by as many Saints and Spouses of our Lord as have ever been put to this task, and particularly by St Teresa. And we find the self same things to be also now assured by [Lucy Knatchbull] this holy Abbess of ours, in the Relation which she makes of herself.

Significantly, Matthew compiled this work just after translating Teresa's Life for the Antwerp Carmelites. He observes of Knatchbull 'who soever will take the paines and pleasure to read of Saint Teresas Life of the flaming hart will clearly find the truth of that which I am delivering here. For they are as like one another ... as even two dropps of water can be' (Hallett, 2012a, 194). Indeed, Knatchbull's Life has 'not a little in common' with the autobiography of Teresa de Jesus (Knowles, 1931, viii). She experienced a personal epiphany on the feast of St Teresa and frequently uses Teresian 'comparisons' to explain her spiritual

---

[1] See Katharine Craik's *Reading Sensations in Early Modern England* (2007, 11–34) for an excellent exposition of emotions and 'the relationship between literary texts and the bodies of English gentlemen' (3). Several of her insights translate to, or are complicated by, observations made of women readers in my study.

[2] See Knowles, 1931 ed., 56. For an edition of the text from a Sepulchrine manuscript, see Hallett, 2012a, 159–217.

favours. As ever with such life-writing it is difficult to decipher where similarities originate and end.

What is clear is that Matthew, Knatchbull and other nuns, are in conversation with commonly-made claims about the role of the senses. We might recall, for instance, Thomas Hobbes' view in *Leviathan* (1651): 'For there is no conception in a mans mind which hath not at first, totally, or by parts, been begotten upon the organs of Senses' (see above, pp. 49, 65). Hobbesian questions about the relationship of mind and matter are answered rather differently by those with contemplative sensibilities, yet we can trace the effects of such approaches in Matthew's writing. He was, of course, friendly with Francis Bacon (1561–1626) to whom Hobbes acted as assistant from around 1620.[3] Matthew oversaw the translation and publication of some of Bacon's works on the continent, and his discussion of natural philosophy is often in tacit dialogue with Bacon. In 1605 Bacon sent Matthew an advance copy of *The Advancement of Learning*, 'at the swaddling thereof you were', and in 1610 sent a 'little work', mentioning in the accompanying letter 'My great work goeth forward', namely *Novum Organon*, published in 1620 (Mathew and Calthrop, 1907, 47, 118). Bacon considered 'by far the greatest hindrance and aberration of the human understanding proceeds from the dullness, incompetency, and deceptions of the senses' (*Novum Organon*, I: 50). Yet, 'the human senses and understanding, weak as they are, are not to be deprived of their authority, but to be supplied with helps' (67).[4]

Matthew therefore considered the same questions as Bacon and Hobbes, deducing a different, divine 'immediate way' of instilling truth into the soul. In his writing and networks, shaped by his encounters with the nuns, we have one of many meeting points of empirical, inductive and contemplative method. His theological statements, infused as they are with precepts drawn from the work of Teresa de Jesus among others, illustrate the part the women played in what has often been represented as a predominantly male debate. Again, we can see conceptual as well as personal connections with Margaret Cavendish's own ideas and the geographical and cultural circles in which she moved; her intellectual interests shared with the nuns across otherwise reformist boundaries and their common precinct wall.

---

[3]   On Hobbes' connections with the Cavendish family, see pp. 17–18. On connections between Hobbes and Bacon, see Martinich, 1999, 66; Matthews, 2008, 234. William Cavendish (1591–1628), second Earl of Devonshire for whom Hobbes also worked, was remembered by Bacon in his 1621 will (Kiernan, 1985, rep. 2000, lxxxix). Malcolm notes traces of Bacon's influence in William Cavendish's *A Discourse Against Flatterie* (1611) a copy of which in Hobbes' writing survives at Chatsworth, but claims 'it is hard to find any evidence of a strong or direct Baconian influence on the substance of Hobbes's later philosophy' (1996, 17–18). See also Huxley, 2004, on links between Bacon, Cavendish and Hobbes in relation to *The Aphorismi* and *A Discourse of Laws*.

[4]   In other words: 'With careful guidance, and compensating techniques for the failings of the senses, certainty can be attained' (Jardine 1974, 80).

Matthew's Life of Lucy Knatchbull lays bare, then, the effects of ideas and books on Lives. I use his observation on 'the Ministry of our Sences' to illustrate two interlocking facets of bookish experience as described by the nuns themselves: the role of reading in shaping sensory behaviour, and the route of the senses into and out of the body.

Anne of the Ascension: a 'living book'

The 1611 version of the Life of Teresa de Jesus, published in Antwerp, contained a dedicatory epistle from Luis de Leon to Anne of Jesus, a Discalced Carmelite in Madrid, praising the 'liuely pictures' Teresa left for her nuns: her 'children' and her books.[5] He commends 'the fyre which shee enkindleth with her words in the heart of the reader ... to inflame them in the loue [of virtue]' (6).[6] Teresa herself had explained:

> When once they tooke manie Bookes, written in Spanish from me, that I might not reade them, I was much troubled at it, for, some of them, serued me for recreation: and now I was not able to reade them, because there was none left there but in Latin. But then our Blessed lord sayd these words to me: *Be not troubled: for I will giue thee a Liuing Booke* ... his Diuine Maistie, hath been that true Booke to me, wherein I haue indeed seen Truths ... And now blessed be such a Booke as this which leaues that imprinted in the verie hart which is to be read: yea and so as that it can neuer be forgotten. (*Flaming Hart*, 363)

In Aristotelian, rhetorical and Christological terms, *logos* is literally embodied and ethically embedded. The *species* of the image within the text can thus be assumed, incorporated, internalised: taken to heart. This is, in true Teresian style, a sensory effect achieved through denial of the senses: assimilation as digestion.[7]

The Lives of Teresa de Jesus' early successors stress their effective embodiment of her ideals. Anne of the Ascension both wrote guidance and encapsulated it in her own far-from-easy passage to perfection. She was, her contemporaries noted, 'naturally of a hott temper', yet by the end of her life she 'had overcome herself

---

[5]   'imágenes vivas que nos dejó de si' (cited Carrera, 2005, 3, who discusses the aesthetic of imagining).

[6]   In the same spirit, the compiler of the Antwerp annals did so 'to the end that those present and those who follows may be animated with the primitive spirit and fervour couragiously to follow the examples of these their predecessors' (*A1*, x). On the debate about the editor of the 1611 Antwerp Life of Teresa de Jesus, simply designated as 'WM' in this edition, see Spinnenweber, 2007.

[7]   'puesto en un plato, y él mesmo digerido y cocido en el estómago' (Luis of Granada, quoted by Carrera, 2005, 32).

[an oft-repeated claim in these papers] so much, that she seem'd all meekness, and on this account the Religious used to call her Moyses' (*A1*, 45).

Certainly Anne Worsley was a spirited young woman. Living in exile with her family, aged around 15 she 'began to take delight in ye world, and to be in company', becoming preoccupied with the social disadvantage of her situation: 'I was troubled yt my parents could not maintain me as I desired; and that wee were in a strange countrey & had no friends nor kindred as I saw others had loosing thereby many occations of pleasures. Being troubl'd I thought the only way to come to some preferm[ent] was either to goe in to England, or to serve some Ladys ... To goe in to England I durst not, fearing to lose my soul by Heresy: the other I resolv'd upon' (*A1*, 1). A frightening dream or vision (see p. 46) changed all that; she decided to become a nun, eventually settling on the Carmelites despite fearing 'yt ye rudeness of Spanish natures was not fitt for me' (2). Naturally anxious at every turn, 'opprest & grieved' when she arrived at Antwerp, she drew comfort from attachment to her Superior, Anne of St Bartholomew (1549–1626), companion to Teresa de Jesus, under whose authority the English community was founded. The two women travelled to Antwerp to establish what became known as the 'Spanish' Carmel in 1612. In 1618/19 a house was purchased for the English foundation, and five English nuns (from Antwerp, Brussels and Louvain) moved there. Anne described herself as overwhelmed by emotion when the two women were eventually separated, the young nun being sent away to another community on the orders of a priest whom she had defied. Although she gained temporary comfort from perceiving a holy presence, she remained overcome by emotion: 'for ye present my nature was so fraile that I sounded [swooned] divers times that afternoon in ye way wth extremity of grief' (9).

This is hardly exemplary conduct. Yet her own papers, and the testimonies of nuns whom she eventually governed as Prioress from 1619 to 1644, suggest she successfully managed to take control of her passions. Helpfully for us, she documented her process of self-discipline. The Antwerp annals draw on Anne's 'manifestations of conscience' (a common confessional mode) written by the nun for her spiritual advisors, 'left in loose papers in her own hand writing'. At times she struggled to maintain the composure required for mental prayer and she was advised to desist for the sake of her health (*A1*, 23). It is remarkable, then, that she eventually presented a demeanour that the other nuns found deeply edifying, becoming, one noted, 'so intirly mortified her passions that in an occatione, which was the greatest, & neerest to her, that could possibley happen to her, in this life, she remained as peacable & quiatt without the least shew or motione, when as wee know for certaine she was tuched to the very hart' (*L1.5G*). Another recorded: 'she was veri considerat prudent and discreet in all her actions neuer any rash word was hard to proceed out of her mouth nor did euer any word or action of hers sauour of pasion for she had so great a comand ouer them all ...' (*L1.5C*). 'I had', she wrote of herself, 'a desire for mortification and was carefull to mortify my senses, as not to hear or see out of curiosity and the like things' (*A1*, 6). In this she was the apotheosis of religious life and of conduct manuals.

Her ideas and mode of being were both summarised in a text she composed for another nun, Catherine of the Blessed Sacrament (Catherine Windoe: 1608–66), during her temporary absence from the Antwerp community when, in around 1631, a new convent was established at Aalst, about 40 miles from Antwerp. Catherine was among a group of nuns sent to prepare the house. Several letters survive from Anne to Catherine, suggesting she was feeling homesick, and Anne also prepared for her use a devotional scapular, three copies of which survive.[8] It is written in two columns on a piece of paper:

Jesus Maria

Being ons in discurs with on that was much illumi nated by God, I was tould by them acecure and short way and short way [sic] to per fection, which is a continuall upholding of ye spiritt and an adheerig to God, which is to be don more by leeuing then working. I mean by [this] a continuall leauing and denying our selves in all things which natuer desiereth. This must be don with great sweettnes and repose of mind, as not as if wee wear to undertak a terible hard and laborius exersys, for it is nothing but a continuall scinking in to our senter, for the more wee incres in being unknowne and estraned to exterior sence and feelling, the more shall wee be drowned and loost in that replenishing fullnes which filleth / all placis with his greatnes. But this wee must not think to obtaine with out taking paines, for wee must put our selus ernestly to it without permitting natuer to take content in any thing, for if wee ar not resouluedd to suffer the continuall want of all feelling sattisfaction, it is but in vaine to undertak this maner of proceeding. Moreouer, wee must all ways cary our selues with an upright and simple hart, remaining steadfast lyck a walle, neuer declining at what so euer may happen, no more heeding the repugnance of natuer in contradiction and aduercity then if it belonged not unto us. In this maner wee must proceed with great care and whach fullnes ouer our interior desiers and affection and exterior actions, for the eye of our soule sayk that must always / be fexed on God in that maner as if thar wear no other in the woreld but God and she alone, being both dome, deefe and blind to all things which tend not to ye per formance of our oblygation toward God, and charitable corispondence with our neabore ... as allso quick and spidy in actes of obedience and charity, mild and affable in conversation, acomodating our selfes in all things to each other, well composed in our exterior cariage. For thay sayd that it was not possible fo[r] the mind to remaine in pese and quiet, except the iestuers and cariage of the body wear acording, for by only leening or going to on side or other, or in seecking our eas, or following sence in the least maner that can be, hindareth yt interior recolection of ye mind, which ye

---

8   Scapulars are small pieces of cloth or paper worn underneath the clothing, hanging from the neck onto the chest, sometimes front and back, mirroring part of the religious habit of the same name. They are considered sacramental, outward signs of invisible action, the wording of which accounts for and directs the intentions of the wearer. Some scapulars contain an image or meditation which might have an indulgence attached to it.

> continuall mortification and faithfullness to God sett downe in this paper doth
> ordinarily bring with it. (*L1.6*; Hallett, 2007a, 268)

This remarkable text bears the patch-worked imprint of multiple sources. It functions as a means of keeping in touch both metaphorically and literally reducing the women's separation, designed as it is to be worn as well as read.

It describes the route to contemplative union through self-negation: 'a continuall leauing and denying our selves' in a paradox of poised relaxedness, 'to be don more by leeuing then working'. We might appreciate the phrase 'continuall scinking in to our senter' not just in terms of a rhetorical ideal of interiority but also as a statement of decorum. Her ethical enjoiner bears the traces of an Eckhartian *gelassanheit* tradition; the self must 'become or sink into nothing'.[9] The scapular assimilates a range of other texts, rather as its writer presents a malleable devotional selfhood, shaped by its ready absorption of, with, the other.

Anne directly references Rodriguez's *Short and Sure Way to Heaven*, the 1630 translation of which has a dedicatory epistle addressed to her. We should, says Rodriguez, imagine ourselves 'in the midst of this infinite *sea of God*, circled and hemmed in by him ... as a sponge in the middest of the sea might be, all bathed, and full of water' (274–5). Whereas popular conceits of the period have water taking the shape of the vessel it fills (Meres, 1598, 35), here we have the vessel assuming as far as it is able the form of the incoming medium, replete with its 'replenishing fullnes'.[10]

We must, writes Rodriguez, use 'constant & continuall *Prayer*' (287) as 'an inexpugnable wall'. Anne, 'steadfast lyck a walle', repeats the word 'continual' five times in her scapular. Repose is not won 'with out taking paines'; it involves training the body to decline exterior influence, in particular 'carefully watching the gats of our senses' as Rodriguez states in his treatise on modesty. One 'ought to be deafe, blind and dumbe, for as much as the gates of his senses should but once be shut, his hart would be pure, and his imagination free and well disposed to treat and conuerse with God Almighty' (1632, 14, 16).[11] Anne writes we need be 'dome, deefe and blind' to things that detract from 'our obligation toward God'.

---

[9]   See Kangas, 2007, 9–10 for an account of the German theologian Johannes Eckhardt (*c.*1260–*c.*1327) and his influence on Kierkegaard. Here Levinas' theories are also apposite: 'The ethical encounter with the other brings the subject into being ... the problem of the self-obliterating alterity of the other dissolves because the "other" is there in the "self" from the start' (Jackson and Marotti, 2004, 5).

[10]   Anne makes use of this image elsewhere, quoting another Spanish Jesuit writer, Francisco de Ribera (1537–91): 'wee might be or were in God as in a sponge in the water' (*A1*, 7). Benet of Canfield has the 'Spunge that drencht in the Sea ... filled to the Brim' with desire for union (1609, 43).

[11]   Luis de Granada makes very similar statements: on waking we must be especially vigilant over eyes, ears, mouths (1598, rep. 1600, 8). Teresa de Jesus describes recollection

Prayerfulness arrives with, and is signified by, proper posture which is itself a record of its subject's spiritualisation of space. As with the Prioress' instructions on mortification, we can see traces in the scapular of domestic conduct books here intensified to devotional ends: 'it was not possible fo[r] the mind to remaine in pese and quiet, except the iestuers and cariage of the body wear acording'.[12] Religious gravity acts as 'an excellent sermon' to stir others to devotion (Rodriguez, 1632, 3).[13] Anne of the Ascension accordingly 'euer apiered so great a tranquillity in her countenance that only to behold her was sufficient to quiet a trubled mind'; emblazoning when 'her loue to Allmty God was so exsessiue ... her face would show the flames that burned in her hart' (*L1.5.C*).

Imitation operates in several directions here, and is central to the scapular as to other contemplative texts: 'this paper doth ordinarily bring with it' both intellectual and tactile effects.[14] By these words of grace and through touch the paper is translated, transubstantiated. In turn it has a transformative affect on and between bodies.

We see why it was important to remain steadfast yet also to pursue a charismatic course. Anne of the Ascension's scapular steers a nimble way through tricky terrain, developing what Nancy Bradley Warren has exposed in the Cambrai Benedictine nuns' reading of Julian of Norwich's *Revelations of Divine Love*, the earliest

---

in such terms; it gives 'the soul the desire to close its eyes and not hear or see or understand anything [other than] communion with God in solitude' (*Spiritual Testimonies*, 1976 ed., 426).

[12] As Thomas Wright states, 'a slow pace sheweth a magnanimous mind ... a light pace argueth a light mind, because thereby wee know how the spirits are not sufficiently tempered and bridled ...' (1630, 135). In general terms, instructions appear very similar in texts for male and female audiences. Francis Hawkins wrote in his translation *Youths Behaviour*, 'Runne not in the streets, alsoe goe not too slowly, nor with thy mouth open: Move not to and fro in walking, goe not like a ninnie, nor hang thy head downwards, shake not thine arms ... nor in a stooping, nor a capering, or in a tripping manner with thy heels' (1651, 20). See also Della Casa, 1576, 111 for very similar advice. Rodriguez's injunctions on modesty were not so far from Erasmus' outline on 'the modestie that one ought to haue & to hold in walkynge', 'wherein appeareth grauite, a wayte of authoritie & a trace of tranquilitie' (1560, 51). Similarly, as Anne wrote about hindering recollection by 'leening or going to on[e] side or other', domestic conduct books state: 'bend not thy body too far foorth nor backe thy leg behind' (West, *Booke of Demeanour*, 1619; see Bryson, 1998, 84). In his *Introduction to a Deuout Life*, Francis de Sales advised the pious to concentrate on Christ's 'carriage ... and gestures', to conform and model all actions to his (1616, 158–9).

[13] The *Rule of St Clare*, among other such Rules, specifies that nuns 'shall goe modestly and speake little, to the end that those who see them may be edified by them' (2006 ed., 40).

[14] Tomasso Campanella wrote in *De Sensu Rerum et Magia* (1589/90): '[T]here can be no sensation without the sensed being's acquiring a likeness of the sensed. To feel an external object is to feel, within oneself, the very force of that which one feels outside. It is to be touched by it ... perception consists in a tactile act (*tutti li sensi esser tatto*) which transmits to one being the nature of another' (Heller-Roazen, 2007, 170).

surviving manuscript copies of which were produced in the mid-seventeenth century by English Catholic nuns in northern Europe.[15] Warren claims that, through intense imitation, medieval visionary experiences 'insinuate themselves into and shape other lives', creating an I-figure 'with reference to others' (2007, 371–2). The nuns share Julian's 'bodily sights, her bodily knowledge', and so share in an 'incarnational epistemology' (375), the poetics of which underline a breakdown of the boundaries between words and bodies (383).[16] Anne of the Ascension's scapular, designed literally to touch its recipient, collapses those boundaries still further, performing its own paradox of steadfast dissolution.

That 'My heart should suffer for mine eyes' offence'[17]

We might again recall Tobie Matthew's statement in which he elaborates Thomas Hobbes and others: 'as nothing getts into our Soules, but by the Ministry of our Sences, so nothing can well get out, but by that way'.

By 1651 when *Leviathan* appeared, as already noted, two nuns from the Antwerp convent had moved to nearby Lierre and were undergoing a process of exorcism that appeared to give proof to such claims. Margaret and Ursula Mostyn's case was written up by their confessor, Edmund Bedingfield.[18] Its details bear witness to a contemporary debate about the efficacy of exorcism and the role of the senses in spiritual experience, one indeed played out in and on the women's bodies.

The nature of Margaret Mostyn's domestic discipline has already been mentioned (above, pp. 52–3). Accounts of her early life indicate she was acutely aware of the dangers of sensory pleasure. One might imagine, then, it was punishment enough that Margaret's grandmother should spend extra time in purgatory for encouraging her granddaughter to read *Arcadia*.[19] That one of the devils exorcised

---

[15]   The Cambrai nuns had access to manuscripts of *Revelations* before 1637, probably through Augustine Baker who arrived there in 1624. On Cambrai books, see Wolfe, 2004; 2007. On manuscript and early printed versions of Julian of Norwich's work see Colledge and Walsh, eds, 1978; Riddy, 2004; Summit, 2009; Watson and Jenkins, 2006.

[16]   See also Warren's further study in which she explores 'the multidimensional bonds of identification' between Christ, Julian of Norwich and the Cambrai nuns (2010, 71, 267 n. 28). On the 1670 edition of Julian's text, see Summit, 2009; on a copy of this book in the Lierre convent inscribed with the name 'Mary Frances Somersett' (whose family gave hospitality to Tobie Matthew), and on convent reading more generally, see Hallett, 2012b.

[17]   Michael Drayton, 'To the Senses', from *Idea* (1619), line 4.

[18]   Edmund Bedingfield (1615–80): unusually his Life is included in the Lierre convent's annals (*L13.7*, 99–122), indicating the closeness of his relationship with the community. He wrote two Lives of Sister Margaret, one about her exorcism and the other a posthumous reworking. See Hallett, 2007b for a full account and an edition of these and other documents surrounding the exorcism.

[19]   'Being a bout a 11 years of age and hauing a cosen in the house wh was mightily addicted to the reading of idle historyes as Sr Philip Sidneys Arcadia & c: her grandmother

from Margaret should encourage its victims to derive pleasure from reading 'trivial books' might suggest the punishment did indeed fit the crime.[20] Teresa de Jesus among others warned of the dangers of such material; in her childhood she too became 'addicted' to reading books of chivalry which her mother enjoyed, and this cooled her religious ardour.[21] Carmelite women frequently scorn 'idle' in favour of 'holy' histories.[22]

We might consider the effect on Margaret Mostyn of reading *Arcadia*, a text which itself bears testimony to the pain and pleasure of sensory arousal.[23] Its characters are shown in excitable states: 'This word, Louer, did no lesse pearce poore *Pyrocles*, then the right tune of musicke toucheth him that is sick of the *Tarantula*. There was not one part of his body that did not feele a sodaine motion, while his hart with panting, seemed to daunce to the sounde of that word' (1985

---

would haue her to read them alsoe, for to learne languag & deuert her selfe from adesire unto Religion wh she perceiued daily to encrease in her' (*L3.31*, 3). Margaret of Jesus was led later to believe what her 'grandmother's greatest imperfection had been, and for which she had lain in Purgatory, was for having hindered me from being religious and breeding me in vanities and letting me read vain books ...' (*L.3.34D*, 165; Hallett, 2007b, 21). Philip Sidney (1554–86) wrote an early version of his prose romance *Arcadia* for his sister Mary, Countess of Pembroke, completing it in 1581, with a second version in 1585.

[20]　Lestius, the eleventh demon to be withdrawn, was listed in Bedingfield's catalogue with this attribute: 'in vanis libris legendis multum se delectare' (*L3.31*, 65r; Hallett, 2007b, 93).

[21]　'My Mother was very particularly affected to read *Bookes of Caualleria*, or vaine histories ... I, in the meane time, remained with the custome of reading these Bookes; and that little fault of mine which euen I myself discerned therein beganne to coole my good desires' (*Flaming Hart*, 1642, 7; 8). Henry Coleridge suggests that such books in her extended family home included *Amadis of Gaul* (published in Spanish in 1508) and *Palmerin of England* (Spanish translation 1547); Teresa is herself said to have written a Romance (1893, 11, 13). See Carole Slade on Teresa de Jesus whose 'entire existence ... is organized around, depends upon, and proceeds from books'; her 'surrender of self to the world of the text' (2002, 297).

[22]　Aged around eight years, Margaret Mostyn 'had a very great fayth in beleeuing Holly Historyes especially of our Bd Lady & ordinarily after Suppar spent aboue an houre with great contentment in speaking & reading of them, wh was of great profitt to the Heritick seruants of ye house, two of them being conuerted by hearing her read the Sts liues' (*L.3.31*, 3; Hallett, 2007b, 51). Other Carmelites similarly contrast 'idle' and 'holy' books: Mary of the Holy Ghost (Mary Wigmore: 1622–91), for example, 'never could read out any book or apply her self to learn any thing but only wt honour and good breeding required ... her first enquiries were allways about ye truth of what she heard or read, and when she found any doubt of it, she allwais despised the subject as unworthy her thoughts, or attention, in so much as she had an aversion from the reading of all plays Romances and such fabulous entertainments' (*A1*, 405).

[23]　Katharine Craik discusses Sidney's work and ideas of utilising military anger through fiction which 'may reinforce men's active commitment to country and commonwealth' (2007, 52–72; 52).

ed., 16). Sidney appears to have built into his work a staging of the 'banquet of sense', parodic in its euphoric overload:

> The table was set neere to an excellent water-worke; for by the casting of the water in most cunning maner, it makes (with the shining of the Sunne vpon it) a perfect rainbow, not more pleasant to the eye then to the mind, so sensibly to see the proof of the heauenly *Iris*. There were birds also made so finely, that they did not onely deceiue the sight with their figure, but the hearing with their songs; which the watrie instruments did make their gorge deliuer. The table at which we sate, was round, which being fast to the floore whereon we sate ... the table, and we about the table, did all turne rounde, by meanes of water which ranne vnder, and carried it about as a Mille. But alas, what pleasure did it to mee, to make diuers times the full circle round about, since *Philoclea* (being also set) was carried still in equall distance from me, and that onely my eyes did ouertake her; which when the table was stayed, and wee beganne to feede, dranke much more eagerlie of her beautie, then my mouth did of any other licour. And so was my common sense deceiued (being chiefly bent to her) that as I dranke the wine, and withall stale a looke on her, me seemed I tasted her deliciousnesse. But alas, the one thirste was much more inflamed, then the other quenched. Sometimes my eyes would lay themselues open to receiue all the dartes she did throwe, somtimes cloze vp with admiration, as if with a contrary fancie, they woulde preserue the riches of that sight they had gotten, or cast my lidde as curtaines ouer the image of beautie, her presence had painted in them. True it is, that my Reason (now growen a seruant to passion) did yet often tel his master, that he should more moderatly vse his delight. But he, that of a rebell was become a Prince, disdayned almost to allow him the place of a Counsellor: so that my senses delights being too stro[n]g for any other resolution, I did euen loose the raines vnto them: hoping, that (going for a woman) my lookes would passe, either vnmarked, or vnsuspected. (Book I, Chapter 14)

Sidney is of course exquisitely adept in drawing on contemporary mores for comic effect; this high camp pleasure prevails throughout his work. He is also philosophically assured, drawing on a range of sensory theory to inflect the occasion. Like Chapman in *Ouid's Banquet of Sence* (1595), he draws on classical and Judaeo-Christian sources, dramatising sensory effect through the medium of romance. When the eyes of the character Pyrocles fall on a picture of Philoclea, Sidney enacts Aristotle's ideas of *species* combined with Teresian-like ineffability of words in describing his response: 'when with pittie once my harte was made tender, according to the aptnesse of the humour, it receaued quickly a cruell impression of that wonderful passio[n] which to be definde is impossible, because no wordes reach to the strange nature of it ...' (Chapter 13; 1985, ed., 11).

Devotional manuals to which Margaret Mostyn was later exposed deflect such sensations towards contemplative ends. Chapman's nuptial treatment of such conceits already has the inkling of such potential: 'Never was an sence so sette on fire / With an immortall ardour, as myne eares ... whose species through my sence / My spirits to theyre highest function reares; / to which imprest with ceaseless confluence / It vseth them as proper to her power / Marries my soule, and makes it selfe her dowre' (1595; STC, 2nd ed., 4985). In the hands of devotional writers, at home with Petrarchan and erotic similes from the Song of Songs, such images naturally relate to the *sponsa Christi*. The Capuchin friar, Benet of Canfield (William Fitch: 1562–1610), for example, follows his arousing extensive description of passionate delight with an explanation of Union as God 'knitting itself thereto' the Soul as through visual *species* (*Bright Starre*, 1646, 103; see below, p. 182).[24] Devotional writers rejecting 'idle' literatures nonetheless harness erotic energies to further their own appeal. We can understand, then, the young Margaret Mostyn's enjoyment of *Arcadia* just as we can appreciate the disquiet that, as Margaret of Jesus, she later felt. The superseding of one sensorial impression by another exactly enacts the erasure accompanied by textual or physical gesturing that several instructors advised. Margaret's rhetorical rebuff of *Arcadia* marks the effect of sequential consumption and correctives. Small wonder, then, for every reason that the reformed nun rejected her earlier reading matter.[25]

In line with her responsibility to instruct the community as Prioress, Margaret later turned her *energia* to edifying her nuns:

> ... she would on fiesttiful days, and at other times; find out some pious historicall Booke; and read to ye religious; wch was ye greatest recaration she could giue ye comunity ... for sayd thay though wee haue often read, and heard, these very things before; it must we confesse coming from her Rce it makes anothere manar of impression; for it seemes her words opens our understandings; and changes our very harts. (*L3.29*, 35)[26]

Before they could become exemplary, though, in April 1651 the Mostyn sisters faced the trauma of exorcism.

For several years prior to this the two women had displayed a bewildering array of symptoms that doctors and spiritual advisors struggled to explain and treat.

---

[24]   The English-born Fitch entered the Capuchin Order in Paris in 1587. *The Rule of Perfection*, shaped by exposure to Flemish and Franciscan affective theologies, circulated in manuscript from 1592, then was published in over 50 editions in several languages through the seventeenth century before being placed on the Index of prohibited books in 1689 (*ODNB*). *A Bright Starre* incorporates *Rule of Perfection*. The text follows a process of purgation towards union, in line with many other devotional texts discussed here. On Canfield, see Emery, 1984; 1987.

[25]   For complicating factors surrounding royalist Catholic reactions to Sidney and his association with Protestant nationalism, discussed in Hallett, 2012b, see Duncan-Jones, 1991; Lewalski, 2003; Spiller, 2000, 224; Weiner, 1978.

[26]   This description appeared in a posthumous account written by her sister Ursula in around 1680.

Bedingfield's detailed account of the exorcism and the nuns' own papers written before and afterwards, suggest ways in which their alleged demonic possession was understood. It is clear by implication that part of their agony came from the possibility that they might have brought about their possession by personal negligence, failing sufficiently to guard their senses against demonic assault. The devil, after all, was said to gain access through temptation when he 'doth trouble the senses, and puzle the phantsaie'.[27] According to Martín del Rio in his influential *Disquisitiones Magicae*, published and widely distributed within the Spanish Netherlands from 1595, the devil stirs up black bile and 'drives black specks into the brain and the cells of the internal sense-organs', thereby causing melancholy, epilepsy and other ailments by blocking the route to the brain (2000 ed., 127).

Several explanations were given for the Mostyn sisters' possession. Bedingfield recounts 'how Sister Ursula was once bewiched and Sister Margaret twice'; the first time in 1640 before they joined the convent when the Earl of Dumfries 'made particular love' to Margaret: at a feast-day table 'she received ye liuer & pignion of a chiken, presented by him & eat it unawars. It was alsoe increased by a locke of haire & riban giuen unto him by her mayd by her consent: And lastly by Peachs & a letter wh she sent unto him to present unto ye King then near at hand' (*L.3.31*, 5).[28] Such an exchange of love-tokens was common courtly behaviour. *The Accomplished Ladies Rich Closet*, for example, warns: 'presume not too much on your own strength, by interchanging Gloves, Rings, Ribons, and such things which you may term Trifles, lest, by this kind of familiarity, Love by insensible ways opens a passage to your Heart' (1687, 198).[29] Do not, it continues, give 'Licentious Amorists liberty to meet you in your Walks' (198).

The nuns' later behaviour with the devil disguised as their suitors suggests they indeed faced sensual temptations and fantasised about secret assignations, remembering past lovers.[30] Margaret noted she was troubled 'by ye rememberance

---

[27]   His other routes were through *obsession* when he carried his victims through the air, and finally *possession*, when he became 'predominant over his body and soule' (according to Nathaniel Homes in his sermon after the London eclipse of 1652: cited Harley, 1989, 123).

[28]   The account of the second bewitchment two years later is less specific; Margaret opposed the overtures made by a kinsman, Roger Mostyn, who wished to marry her sister. He allegedly 'procured a double wichcraft' to seduce one of them and punish the second. Another version of events attributes the bewitchment to a witch who had been confined to the convent.

[29]   On the exchange of ribbons as love-tokens see Ranum, 1989, 246.

[30]   Sulphus, the sixty-sixth demon to be exorcised was said to have excited sensual feelings by causing them to imagine kisses (*L3.31*; Hallett, 2007a, 94). The devil 'represented the sisters themselfes most parfectly ... yea sometimes he would comitte unciuell acts with those representations & persuad them that they weer as guilty of the sinnes as if they themselfes had done it'. The devil was said to promise Margaret 'yt she should enioy him as much as if she liued with him in his owne house hauing appoynted the garrett for the place where she spent many hours in receiuing his courtisyes & answearing unto them in all kinds' (*L3.31*, 26).

of pasiges in ye world and also wth dreames of this kind' (*L3.35*, loose paper). The nuns were very aware of the dangers of memory to incite fantasy.[31] Their mnemonic discipline was designed to withhold sensory as well as pre-professional experiential recall.

All in all, then, in their pre- and early post-profession lives the two women might be thought to have failed to be sufficiently guarded: 'The Devil acts in this business, as a thief that is going to break into a House, who finding the Windows too strait for himself to enter in, thrusts in a Boy, to open the Door on the inside. Bad suggestions, want of recollection, too much liberty of our Senses, and a thousand such like occasions, are the engines the devil makes use of, to force a passage into our Soul' (Rodriguez, *Practice of Christian & Religious Perfection*, 1697, 212).[32]

Having gained access, the devil's sensory subterfuge, sometimes through 'melancholic diseases', made symptoms complicated to decipher.[33] Robert Burton's influential compendium on melancholy (published in 1621) reported sufferers' 'senses are troubled, they think they see, hear, smell, and touch that which they do not'; 'Some have a corrupt ear ... they think they hear music, or some hideous noise as their phantasy conceives ... corrupt eyes; some smelling, some one sense, some another.' Nuns, in his opinion, were especially prone to the condition (2001 ed., Part I, 384; 403; 414ff). Such views served to make sufferers doubt themselves and be doubted.

If demons arrived through the senses, they were accordingly withdrawn that way or by realigning sensory purpose to good effect. Bedingfield's narrative pays much attention to entry and exit points and to the body's extremities. The devil's 'chieffe habitation was in [Margaret's] eyes & her Armes' (*L.3.31*, 79–80); 'euery body in this condition doe not moue hand, foot or eye & c' (72). At other times

---

[31] Francis de Sales' *Introduction to a Deuout Life* warns widows 'to resist the imagination which lawfull pleasures, receiued in mariage in former times may breed in their remembrance, their minds therefore being more subiect to vncleane allurements and vnchaste impressions' (1616, 442).

[32] For discussion of the relationship between witchcraft and women's senses in general, see Classen, 2005. For example: 'The basis of the witch's powers was the suspect female sensorium ... witches defied sensory and social norms by using feminine senses of touch, taste and smell as media for self-gratification, rather than self-sacrifice, and as avenues of empowerment, rather than instruments of service' (71). The resonance of such views might be more powerfully felt, we might imagine, in a convent context bent specifically to mortification.

[33] Official guidelines after the Synod of Rheims in 1583 stipulated that priests should 'distinguish a possessed person from other individuals who suffer from melancholia or any other illness (*qui vel atra bile, vel morbo aliquot laborant*)' (Clark, 1997, 394). Teresa de Jesus warned that the devil could cause illness and melancholy, and that both could also have innocent origins (*Interior Castle*, II, 277). She considered that less effective confessors over-diagnosed demonic interference, and told her nuns to choose their advisors well (272).

Margaret was overtaken with uncontrollable convulsions.[34] If we compare her dire situation with that of the poised and still young woman with holly under her chin (pp. 52–3) we can gauge the dread that this loss of decorum caused. Indeed, given anxiety about the possible coherence of actual and imaged materiality, it was presumably very shocking that the shape-changed devil tempted the women 'to comitte unciuell acts with those representations & persuad them that they weer as guilty of the sinnes as if they themselfes had done it' (*L3.31*, 44).[35]

The devil assumed duplicitous forms, sometimes disguised as an angel of light.[36] Potential moments of faith thus became acutely ones of doubt. As John of the Cross noted, spiritual people sometimes

> see the forms and figures of those of another life ... They hear strange words, sometimes seeing those who utter them, and sometimes not. They have a sensible perception at times of most sweet odours, without knowing whence they proceed. Their sense of taste is also deliciously affected ... Still, though all these may happen to the bodily senses in the way of God, we must never rely on them ... inasmuch as they are exterior and in the body, there is less certainty of their being from God ... for the devil has more influence in that which is exterior and corporeal, and can more easily deceive us therein than in what is more interior. (1906 ed., 104)[37]

---

[34] Margaret's convulsions 'became almost continuall day & night, sometimes hauing 20 fitts in 12 hours; her leggs & Arms being almost drawen up together with such vehemence yt when she would rise afterward she was forced to creep upon hands, & feet; her sences frequently failling her so yt she spooke idle ...' (*L3.31*, 20). On another occasion convulsions 'passed from one lime into an other, through their whole bodys ... often times crying out to mee [Bedingfield] for to saue them, or else they should be carryed a way a liue; sometime having such suddaine & vehement twichs, as if the Diuel intended it indeed' (52).

[35] 'About this time Sister Margt was soe afflicted yt in a whole night she could scarce gett an houres sleep being constantly waked a quarter befor 12 with unciuell temptation' (*L3.31*, 56). On Margaret's use of 'uncivil', see p. 55 n. 74.

[36] 2 Corinthians 11:26: 'even Satan fashioneth himself into an angel of light'. See Teresa de Jesus, *Interior Castle*, II, 211; Boguet, 1929 ed., 5, 17; *Malleaus Maleficarum*, 1971 ed., 122–4, all warning of this phenomenon, and see below pp. 191, 198.

[37] Such views were widespread and common to different religious denominations. The rector of Braunston in Northamptonshire, Edward Reynolds, noted in *A Treatise of the Passions* that melancholy men suffer 'gastly apparitions, dreadfull sounds, blacke thoughts, trembling, and horrors', delusions caused by disordered humours or the senses misleading the imagination by 'strange and false *species* cast into it by the devil' (1640, 26–7). Ludwig Lavatar, a Protestant pastor from Zurich claimed that devils could 'deceyve the eye sight, and other senses of man, and hide those things which are before our face, and convey other things into their places' (*Of Ghosts ...* 1572, 45). For a discussion of this and of other areas of doubt concerning vision in particular and the senses more widely, see Clark, 2007, 47, 60–61, 211, *et passim*.

And deceive them he did. 'He very often alsoe tooke good & pious shapes uppon him appearing some times like our Bd Saur crucifyed, like our Bd Lady, St Theresa, their good Angell & c' (*L3.31*, 42). He taunted the women, calling their names and mimicking those they knew well, including Bedingfield himself.[38] Demons buzzed like flies around their heads. More dramatically, the devil appeared to Margaret as a black horse, 'stamping shaking or breathing' or crashing like a collapsing wall (80).

Sounds and voices feature significantly in the exorcism narrative; the mouth alone is mentioned 17 times and at key moments; 'speak' appears 26 times and 'word(s)' 31. While the primary strength of the exorcist was in commanding each demon by name, many of Margaret's agonies related to her loss of language or control of her mouth. 'Phalasius told mee' wrote Bedingfield, 'yt his residence was chieffly in her head & tong' (81). The women were unable to pronounce sacred words (a sure sign of possession according to contemporary lore). Bedingfield meanwhile read aloud the exorcism prayers and the women suffered agonising 'contradictions', often unable to utter anything meaningful, making mere sounds and moans. When devils were withdrawn, a 'siluer sounding bell [was heard] distinctly to strike one wh[ich] filled us all with teares of ioy' (61). The women were finally able to speak coherently, and Margaret eloquently, when 'she bound the Dumb Diuel in cheans, and [he] gaue them freedome of speech' (71).

Other sensory orifices were similarly attacked. 'Vochiel the diuel of the stomach & wichcraft' tormented Margaret with vomiting.[39] Whereas before their exorcism, the women had found food tasteless, afterwards their appetite was restored, along with an ability to sleep.[40] Demonic presence was signalled by the smell of brimstone; clouds and flies which Margaret 'knoweth to haue bin the

---

[38]   'He alsoe appeared unto her frequently in shap of her confessarious making use of all my words & action: yea once ringing the Bell at the turne after his fashion, & Sister Margt hauing a great desire to speake with mee came runing with Deo gratias in her mouth but found nobody at the turne, but she was noe sooner gone but she heard the bell ring agayne thought yt she was mistaken wherfor coming the 2d time with out Deo gratias asked who was there, & he replyed you are she I would speake withall: And begun to tell her how he had recomended her businesse to God, & yt att length he understood her very well & yt her case was with out remedy & yt heauen was onely for those yt did indeauor to amend & serue God soe yt she might doe what she pleased & yt she should come noe more near him it was but in vaine he could but compassionate her & soe farwell' (*L3.31*, 43).

[39]   Vochiel also gave Ursula serious menstrual problems, often confining her to bed. He was said to have been a stubborn demon to withdraw. Once he was expelled the Virgin told Margaret that the women 'should eat flesh until our Bd Ladys glorious Assumption & forbear from eating cold things, drinking win[e] moderatly' (62). They had previously been treated by 'hauing Hollowed thinges alsoe mixed with her dyett & often times eating pieces of Agnus Dei' (19), that is, wafers or discs (often of wax) impressed with the figure of a lamb and blessed for sacramental use.

[40]   'Et cum antea vix duas horas, tonini per integram noctem caperent, nec cibus ipsis, vel potus qualiscunque saperet, iam sicut catera sorore tota nocte dormiunt optimo appetitu comedunt' (*L3.31*, 39r).

diuel Diaspas who is alsoe one of ye region of ye Ayre' (81). This was in contrast to the 'odoriforous' smells witnessed by several people when the exorcism was successful (73).[41]

Touch features strongly in this story. Hands and fingers are mentioned some 16 times in the account, frequently said to be contorted, gripped shut.[42] The women were given blessed beads to hold to divert the devil from 'putting things into their hands for to kill them selfs' (41). Simply by taking hold of her beads, Bedingfield claimed, Margaret was able 'to know the infalible truhe wh[ich] serueth mee daily in these writtings' (75). The nuns' hands were tied during the exorcism (71). Most strikingly of all, Bedingfield instructed Margaret 'to confirme a falcity or deny any verity as often as I put my fingers a crosse into her mouth'.[43] Margaret's oral and tactile gesture thus replaced her language at key moments. The successful exorcism was (according to instructions from the Virgin via Margaret) to be recorded in a votive image of 'two flaming hands lincked together & holding them alsoe in a cheane with ye other ... because she bound the Dumb Diuel in cheans, and gaue them freedome of speech' (71).[44]

All in all, this extraordinary document records perception *in extremis*, charting loss then regain of sensory control: the young Margaret Mostyn moving through a phase of being 'addicted to the reading of idle historyes'; 'pinned up' in ribbons and holly; exchanging love-tokens, then being so afflicted that she was in the depths of suicidal despair. The narrative maps mishap and recovery so that eventually the nuns were models to their community, one after the other Superiors at the convent (in total for 45 years). Margaret moved from being a dissident to an exemplary reader: 'her words opens our understandings; and changes our very harts'.

---

[41]   'the signe was a most odoriforous sweett smelt somewhat like Lillys, with which she [Margaret] was recreated ... And this sweet smel continued with them by fitts for many dayes after, the Mother [Superior] once her selfe participating of it in their presence' (*L3.31*, 73). On brimstone and the devil, and miraculous smell more generally, see Chapter 6.

[42]   'Their armes & hands were soe strangly contracted, and soe extreemly cold that they represented a carkas rather then a liuing body' (52). Demons marked the women's skin with spots that moved under signs of the cross.

[43]   The relationship between Mostyn and Bedingfield is fascinating at such moments. Jodi Bilinkoff has observed 'The bonds of understanding and empathy forged between priests and penitents also found physical expression manifestations in body as well as soul. ... For some religious women, it was as if the vow of obedience they made to their confessors conferred upon these priests an almost thaumaturgic power. The men to whom they submitted their wills could also control their bodies' (2005, 86, 87). Here the gender relationship appears reciprocated. As the exorcism continues, it is the woman who assumes elements of somatic power, signalling meaning; the verbal-textual translation of her experience remains the priest's (on authority of the Virgin via Margaret).

[44]   In a different context Katherine Rowe observes that 'anatomical illustration, drawing on a traditional visual representation of God's hand, returns repeatedly to two clasping hands: suggesting the interlaced and mutual nature of divine and human agency' (1997, 288).

Although Margaret initially appeared powerless in the face of the drama unfolding around her, gradually she assumed some authority. Bedingfield's gesture of touching her mouth with his fingers is especially powerful, culturally as well as ritually when the hand thus 'moves to the chiefest orifice of the mind', as John Bulwer explained in his *Chirologia: Or the Naturall Language of the Hand*, (1644, 87).[45]

Touch, then, sometimes regarded as the least stable of the senses, afforded Margaret interpretive authority and a certain kind of expressiveness. It is to touch that we will now turn to investigate further its special place within the Carmelite sensorium.

---

[45] This 'natural' language is of course a highly choreographed and culturally specific system. Bulwer is here discussing kissing the hand (a gesture considered here in more detail in Chapter 3). He also explains that biting one's own finger signifies anger, and putting your hand to your mouth suggests astonishment (1644, 160, 168).

Chapter 3
Titillation and Texture: The Sixth Sense of 'Handsome Handid Nuns'

Although (or perhaps because) Touch was often regarded as 'the lowest of the elements', the fifth or even sixth sense in most computations, Carmelites have a particular preoccupation with this sense.[1] Personified, it brings about the erotic finale in early modern masques of the senses, the least guarded of routes into the body since 'Through euery liuing part it selfe doth shed / By *sinews* which extend from head to foote, / And like a Net all ore the body spred' (Davies, 1653, 45). Indeed, it is often represented emblematically in early modern culture by the spider.[2] Ambiguously, perhaps, Touch is also the 'sences ground-worke', 'sences emperor' (Chapman, 1595, 39): 'Lifes roote' (Davies, 1653, 45).[3]

By way of introduction and reprise, I offer six (or more) things about Touch, some of which have already been mentioned in passing, some are yet to come; all of which happened in the convents under discussion here.

---

[1]   The commentary on Plato's *Symposium,* by Masilio Ficino (1433–99) for example, an influential text reprinted from 1474, presents a typical hierarchy: 'Reason, which seeks the Celestial, has no seat in the body; Sight, as the noblest of the senses, is placed highest in it. Next comes Hearing and Smell, and then Taste and Touch, corresponding to the lowest of the elements. Counting reason as a sense, three senses appertain to Body and Matter, and three to the Soul. Reason, Sight and Hearing nourish the Soul; Touch, Taste and Smell the body' (Kermode, 1971, 94). Kermode points out that Aristotle places them in the order Vision-Hearing-Smell-Taste-Touch, with taste a form of touch (*De Anima* II.vi–xii).

[2]   On the place of Touch in 'a complex, shifting and sometimes contradictory position in the representation of the five senses in Western culture', see Harvey, 2003, 1. On *tactus* in erotic representation see Benthian, 2002, who notes Touch appears at the conclusion of a pictorial series on the senses; in preceding scenes 'the various senses are being sharpened and stimulated', and the final one 'represents the goal and climax of this stimulation' (190). Original sin was often artistically represented as that of grasping (rather than tasting) the forbidden fruit (see Boyle, 1998, 111). See Helkiah Crooke *Mikrokosmographia* (1615, 730–31) for a description of grasping as the 'office of the Hand'; 'the most noble and perfect organ or instrument of the body' (see Rowe, 1997, 290; Kemp, 2000, 25).

[3]   Aristotle wrote: 'Other senses such as colour, sound and smell, do not destroy the animal by excess, but only the sense organs ... but the excess of tangible qualities, such as heat, cold and hardness destroys the animal ... without touch an animal cannot exist ...' (*De Anima*, 435b, 7–9; see Mazzio, 2003, 181). Brathwaite wrote of 'the liuing Sence', it 'hath a certain affinitie with the essence of man' (1620, 27).

One: things that touch each other do not necessarily feel: *viz* a spoon on a plate. Two: of things that come into contact, one part of the pair might be more sensitive than the other: a woman touching a rosary, say. Three: the effect of touch can lead to a dermal reaction even in the absence of touch itself, as with 'scraping of trenchers'.[4] Even memory of such sensation years later can cause a reaction anew. Those who only hear it reported can also experience or imagine the sensation at several removes as if it were their own.

Witches too can make their touch felt at a distance, for example by infecting food or handling items of clothing.[5] Conversely, but with similar process, relics that are put to touch diseased bodies might be felt to bring curative presence, metonymic of a saint who is no longer physically alive or present. Even a small sliver of flesh can be felt to have miraculous effect on a whole body. Even a piece of paper or cloth that has touched the cloth that touched the saint can bring the impression of touch via several bodies. It does not necessarily have to be in direct contact with the ill person in question for it to have an effect.

Four: To have touch is to have confidence: 'Of all our senses, touch is the one considered the least deceptive and most certain' (Descartes, *The World or Treatise on Light*, 1664; 1985 ed., I, 81). Edmund Bedingfield put his finger into the mouth of Margaret of Jesus 'to confirme a falcity or deny any verity'. Margaret bit his finger. Both of them felt something. This might or might not have resembled the object producing the sensation.

A nun feeding another nun in the infirmary sensed (we assume) the spoon, the trencher, the touch of the cutlery on the lips of the patient; the patient felt the spoon on her mouth, the food on her tongue. Even at such an intimate moment, both scenting the same cooked chicken, they are sensually apart; their pleasures are different. The sick nun was allowed meat (a rare component of the convent diet); her companion might crave it (or not). Likewise, even when they touch each other, those in pain cannot be fully comprehended by those who are not.[6] Pain is manifested on the skin's nerve-ends even if the cause is not proximate.

A nun feeding a cordial to another sick nun used a feather to administer the liquid. 'Do you think the idea of tickling which [s]he conceives resembles anything present in this feather?' (Descartes, *The World or Treatise on Light*, 1664; 1985 ed., I, 81). Ideas formed in the mind as a result of sensation might bear no resemblance to the bodies causing it. So, to have touch might be to have *un*certainty as to immediate cause.[7]

---

[4]   Galen considered that skin only responds to tactile stimuli if it is in direct contact with the source of stimulation (Siegel, 1970 in Krueger, 1982, 7).

[5]   'The touch of a witch is noxious and fatal', wrote Nicholas Rémy in *Demonolatry*. On witch's powers in 'the suspect female sensorium', the most dangerous of which was touch, see Classen, 2005, 71.

[6]   'To have pain is to have *certainty*; to hear about pain is to have *doubt*' (Scarry 1985, 13).

[7]   Hence in Thomas Tomkiss' 1607 play, *Lingua, or the Combat of the Tongue and the Five Senses for Superiority*, performed at Cambridge and reprinted five times to 1657,

Five: We can explain pain and pleasure by identifying the mechanics of response. If a feather touches lips or hands agitate the sensitive soles of the feet, skin moves, muscles twitch 'just as when you pull one end of a string, you cause a bell hanging at the other end to ring at the same time'; we might 'feel a certain bodily pleasure which we call *titillation* ... very close to pain in respect of its cause but quite the opposite in its effect' (Descartes, *Treatise on Man*, 1664; 1985 ed., I, 103).

Six, and perhaps most important: two people touching (one causing the twitch) will have different sensations, one drawing on their 'inner sense' to coagulate sensation, on their intellect to interpret, standing aside from sensation whilst simultaneously feeling; the other is simply agonised (or full of pleasure, depending on the cause). 'By *touch* the first pure qualities we learne, / Which quicken all things *hote, cold, moyst,* and *drie*; / By *touch, hard, soft, rough, smooth,* we do discerne; / By *touch, sweete pleasure,* and *sharpe paine* we trie' (Davies, 1653, 46).[8] So, in diagnosis, a nun feeling the temperature, febrility or pulse of a sick Sister can evaluate to some extent her condition; and a nun touching a dead body might be alarmed to find the corpse still sweating after several days, the moistness returning in the presence of eye-witnesses who also note that the nun does not smell of corruption. Touch validates or thwarts the observations of other senses. It seems indeed to cohere the body 'and cannot be separated or taken away without the detriment or vtter decay rather of the subiect wherin it is' (Brathwaite, 1620, 27).

Finally, for now: Touch can replace or reinforce other senses in a way that others apparently cannot. Blind nuns find their way around the convent by touch: 'they see with their hands, or ... their stick is the organ of some sixth sense'. This is also proximate at one remove: 'when a blind man feels bodies, nothing has to issue from the bodies and pass along his stick to his hand; and the resistance and movement of the bodies, which is the sole cause of the sensations he has of them, is nothing like the ideas he forms of them' (Descartes, *Optics*, 1637; 1985 ed., I, 153).[9] Deaf nuns use or receive sign language, some of it tactile, some of it visual: gestures cut across several senses, representing touch in its absence, like language itself which can from afar be perceived to (or actually) cause hurt or sacramentally salve.

Tactus is represented by Mendacio, the lie (see Mazzio, 2005, 88–9, who notes that Oliver Cromwell played Tactus in an early production).

[8]   Aristotle explained that every sense contains one set of opposing sensible qualities: bright and dark; loud and soft; bitter and sweet; 'in the object of touch there are many pairs of opposites: hot and cold, dry and wet, rough and smooth ...' (*De Anima*, 422b, 23–7). He extended this further in *De Generatione et Corruptione* to include heavy and light, hard and soft, viscous and brittle, thick and thin (see Heller-Roazen, 2007, 29).

[9]   *Species,* in other words, do not move through intermediaries (although reports of the effect of *species* can leave an impression on different senses). On the relationship between touch and sight, and the idea that 'touch was only intended for the final stages of visual perception' see Clark, 2007, 340–41. Margaret Cavendish refuted aspects of Descartes' theory, rejecting the idea that 'the sensitive organs should have no knowledge in themselves, but serve only like peeping holes for the mind, or barn-dores to receive bundles of pressures ...' (Letter 35; Anderson, 2003, 191).

All this throws up the question what 'is the sense organ for touch? Is it the flesh ... Or is flesh, on the contrary, the medium, while the primary sense-organ is something internal?' (Aristotle, *De Anima*, chapter 11, 422b17; Durrant, 1993, 44).

This chapter will deal with each of these issues in turn, considering the nuns' ideas of touch itself; of texture; of proximate and remote touch; of hands (dead and alive); and flesh (dead and alive); of gesture, language and its tactile attributes.

First: *Noli Me Tangere* and Palpable Satisfaction[10]

Touch in convents is constitutionally conditioned. It comes within a range of prohibitions relating to enclosure more generally, including conversation with other religious and with seculars outside the cloister. The Carmelite Rule specifies 'That none of ye sisters imbrace one another, or touch face or hands.' This embargo comes in a section of the constitutions which also deals with mealtimes and refection, occasions when the nuns socialise. The statement continues with injunctions against 'haueing particular friendshipe'; 'This point of louing one another in generall is of great importance' (*L3.34*, Chapter 4).

The contextual connection between social association and touch suggests a concern to prohibit undue intimacy of any kind. This is underlined in 'Chapter 20: Of the Most Grieuous Fault' where false witness and the sin of sensuality (both breaking rules of conceptual containment) are severely punished. The offending nun 'shall doe her pennance at ye time of refection being wthout a cloake, haueing nothing but her scapular, upon wch there shall be sewed tow tounges of white cloath before and behinde in different manners;[11] and being in ye midest of ye Refectory she shall eate bread and drinke water upon ye ground, to shew yt this pennance was giuen her for ye great vice of touching and thence she shall be brought to prison; and if any time she be deliuered, she shall haue no voyce, nor place' (Hallett, 2007a, 259).[12]

---

[10]   John 20:17, the words spoken by Christ to Mary Magdalene after the Resurrection: 'Do not touch me: for I am not yet ascended to my Father' ('noli me tangere nondum enim ascendi ad Patrem meum'). Later in the same chapter Thomas is invited by Christ to touch his wounds (John 20: 24–9). John Bulwer accounts for this in *Chirologia*: 'Hence *manus occulata* the adage; and verily we may well believe this occular test or feeling eye of the *hand. Thomas Didymus* as diffident as he was, received a palpable satisfaction by this way of silent information' (1644, 172).

[11]   This is presumably for modesty, the scapular being 'four fingers shorter then ye habitt'. The prison mentioned in this passage is a special place designated within the convent. Punished nuns were disenfranchised, losing their vote (voice) and place as choir Sisters.

[12]   Clearly some aspects of the liturgy required touch. At times it is sacramentally compulsory and ritually regulated, for example in handing out the Eucharist or in anointing a dying nun with sacred oil. 'Salves, oils, unctions, unguents, lotions, liniments, embrocations all involve not an arresting of a state of matter into a skin, but a harnessing of the power

We might recognise therefore that special conditions surrounded the case of a nun who, having suffered painful surgery to her jaw, asked Mary Xaveria 'to strock my face with her hand in wch St Xaverius had left ye mark of his cure, and presently it grew much better, ye wound soon healed up without leaveing any scarr' (*A3*, 384).[13] Given the injunctions against general touching, we might also feel the frisson of Anne of the Ascension's description of separation from her beloved Superior when she had her hand on the veil to lift it back from the older woman's face.[14] If we also understand the prohibitions surrounding entry to the enclosure, we can gauge the urgency behind Edmund Bedingfield's action in going to the bedside of the nuns during the exorcism, and in touching Margaret's mouth.[15] Clearly this was, quite literally, a case of must needs.

When touch is mentioned in the convent papers, therefore, it has a range of significances attached to it, none of them casual even if they are work-a-day. We might consider what the nuns touched in their daily lives and why.

'Handsome Handid' Nuns: Licensed Touch in the Convent

Much emphasis here is on exemplary effort. In descriptions of labour performed in adversity, for example, the nuns' tactility underlines their martyr-like mortification in which they are presented as always occupied, the devil manifestly kept at bay by the women making their own work for idle hands. In particular, there are

---

of certain substances to change state' (Connor, 2004, 179). Patristic writers paid much attention to the liturgical powers of human hands. 'Great are the deeds for which the hand is eminent. The hand is placed on the holy altars as conciliator of divine grace. Through it we offer as well as partake in the celestial sacraments. It is the hand which performs and at the same time dispenses the divine mysteries' (Ambrose, *Hexameron*, 6.9.69, cited Boyle, 1998, 108). Clearly within the liturgy there are gendered differentials in place; women are not permitted to dispense sacraments.

[13]   The nuns were clearly aware of claims about the power of royal touch. The Lierre papers include an account of the case of Mary Newman the bones of whose legs were 'displaced' as a child so she went on 'stumps of knees', trying numerous cures across and visiting baths across Europe. She was unsuccessfully touched by both the English and French kings and was finally cured after a visit to St Winifred's well in Wales in 1666 (*L3.35*, loose paper). On St Winifred's well, close to the Mostyn family home, see Seguin, 2003.

[14]   'Being at ye gate to goe forth I turnd back to see our Dear Mother once more for ye last time, as I had my hand on ye vaile wch hung over her face (because there were People she was coverd), the Provincial call'd me to come without Delay, so I left ye vaile with grief not to see her more ...' (*A1*, 8; Hallett, 2007a, 48). On this incident, see above, p. 72.

[15]   Outsiders could not enter for purposes of work and for medical reasons: 'saue only in case of necessity ... ye phisitian, surgen, or ye lik'. 'In noe case ye Confessour ought not to enter ... if it be not to confesse ye sicke when ye phision shall say yt it is necssary, and to minister unto her ye Bd Sacrement and extrem unction, when tis time' (*L3.34*; Chapter 3, 'Of Enclosure').

innumerable accounts of nuns sewing, that advertisement above all of female virtue in secular and religious life.[16] Some women indeed are said to have learned their craft before they arrived in the convents, cutting and shaping linen there for instance, then afterwards taking responsibility for 'plain work' and embroidery in the cloister, 'curious worke' being prohibited by the Constitutions.[17] The Antwerp and Lierre annals lay particular emphasis on this and related occupations. Some references suggest habitual practice,[18] others border on the saintly-heroic: on her death bed, 'her strength dayly diminishing & being never able to change her posture', Teresa de Jesus (Bridget Howard: 1694–1764) 'was continually employd either in praying reading or working bobbin to trim beads with one hand which

---

[16]   On losing no time in association with domestic handicrafts see Orlin, 1999.

[17]   Some textiles were used by the community, either for practical purposes or to decorate the chapel; some products were sold to visitors to raise important revenue: 'lett euery one endeauour to worke yt ye others may be nourished' ('Of Labour and Handy Workes', *L3.34*, Chapter 9). Margaret Teresa of the Immaculate Conception (Margaret Mostyn: 1657/9–1745) had learnt 'to Guild & Japan; her first years were spent in making several fine pieces of work for ye odorment of ye church' (*L13.7*, 281). See Walker, 1999 on general production in the convents.

[18]   The convent oblate Mary of St Barbara (née Leymons: 1701–77), for instance, 'when at home on her wheel, when to answer the Bell she immediately took up her knitting not to lose a moment of her time' (*A2*, 320); Mary Gertrude of the Annunciation (Gertrude Aston: 1637–82) who came to Lierre with 'an impeaddiment in her head, wch was by ill surgence in ye cure unfortunatly poysened', 'would neuer goe to ye grat wth out her basket, or spargat worke' (*L13.7*, 141; that is making the nuns' sandals). Eugenia of Jesus sat up many hours at night mending sandals, presumably helped by Teresa Maria of Jesus (Bridget Kempe) who professed at Lierre in 1651; she was also 'very handie att all qurrious workes' (*L13.7*, 31), whereas 'Oh that I were but handsome handid' lamented Catherine of the Blessed Sacrament, the nun for whom Anne of the Ascension prepared the scapular (Chapter 2), renowned for her utter humility and wearing patched clothing. Frugality indeed is marked by the nuns' choice of old and discarded habits, and by their care in preserving material: Mary of St Joseph (Mary Vaughan: died 1709) was 'diligent in those daily needle works wherein the sisters usually pass away their time after Dinner and supers' finding a use for 'what others knew not what to do with, she would always bring to pass some thing or other, and Bitts of old rotten fringes Laces, Silks, Purles which the sisters flung away, she would gather together and trime up Beads and make them and everything serue some way or other for the use of Poore and ordinary peeple' (*L13.7*, 240). Anne Teresa of Jesus (Catherine Nelson: 1642–1700), noted for 'mortifien her passions yt she soone brought ym under sbuiction', 'noe would she kepe bye her moer Thred, Needles, Sheuers, Thimbels, then what iust needful for hir present work' (*L13.7*, 208). Mary Anne of Jesus (Mary Forster), who professed in 1629, 'estemed nothing hard or two rigurous in a religious cours; altho in ye world, she was of a tender complextion'; 'would wth Leaue of her superioure lose her sliepe, and spend meny oweres; when ye reast ware att rest, to pach and mend ye religious stookings, and neuer was heard to repine, or think it much when out of negligence, thay war burned and disgustfull, but she would be ouer joyed, to haue them to doe, and say ye more ye better' (*L13.7*, 34–7).

was the only limb she had the perfect use of' (*A2*, 290). The aged Teresa of Jesus Maria Joseph 'tho blind she was always occupy'd, wou'd trim beads, threads purl combe silke, weave strings ... wholly by guess custome and attention of minde'.[19] This suggests a 'haptic continuum of the self' (Pallasmaa, 2005, 11)[20] found too in Mary Frances of St Anne (Mary Somerset: 1667–1745); though blind, in 'continual darkness' and confined to the infirmary for fear of accident, she remained 'skilful in knowing the pulse' (*L13.7*, 293).[21]

Beyond this, the nuns were engaged in all sorts of other domestic handywork and are described gardening, sweeping, whitewashing, making beds, trimming and carrying candles, cooking.[22] Writing, of course, was part of daily practice for some nuns, particularly Prioresses. Many women compiled spiritual confessions or 'diaries'. Various degrees of literacy are recorded, and tools are sometimes mentioned: Mary of St Joseph (Mary Vaughan: died 1709) 'writ a larger sort of book of priuate devotions ... with an old pen, and made use of the same pen for seven years together' (*L13.7*, 236).[23]

Most particularly, there are many accounts of nursing, the nuns taking care of each other in the convent infirmary about which we have quite vivid detail, of the heat of its fire, of its cold during winter, of smells and sounds; nuns helping

---

[19]   This was the nun who was born prematurely (see p. 31 n. 18). When she eventually was unable to sew even by habit 'she wou'd stich spargets for the lay sisters and do other coarse work' (21). Here touch and memory coalesce rather as the dying Edmund Bedingfield is movingly described with 'his hands always one his beads wch hung a bout his neck, and his mouth went continually as if hee ware saying them' (*L13.7*, 110).

[20]   On the heightening of haptic intensity in people who are blind, see Krueger, 1982, 7.

[21]   On Touch in medicine, see below p. 119. A Lay Sister, Marie Teresa of St Albert (1638–1701), was by illness rendered incapable of any labour 'ore so much as lefting up her armes thefoer could only paer Apells and ... could doe little with her Needle by reason of soer Eyes' (in fact it emerged she was blind in one eye and had not thought to mention this on entry; *L13.7*, 218).

[22]   The Constitutions required the nuns 'to helpe themselfes wth ye labour of their hands' (*L3.34*, Chapter 7). Some references give vivid example of this work: Paula of St Joseph (Elizabeth Poulter: 1613–72) 'was struck with a fit of palsey as she was with a brush in her hand, whiteing the walls near the Reffectory dore, and one of the religious passing that way, seeing her hand shake, asked her what ailed her. She answered 'I am struck, it is my death, but God's will be done', and never spoke one word more ...' (*L13.7*, 400). For an account of Lay Sisters' labour, including bread and butter making, wet and dry cleaning, gardening, laying tables and kitchen work, see Hallett, 2007a, 111–12.

[23]   Before she entered the convent Agnes Maria of St Joseph (Mary Basson: professed 1651) lived as an adult 'in the world' for many years: 'her parents being dead, she toke uppon her the care of her three Brothers, and ye manigment of thers, & her owne affaers, for she was notible in bussnes, and good witt a great memory, and very industtrus & skillful in ye Law, & writt two or three hands admierable well' (*L13.7*, 163). No doubt this skill was well used on convent business. On a devotional book bearing a signature of the same name, see p. 60 n. 86.

each into bed or to turn in the night; fat nuns are lifted with great difficulty by several Sisters;[24] thin nuns are noted for being merely skin and bones, 'more lick to an nottimie' (a corpse; *L13.7*, 153).[25] They describe touching each other in this context, their focus of attention to particular ends. Mary Poole, for instance, who sewed when blind, had previously been convent apothecary and was said to be good at dressing wounds, preparing salves and poultices, having been taught by her brother, a physician. Notwithstanding their awareness of the contagious hazards of touch and the need on occasion to isolate very sick nuns,[26] the papers attest to acts of tenderness and close tactility. On Easter eve 1752 a nun died as the Infirmarian was putting on her nightgown;[27] in March 1789 a nun who was disabled by strokes was seen just before she died by one who had called in to wish her good night 'sitting up very chearfull, helping the Infirmarian rub her leg wch was particularly affected by the palsey'.[28]

There is a particularly moving account of the illness of Mary Anne of Jesus (Mary Forster: 1601–79) who 'to ye very last lay upon a straw bed in ye Dormetary'. In her final agony when the nuns were 'laying her one a palet bead, she recouered her parfect siuncis ... and helped to unclothe her self, one of ye strs goeing to pull of stookins, being afraid to hourt her fore lege, she called to her, for ye loue of god make hast, pull of skine and all good str be not a frayd of hurting me' (*L13.7*, 39).

---

[24]   Weight is another aspect of tactile discernment. When the Mostyn sisters were being exorcised it was noted 'it was 4 or 5 hours befor they could be carryed up unto their chamber, each one seemig to weigh as much as three' (*L3.31*, 52). Conversely, when a heavy statue was brought to the bed-side of an ailing Sister Ursula, the Dominican father who carried it there noted that it was afterwards 'as light as if it had been made of wicker, or basket' (*L13.7*, 200).

[25]   Mary Magdalen of Jesus (Magdalen Leveston: 1619–92).

[26]   'Contagion is an evil qualitie in a bodie, communicated unto an other by touch'; 'the most hazardous of senses' (Lodge, 1603; Healy, 2003, 22). When Teresa de Jesus (Howard), the nun who continued to work her bobbin while ill, was taken ill in 1764 'the fatal distemper shewd itself & proved the small pox & of ye worst sort. As several had never had it, the community was obligd to be separated & she deprived of the assistance of some of those she was accustomed to ... who had attended her during the whole time of her illness ... This was indeed a severe trial to all ...' (*A1*, 292).

[27]   Mary Constantia of the Assumption of the Blessed Virgin Mary (Laura Bulstrode, 1680–1752; *L13.7*, 298), the nun who could mimic activity at the royal court, see p. 12.

[28]   Mary Joseph of St Ann (Anna Maria van den Wyngaert, 1720–89); the author continues 'she talk'd to me as usual but seem'd much fatigued and oppressed, about half an hour after going to bed, just as she was lying down, she call'd our *I am going*, they came in hast to me, I found her alive but death in her face, she calmly expired before our confessor cou'd reach the Infirmary' (*L13.8*, 12). The Constitutions instructed the nuns 'must visit those who are sick and cheer them' (*Constitutions*, III, 226).

All in all, then, we have vivid descriptions of the materials and surfaces that the nuns touched and of their own responses to physical handling, to tenderness or the pain of surgery under 'doctor's hands'.

Differently, they mention kissing the hands of noble patrons, for instance during the enclosure ceremony of a new convent (*A1*, 64), so we might suppose they performed similar gestures of respect to other aristocratic and royal visitors. (The nuns' use the same gestures of veneration in their interactions with holy hierarchies.) Enclosure ceremonies involved a procession outside the cloister and elaborate staging to ritually inscribe the sacred space and its links to rich patrons and supporters. These were multi-sensory occasions. The nuns were carried by coaches to the new enclosure, in mantles and 'great vailes', then processed singing, with wax candles in their hands. Bells rang to call everyone to the convent along with 'such other demonstrations of joy and triumph, the more the better'. There were hymns sung in harmonic parts, and a sermon preached, then the 'great bell' rang, and the nuns showed their gratitude to their noble patrons by kissing their hands.[29]

As John Bulwer explained, hand-kissing is an 'obsequious expression who would adore & give respect by the courtly solemnity of a salutation or valediction ... There is no expression of the *Hand* more frequent in the formalities of civil conversation ...' (1644, 87–8). Convent rules prohibiting human touch therefore on occasion meet more secular mores, and compromise is reached in the interest of good manners, to ritualise a contract with patrons on whom the nuns relied for finance and protection. In fact, all sorts of accommodations were needed for the nuns to adapt their tactility to the convent environment. I turn now to ideas of texture, the nuns' most immediate encounter with the rough and smooth of convent life.

Touching Feeling

In her powerful exploration of emotion and expression, Eve Kosofsky Sedgwick (in her book of that title) discusses texture and affect, 'how physical properties act and are acted upon over time' (2003, 13). In Aristotle's terms (echoed by John Davies in *Nosce Teipsum* quoted above, p. 89), she can judge the 'qualities of a thing',[30] then 'hypothesize whether a thing will be easy or hard, safe or dangerous

---

[29]   These details are included in an obituary of Anne of St Teresa (Anne Leveson) who professed in Antwerp in 1627 and went to establish the new foundation at Dusseldorf in 1643/44, thence to Newburgh. Like clothing ceremonies and other liturgically inflected occasions, this is a performative event, effecting as well as celebrating the events it contains.

[30]   Bulwer wrote: 'To feel with the fingers ends, is their scepticall expression who endeavour to satisfie themselves by information of the Tact, in the qualities of a thing. ... we know our *Hand* to be the judge and discerner of the touch, for although this touching virtue or tactive quality be diffused through the whole body within and without, as being

to grasp'. 'Even more immediately than other perceptual systems, it seems, the sense of touch makes nonsense out of any dualistic understanding of agency and passivity.' Through touch she says, we can most understand natural forces or other people, if only to know they have created textured objects (14).

Sedgwick draws on Walter Benjamin's analysis of nineteenth-century bourgeois texture. His observations are oddly apposite to the conditions of those wealthier early modern nuns who struggled to adjust to the austerities of convent materials and shared property, having been used to households full of luxury objects. The bourgeoisie, says Benjamin, 'prefers velvet and plush covers which preserve the impression of every touch'; the dwelling is 'a kind of case for a person and embeds him [*sic*] in it together with all his appurtenances' (1983, 46). We can infer a different kind of 'embedding' in the casing of the convent, one which advertises the textural dissonance of its occupants: 'to wear Hair-cloths, to take Disciplines, to suffer the incommodity of going bare-foot' (Rodriguez, *Practice*, 1697, First Treatise, 33).[31] Conversely, we can appreciate the small degree of comfort in the case-change of a disabled nun who for years before she joined the convent 'sufferd much with waering Night & Day Ieron Bootes and Bodys', removing them when she was clothed, only keeping her lame leg 'allways swaded' (*L13.7*, 213).[32]

Equally useful is Sedgwick's reference to Renu Bora's essay, 'Outing Texture' which states 'smoothness is both a type of texture and texture's other' (1997, 99; Sedgwick, 2003, 14). We might imagine abrasive reverse otherness when nuns moved from relatively lush surrounds to the harsh functionality of the cloister. They might register their response as that of 'unequal tug' in Descartes' explanation of the mechanics of texture: when muscles' fibres 'are pulled equally and all together they will make the soul perceive that the surface of the body touching the limb where they terminate is *smooth*; and if the fibres are pulled unequally they will make the soul feel the surface to be uneven and *rough*' (*Treatise on Man*, 1664; 1985 ed., I, 103). This causes exquisite sensation: 'however slightly we touch and move the spot in these places where any one of the fibers is attached, we also

---

the foundation of the animal being ... we doe more curiously and exquisitely feele in the *Hand*, then in the other parts, and more exactly where the *Epidermis* or immediate organ of the outer touch is thinnest ...' (1644, 171–2). Sedgwick notes, 'I haven't perceived a texture until I've instantaneously hypothesized whether the object I'm perceiving was sedimented, extruded, laminated, granulated, polished, distressed, felted or fluffed up' (2003, 13).

[31]   The Life of Edmund Bedingfield records that 'wee may well say hee liued ye life of a carmellet – [he] lay one a poore straw bead ... continually wearing of heire cloth, and a haire gerdle full of knots, yt would some times eat in to his flesh, att other times a chaine, & dissiplines of Iorne, wch hee did frequently uise'. On his death bed the nuns discovered 'about his medle, a courd full of knots teyed so strayt yt thay ware forst to cut it' (*L13.7*, 109–10).

[32]   This was a niece of Edmund Bedingfield: Anne of the Angels (Anne Bedingfield: 1650–1700) who suffered from a range of childhood diseases including rickets. She was a cousin of the Eyre sisters (Chapter 2). We are told that her lame leg was 'bent like a Bow so that one would think it would break & yt the bone would come throw ye skine' (*L13.7*, 213).

move at the same instant the place in the brain from which it comes; just as pulling one of the ends of a very taut cord makes the other end move at the same instant' (*Optics*, Fourth Discourse, 1637; 2001 ed., 89).[33]

Texture thus links mind and body. To feel, for Sedgwick, is to register 'a particular intimacy that seems to subsist between textures and emotions'; 'Attending to psychology and materiality at the level of affect and texture is also to enter a conceptual realm that is not shaped by lack nor by commonsensical dualities of subject versus object or of means versus ends' (2003, 17; 21). Dualities indeed are complicated by the 'multimodal' quality of texture perception, involving several different sensory channels: 'In addition to cutaneous and thermal input, kinaesthetic, auditory, and visual cues may be used when texture is perceived by touching a surface' (Lederman, 1982, 131); some surfaces are smoother to cool skin; some elicit 'touch-produced sounds' (134).

We might wonder which of her senses was most assaulted when Margaret Mostyn altered all over when she touched wool (p. 2), and which traces were stored in her sensitive memory; whether perception was caused by her hand's movement, the sound of rasping; by grasping or by static touch; whether, as I have already suggested, her response is partly bourgeois, a classed reaction to inhospitable textures; whether she had been over-sensitised as a child through ordeal-by-holly (pp. 52–3); whether after clothing her alteration relied on sequential encounters with 'texture's other' which was not the smoothness of silk.

The successors of the Lierre Carmelites (afterwards at Darlington in England) have portraits of the Mostyn sisters before they entered the convent. Both are reproduced by Anne Hardman in her 1937 study of Margaret of Jesus. They show the two women in fine clothing, their long loose hair adorned with braids and in Sister Ursula's case with a diadem; she has pearls around her neck, and an arrow pointing to her heart *qua* Teresa de Jesus' transverberation. The texture of their garments is evident even in photographic copy of the original. So too is that of the Carmelite habit worn by Margaret in the frontispiece portrait, her hand holding a book in emblematic gesture (see p. 123). She is wearing the statutory clothing set down by Teresa's Rule:

> The habitt must be of course stament of a darke brownish couler wthout dye, called in Spanish xerga [serge] or sayall ... that ye sleeues be straite and no langer at ye one end then at ye other. That ye habitt be round wth out pleats, noe longer before, then behinde and downe to ye feet;

---

[33] He continues: 'For, knowing that these fibers are so enclosed in the tubes which the spirits always keep slightly inflated and open, it is easy to understand that, even if they were much thinner than those spun by silkworms, and weaker than those of spiders, they might still be extended from the head to the most distant parts without any risk of their breaking, nor would any of the various positions of the limbs impede their movements' (*Optics*, 1637; 1965 ed., Fourth Discourse, 89).

> The scapular shall be ye same, four fingers shorter then ye habitt; the mantle
> of ye quire as long as ye scapular and yt as litle stuffe be spent as may be ... The
> tuckes or head cloaths shall be hempe or corse linnen, not playted [pleated], and
> ye scapular a boue it. The tunicks shall be stamett[34] ... The shoes of breaded
> hempe and cordes, called alspargates and for decency ye stockings shall be of
> some course linen ... (*L3.34*, Chapter 8; Hallett 2007a, 248–9)[35]

The nuns' clothing ceremonies symbolically marked their transition into egalitarian religious life. They were a prelude to their eventual profession a few years later, replicating in many ways the rituals of secular marriage.[36] The convent annals suggest just how sensuously stimulating such occasions were. Some women entered to the sound of kettledrums, walking on rich carpets on which they then lay prostrate. Rich patrons often provided fine food, as in the case of Margaret Mostyn who was clothed at Antwerp with great ceremony in 1645, as recorded in the Lierre annals: 'my lord Bishop was pleased to examine and cloth her wth his owne hands, tho a thing not uissall wth him; ye ould countis of Arandall[37] liueing then att Anwarp, and ye Lady Chatrine Houord, dressed and adorned ye Brydes, wth her rich & pressious Jewelles, of wch her honner had great plenty, and allso out of her great bounty, gaue all things to ye conuent for ye marige feast, and was ye parsone yt lead her in to ye monastary, and assisted ye priourse to put on ye habit ...' (*L13.7*, 47).

Clothing of course shapes as well as advertises those who inhabit it; re-clothing reshapes.[38] The abrupt transition into uniform requires (potentially at least) some dramatic re-visioning of the self whose skin is touched by unfamiliar cloth throughout the body, its textures varying according to angular frictions or skin quality. Some nuns used clothing to mortify their bodies, choosing patched or ill-fitting habits, supplementing this with sharp cords that cut into their skin, or haircloths that irritated them. Margaret of Jesus, for example, committed herself

---

[34]   'Stammel' is a kind of woollen cloth, often of a reddish-brown colour.

[35]   We might imagine the texture felt not only by the hands but by bare soles on stone, on wood, via the hemp of sandals. 'Gravity is measured by the bottom of the foot; we trace the density and texture of the ground through our soles' (Pallasmaa, 2005, 58).

[36]   Of Anne Somerset's clothing, the annals recorded that her father 'most generously declared that he would give her no less, who had espoused the King of Heaven, then he did to his other children who married according to the ... world, which he effectually did' (*A1*, 395). See pp. 14–15 for Margaret Cavendish's role in one such ceremony. On typical ritual involved, see Kuhns, 2003, 22–5.

[37]   That is: Althea Talbot Howard.

[38]   On the role of (secular) clothes in imaginative and idealized visualisations of the body, see Hollander, 1975; on clothing and accoutrements in early modern cultural identity, see Fisher, 2006, 11–17; on the necessity of writing histories of clothed bodies, see Jenner, 1999, who lamented 'It is astonishing and disturbing how far the history of the body has focussed upon the *naked* body' (151).

on three days of the week 'to wher a chan [chain] ye spaces of 2 hours each time'. In 1652, the year after her exorcism, she asked Edmund Bedingfield (in line with normal procedure for additional mortification), for permission 'to wear a bout my middell 3 lettle courds', and to undertake other painful acts such as flagellation with spikes (*L3.35*, loose papers).

Like Anne of the Angels (Anne Somerset: 1631–51) who had entered the Antwerp Carmel the year before the Mostyn sisters 'with great splendor & ceremony, cloathed in black velvet almost covered with pearl' (*A1*, 395), we might imagine the textural shift of re-clothing and the austerity of convent conditions to have been something of a sensory shock. At night nuns slept in beds that the Constitutions stipulated 'shall be without mattresses and only canuesse filled wth strawe'.[39] Some nuns refer to woollen sheets.

Discalced Carmelites were required to wear serge underclothing as well as habits, although apparently novices only took this once they had adapted to the roughness of the outer garments. It was seen in retrospect as a sign of her incipient blessedness that Mary Margaret of the Angels (Margaret Wake: 1617–78) pleaded straightaway to wear hers, it being delayed because of her 'tender complexion'. To test her obedience her Prioress, Anne of the Ascension, instructed her to put the under-tunic over her habit and to stand at the Refectory door in full view of the community (Hardman, 1939, 133).[40]

An Antwerp portrait of Mary Margaret shows her on the day of clothing ceremony, wearing a dress of elaborate frills and bows, with a necklace round her bare neck (Hardman, 1937, facing p. 54).[41] We can gauge the enduring allure of fine material when we read that some 36 years after her death this nun's body was found to be intact (a moment we will return to later in this chapter) and was 'dressed up' by the nuns 'in a habit of silk, which a devout lady was inspired to give'. Soon after the discovery of this body (found 'perfect from head to foot' still covered in 'thin tiffany or gauze'), in token of her respect for the nun, the wife of the regional governor 'took the ring off her own finger and desired ye director of ye monastery to put it on ye finger of ye holy body, where it yet remains: it has a

---

[39]   Mary Anne of Jesus 'to ye very last she lay upon a straw bed, in ye Dormetary, tho amungst her meny mâladys, she was subigect to a continiall sweting and faintnes' (*L13.7*, 37).

[40]   Mary Margaret of the Angels exemplified the virtues of the ideal nun. She was said to have kept such strict guard over her senses that in 16 years 'she could never accuse herself above twice of having cast up her eyes in the refectory'. In one of her rare notes on spiritual life, she referred to 'a book called *The interior and exterior will*' and echoes Rodriguez's *Short and Sure Way to Heaven* in her analogy about free will 'as with the vessel of clay in the hands of the potter' (Hardman, 1939, 134–9): 'Conformity with the will of God', wrote Rodriguez, 'whereby a man is wholly submitted and resigned into the hands of God, as a peece of clay into the Potters hands' (1630, 21).

[41]   This portrait is now at St Helens Carmelite convent in Merseyside, England. Margaret Wake was born to an expatriate merchant family in Antwerp: on her father's business see Arblaster, 2004, 99.

ruby in ye middle, set round with daimands' (*A3*; Hallett, 2007a, 165, 167). Again, we will return to this gesture. For now we should simply note that it suggests the vestigial values the nuns retained even after their disciplinary practices had mortified attachment to material and bodily comfort, much less ornament of any kind.[42] After all, it is only by contrast that the extent of their subjection could be felt; a continual reminder via memory of tactile alternatives is a sure means of meditating on humility's (as well as texture's) other.

Attitudes shown towards dead bodies, and tactile experience of them, are particularly revealing about attitudes to living ones. Let us turn, then, to the representation of this and other intact bodies to consider the messages they give about Carmelite spiritual somatics.

The Case of the Severed Hand; Proximate and Remote Touch

Teresa de Jesus died in 1582. Nine months after her death the nuns at Alba de Torres, the Spanish convent at which she had died, opened her coffin, stirred in their desire to do so by the sweet smells that emanated from her tomb even though it was immured within a thick heap of stones and mortar – all this according to the account appended to her *Life* by Franciso de Ribera (1537–91), a Jesuit teaching in nearby Salamanca. He viewed Teresa's body and wrote one of her earliest eye-witness biographies. His book was completed in 1590 and had a wide circulation; a copy of it was owned by the Lierre Carmel and most likely by the Antwerp too. It summarises the early tradition of miracles associated with Teresa and embedded a representational system that runs through later Lives of the Saint and those of her Carmelite successors.[43]

Ribera has all the skill of a novelist. He moves back and forth through events to create dramatic tension, all of it leading to the place where it effectively began: the recognition of blessedness predicated on the discovery that Teresa's body was intact, with all the assumptions of miracle that this suggested (Ribera is at pains not to pre-empt due process). Having described her burial, what happened before and after death, Ribera writes 'Leave we now our *Teresa* at rest in her Grave a little' turning to enquire about the wonders that had occurred before, of which the preserved body is in effect the sum. His chapter concludes with the assertion that this is all 'unquestioned truth', 'for the Body is yet to be seen with eyes and

---

[42]   The votive to commemorate the Mostyns' successful exorcism was to be of 'plate upon black velvet', according to the instructions from Margaret of Jesus, conveyed to her by the Virgin herself: 'black silk velvet, panné in French' (*L3.31*, 130).

[43]   For a comprehensive account of the death and posthumous treatment of Teresa in various sources including Ribera's *Life*, see Eire, 1995, 401–501.

touched with hands' (1669, 272).[44] Ribera then takes us sensorially to witness the recovery of the saintly corpse.

Despite the fact that moisture had damaged the coffin; that it was covered in stones and a quantity of lime; that the clothes were rotten and damp, the body was covered in earth which had come through the putrefied and mossy coffin – despite all this, the body 'yet was it self as perfect, and entire, as if it had been but lately buried' (273). Ribera was given some of the surrounding earth by friends; it continued to 'exhale' strange and mysterious sweetness. He and we witness events simultaneously, in the enduring present.

Ribera's account and others like it were drawn on during Teresa's canonisation process. Naturally enough the iconography of this intact body was central to Teresian tradition and symbolically central to much early modern Carmelite representation. Within this, her hand had particular significance.

'Hands have histories' (Pallasmaa, 2005, 56). Before it was the hand of a would-be saint it was of course the hand of a nun, and before that (and later simultaneously) the hand of a woman, young then mature. We can assume she was occupied in activity much like her successors, described above. Teresa mentions her hands very many times in her writing; they are emblematically central to her narratives. As in the case of later Carmelites, we can chart her gradual detachments from matters of the body by tracing references in her writing (which is of course designed to document that very course). She recalls her early life, mentioning in the same breath as 'that little fault' of loving books of *Caualleria* that 'I beganne also to make my selfe fine; and to desire, to grow acceptable, in seeming handsome; and I tooke much care of my hands, and of my haire, and to get choice perfumes ...' (*Flaming Hart*, 1642, 8). Her gradual detachment is marked by a rhetoric of de-feminity:[45] 'In fine, I am a woeman, and no good woeman' (220). Her contemplative progress is marked by her gradual distancing from gendered accoutrements, even as she emphatically presents her claims for female spiritual weakness.

It is also marked by her increasingly rapturous experience of union or near-union. In Chapter 6 of her *Vida* she describes four days of 'Agonie, or Trance':

> Me thought, I was totally disioynted; and my head in extreame disorder. I was also, as it were, all rowled vp, and contracted, as if I had been a Bottome of a Packthridd; for in this, did the torments of those days fixe themselues, with my being able, once to stir, either hand, or foot; arme, or head; (vnlesse they moued me) anie more, then as if I had been dead. Only, I thinke, I was able to wagg one single finger of my right hand. (48)

---

[44]   The juxtaposition of touching and intactness that runs through this narrative has a linguistic as well as conceptual neatness. Carla Mazzio (2003, 169) observes that the word 'intact' comes from *in* (not) and *tactus* (touched).

[45]   See p. 6 n. 12 on Teresa's 'rhetoric of femininity' (Weber, 1990).

Teresa's ecstasy (like that of other mystics) is often marked by sensory failure and paralysis: 'as that the Creature is now not able, so much, as to moure her hands, but with much paine. The eyes are also closed, though without anie purpose to shut them ...' (224–5); 'sometimes I am, in effect, without anie pulse at all, as my Sisters tell me ... And the bones of my verie armes, to which the ioynts are fastned, grow then to be euen opened; and my hands are so starke, and stiffe, that I cannot possibly, sometimes, bring them togeather' (260); 'the Bodie remains apart, as if it were vtterly dead ... so it remains, whether it be sitting, or no; or whether it haue the hands, either open, or closed' (264).[46]

When her visions increased, it was suspected at times that the devil was appearing to her disguised as Christ, and her confessor instructed her to cross herself and also make a 'signe of scorne', as Tobie Matthew translates it (411, 412); 'dar higas' in the Spanish original signifies holding up a closed fist with the thumb showing between the first and second finger (Peers, 1944 ed., I, 189).[47] Perhaps understandably, Teresa describes herself as 'afflicted' by this suggestion, instead taking into her hands the cross at the end of her rosary. On one occasion, she recounts, Christ took this same cross into his own hands and returned it in the form of 'foure great Stones' with the five wounds in them; thereafter 'I no longer saw the wood, whereof the Crosse was made, but only these pretious Stones' (*Flaming Hart*, 413). As so often in these accounts, like is replaced with almost-like. Teresa's preoccupation with her own hands is turned to meditation on Christ's: 'being one day in Prayer, it pleased our Blessed Lord, to shew me his Hands, and nothing but his Hands; and they had such an excesse and heigth of beautie in them, as I am not able, by anie meanes, to expresse' (387). A few days later she sees his face, and wonders why he reveals himself 'little by little', realising eventually that he conducts her 'according to my naturall weaknes', 'for the beholding of a Face, and Hands, which were so beautiful' (387). These she insists are visions of the mind's eye not of the body, on which the editor (Matthew himself or the printer) comments in the margin: '*Imaginary Visions represented to & by the senses are of the lowest ranke & most subiect to danger*' (389).

There is repeated mention in the *Vida* of cross-sensory marvel. Once (Chapter 39) when Teresa was asking Christ to give sight to an almost-blind man, he appeared to her as he often had and showed her the wound in his left hand, with the right hand drawing out the nail embedded there: 'I saw well, how great paine

---

[46]   For similar descriptions of Margaret of Jesus and Mary Xaveria in paralysed rapture or agony, see pp. 35, 81.

[47]   Bulwer describes 'The putting forth of the middle-finger, the rest drawn into a fist on each side, which is called by the Greeks, vulgarly *Higa* ... a naturall expression of scorne and contempt' (1644, 173). He also mentions those who vent their spleen by locking 'the Thumbe between the next two fingers', noting that 'moderne Spaniards' know this gesture (183). According to Isidore of Seville, the middle finger is called '*impudicus* or shameful precisely because it was used in obscene gestures' (Boyle, 1998, 23).

it did import; and it afflicted me much' (611). A few days later the man's sight was restored.

The hands of Teresa are literally (well, literarily) central to her self-writing, and figuratively central to her posthumous iconography. Scholars have long noted that Teresa's earliest portraits showed her 'not only with the palm branch of her personal virtues but also with the golden pen of her rhetoric' (Weber, 1990, 5).[48] More than this, posthumous narratives stress and indeed transfer the materiality of her hands, translating between text and form and linking the two in significant ways.

Ribera's narrative laid the foundations of this association. In his account Teresa's hands (one in particular) and the arm that linked it to the body were central to events that unfolded and which extended after the story itself ceased, in their extra-narrative influence.

The body of Teresa, like so many of her Carmelite daughters into and beyond the seventeenth century, is described as having a textured beauty in death. The face is 'without any wrinkles at all', her flesh 'you would say it was a smooth polished *Alabaster Statue*'; the limbs 'when touched, were as limber, and flexible, as a Childs are, both for smoothness and softness' (1669, 268–9): texture's other indeed.

The smell from this body was all-pervasive, representing the traces of touch at several removes: 'And this so strongly, that many days after [her death] a *Sister* smelling this sent in the Kitchin, and inquiring curiously whence it came, found at last a litle *Salt-celler* in a Chest, having then some Salt in it, wherein remained the print of the *B. Mother's* fingers; when it was brought to her, in her sickness, and from thence this smell was perceived to come' (269). The person who buried Teresa likewise found the scent on her hands, even after washing them (a recurring motif). Teresa's companion Anna of St Bartholomew too, who was 'ever and anon devoutly kissing her feet, and hands' (269–70). Miraculous sensation translated between people and orifices. Another nun, 'having lost her smell was exceeding sad, that she could not perceive that fragrancy ... whereupon kissing her feet devoutly and reverently, she immediately recovered her sense, and smelt that which the others did: and the sent remained in her Nose the space of many days after, as likewise in her Hands':

> Another was ill of a great pain in her eyes so that as she went about still she held her hand to them; for the violence of her distemper was such that unless she pressed them with her hand, she could not walk. She had likewise for four years been afflicted with a continual Head-ach. Yet, when she had applied the Fingers of *Teresa* lately dead, to her eyes, and put her hands to her head, without using any other remedy, she felt her self cured of either malady. (270)[49]

---

[48]   See also Thøfner, 2008 on Teresa's visual hagiography.

[49]   For 'cures as drama' generally, see Duffin, 2009, 145–82; she mentions miracles associated with the Carmelite Maria Maddelena de Pazzi and John of the Cross (159). According to Bulwer, applying hands to orifices (mouths as well as eyes) had a particularly powerful effect; pressing hands (a gesture of both lovers and the devout) 'is a naturall

And so it goes on, cataloguing the miracles associated with the dead woman until (the finale Ribera so carefully prepared in his narrative), the intact body was uncovered in 1583.

Teresa's body continued to diffuse scent all over the house, even after it had been washed. It was then wrapped in linen (much attention is given here to the nature and texture of the cloths in which the body is encased, presumably to suggest their relative softness and porosity) and exposed to in the church for all to see. 'Yet before it was coffined up, *Father Provincial* took off the left Hand, which he carried afterward to *Lisbon*, to be kept in a Monastery of *Discalced Nuns*' (274).

Ribera describes the squabbling between different convents as to which should retain parts or the whole of the saintly corpse, Alba where she died or Avila where she made her first monastic foundation. On the day the body was to be removed to Avila, those waiting 'heard three Knocks' and noises from the coffin, and there ensued what Ribera claims ('in my opinion') were two more miracles. The clothes on the corpse were seen to be rotten again, though the body remained incorrupt; 'whereas at her death *Teresa* bled exceedingly,[50] [so much so] that it coloured the new white Woollen Garment, they had put on her, the very same Blood three Years and two Months after smelt notwithstanding fresh and odoriferous: and when a piece of this Garment was put into a Linnen Cloth that also grew by little and little red, and died with the colour of blood. I saw this piece of Cloth ...' (275). The second miracle he claims occurred when a friar next to the open coffin 'drew a Knife, that he had hanging at his Girdle, to cut off her Arm, which he was to leave at *Alva*, and had entred it already in her left Arm, (being that, which was put out of joint, when the Devil threw her down the Stairs of the *Serviceroom*) which had the Hand taken away from it before, he with very great ease, without putting force too it, as if he had been slicing a *Melon*, or new Cheese (as himself affirmed) cut down from the Shoulder-joint as readily, as if he had tried it often before. Thus was the arm severed from the Body' (275–6).[51]

Ribera's descriptions echo some of the detail of anatomical treatises of the period which stress the fleshy muscularity of the hands, arms and shoulders.[52] This suggests how far his work is informed by a need to satisfy both the legal

---

insinuation of love, duty, reverence, supplication, peace and forgiveness of all injuries'; 'this speaking touch of the *Hand*, a piece of covert courtship whereby they seem to strive to imprint upon their mistresses *Hand* a tacit hint of their affection ...' (1644, 117).

[50]   This is generally taken to indicate that she died in rapture. Her biographer Diego de Yepes considered it to be proof of holy consummation (Medwick, 1999, 246).

[51]   In testimony towards canonisation, Mariana de San Angelo compared the action to slicing bread (*Procesos de Beatification* ... I, 55; Eire, 1995, 437). Homely images of this kind appear elsewhere; Teresa's flesh is compared with figs or dried beef.

[52]   See for example Helkiah Crooke's *Mikrokosmographia, A Description of the Body of Man* (1615, 787): 'The first Bender ariseth with a round beginning and large, mixed of a fleshy and Nervous substance, from the internall protuberation of the arme under the heads of the Palme-muscle and those two which bend the Wrist ...' (see Rowe, 1997, 297).

framework of the canonisation process and the associated scrutiny of medical authorities. That Teresa's flesh offers itself so readily to slicing, suggests it invites its own severance.[53] Gory detail adds credence to the account.

Teresa's body was accordingly transported to Avila. The Alba nuns are reported sad 'having now only an Arm, and a piece of bloodied Cloth, whereas they had hitherto possessed the whole Body entire' (276). And so the controversy continued about the rightful residence of Teresa with or without her severed arm. Eventually, going through various changes of cloth, now wrapped in a blanket, the body was again returned to Alba 'with the Arme' where it stayed 'From that time to this present', to the chagrin of the Avila nuns 'and the whole Corporation' of the city (280).

Incorporation is indeed crucial to this narrative and the Carmelite life-writing that followed. Ribera dramatises this and completes his story with astounding detail, once more having raised suspense about the eventual outcome of events. At the very end of his text he presents 'A Description in what state the Body and Arme are at present'. This material is as aesthetically rewarding to the sensory historian as it was we assume to the faithful:

> Those who shall have read this, probably will desire to know much more particularly in what condition the Body at present is ... The *Arme*, from the *Vertebra* of the Shoulder, is perfectly entire, save that it wants the *Hand* which, as I sad before, was carried to *Lisbon*. It is (being that, which by falling down Stairs once was disjointed, and broken; and also by cutting off the Hand, some Vigour and Vital Vertue being gone out of it) less fleshly, than that, which is still joined to the *Body*; yet hath it flesh enough, though it had more formerly; for it is now somewhat dried ... Yet it continues entire still, covered over with its own down, which I have often seen and felt. It is kept by the *Nuns* always wrapt up in a clean Cloth, which by degrees is moistened with a certain unctuousness, or Oile coming from it ... Several Clothes have been died with it; and given to several Persons, as certain sacred Reliques ... Besides no putrefaction can ever totally wast this flesh, as though it were of Brass or steel. For, the least piece of flesh, though but half the thickness of ones Nail, even in the greatest heat of Summer, though worn about ones Neck, or in ones Bosome, or any other place extreme hot, never loseth its smell, if well wrapt up. ... When I first took that *Arme* into my hands, it was one forenoon; and the same Sent stuck to them, that comes from the flesh; which pleased me so, that being to go to Dinner, I would not wash, that they might not in the washing lose that sweetness. But the fear was needless: for even washed they retained the same still; nay, at night after I was in Bed, my Hands kept that smell ... (282)

---

[53]   Rowe discusses anatomical illustrations that show the palm open, fingers spread 'as though freely offering'; 'Their liberal gestures suggest a body inviting its own dissection' (1997, 301).

Ribera bolsters his account by exact references to the body in life (the arm broken by a fall down stairs, for instance; the effects of the veil); to the body he sensed in various ways; to the times of day at which he witnessed its effects. He saw it 'at leisure', he records, on 25 March 1588; 'I am able to describe it exactly':

> It is (then) upright, and extended in length, though a little inclining forward and bending, as the posture of decrepit Persons useth to be; but by it one may easily gather that she was notwithstanding tall of Stature. Withall, so solid and consistent, that by putting one Hand under the Arm-pits, it is able to stand on its Feet, and may be dressed, or undressed, as it living. It is of a Date-colour, as is the *Arme*, I spoke of, yet in some places a little more inclining to white. No part of it is yellower than the Face; for being always covered with a Vale and sullied by gathering much dust, it fared worse, and hardlier than other parts of the Body. Yet it continues entire, and not so much as the tip of the Nose is broken, or impaired, nor one Hair shed off her Head ... The eyes are dried; the humour they had being wasted; yet they are entire and unblemished. The Warts which were on her Face, as we said, are perfect and unaltered, together with the Hairs on them.[54] The Mouth is so close shut that it can by no means be opened. The Body is fleshy, and full of Muscles, especially about the shoulders. Out of that part which the *Arm* is cut off from, there distils a viscous and tenacious Moisture, which stickes to ones hand, if touched, and sends forth the same smell, as of the rest of the Body. The Hand is well-shaped, in the manner of one blessing, but hath not all its Fingers: those that cut them off I do not commend; for that hand, that did such wonderful works, and which God was pleased to have continue entire, I should judge it a crime to mutilate ... (282–3).

The dead hand of Teresa continued to have agency even when severed and kept apart from her body.[55] The adventures of this hand, and the continued effects claimed for it, underline many facets of early modern and saintly identity. Dead

---

[54]   See Adriaen Collaert and Theodor Galle's illustrations of *Vita S. Virginis Teresiae* (Antwerp, 1613) which also include 'the characteristic moles beneath her nose and on her cheek. These lend a certain credence to the image. Through the inclusion of such idiosyncratic facial features, the portrait declares itself to be unadorned and thus somehow closer to the real' (Thøfner, 2008, 66).

[55]   Having been transported to Lisbon, it was eventually 'looted' by republican forces during the Spanish Civil War after which General Franco was said to have kept it at his bedside as a talisman, a nationalised sign of victory. It is now displayed in a hand-shaped reliquary, its fingers pointing upwards, palm out, in the Discalced convent at Ronda. On sacred relics metonymically and prosthetically representing the whole body: see Bynum, 1992; Hills, 2008, who notes 'the suggestive relationship' between enclosed nuns, convent architecture and reliquaries (33). MacKendrick's short essay discusses ways in which 'the divided body of the saint retains its miraculous vitality across its scattered locations (2010, 1); here 'wholeness means not reunification but multiplication' (4).

hands indeed complicate the 'logic of kinetic self-possession'; 'They disrupt the familiar connections between cause and effect that permit us to attribute and interpret actions' (Rowe, 1999, xi). Teresa's hand is different however from those which Katherine Rowe claims 'symbolize the loss, theft or withering of an individual's capacity to act with real political or personal effect' (4). Teresa's after all is not any hand; it is the transubstantiated hand of a saint that continued to display the real effects of its originator (God via Teresa) on the bodies of those with whom it came in contact. It represents a continuous challenge to the 'Main-de-Gloire' of European witchcraft (the severed hands used by witches to effect their charms).[56] It altered those who touched it, causing a reversal of fortunes at the deepest level of cure. For those who kiss it, as we witnessed, sensory and other capacity is restored; agency is here unexpectedly reversed, the dead giving something in return for the sign of lips' fidelity. The hand after all emblematically connects to the heart, the two said to be linked via a nerve or vein that ran down to the third, wedding-ring finger.[57] This may well underlie the gesture of the aristocratic woman who presented the ruby and diamond ring to the Antwerp convent to be worn on the hand of the intact Mary Margaret of the Angels in a form of posthumous nuptial (see above, p. 99).[58]

It is to the body of Mary Margaret that we will now turn to trace its role in continuation of Teresian influence for the Carmelites in Antwerp and beyond.

Dead Hands and their Stringencies[59]

I am interested in the conditions and standards of performance of hands, the role of touch of the living and of the dead in the seventeenth- and early eighteenth-century Carmelite communities. To discuss this, I will focus on an incident that took place in Antwerp in 1716, two years after the death of Mary Xaveria of the Angels Burton whose own reputation for blessedness was upholstered by the events that unfolded.

At this time the nuns wished to enlarge their burial space and, on the strength of funding from a generous donor whose daughter was a nun at the convent[60] they employed builders to work in the crypt. Amongst the many corrupted bodies

---

[56]   I am grateful to Mark Greengrass for making this connection in discussion of this particular hand.

[57]   See Will Fisher's powerful analysis of the hand that gave away the heart of Desdemona in *Othello* (2006, 52); and consider the hand-kissing scene in Webster's *Duchess of Malfi*, on which see Rowe, 1999, 86–110. For the hand as a 'conduit of extraordinary energies' on the Shakespearean stage, see Neill, 1995.

[58]   The iconography of the marital hand-clasp (among other inferences) may be behind Margaret of Jesus' instruction for a commemorative votive (*L13.7*, 71): see p. 84.

[59]   See Sylvia Plath, 'Ariel' in *Ariel*, 1965, line 21.

[60]   Thomas Bond, the father of Teresa Joseph (Mary Charlotte Bond: 1690–1735).

uncovered, they found one intact, that of Mary Margaret who had died in 1678. 'The community was much surprised to find ye body perfectly entire, fleshly and firm.' The account of this discovery is contained in two main documents from the Antwerp Carmel: in an appendix to the Life of Mary Xaveria (some other aspects of which have already been discussed) and in a book-length Life of Margaret Wake written by Percy Plowden (1672–1745) who was spiritual director of the nuns for several years.[61]

There had been many signs of impending miraculous-ness surrounding Mary Margaret's body. Testimony relating to them is built into Plowden's narrative. One includes a dramatic near-miss linked to the life of Mary Xaveria. It relates to Winefrid of St Teresa (see pp. 44, 139), a Lay Sister of longevity who, as Plowden says, 'remained always at Antwerp where she still lives, ready to attest the truth of all I have written'. Winefrid's witness statement is included in the catalogue of events that precede and follow the discovery of the intact body:

> ... Sister Winefrid of St Teresa Linghen being yet a young religious and going upon some occasion with a light into the dead cellar, knelt down before ye place where her dear Superiour [Margaret Wake] had been lately buried ... about 5 or 6 weeks after ye Rd Mors death, to ye best of Sister Winefrid's memory as she has often assured me, whilst she was praying & looking fixly upon ye place, she saw a little streake of blood upon ye wall, just in that where the Rd Mor lay ... She clearly perceived it was fresh blood, and saw it sensibly runing down, thô not very fast: she wiped it off with her finger, and still found by the staining of her finger, and ye wall, that it was truly blood ... Fearing perhaps she should be chid or laughed at in ye community ... she never made ye least mention of it, or even thought of it more till many years after when yt Superiour [Mary Xaveria] [investigated] to whom God was pleased to reveal that there was an incorrupt body in the cellar ... Sister Winefrid interposed and said 'No dear Mother, do not open that grave for I am sure ye body ... cannot be ye uncorrupted body you seek ... I saw fresh blood coming out of her grave ...' (*A4*; Hallett, 2007a, 169)

The apparatus of doubt is superseded by the assurances of faith that echo detail of Teresa's rapturous death-bed haemorrhage. She too was said to have continued to bleed after death (Yepes, 1946, 436; Eire, 1995, 436). Winefrid's finger, stained by blood, authenticates what the reasoning eye doubts. She is sensitive to scepticism and presents herself as rationally faithful in the knowledge that others will chastise or laugh at her. Several narratives, including Hunter's Life of Mary Xaveria, in this way adumbrate a dubious reader who will be drawn to witness extra-sensory happenings that defy their own prejudice. Here cultures of curiosity meet rhetorics of reluctance. In this story touch plays a particular part in validating claims that would otherwise seem doubtful.

---

[61]   Margaret Wake also receives a brief mention in the Antwerp annals which refer to the longer Life being prepared.

According to Hunter's version of events, being eager to touch the body, one of the nuns (perhaps Winefrid herself who engaged in such searches at other times)[62] broke through the covering over Mary Margaret's body. On discovering it was intact, 'not knowing how far this incorruption of her body might be attributed to natural causes' the nuns called on the expertise of physicians, Dr Trohy an Irish medic who was uncle to one of the Antwerp nuns, and 'Myn-heer Vrylings one of ye best doctors of ye town' who came with him. 'They both examined ye body, and were strangely surprised to find it so sound flexible & c'. Within an hour the Bishop of Antwerp arrived with his secretary, three doctors and a surgeon: 'he order'd ye surgeon to make an incision in ye pit of ye stomach, through wch they discouer'd ye diaphragma perfectly sound. The Prelate put his hand into ye wound … and perceived a balsamick smell proceeding from ye body wch his fingers retained two or three days tho' he washed them several times' (*A3*; Hallett, 2007a, 166).[63] The Bishop also put his hand into the other coffins found in the damp cellar, discovering that those most recently buried were 'all in corruption', others entirely consumed. The intact body and its casing surrounds are thus penetrable by the proof-seeking hand.

Pathological examination naturally necessitated handling the corpse, and was by nature multi-sensory. Canonisation processes (which this case evidently anticipates) are commonly described in many Catholic texts, and there is a high degree of correlation between this and other cases. In Carmelite documents such details are arranged particularly to draw on the memory of Teresa de Jesus, to re-impress her in corporate consciousness and make links that stress a line of saintliness within the female Order. The new dead nun is seen to be a kind of figurative reincarnation of the woman at the centre of the main mythologising urge.

It was clearly in the nuns' interests to promote the finding of such a body, extending the reputation of their convent and of the Order more generally. Several new vocations, with resulting dowries and donations, were said to have resulted from the discovery. Indeed the 'publishing' of the news 'drew vast numbers of people about ye monastery who, once or twice at ye opening of ye gate upon some necessary occasions, surprised ye religious and rushed in, in great numbers, insomuch that they were several times obliged to call soldiers from ye cittadell to guard ye inclosure'. Soon,

> the concurse of ye people who came even from ye neighbouring towns was so
> great yt the nuns could not for some days upon any account open their gate.

---

[62]   A document from the Lierre Carmel suggested it was a Lay Sister who made the discovery and 'in a transport of joy eagerly took of[f] the linen that had been put on her face' (*L4.41*). See Hallett 2007a, 165; 64, 70, 163–9, for Winefrid's role in this and other discoveries.

[63]   Although the text asserts that Mary Margaret's body was not embalmed, balsam (commonly used medicinally for its healing properties) is also used to preserve corpses. In other Carmelite accounts, bodies remain intact after they have been covered with lime.

They cry'd out in ye streets yt God had not given ye Saint for ye monastery alone, but for them all ... When they saw they could not find access they sent in such numbers of beades, meddals, pictures & c. to be touched yt it was sufficient imployment for one or two of the religious for some dayes to comply with their request in touching ye body and bringing them back. (167)

Again the effects of touch are felt at some considerable distance: 'A boy in England was instantly cured of sore eyes by applying some of ye linnen that had touched the body.'[64] Just as Ribera placed his narrative in the continuous present, with Teresa's body 'even now' intact for us to see, so Plowden and Hunter invoke readerly authetication: 'ye Reader may easily satisfy his own curiosity or devotion by becomeing an eye wittness of it when he pleases'.

The intertextuality and intactness of this tradition is crucial to Carmelite historicising. The writer of the Antwerp annals noted of documents surrounding Mary Margaret's life: 'We must still lament our misfortune that the particular relations which has been left writ of many of our religious are lost and taken away by those that went to severall foundations etc which deprives us of many more great examples of vertu and sanctity of this Venble Mother ...' (*A1*, 298-9).[65] Of her body 'Nothing is missing, not even a nail on the hands or feet, and by supporting it with one arm the body can stand upright' (Hardman, 1939, 156). Somatic and textual integrity is crucial here. The nuns resist hermeneutic disintegration which erodes their authority, most particularly in the face of challenges from the male members of their Order. As one nun put it, describing Anne of the Ascension's refusal to concede to the friars on matters of constitutional importance, she 'ded refues to accepe any one pointe hose lettel soeauer it wear knowing well that if thay coulde get but one finger thay would encleud thae wholl body' (*L1.5.H*, f1r).

---

[64]   There follow numerous examples of cures related to touching the body, for example: Joanna Catherina Truyts, on 18 February 1717, with a broken leg, found herself afterwards able to walk without crutches; Charles le Brun recovered from a fever when dust taken from the coffin was mixed with wine and drunk; Charles Quise, a soldier at Antwerp castle, recovered from malignant ulcers on his legs when touched by linen that had touched the body; Elizabeth Vandegraef, a beguine of Antwerp, who had suffered with crippling rheumatism for many years that visits to Aix-la-Chapelle and other places could not cure, touched the body and 'now could carry a pitcher of water with yt very hand with wch before she could not so much as stick a pin or hold a glass of bear' (*A4*; Hallett, 2007a, 169).

[65]   Mary Margaret, following closely the maxims and example of St Teresa, was said by religious witnesses to have been 'a living book in which [the nuns] could read all the Constitutions, Rules and practices of the Order, though the material books in which these things are contained were all burnt and destroyed' (Hardman, 1939, 135) and see above, p. 71.

Textual Touch and Tradition

Carmelite historicising accordingly places particular emphasis on tactile textuality. Authenticity is inscribed by and on the hands of the faithful. Carmelite documents stress their own particular precision of transmission in a narrative line that replicates physical patterns of the female religious. The Antwerp (and from it the Lierre) tradition owed its inception to Anne of St Bartholomew in whose arms Teresa de Jesus was said (repeatedly) to have died. Anne passed the baton of saintly authority on to Anne of the Ascension whose own Life in the Antwerp annals incorporates documents delineating Teresa's licence to her nuns, refuting the friars' allegedly false claims and fraudulent documentation. Since their early modern history was so shaped by this struggle, it was important for the Carmelite nuns to establish an overarching narrative that secured their position and that of their successors. They did so in relation to textual touching of a literal and interlinking kind.

The Lyf of the Mother Teresa of Iesus published in Antwerp in 1611 is indicative of the general pattern.[66] In his dedicatory epistle to the original text, Luis de Lyon records how he pored over the copies of Teresa de Jesus' works:

> for I haue not only laboured in seeing & examining them ... but also in conferring them with the originall, which I had in my hands many days, and in reducing them to their proper purity, with which the holy mother left them written with her own hand, without changing them eyther in words or matter: From which the coppyes, which were caryed about, varied not a little, eyther by the negligence of the writers, or else by udacity & error. For it was an exceeding great presumption to make any mutation in those things, which were written by her, in whose breast God liued, and moued her to write them ... (1611, 7)

There is much emphasis here on writing in Teresa's (and others') 'own hand'. The purity of the textual tradition, like maintenance of Teresa's reform of the 'primitive' Order, is crucial to ideas of heritage at the heart of Carmelite writing. Anne of the Ascension is accordingly praised: 'to em[p]rent her pius documens in our harts she wold be plesed to giue some sentence of her Rce hand writing that all our thought words and deds should be to the greatter onar and glory of Goid' (*L1.5.D*, loose paper).[67]

This spirit runs right through the Antwerp annals. The initiative to compile them appears to have come after the discovery of the body of Mary Margaret, a few years before the centenary of the convent's foundation. The Prioress at the time was Mary Frances Birkbeck (see p. 61) who recorded her ambition to recover 'the many remarkable things [otherwise] buryed in oblivion' (*A1*, ix). She

---

[66]   Discussed above, see p. 71.

[67]   On the implications of this claim for subsequent editorial interventions, see Hallett, forthcoming.

commissioned the writing of three texts, the annals themselves and the Lives of Mary Xaveria and Mary Margaret of the Angels. Under her instigation the first compiler of the annals, was Mary Joseph of St Teresa (Mary Howard: 1688–1756). She too emphasised 'constancy in the practices of our Holy Mother', 'all which our first Superiour Rd Mother Anne of the Ascension took from the companions of St Teresa under whom she was professed and lived several years with ...' (x).

Mary Joseph's personal testimony is included in her obituary within the annals. She exhorts her sisters to 'remember your tread upon Holy ground', sanctified by Carmelites in 'a paradise upon Earth' (*A2*, 263).[68] The handing-on of a spatialised and somatically-infused authority is central to this storying; nuns are said to have been professed 'at the hands' of Spanish nuns who had lived with Teresa.[69] This and the recurring reference to the uncovering of Mary Margaret's body (which preceded the compilation of many of the lives recorded in the annals), and the search for other intact corpses, are the predominant *leitmotifs* of the Antwerp annals.

Towards the end of the Life of Anne of the Ascension (the first in the annals), Mary Joseph lists 'reasons to shew our Holy Mother made our Constitutions' claiming that the friars 'write several things otherwise than they are, even the life and writings of our Holy Mother as appears for the books wch now are printed doe not accord with the old, and have blotted out some of our Holy Mothers own hand writing. They have printed things in the life of Mother Anne of St Bartholomew wch I have often heard her to relate quite contrary' (*A1*, 75). They 'falsifyed in ye French translation as it appears by ye Spanish original' (76). No wonder, then, that the author of the 1611 *Lyf* and the nuns in their annals were so keen to emphasise their credentials.

Mary Joseph's narrative impetus is one of communal commemoration and integrity: 'It is morally certain that if ye Convent had remain under the govermt of the Fathers, it would not [have] continued in that union as now it doth, all being of one heart and one mind' (74). In Anne of the Ascension's Life, she quotes a letter from Teresa, recording:

> Our first Mother Anne of Ascencion has write upon the back of this letter that we have an Authentick coppy taken out of our Holy Mother St Teresa's own hand writing, this letter we have allso in Sr Toby Mathew who did not only translate all St Teresa's works, but went into Spain on purpose to visit all the Monasteries she had founded, to be the better informed of all the particulars not mentioned by her self ... He composed 3 different books which we have still in his own hand and keep as a great treasure, the more because her works are of late so much

[68]   She echoes this phrase from Teresa's own writing, in a letter she quoted when transcribing the Life of Anne of the Ascension.

[69]   For example, Teresa of Jesus (Frances Ward: 1590–1649), sister of Mary Ward who founded the Bar convent in York, like Anne of the Ascension professed at Mons 'in the hands of the Ven Mo Isabella of St Paul, one of the five Spanish mothers who came to found in France and ye Low Countries and who had lived with [Teresa]' (*A1*, 454).

falsifyed; he printed the life of our Holy Mother at his own charge about the year 1642 and did designe to have printed the rest but was prevented by death. He was on all occasions a most true friend and geat lover and esteemer of this Community ... (79–80)[70]

Tobie Matthew is, then, part of a crucial historicising chain. In 1642 as part of his gifting to the nuns of *The Flaming Hart*, he also presented to them a relic of the heart of Teresa de Jesus pierced by the fiery dart of divine love, her familiar iconography. To this relic he attached a statement (dated Antwerp, 21 September 1642) attesting that it came from the Carmelites at Alba, via a friar, who took the reliquary from around his neck and put it round Matthew's. I have, he wrote, 'perpetually worne [it] next mine owne hart above these thirtie years. And having lately translated that Life which she wrote, with her own holie hand, into English' for the Antwerp women 'I have thought fit to give them my aforesaid, undoubted Relick of the verie hart'; 'All this ... I affirme, and declare to be expressly true; and I will heer signe, and assure it under my hand and seal' (Hardman, 1936, 76–7).

Matthew claims his incentive is 'in the service of my Nation'. For the Antwerp nuns, this evangelising mission continued in their onward transmission of the relic. Some 46 years later, on 23 May 1688 the then Prioress at Antwerp, Mary of the Holy Ghost, sent a letter to the pregnant Mary of Modena, wife of James II, who it was hoped would produce the much longed-for Catholic heir, heralding the return of the state to Catholicism, and consequently of the nuns to their homeland. Included with the letter, which has all the rhetorical paraphernalia of an address from a pious and loyal subject, was a relic of Teresa to protect the queen in childbirth, asking 'The Diuine spirit whose fruites and gifts adornes soe much your Royall persone, I beseech to liue euer and animate the hart and soule of your sacred maiesty whose example and illustrious vertues are sufficient to reduce to the waie of truth & sanctity the whole nation.'[71] She assures the queen that they pray for her, and commends the queen's devotion to Teresa, 'whose Relique a peece of her flesh I presume to present, beseeching your maiesty to weare it in your labour' (BL Add. MS 28225: 276–7).

This is a powerfully somatic (and extremely generous) gesture. It was not peculiar to the Carmelites as such, for the Queen received many such letters from

---

[70]   Matthew made a legacy in his 1647 will, 'that out of the first money' after payment of debts 'all the works of my glorious Mother S Teresa (whereof I translated the most part of ...) may be printed to the glory of Almighty God ...'. He bequeathed other written material to his friend, Walter Montague, 'that such of them may be printed' as his advisors saw fit (Mathew and Calthrop, 1907, 339).

[71]   James Daybell identifies in similar letters a 'distinctly 'feminine' mode of petitioning' (2006, 3). See Walker on letters seeking patronage, and 'imbued with considerable political significance' (2004, 230); and Walker, 2000 on the roles played by English nuns in Restoration politics. See also Morrissey and Wright, 2006 on the 'role of women as givers and receivers of spiritual advice and encouragement'.

her pious subjects abroad seeking to link their Order to the royal succession. This letter however distinctively and textually formalised their affinities, from hand to heart to eye, and onward. Like Anne of the Ascension's scapular, this is another worn text which 'doth bring with it' various effects; like Tobie Matthew's audit trail, the letter practices what it preaches.

The wearing of sacred text or image was not simply emblematic or aspiration-advertising therefore; it also linked to the physical apparatuses of pious alteration.[72] In this philosophy, the skin transmitted not only signs of a reality hidden beneath its layers but also of an ethereally beyond; it was also the conduit of transmission to that ethereality. It is therefore to Carmelite skin that I now wish to turn.

Common and Uncommon Borders

Skin has been said to be the 'milieu' of the other senses, the place where they all meet; 'through the skin, the world and the body touch, defining their common border' (Serres, 1998, 97, in Connor, 2004, 28–9). Yet this border is also uncommon: acutely sensitive to all manner of change, including those caused by stimulus to other senses than touch, the skin is yet imprecisely tangible, even when the object of touch is oneself (itself), 'the touching is never exactly the touched' (Merleau-Ponty, 1964, 307, in Heller-Roazen, 2007, 295).

This wholeness/partness of the skin's centrality has posed a long-standing and perhaps intractable philosophical dilemma. There is no coincidence of self even at the point where the most sensitive membrane of the body is caressed or pinched. The one stroking (even if she strokes herself) watches even as she feels the acute tincture of touch. She observes her smoothness with a sense of herself as other, the one who is smooth. How much more are we apart from those others who stroke us or whom we caress? To touch is to experience hiatus, delay, disjunction in Aristotle's terms. There is an interval between touching and perception: 'It is in the imperceptible space [temporal and physical] between that which touches and that which is touched that one body can be felt, no matter how closely, to be different from another' (Heller-Roazen, 2007, 27). Flesh is thus the medium of touch, the light-equivalent of sight. Things pass through it and over it, and then things are felt to have done so; we sense the tangible 'simultaneously with the medium' (28), then incorporate sensation afterwards.

The Carmelites like those in other contemplative groups ponder on the various meanings of touch, as sensation and as significant. In their descriptions of skin they express continual respect and bewilderment for the exemplary other who is within a skin, both human and blessed, reflecting a distancing via intimacy.

---

[72]   The skinny nun, Mary Magdalen of Jesus ('lick to an nottimie: p. 94) was celebrated for having 'keept a Picture of them [Our Lady and Mary Magdalen, her name-saint] in her bossume on theire days, next her hart' (*L13.7*, 157).

Ecstatic touch (that is, the sense of touch within rapture) has a certain kind of significance, of course, given the primacy of this sense in secular and devotional erotic literatures. There is a special interest here is the detextured othering in which poetically the Son and the Bride come together, first in the Incarnation (of which John of the Cross wrote 'His arms embraced closely / The Bride He brought in / Whom the radiant mother / Laid down in a crib'),[73] then in spiritual union ('With his unhurried hand / He wounded my neck / And all my senses suspended there').[74] In his *Cantico Spiritual* he accounted for the Song of Songs 5:4 in which the hand of the bridegroom is on the latch of his beloved's door: the lover's touch was his love, his hand signifying mercy, the manner in which he penetrated his beloved. Post-coitally, 'Her neck reclined / To rest upon the Loved One's gentle arms' (25:6; 22:139–40; Boyle, 1998, 202).

This kind of description, figuratively linked to contemplative endeavour, was transposed to a literal happening in the Lierre annals account of Lucy of the Holy Ghost (Elizabeth Mostyn: 1654–1707), a niece of Sisters Margaret and Ursula:

> ... she made known to her Mistriss who taught her Latin, how litle Jesus had been pleased to giue her a visit and was so kind as to let her take him into her armes permitting her to embrace him, and he embracing her with a mutual kindness, endeavouring to express how sure she seem'd to be of the reality of his appearance, she said his Little Prity Hands were so soft, so very soft, that she never felt any thing so pleasing and agreable to her Feeling in all her Life. But these fauour she only discouerd att this occasion, if any other she might perhaps haue receiued at any other time she kept closs to her self shut in the Priuate closset of her own heart ... (*L13.7*, 233)

The interior and exterior meet here (Lucy's own, and hers with another) in acutely sensitive ways; 'reality' is underlined by sensory knowledge whereas generally it is said to be directly intuited. Familiar poetic analogy is made real and taken again into the interior, reserved in the closet of her heart, that space of contemplative encasing and withdrawal.[75]

In the Carmelite papers such discussion of the othered skin sits alongside more subjective accounts, most particularly related to pain. Here references are literal as well as allusory.[76] Mary Xaveria Burton described her childhood agonies including blistering and blooding in this way, having endured these procedures for many

---

[73]   'In principio erat Verbum', cited Boyle, 1998, 201.

[74]   John of the Cross,'Niche oscura', cited Boyle, 1998, 201.

[75]   See also below, p. 183, for discussion of the synaesthetic qualities of this experience.

[76]   Anne of the Angels, Edmund Bedingfield's niece (see p. 96 n. 32): 'her limbes waer stife & could not sture one Joynt about her. for sometimes thay remained whole weeks together so lame you might sooner break then bend them. yet would she at the same time saye. tho I can't sture hand nor feet. thay are not nailid to a Cruxefes as my Sauouers was' (*L13.7*, 213).

years until her skin was ravaged: 'now no plasters would take place on my feet or leggs, but put me to a great deal of pain, tore of the skin and burnt up ye flesh without drawing any blisters; they often took them of, renewed them, & rub'd ye places with vinegar, wch put me in mind of something ye martyrs suffer'd. When they could fasten them no where els, they order'd the top of my head to be shaved, and a strong blister to be laid there, to draw out what the chymist had drawn into my head; after some hours, this putt me to intolerable pain; I did not ask to have it taken of, but my Aunt and others, seeing ye torture I was in removed it, I endeavour'd to bear it: with all the patience I could, and to think of ye Crown of Thorns' (*A3*, 39). Such medicinal application (Burton also refers to 'bleeding' and the use of 'witch water' as well as the application to her neck, arms and legs of 'spanish flyes', a preparation of cantharides made from dried bodies of Spanish fly or blister-beetle: *A3*, 35, 42) indicates knowledge about properties of the skin and its sensitivity as a purgative or entry route.[77]

On the one hand, then, suffering is achievable through imitation, on the other it isolates the sufferer. Teresa of Jesus Maria (Elizabeth Worsley: 1601–42), the sister of Anne of the Ascension, was represented as separated from her sisters by pain, beyond even her own expressiveness except via metaphors of martyrdom. She was transcendent; untouchably touched in her agonies:

> ... she would say with great resignation it seems to me as if my breast was pearced with nails and all my flesh and internalls were pulld in peaces, which we found to be so in effect for she was consumed to nothing and her bones was only held toghether by the skin and sinnews ...

> ... it seemd in this nineth hour she went with our Dr Lord into the garden there to begin her approaching agony with a general courage inflamed like a seraphine raysing herself up as lightly as if she would have flown to the combate, her countinance sweet & venerable and her face more beautiful then we had ever seen her before but particularly her eyes which even sparkled with brightness ... wee kneeling round about her ... (*A1*, 175)[78]

---

[77]   The Italian botanist Paolo Boccone noticed that nursing women placed a bunch of 'solanum hortense' next to a baby to induce sleep: 'The cause of this effect must be attributed to the narcotic effluvia, and also because the pores of the babies are susceptible and they are more capable of receiving the effect of these plant effluvia than adults' (Camporesi, 1989, 24). See also Francis de Sales' simile of skin and mushrooms, 'being spongie, and full of wide pores' (*Introduction to a Devout Life*, 1616, 649–51), above p. 61.

[78]   The account continues with a description of the public response to this blessed death in which touch, as ever, plays a central role: 'the next day her body was brought into the quire and placed before the grate where it remaind tell Wednesday afternoon and as her vertue and sanctity was held in great opinion in the town so it caused a great concern to people who flocked to the monastery and it was wonderful to see the great devotion with which each one desired to have some thing that had tuch'd her Body, so that there

We have already noted the interplay between Carmelite textual bodies. It may be a cliché of postmodern theory to claim the body is a book, but this idea took particular form in early modern devotional writing. If faces were there to be read, the nuns were agents who also wrote them in their behaviour and their testimonies. It was important therefore to regulate the flesh as well as the features, to present a textured self: 'that as we cannot Write upon a Skin of Parchment if it be not well and even shav'd, and all Flesh taken off, so if the affections and bad inclinations of the Flesh be not all Rooted out of our Mind ... for our Lord to Write and Imprint upon it, the Characters of his Grace and Wisdom' (Rodriguez, *Practice of Christian & Religious Perfection*, 1697, First Treatise, 2). Religious carry on their flesh advertisements of their demeanour; he criticises those going about their holy business 'who have Sorrow Printed upon their foreheads' (Sixth Treatise, 414).[79]

The state of the skin thus signposts interior geographies; it shows where the face has been as well as is. 'Do not Flout, nor be loud in laughter' might be a line from a manual on devotional decorum were it not for the rest of the sentence: 'lest, by straining your Mouth, Wrinkles appear in your Cheeks and Forehead, you thereby become deformed, or appear much older than you are' (*The Accomplished Ladies Rich Closet ...*, 1687, 199).[80]

'If time writes the skin' as Steven Connor suggests (2004, 90), then those who have time's marks erased are signified as timeless. The dead Teresa de Jesus had all the scars of life on her skin, its moles and yellowness, yet her face was suddenly without wrinkles, her flesh smooth as stone. She is sculptural in her stasis, poised mid-point between where her body is heading (corruption) and where it was (alive). Her Carmelite successors are similarly described.[81]

---

was things without number flung in at the grate and given in at the turn for this purpose, as beades medalls reliquarys & c. ... which lasted so long that when the Body was put into the grave it was necessary to hold up the lid of the coffin that we might touch what was continuelly given ...' (*A1*, 175).

[79] The appearance of stigmata, of course, was the ultimate imprinting of faithful imitation on flesh. Paul of St Ubald wrote of St Francis for whom Christ's wounds 'were not only fixed in his mynd, but also printed in his very flesh to be seene, in his hands, feete, and syde', so he hardly used his outward senses (1654, Part 2, 249). There is no mention of the appearance of such signs in the Carmels under review here.

[80] Lest one disobey this instruction, this text also has advice on how 'To take away Wrinkles, and make the Face look youthfull' with a recipe comprising brandy, bean-flower, rosewater, bryony juice and figs (55). It also has a scheme for breast reduction (63). On 'the arts of beautification' see Jenkins, 2009, 77–8.

[81] It was written of Margaret of St Teresa (Margaret Downs: 1600/03–82) that 'to see ye corpes, could not beliue, she was more then 50 yeares ould, nather could one desarne, one rinckle in her face, of wch she had meny persepttable ones, when she was liueing' (*L.13.7*, 134); of Agnes Maria of St Joseph (Mary Basson: 1614–92) 'she looked so young & smoue wth such a fresh coluer in her cheekes yt you would haue thought her a sleepe & we ware euen afraid of naylen up ye coffen, tho ye corps had laine 24 howers & was as stife as a boord' (*L13.7*, 166).

There is significant correlation in the ways the nuns describe the skin of such corpses. Presumably in fact preserved bodies do resemble each other. Certainly narratives stress similarity, naturally enough recalling the body of Teresa de Jesus herself. That the Antwerp Carmelites actively searched for intact bodies in their dead-cellar suggests just how normalised the possibility was, and how important to their historicising evangelism. The Antwerp annals describe several such excursions. On discovery of a corpse, for authenticity it was important that the individual nun's remains resembled the same woman when alive ('her Countenance so much her own that had she not seen her taken out of her grave, she could have been certain that it was she')[82] and also that it recalled the sensory signatures of saintly precursors: 'the aforesaid hands feet and head they put decently up in a cloath and lock them in a Room, where they soon grew dry, & has an agreable smell like to that of our Venble Mother Mary Margaret, and ye same couler, but rather whiter' (*A1*, 188).

The skin of one dead nun recalls that of another. Teresa de Jesus' body, according to Ribera, was 'of a Date-colour ... in some places a little more inclining to white', still covered in its own down he had often seen and felt (p. 106). Mary Margaret 'appears of a brownish complexion, but full of flesh, which like a liveing body yeilds to any impression made upon it, and rises again of it self wn it is press'd: ye joynts flexible, you find a little moisture when you touch ye flesh' (*A3*, 462). These are textured encounters. We might (rather horribly) apply differentials of touch outlined by Avicenna in his *Book of Definitions* which distinguish the surfaces of solids: Mary Margaret is 'a solid which receives this push with ease' as opposed to 'a sold soft which is ready to come apart' (cited Heller-Roazen, 2007, 291).

Just as the nuns were highly interpretively aware of the various tones of skin and flesh in death, so they were in life. Smallpox (outbreaks of which were common, and from which some nuns survived) left its mark on the skin; measles came and went, as did (we presume) the skin-marks of Mary of the Holy Ghost who so mortified her passions 'once to that degree her [Novice] Mistress found her att night all covered with red spots' (*A1*, 407). Some skin conditions are described in queasy detail: when Anne Teresa of Jesus died, 'she being much spent and worne a way with a violent humour in her head & forhead wch was all of a scrufe & some 2 months befoer her death became an intyer scab & all downe her Temples runing a vast quantety of theitk green and yellow matter. which ye Doctors and surgings sayd was a sort of a Leperos' (*A1*, 209).

If disease and rapture marked the skin, so too did the effects of witchcraft. Margaret of Jesus and Ursula of All Saints were said to have been marked by

---

[82]   Anne of St Bartholomew (*A1*, 187). These later Carmelite bodies add a further dimension to Eire's claims about Teresa's body as an hierophany, 'the fulcrum of paradox': 'Though it continued to remain very much as it once had been, it obviously had become *something* else; though it still occupied a limited physical space, its presence was desired everywhere; though its integrity was its preeminent distinction, its mutilation and dispersal became most desirable' (1995, 431).

the devil himself, who would 'kick & trample uppon them for a long space: some times to make their body black & blew with stripes' (*L3.31*, 41). Margaret also reported the sensation of crawling on her skin.[83] Dr Lazarus, the Antwerp physician, had previously advised that 'an issue' (a counter-irritation technique placed beneath the skin) be inserted into Margaret's left leg. During the exorcism this suddenly caused her extreme pain which lasted 'untill the boule or little bead of wood was taken out'. It must have been in place for at least three years and was 'almost couered ouer with flesh, soe yt she could scarce gett it out, the flesh forcible seeming to cease up of it selfe' (73).[84]

In line with long-standing diagnostic practice, skin was examined for symptoms, probed inside and out for speculative cure. The nuns, as we have noted, took each others' pulses, Galenic understanding of which suggested a range of closely-observed differentials: speed, vigour, smooth- or hardness, the nature of motion, intervals and evenness. Galen noted variation in the qualities of pulse in well-fleshed and thin people.[85] Nuns' encounters with skin surface thus gave them insights into their Sisters' interiors.

With what is seen as a rise in anatomical interest in the early modern period 'came a reawakening of interest in the body's *penetrable* nature' (Sawday, 1995, 87).[86] This interest has been recognised as marking the overturn of Aristotle's idea that skin could not feel: 'The understanding that the outside of the skin is directly rather than mediately involved in the apprehension of the touch ... was an important stage in bringing the skin to life' (Connor, 2004, 15). Carmelite description of agonising incisions and surgery (such as that performed on Mary Xaveria, p. 35) indicate that the nuns had always known this was so.

---

[83]   Demons were said to have caused 'a black spot to appear in [Margaret's] little finger' (*L3.31*, 65). At other times 'ye diuels began to be soe exterieur yt they could not imagen but that they had fleas hopping up & downe' (62). Given Margaret's propensity to bladder stones (once miraculously shifted: see Chapter 4), it is possible that she suffered from the symptoms of urinary or kidney infection which were manifested in this way, often described as feeling like ants crawling on or under the skin.

[84]   Issues were commonly used to relieve the effects of gout (again caused by the build up of uric acid, so Dr Lazarus might have been close in his diagnosis; he also suggested exorcism as a cure), arthritis or joint pain. Physicians cut the skin with a lancet and inserted a small ball, often gold or silver, sometimes a dry pea, in this case made of wood. Occasionally, too, a seton of horsehair or silk would be run through the skin and left there to allow suppuration or hyperaemia (Copeman, 1960, 149). The papers mention that the bead, like a bandage used by Margaret that was discarded in the latrine then retrieved, afterwards was regarded as a relic.

[85]   See Galen's instruction on 'The Pulse for Beginners', 1997 ed. 325–44.

[86]   Sawday includes some examples of sacred anatomy in his study of the Renaissance 'culture of dissection', noting 'The uninhibited familiarity with which the nuns ... opened corpses' (citing Camporesi, 1988, 7; Sawday, 1995, 100). See also Park, 2006, 39–76 on 'Holy Anatomies'; Bynum, 1992, on 'Material Continuity, Personal Survival and the Resurrection of the Body', 239–97.

In such descriptions, the reality and the sanctification of pain are frequently juxtaposed; martyrdom and the everyday coexist in this environment, so penetrated skin is simply known from experience (for instance by partially-sighted nun who ran an awl into her hand requiring surgery: *A2*, 182) and symbolically remote (brought close in affective meditation). For those living in a Christian community, ideas of skin piercing had particular resonance of course, the crucified body being the organising icon of their devotion. In mental prayer they imaged it closely; in visionary experiences it featured strongly.

Their parallel object of veneration, meanwhile, was the immaculate virgin who the nuns' own enclosed bodies conceptually mirrored. Penetration was something one imaginatively watched and vicariously experienced through empathetic meditation, while the impenetrable was a given, integral. This again suggests a system of dislocation between the personally felt and the seen body, the experience of one's own and that of the objects of devotional desire. This serves to distance figures that are only brought into contact during meditative exercises, however intense the emotional affectivity. The devout person therefore moves back and forth, away and towards the skin of the holy figure, literally or imaginatively touching it at moments of pious intensity, and withdrawing to gaze in delight before and afterwards.

For the devout person herself, spiritual pleasures are revealed on the skin, most markedly when the ecstatic body is otherwise immobile or silenced.[87] Although skin flush was explained in various physiological ways by religious and philosophers alike,[88] in Marian representation it was associated with the blessed blush of the incarnation, 'a sign simultaneously of innocence and knowledge' (Clarke, 1996, 119).[89] Hence, although those seeking to control their bodies and spiritual states might hope 'To hinder the motions of choler ... the blood not to rise in the face' (de Sales, 1632, 132), for those rapturously beyond control and the reach of sensory stimuli, blushing was reflex and exemplary.

---

[87]   Anne of the Ascension's 'loue to Allmty God was so exsessiue that she could neuer speack of any thing which conserned him but her face would show the flames that burned in her hart' (*L1.5.C*); Margaret of Jesus was observed writing, 'her face inflamed as her Rce was wont to be in prayer' (*L3.29*, 109); as she was about to receive the Eucharist 'her face began to shine with an unusual beauty, darting out resplendent rays' (*L3.30C*).

[88]   Wright said that those who blushed betrayed their errors: 'they blush, because nature being afraid, left in the face the fault should be discouered, sendeth the purest blood, to be a defence and succour' (1630, 30). Descartes considered joy also caused blushing 'because it opens the valves of the heart and causes the blood to flow more quickly in all the veins'; conversely, when we are sad 'the blood trapped in the face makes it red ... indeed redder than when we are joyful, since the colour of blood is all the more conspicuous when it flows less rapidly, and also because more blood can collect in ht veins of the face when the orifices of the heart are opened less widely' (*Passions of the Soul*, 1649; 1985 ed., I, 368–9). On pallor, see pp. 29–30.

[89]   Clarke notes 'a high concentration of the use of the word "blush" as an important attribute of the Virgin Mary' in many texts of the 1630s (1996, 118).

Sweating similarly shows its affects on the skin's surface, and the nuns were ever-watchful for it in as a sign of medical or miraculous alteration. Again, Galenic medicine sought to detect illness by skin temperature, tracing 'differences in the quality of the heat'; Anders Celsius (1701–44) likewise examined the surface of the skin, feeling for dryness, patches and pulse change, examining colour and texture (Wootton, 2006, 53). Some common treatments induced sweating to assuage the effects of fever.[90] More marvellously, the Maryland-born Mary Rose of the Sacred Heart of Jesus (Mary Boon: 1718–58) continued to sweat after she died, to the consternation of the Lierre nuns. Doctors were unable to find any sign of life so she was prepared for burial when the nuns again saw sweat on her face. Since the 'dead bells' had rung to summon members of the public to her funeral, the nuns proceeded to carry her to the dead-cellar, then disinterred her when they had gone. In the infirmary 'methods was taken to bring her to life. but in vain. att night she was carry'd to the dead cellar again; 3 days after ye mason went to stop up ye oven; when we found her fresh without ye least smell; & her face with ye same drops of sweat on it, which was wiped of[f] several times & still came on again ...' (*L13.7*, 302).

It is clear, then, that skin in various ways was thought to reveal (or refuse to divulge) interior truths, whether medical or miraculous, advertising both itself and the cause of its change. Whether it is the organ of touch or the place where touch is most apparent, it has a certain centrality and palpability in the intimate expressiveness of a close-living community.

In the final stages of this chapter I should now like to turn to other aspects of the impalpable components of tactility, to touch's palimpsest, the visible representation of its near-absence: the gestural hands.

The Speaking Touch of the Hand[91]

'Discovery of Passions in gesture' is such an ample subject it would require a whole book, according to Thomas Wright. I will therefore confine myself to hand gesture

---

[90]   Edmund Bedingfield who was given 'my Lady Kempts powder, and hee sweat very much, and was well affter it so yt ye Doctur, found him wth out ague' (*L13.7*, 118) 'The Receipt of the Lady Kents powder, presented by her Ladyship to the Queen' was included in *A Queens Delight; or, the Art of Preserving, Conseving and Candying* (1671, 80). Clearly the recipe was known before this: Robert Boyle advocated the use of it in *Some Considerations Touching the Usefulnesse of Experimental Naturall Philosophy* (1663).

[91]   This is a quotation from Bulwer, 1644, 116. He describes a lover's 'piece of covert courtship whereby they seem to strive to imprint their mistresses *Hand* a tacit hint of their affection' (see Fisher, 2006, 48 for the implications of this in *Othello*). On the issues facing historians using books of manners [and, we might think, pictures] to elucidate taxonomies of early modern gestural code see Walter, 2009; on the politics of gesture see Braddick, 2009.

in Carmelite contexts although clearly the topic could be widened.[92] Here as in other behaviour the nuns conducted themselves in line with social and devotional etiquettes.[93] Since positions of the body were thought to influence as well as reveal emotions, accounts of gesture were especially careful as well as descriptive; if they appeared in portraits of nuns or were woven into commemorative convent documents, they would be on permanent (if restricted community) view.

Some gestures were said to be suitable for a contemplative environment, appropriately reinforcing or replacing mental behaviour. Augustine Baker, for instance, suggested a pious person should turn away from temptation: 'She may doe well also by *words* or outward *gestures* to signify her renouncing and detestation of them ...' (1657, 385).[94] Rodriguez, rather, laments that those facing temptation 'press their Temples very hard with their Hands, knit their brows, shut their Eyes, and shake their Head, as if they wou'd say hereby, that they will give 'em no entrance' (1697, Fourth Treatise, 367). Although this gesturing is partly acceptable in secular life, the proper remedy in devotional contexts is rather to make a sign of the cross on the forehead and over the heart (221).[95]

The Carmelite papers frequently mention hand gestures of different kinds, and portraits of nuns naturally reflect these. Although I am primarily interested in literary representation, we might note the correlation between visual and textual gestures. For example, a depiction of the Virgin's cure of Ana de Jesus (in the Brussels Carmelite convent) shows her pointing with index fingers to her head and her mouth. Pictures of Teresa de Jesus blessing Ana de San Bartolomé and Ana de Jesus (at convents in Madrid and Brussels respectively) show the nuns each kneeling at the feet of the saint, Ana de San Bartolomé's hands held together in prayer, and Ana de Jesus' folded across her chest in humility (Wilson, 2006, Figures 3, 7, 8). Other portraits show gestures of wonderment, praise, contrition (see below, Chapter 7), all of them consistent with Bulwer's outline of signs. Here holy and human figures use the same modes of expression for easily understood reasons. The hand's 'natural language' according to Bulwer had a purity that eluded Babel's confusion since it was 'made a holy language by the expressions of

---

[92]   'The gestures of the body may be reduced vnto these heads; motions of the eies, pronunciation, managing of the hands and body, manner of going' (Wright, 1630, 131).

[93]   Directions for behaviour outlined in *The Accomplished Ladies Rich Closet* likewise outline advice on hand movements (no pointing with the finger especially in the company of social superiors, for example: 1687, 193).

[94]   Baker suggests that temptation is best resisted by neglect rather than force: 'For by neglecting of them the *impression* that they make in the imagination will be diminished' (1656, 385). This suggests how impressions (good or bad) might become more ingrained in the memory by repeated recall.

[95]   Bulwer, for example, suggests that 'To apply the hand passionately unto the Head is a signe of anguish, sorrow, grief, imaptiencie and lamentation' (1644, 84). *The Cloud of Unknowing*, a fourteenth-century mystical text, copies of which circulated among the English convents, satirised the excessive gestures of ascetics, advocating stillness (Chapter 53).

our Saviour's *Hands*; whose gestures have given a sacred allowance to the naturall significations of ours. And God speakes to us by the signes of his *Hand*' (1644, 7). Sights, we may consider, are not merely gestural in a devotional context; they might synaesthetically cause the sensation that they signify.

Books feature often in such representation, clearly not unique to Carmelite typology and familiarly echoing (*inter alia*) images of the Virgin at the Annunciation, her hand mediating between text and experience.[96] Anne of the Annunciation is depicted in this way in a full-length Antwerp portrait (Hardman, 1936, facing 166); three-quarters turned, in her left hand she holds a closed book, her fingers apparently between its pages, while her right hand rests on a surface, behind which is a crucifix. Texts replicate similar stances. One nun, temporarily absent from the convent, described a vision in which she was 'suddainly transported into the Liberary of Antwerp with her hand upon a Book' (*A1*, 482).[97]

Typically (understandably) literary descriptions represent polite gestures, familiar from secular as from religious life. Indeed, apart from the most specifically liturgical signing, most gestures appear to relate to both arenas. For example, when nuns entered the kitchen, a Lay Sister greeted them 'with a Chair in her Hand in ye most respectfull & affecyionate manner'; if it was cold she 'placed it at ye fire in ye most obligeing terms; she had an education which made her Mrs of civility & good manners' (*L13.7*, 275–6).[98] Again, as we might expect, such *gentilesse* was said to carry over to supernatural areas, in dreams and of visions: 'I saw our Blessed Saviour standing some distance from me reaching out his hand to me, and sayd Follow me ...' recorded Anne of the Ascension (*A1*, 4). Of course, it would be very odd if signs there were in anything other than explicable form; although some nuns are initially perplexed by the implications of their holy revelations, they generally recognise the gestures as human.

Some reporting has poignant features, drawn as it is from convent necrologies. In 1692 when Anne of the Ascension (Anne Cobbes: *c*.1650–92) was dying, one of the nuns remembered she had special veneration for the image of the *Ecce Homo* (Christ with Pilate during the Passion) and ran to fetch it. She 'had scarce braugh it

---

[96]   The Virgin is commonly shown in medieval and Renaissance art kneeling at the Annunciation, her hand on book, textually marking with her fingers as if interrupted reading her own prefigured history. Time at such moments is pictorially present: past and future coalesce in the present figurative reality. It is as if she read ahead about her own destiny then recognised it when it arrived. Despite this particular contextual association with feminine humility and compliance, the inclusion of books in portraits was not generally gender specific. See Filipczak, 2004, 72–7, on hand positions that were equally acceptable for men and women, and for discussion on folded hands as a sign of 'intention of the soul' in Leonardo's Mona Lisa.

[97]   Teresa de Jesus (Catherine Wakeman: 1636–98), one of five sisters to join the Order. See Chapter 7 for discussion of the correlation between visual images and visions.

[98]   This was Joseph Teresa of the Purification (Catherine Quinigham: 1682–1738). She was the niece of Dr Trohy, one of the witnesses to the autopsy of Mary Margaret of the Angels, p. 109.

in to ye rome but she spid it, and smilling clapt her hands wth excesse of joy say'd there is my Beloued Lord' (*L13.7*, 172). This may seem an unguarded gesture (even if we can forgive one at the last stage of her life for indecorum); certainly applause was sometimes regarded as 'vulgar'.[99] That it could also be edifying is suggested by the Life of the Florentine Carmelite Maria Maddalena De Patsi who is described as using 'pious gestures as kindled in the beholders an vnspeakable deuotion; sometymes she would spread her armes abroad, sometimes she would clap her handes togeather' (Puccini, 1619, 53).

Kneeling, of course, was the main posture of prayer and of humility as was being prostrate, both entailing particular positioning of the hands. Neither posture was necessarily fixed, with rituals being subject to change.[100] Kneeling was not necessarily static,[101] the hands being moved according to the meditative moment (the liturgy of course itself systemised gestural repetition). Margaret of Jesus' devotions for 1652 mention that she knelt with her 'armes a cross each other staying in posture' (*L3.35*, loose paper).

'To raise the Hand conioyned or spread out towards heaven is a habit of Devotion', Bulwer explains; 'Thus we acknowledge our offences, aske mercy, beg reliefe, say our vowes, imprecate, complaine, submit, invoke and are supplicant' (1644, 14). So we might read the report of the childhood reaction of Monica of St Laurence (Anne James: 1606–78) whose family estates in Monmouthshire were confiscated during a period of religious persecution. She is said to have called her siblings to where their father was taking horse, 'they all knelt down with her, holding up their little hands, and she beged him in the name of them all that he would do nothing against his Conscience for their sakes' (*A1*, 388). So too might we understand the histrionic account of Agnes Roosendaell (1615–42), an Antwerp woman who later professed as Agnes of St Albert having broken into the convent in defiance of her family. Clearly prone to passionate excess, she was always 'extraordinarily moved and inflamed whensoever she did but come in to the very sight of the House'.

The account of her arrival is suitably dramatic:

> ... having laid laid her upper garments aside [she] crowded herself into the turn, which yet she did with difficulty enough because the place is incommodious and straight, and tho she were but 16 years of age and farr from being of full growth att that time, yet she made a hard shift, and turned herself in as soon as ever she was in the monastery, she felt her whole heart full of joy ... the Porteress being

---

[99]   Bulwer refers to the Roman populace producing 'noise' of this kind (1644, 30).

[100]   Anne of the Ascension mentions that when she saw Christ reaching out his hand, 'I was prostrate *as we used to be* after ye Elevation of ye Mass' (*A1*, 4; my emphasis).

[101]   The aged Mary Magdalen of Jesus is commended for remaining steadfast in position: 'uppon sondays & other feastiall days she was faithfull in hereing all ye Massis uppon her knees upright wth out leaning against any thing for 3th or 4 howers in ye same possture' (*L13.7*, 156). For Margaret of Jesus kneeling on boards, see Chapter 7.

then by accident not verry far and hearing an extraordinary noise and busseling about the turn, went towards it, and seeing a young creature there in secular attire, half uncloathed found the sight very surprising and ran presently to tell Mother prioress of it, who with other religious coming from the Quire hasten'd towards the place, and saw this young creature there upon her knees and begging with her hands held up to heaven that for Almighty Gods sake they would have compassion upon her, and receive her; and the self same diligence she used to everyone of the religious, who by this time was order'd to injoy their severall parts of this strange spectacle. (*A1*, 269–70)[102]

It is difficult to know which came first in the relationship between textual and behavioural script. Either way, description of the gestures suggests a literary embedding of stylised acts. Although such accounts might appear to owe more to hagiographies that accept passionate overflow in a worthy cause, similar hand gestures appear in visual art in the same vein.[103]

The Carmelite papers mention other kinds of familiar gesturing, such as when a secular woman (a fake Countess) sought to entice a nun to leave the community, appearing in the speak-house 'making signs', some of silent indignation (*A1*, 569). The dying Teresa de Jesus Howard, the nun who worked bobbins (p. 92), after a stroke had deprived her of intelligible speech, 'not long before she dyed, she made a sign for a pen & ink, & wrote down something she wanted & which she could not make them understand by speaking (*A2*, 292).[104] At Lierre, the deaf Margaret of St Francis (1594–1678) 'when she grew holy empotent that she could not hear nor scarcs understand us when we spooke to her ... if we pointed up to heuen, she would be ouer ioyed' (*L13.7*, 30).[105]

While much of the gestural activity of the nuns is an undescribed given in their texts, it is referred to at moments of extremity. Making the sign of the cross, for

---

[102]   John Falconer's *The Mirror of Created Perfection* (1632), a copy of which survives in the Lierre Carmelite archives (Darlington Book 4) is dedicated to this nun. The Antwerp annals, written later in around 1731 echo some of the style and detail of the *Mirror*'s dedicatory epistle. (Frances Dolan mentions this book: 2003, 333, note 13).

[103]   For example, in the fresco of Michelangelo Buonarotti (1475–1564) in the Sistine Chapel Eve's gesture of joined hands imitates the servility of the Pope at the altar, according to Boyle, 1998, 108.

[104]   Amazingly, the small slip of paper has survived, tucked in between the pages of the book at this point. It has spidery, barely legible writing on one side, from which can be made out the word 'candle'; on the reverse it reads 'This was wrote by Dr Mother 3 or 4 hours before she dyd.' For me, touching this paper was very emotional. The pleasure of our tactile intimacy was barely reduced when I turned the page to discover that she had died from a virulent form of smallpox.

[105]   The pointing finger, as Bulwer notes, sometimes 'stands for an Adverbe of place' (1644, 165). There appears to be no direct reference in the papers to more systemized sign languages for the deaf depicted in manual alphabets of the period (Sherman, 2000, Catalogue 52–4).

instance, a repeated action throughout the day, is only referred to when the nuns describe anxiety or fear.[106] Nuns who are exemplary in death distil a frozen gesture almost in pageant form, clutching a range of devotional paraphernalia.[107]

Rosary beads, of course, have a special place in Catholic tactile schemes. Paul of St Ubald among others recommends their mnemonic use in maintaining devotional focus: 'to make you mindfull of it: as a few stones of beades to hang where you most visually put your hands, that touching them, you may call to mynd, what you intended' (1654, Part II, 43); 'you may likewise were [wear] a ring on your finger, with some notable marke, to that same purpose; or a string vppon the wrest of your hand ... to keepe you mindfull' (139).

The nuns clearly used such systems in their devotions, as well as drawing on long-standing haptic schemes for prayer, such as using fingers to indicate meditative stages.[108] Margaret of Jesus seems to refer to a relatively simple system when she noted her method 'to keep our thoughts recollected in the time of Mass', resolving each day also 'allwayes to visite the 5 wounds of our Bd Lord praying & offering to euery onne of them to these following things the ane is the Conuersion of soules, to ye right hand, to ye Lefte ye distressed Catholicks of England' (*L3.34*.C).

There are, then, many ways in which the 'speaking touch of the hand' functions in liturgical and extra-liturgical actions within the convents. The Carmelite papers

---

[106]   For example, when Margaret of Jesus was 'violently set upon by an Evell spirit', she reported to Edmund Bedingfield 'I know not what inspired me and assisted me to obey your Reverene in making the signe of the cross, which I did five times together, with much contradiction, for when I saw it remaine, I was possess'd with a deep Apprehension it was really God' (*L13.7*, 193).

[107]   Margaret of St Teresa (Margaret Downs: 1600/03–82), who was unwrinkled in death (see p. 117 n. 81) 'sweetly departed' 'hoalding her crusifex in her right hand, upon her hart, so close and fast, yt wee had some dificulty, to get it out of her hand' (*L13.7*, 68). Mary Magdalen of Jesus was found dead in bed surrounded by medals, badges and pictures, 'her boody in a possture most mouing as if she had layed her selfe for yt porposse her Eyse swetly cast done wth a smielling countance wth her head raysed tourning as if she answaring her spousses call ... her Crucifix in one hand, & a pare of Beads in ye other & a holoued Candell under her pillow' (161).

[108]   Some Carmelite descriptions appear to be in line with material included in *Writing on Hands*, an exhibition on memory and knowledge in the early modern period. This noted 'the centrality of the hand to the acquisition and dissemination of knowledge' and 'the hand as a meeting place of matter, mind and spirit' (Sherman, 2000, 7; 21). It included woodcuts of the hand as a mirror of salvation, each finger representing a different meditative stage: '[T]he thumb, the master digit, signifies God's will; the index, examination; the middle finger, repentance; the ring or medical finger, confession; the smallest or ear finger, satisfaction' (Catalogue 1). It also represented a 50-place system of mystical meditation on Christ's suffering, each hand being divided into sections culminating at the tip of the smallest finger (Catalogue 2).

bear out systems in use elsewhere and also indicate the particular ways the nuns made use of the hands to convey, control or affirm spiritual truths.

Hands, of course, are not the only sensitive surface to come in contact with stimuli. Tongues also convey sensation directly: for 'taste also must be a sort of touch, because it is the sense for what is tangible and nutritious' (Aristotle, *De Anima*, 1941, 601). Touch and Taste indeed are frequently connected in the early modern period in both sensory and conceptual terms; for Bulwer, after all, the hand was 'the *Substitute* and *Viceregent* of the Tongue' (1644, 3). Let us turn then to the Regent itself: to the tongue and its role in Carmelite sensory schemes.

Chapter 4
Of Taste and Tongue:
'a very slippery member'[1]

Q. How many are the vses of the Tongue?

1 *A* Three; the first to frame the speech.

2 The second, to helpe the taste.

3 The third, to prepare the meate that is chewed in the mouth, for the nourishing of the body. (Nixon, 1612, 17)

The first two uses (Nixon's third relating to his second) will form the sections of this chapter, here in turn Taste then Speech.

The tongue, Nixon explains, 'is a fleshy member full of *Sinewes, Arteries and Veines. Sinewes*, by reason of the sundrie motions it hath, and the *Sense* of *Tast* and *Touching* ...' (19).[2] While Descartes considered Taste to be the least subtle sense after Touch, the *Experiments and Observations About the Mechanical Production of Tast[e]* conducted by Robert Boyle (1627–91) found fine distinctions, dependent on the shape, size and motion of the tasted item (1675, 5).[3] He created mixtures to stir bitter, sweet and salty sensation on the 'spungy organs of Tast' (15), noticing 'how much Tast may be diversified by, and consequently depend upon, Texture' (19), and how maturation mellowed vegetable matter including 'the Fruit they call

---

[1]   'For the tongue is a very slippery member, which slippeth very quickly into many kindes of filthy cholericke, boasting, and vaine words: yes, and sometimes also into lying, swearing, cursing, slaundering, flattering and such like' (Luis de Granada, *Memoriall of a Christian Life*, 1599, 646).

[2]   'The tongue perceives all tangible objects with the same part with which it perceives flavour' (Aristotle, *De Anima*, 11, 423a, 19–20; Durrant, 1993, 45). In common with many commentators, Nixon (about whom little appears to be known: Ennis (1940) refers to him as a 'plagiarist and hack'; his statements provide insight if so into early modern truisms) considers Taste to be a form of Touch. This idea did not pass uncontested in the early modern period. Helkiah Crooke, for example, argues that if Aristotle 'had meant that the Tast and the Touch did not differ in *Specie*, hee would neuer haue sayd that *Gustus* was *Tactus quidam*, but simply and plainly *Gustus* is *Tactus* ... that Tast is a Touch'; 'But because the Sense of Tasting is not always found where Touching is, and where it is found there is no other Faculty of sensation: I conclude that not onely all the other Senses but the Taste also is a distinct and different Sense from the Touch' (1615, 716; 718); see Mazzio, 2005, 94–5.

[3]   For Descartes, see *Principles of Philosophy*, 1647; 1985 ed., I, 282.

Bananas' whose colour and pliability were altered by air and temperature (31).[4] The nuns' writing shows their awareness of variety and of the complexities of pleasure and of pain surrounding this as other senses. For them Taste in particular was closely bound up with conceptual as well as sensory distinctions, between feasting and fasting, between human and holy food.

'Do we not still tast the bitter fruit forbid?'[5]

'This *Sence* makes mee weeppe ere I speake of her; sith hence came our greefe', wrote Richard Brathwaite; '*apples* are suspicious to me' (1620, 45).

If the effects of the Fall were thought to be rectified through the Crucifixion when typologically the first Adam was answered by the second (Christ), so the senses' lapsarian roles were figuratively redeemed by contemplative consummation, described in lyrical paean. The stupefied Bride aroused from heavenly inebriation murmurs to her Spouse: 'Thy breasts are better than wine'; 'one drop of which makes me forget all created things, and withdraw from the creatures and from myself and no longer desire the satisfactions and joys which until now my senses have longed for'. Teresa de Jesus' commentary on the Song of Songs, probably composed between 1571 and 1573, draws out the 'tremendous secrets' of higher spiritual stages in which the ecstatic embrace is signified by a range of sensory pleasures including a 'delectable feast'. 'Oh, my daughters, may Our Lord grant you to understand – or, rather, to taste, for in no other way can it be understood – how the soul rejoices when this happens to it' (*Conceptions of the Love of God*, II, 383–4; 385):

> ... the Lord is giving her the fruit from the apple-tree with which she compares her Beloved: He picks it and cooks it and almost eats it for her. And so she says: 'His fruit is sweet to my palate' ... He watered this tree with his precious Blood! (389)[6]

---

   [4]   On Boyle's championship of experiments, see Hunter, 2009.

   [5]   In common with many other writers, John Davies associates the Fall with the sin of Taste as well as Sight (then to other sensory slips): Man 'by tasting ... himself was slaine' (1599, 2).

   [6]   On the controversy surrounding Teresa's text see Peers, 1946 ed., II, 353–5). The manuscript was apparently confiscated during Teresa's lifetime since one of her Confessors ordered the book to be burned, considering it 'a new and dangerous thing that a woman should write on the *Songs* ...' (355).

Teresa's thinking is clearly shaped here as elsewhere by Francisco de Osuna. For him, knowledge (*saber*) comes from tasting (*sabor*) the *gustos spiritual* (*Third Spiritual Alphabet*, 12.6).[7]

Unsurprisingly the Eucharistic moment was frequently one of spiritual epiphany. On Palm Sunday in around 1571, a desolate Teresa de Jesus found herself unable to swallow the Host: 'I really thought that my mouth was full of blood. I also thought my face and whole body were covered with it, as though the Lord had just shed it. It seemed warm to me and made me feel exceedingly tender' (*Spiritual Relations*, I, 346–7). In fine imitative fashion, it was at such a moment that Margaret of St Teresa (Margaret Downes: 1600/03–82), the first Prioress at Lierre, became assured of her own vocation: 'going to communicate upon palme sonnday I found that I could not by any meanes swallow the sacred host although I procured to doe it for ye space of three misereres ...' (*L4.39*).[8]

Teresa de Jesus reveals herself accordingly as devotionally ideal, proposing the sorts of techniques that foster figurative renewal made real, the imagination's success being marked by the stimulation of senses it sought to assuage. Rodriguez similarly suggests that the devout should at such times imagine themselves present at the foot of the Cross, 'recieving by their mouth, with extreme sweetnes, those drops of *bloud*, which ran' (1627, 278). Although mouths like the other sensory orifices should otherwise be closely guarded, when they are appropriately open they are said to be a route to the sublime. A Cistercian monk whose stomach turned at the idea of eating coarse brown bread was presented by Christ with a piece of it: he 'Dipp'd it in the Wound of his sacred Side and then Commanded him to Tast it' (*Christian Perfection*, 1697, 5th Treatise, 340–41). As so commonly in such writing, daily bread is transformed and replaced by holy flesh. The nuns' last meal to celebrate their clothing was sumptuous as a wedding feast; their first sustenance in a new enclosure was through Communion, 'the food of eternall life' (*A1*, 235).

Of course nuns, like other religious people, used fasting and abstinence to advertise piety and to prepare for spiritual replenishment. Denial of the pleasures of Taste was said to lead to diminution of both appetite and sensation. As in secular life, meal times were the occasion, and dining rooms the spaces, for staging a certain kind of decorous selfhood (see p. 53). Nuns who forgot to eat were accordingly feted; the refectory itself was used a place of correction as well as refreshment.[9]

---

[7] See Tyler, 2011, 117. De Osuna equates books with 'food that will not fill the stomach' (ibid., 119).

[8] On temporal markers and treatment in the convent (here referring to the length of time it takes to say a prayer drawn from the Vulgate Psalm 50:3, 'Misere mei, Deus'), see Hallett, 2012c. See Bynum for discussion of the Eucharistic miracle as 'a female genre' in the Middle Ages having 'a special effect on the senses' (1987, 76–7).

[9] Anne of the Ascension 'sum times she for goet her ordenare sustenane and so wold com in to our recreation with out remembaring that she had not bin in the refictore' (*L1.5.D*); Margaret of Jesus was commended for never complaining about ill-seasoned food or for asking for vinegar or mustard in the refectory (*L3.30E*). Ever sensitive to the dangers of

The Carmelite Constitutions stipulated that aberrant nuns should be whipped there. One convicted of 'grievous fault' should sit apart from the others 'in midle of ye refectory upon ye bare boards wth her mantle; and shall haue but bread and water ...' (*L3.34*, Chapters 3, 4, 19, 20). As in other respects, mortification appears to be most effective through its potential contrast, when expectation or symbolic content are ritualistically thwarted. Isolation is thus emphasised because it happens within the community; the mouth is put to the same kind of use as it might be for pleasure, yet employed for penitential rather than sensory satisfaction. Hence, the divine mouth of spiritual union is absent-present when a Prioress requires a nun to kiss the ground, other nuns' feet, 'a post ore a pane in the kitchen' (*L3.5*, 1). Likewise, by redirecting her gratification to distaste, the nun is reminded that the taste of human food falls far short of holy food, the near-repeat of the rituals surrounding both underlining a painfully edifying dissonance.

Mortifications around food were accordingly widespread within the religious Orders.[10] Augustine Baker, for example, gave advice on how to become as 'perfectly spiritualized' as a Franciscan who 'lost all perception of tast in eating' (1657, 353). Some nuns followed the types of routine set out by manuals, making food unpalatable by meditation on its disgusting qualities or by physical adulteration. Paul of St Ubald, for example, suggests rejecting 'good meates and sawces' and adding ear-wax to food to make it taste bitter (1654, Part 2, 223). It was said to be a mark of personal detachment not to notice even the most horrible of tastes. Such was her sensory martyrdom that when the Antwerp Infirmarian mistakenly gave Martha of Jesus (Rose Fisher: 1600–*c*.1640), 'a Glass of vinegar in place of beer' she drank it without saying a word; 'whether this had any bad effect or no, we cannot judge' (*A1*, 300).[11] On another occasion a young novice, Angela Maria of St Joseph (Catharine Kingsley: 1707–84) who almost died from malnutrition as a baby at the hands of a negligent wet-nurse, complained about flat beer at which her Novice Mistress waspishly replied 'Drink your own water' (*A2*, 328). That the young nun did just that suggests how habitual dietary sufferance was. Other women were praised for eating leftovers; a toothless old nun expressed herself

---

devotional excess, Teresa de Jesus advised that even those who sought to forget themselves should not neglect food or sleep (*Way of Perfection*, II, 339). For women especially, she said, food was a cure for physical languor (*Interior Castle*, II, 246).

[10]   The Benedictine Gertrude More (1606–33) 'resigned to loose all pleasure, delight and Gust in the sense of Tast soe that I may finde noe more tast in the pleasantest meate, then I should doe in eating a chip, or a stone', renouncing 'all affection to meates, and drinkes as to any pleasure, or delight that I willingly intend in them', desiring to be relieved of the need for either (1657, 163, 195).

[11]   This incident echoes similar occasions in devotional manuals, when the devout turn accidents to pious advantage. Rodriguez, for example, mentions the case of an Abbot who mistakenly was given linseed instead of sweet oil in food; the guilty Infirmarian afterwards called himself 'a Poysoner', while the Abbot appeared not to notice (1697, Part I, 545 on 'Conformity to God's Will').

thrilled to receive hard crusts.[12] Most poignantly, the elderly and infirm Catherine of the Blessed Sacrament even as she died could only be persuaded to drink when reassured it was her Superior's express command that she should do so.[13]

Partly, conditions for consumption themselves affected experience. According to research on the effect of background noise on oral perception, sound and taste may interact; gustatory intensity is dampened by noise, though sound-mediated food cues (suggesting freshness for example, saltiness or sweetness) were found to be more intense in noisy situations (Woods et al, 2010). One might imagine that the nuns' sense of Taste was indeed altered in such conditions. They seldom had the opportunity to concentrate on tasting as such. In the refectory at meal-times they heard devotional readings as they ate, habituated by manuals that suggested they should imagine themselves at the family scene in which Jesus ate with his earthly parents (Molina, 1623, 62). Notwithstanding the symbolic and penitential pressures around food and their likely affect on the experience of taste itself, we might consider briefly the general understanding of the mechanics of oral sensation, then its relationship to what the nuns actually ate and how they described their responses.

The Anatomy of an Early Modern Tongue

Anthony Nixon echoes other commentators when he considers the tongue is structured to ensure that the body is well nourished. In his catechismic scheme the question 'What is the use of spittle' is answered: 'Although it be an excrement, yet it is profitable to wet and moisten the *Tongue. There are two kindes of Kernels*

---

[12] Mary Magdalen of Jesus, known also for her acute sensitivity to smell and sound (p. 167), 'was also very dellicate & nise in her dyet, both for ye goodnes & clenlynes of it, yet was neuer known to complaine or haue any choys, saying it was all tow good & when it was in her power, made choys of the worst & hardest crousts tho she had not a tooth in her head' (*L13.7*, 154). Of Teresa Maria of Jesus (Bridget Kempe, professed 1651) it was said she preferred 'the scrapes and leauings of otheres, in so much that when she was dispencer, she left it for a maxceme in the kichine; when there was any scrapes left ore what others did not eatt; give that to Sister Teresa Maria' (*L13.7*, 31). The Lay Sister Alexia of St Winifred, though as cook she had access to the kitchen's choicest, 'allways eatt but lettle, yet neuer was seene, to cherish her selfe, but made choyes of ye worst, and fasted constantly most rigourosly' (147). The recycling Sister, Mary of St Joseph (see pp. 92 n. 18, 93), 'gave her self nothing but such Bitts and scraps, which others would have giuen to the catts' (240).

[13] Her Prioress 'desiered her to obstaine from drinking as much as she could, affter-wards her sickness growing to a continuall high feaure, she would neuer call for any refreshment, but when the Religious would offer her bier, ore othere things for her solies, she would aske; would our Mother haue me drinke; and when they answeared yeas, and that the Glass was att her mouth, she would pull it a way, saying; doe you thinke our Mother had rathere I should obstaine; and till they assured her it was the will of her superiour that she should refrlshe her-selfe' (*L13.7*, 21).

underneath the roote of the Tongue, called *Almonds, which serue to moisten the whole mouth'* (1612, 20). It enabled food to be chewed, for nourishment.

This, linking the mechanisms of taste and digestion through reference to the veins and sinews of the tongue, is implicitly a much shortened version of Galenic precepts in which food was concocted in the stomach, transformed into milk-like 'chyle' then again via the mesenteric veins to a blood-like substance. Food was thought to modify natural humoural states, and responses to it crucially altered personal dispositions. It was therefore central to Galen's physiological schemes and to medical texts that embraced them: 'Not only the flesh but also the mind was affected by the type of food that was eaten' (Wear, 2000, 171–2, from whom this summary of Galen's ideas is taken).[14]

For writers preoccupied with the relationship between body, mind and soul, clearly diet was also important to spiritual health. Committed as he is to subjecting the senses, and especially the tongue, Rodriguez attributes 'irregular Passions and bad Inclinations' to over-eating which disrupts sleep 'because the crudity and indignation that remains in the Stomach, and the gross Vapours which the Meat sends continually to the Brain, do's so disquiet him' (*Christian Perfection*, 1697, 5th Treatise, 4). In prayer, the same thing happens: inordinate passions from over-indulgence 'excite such Vapours in us, and produce such fancies in our Imagination, that we cannot recollect our selves, not have our Mind's united unto God' (4). Pleasure in Taste was therefore to be quelled at source, the tongue subdued in pursuit of spiritual as well as physical wellness.

The Carmelite nuns responded to such theory, and also show awareness of the effects of diet on taste itself and on health more widely. Given the capacity of bad diet to cause suffering, they were also mindful of its potential for a different form of mortification, through deliberate self-neglect.

Eating and Drinking in the Convent

Occasions for dining in the convent were also occasions in which the nuns came together, and so they were highly regulated to ensure that communication was minimised. The women were summoned by bells at 11 o'clock for dinner on fast days of the Order, 11.30 on fast days of the church, at ten in the summer. They were forbidden to eat without permission outside these set times, and were punished if they did (*L3.34*, Chapters 4, 16).[15] On fasting days, the basic food was neither eggs 'nor whit meates'. Between September and Easter the nuns 'ought

---

[14]   See also Hampton, 2004, 277 on the relationship of diet to other environmental factors in Galenic thought; Wood, 2009 on 'changes in the caloric [which] can lead to the temporary imbalance of the humors' (20).

[15]   Edmund Bedingfield was praised for adhering to such rules, although he did not need to do so: in his 20-year association with the Lierre Carmel 'he 'scarce drunck a coupe of beare between mieles, all tho hee had ye fridome to comemand what hee pleased in ye

neuer to eate flesh, unless it be for necissity'. The Prioress could dispence with rules 'wth ye sicke and those wch haue neede and wth whom fish doth not agree' (Chapter 8) – presumably the case for the nun who ate chicken in the Infirmary (pp. 47, 88). The experience of taste was, then, mapped on to both the agricultural and the liturgical season.[16]

Several nuns describe their extreme difficulty in adapting to a convent diet. Others, like the aristocratic Mary Gertrude of the Annunciation (Gertrude Aston: 1637–82) from Tixall in Staffordshire slipped surprisingly into their new regime: 'she was able to passe, wth only bread and water, tho she allways had a good stomake, and was ussed to dainty fare, very diffarent from what, she could expect in religon' (*L13.7*, 140). Indeed this nun like many others of her class in the convent was probably accustomed to the sorts of food and drink described in fashionable recipe books of the period such as Hannah Woolley's *Cooks Guide* of 1664, in part copied (unattributed) during the 1680s in *The Accomplished Ladies Rich Closet of Rarities*. On the evidence of richer household accounts, Gilly Lehmann (2003) suggests that by the mid-seventeenth century there was increased consumption of vegetables and fruit, and some adoption, or aspiration to follow, continental recipes, the fashion for richer Catholics presumably stirred by travel abroad and contact with the court in exile. The *Closet* provides advice on table-manners and for carving food (see p. 53), including the use of a fork, an innovation said by some to affect taste as well as modes of eating.[17] It also describes seasonal foods and recipes, mentioning more unusual fruit like apricots which were presumably available in England from hot-houses. The relative rarity of such fruit is indicated by the roles attributed to them in the nuns' writing, especially in relation to seduction. The annals Life of Teresa Joseph Maria of the Sacred Heart of Jesus (Catherine Howard: 1722–75) to whose unfortunate death we will return (p. 170), for example tells us that before profession she successfully repelled a would-be suitor: 'one day a gentleman offering to give her a few cheries privatly, she refus'd to take them, saying Oh! Satan don't tempt me' (*A2*, 304). In the case of Margaret Mostyn, her alleged bewitchment in the 1640s was attributed in part to the exchange of love-token peaches (see p. 80), the gifting of which again suggests their relative rarity.

If seasonal fruit was included in domestic diet, it was far less integral in religion, at least if denial is evidence of potential consumption. Mary Xaveria Burton told how, as a young woman in Suffolk she tried to follow Carmelite diet: 'yet I thought it very hard at first not to eat nor drink, but at ye ordinary hours

---

house, conforming him selfe in all to the customes of ye place not to be singular from ye rest' (*L13.7*, 110).

[16] The recipe book of the English Poor Clares convent from Gravelines, with its seasonal variations, typically represents the diet and mode of preparation in these religious communities (Hallett, 2012a, 319–35).

[17] 'How can I taste my salad if I don't eat it with my fingers?' a question attributed to the poet Johann Michael Moscerosch (1601–69): see Jütte, 2005, 178.

of dinner and supper, and to forbear fruit wch was a great mortification: It often came into my mind how Adam was overcome by eating an Appell, so I thought I was inspired by Alm: God to mortify my appetite in these things' (*A3*, 20). She followed a strict regime, in part because of sickness, though as ever it is difficult to determine which came first, her digestive problems or her fasting.[18]

When fruit is mentioned in the convent life-writing it is in reference to unusual occasions. We might wonder when Anne of St Bartholomew (Anne Downs: 1593–1674) laughed out loud at the sight of the Infant Jesus going from cell to cell in the convent distributing sugar-plums to the nuns from his apron (*A1*, 184), whether it was the donor or the nature of the gift that elicited pleasure. It is therefore striking (and intriguing as to the source of supply) that when Margaret of Jesus' 'stomak was growne so weeke yt she could not digest ye quantytie to one ege in a day, but liued meny munths, wth only ye raie piles of orringes' (*L13.7*, 51).

Barbara Harvey alleges that monastic food and drink 'was a form of upper-class diet' (1993, 34), at least in the case of a male community in England in an earlier period (Benedictines at Westminster, between 1100 and 1540). Post-Tridentine women sought (or advertised themselves as seeking) to follow an austere diet, the health-giving advantages of which were emphasised by a number of writers, among them Leonard Lessius (1554–1623), a Jesuit theologian. He also wrote texts on asceticism, science and piety including the influential *Hygiasticon: Or, The Right Course of Preserving Life and Health Unto Extrem Old Age, Together With Soundnesse and Integritie of Senses, Judgement and Memorie*, first published in Antwerp in 1613 and reprinted in English from 1634. He recommends a monastic diet, citing the collations of 'Abbat Moyses' as exemplary, and reporting the longevity of nuns who 'upon a most spare diet they live to 80 or 90 yeares; so that those of 60 and 70 yeares old are scarce accounted amongst the Aged' (1634, 126–7).[19] Such sobriety of diet, he claims 'ministreth soundnesse and vigour to the outward Senses', helping to maintain the optic nerves and preserving hearing which is otherwise hindered by 'the flux of crude and superfluous humours' caused by over-rich and varied food (145). 'In like manner, good Diet conserveth the

---

[18]   She wrote: 'my stomack was so weak in ye begining of my illness, and I had such a loathing of flesh, broath and eggs, yt ye very nameing of meat was almost enough to cast me into a swoon' (*A3*, 36); 'in three weeks time I never eat anything I know of but once a peice of bisquett as big as ye end of my finger and it lay like a stone all night on my stomack' (64); 'I lay a month and some dayes speechless, without being able to speak one word, or swallow anything but only once in four and twenty hours ... I had power to swallow for about half a quarter of an hour, what I commonly took was either beer or ale or silly-bubb ... once I think I tried to take part of a candle ...' (46). On nourishment received by Smell alone, see p. 168 n. 13.

[19]   See also Lemery, 1745; Muldrew, 2010 on diet and calorific consumption of labouring classes. On the longevity of nuns in Florence see Brown, 1999. The English edition of Lessius' text was published by Cambridge University Press, the fellows of the institution presumably enjoying his endorsement of college and university diets as well as monastic.

Senses of Smelling and Touching' (149). He claimed that Taste itself was adversely affected by over-stimulation of bitter, tart and salt substances (148). If his claims are proven, then we might imagine that Carmelite sensation was especially acute.

Such ideas on diet were firmly embedded in devotional manuals. Francis Sales' *Introduction to a Deuout Life*, read both before and after entry to the convents, advised against hot, spicy foods which, being 'fumy, and windy' 'endammage our health, or trouble the spirit' (1616, 560). He counsels against over-fasting as well as over-indulgence, and considered it 'a greater virtue to eate without choice', 'for thereby one renounceth, not only his owne taste, but also his owne Election withall' (558). Such subjection 'exceedingly befitteth a ciuill life'. Carelessness about what one eats is likewise a sign of conformity to Christ's rule. Such texts combine medically-related advice with spiritual guidance, and both aspects appear to influence the nuns' consumption and experience of food within the convents.

Although some nuns like Mary Gertrude Aston adapted themselves with apparent ease to a religious regime, others struggled. Several express extreme aversion to the Flemish diet, 'ye grosse fare of these parts' as the Lierre annals writer described it (*L13.7*, 110). Such disdain is also expressed by English nuns in other communities. The chronicler of St Monica's Augustinian convent in Louvain, for example, notes that women brought up 'tenderly and daintily' submitted to the 'simple diet of the cloister, dressed after the Dutch manner, which indeed was so very mean as to deserve to be recorded to posterity'. She describes meals of coarse rye bread, sodden porridge, meagre portions, peas 'dressed with lamp oil', celebrating a rare dinner provided by the mayor's wife: 'a portion of salt-fish about the bigness of three fingers, with a little spoonful of salad oil, which was accounted great cheer' (Hamilton, 1904, 34–5). The women's attitudes to foreign food suggest that they linked Taste with the superiority of their own national standards. Some Lay Sisters were accordingly commended for learning new recipes to please the nuns. Two natives of Brabant received particular praise for this, one 'applyinge her self to the English manner of cookinge'; the other, originally Edmund Bedingfield's servant before she joined the community, would ask the nuns at the turn 'for instructions to the cooking some particulars for her masters table after the English way' (267).[20]

Clearly, then, the women encountered mainly 'foreign' flavours as well as some familiar styles of preparation, although local ingredients and ambient conditions would naturally alter the taste of even recognisable food. Most particularly, since bread was a staple, unusual grains and methods of making dough were something

---

[20]   The first of these Lay Sisters, Anne Therese of the Presentation (Anne Lysens: died 1723), also 'loued much more to speake English then her owne naturall language Dutch being very attentive when ever she did but hear the sisters speake aney words wch sounded, as she imagin'd, fine and not common, those she would carefully retaine in her mind to bring out in the first occasions, tho' maney times so improper to what she was sayeing, with which she hugely deuerted the community' (*L13.7*, 266). The second woman was Anna Maria of St Joseph (Petronella van Dyck: 1650–c.1724/5), on whom see p. 192.

of a shock to those with delicate palates. An account of the duties of a Lay Sister included in the Antwerp annals indicates that meal flour was leavened and 'boulted' (to remove bran from grain using a cloth stretched between several people or held taut by the 'boulter' above a vessel), suggesting a certain type of relatively refined recipe for the dough, albeit strange to English tongues (*A2*, 144–5).

Mary Xaveria recorded in some detail her adaptation to the convent diet. She was said only to have overcome her aversion to eggs with help from her name-saint, and she recalled the novelty of salads:

> when I took ye Habit ye Rd Mother understood ye day before my enterance yt I had an aversion from eggs and upon demand I told her I had not eat one in seaven yeares ... she thought it impossible for me to comply with our constant rule of abstience from flesh, egges being ye cheif part of our diet ... she told me afterwards some of ye Community wondered she durst venture to admitt me, seeing I looked pale and thin and could not eat eggs ... I was order'd [by St Xavier] to try to eat an egg at dinner ye day before I entered I took one into my hand, but my stomack immediately turn'd to yt degree yt my Confessor ... made me lay it down ... ye first day I came to dinner with ye community my stomack was so much alter'd yt I longed tel they gave me some eggs wch they did that day and I eat ym heartily: ye Rd Mother was transported with joy saying St Xaverius had done this for me ... I continued after this constantly to eat them with as good an appetite as ever I did any thing in my life. My Mistress asked me how I liked ye other fair as sallets & c: I could not but own I had never been accustomed to eat them, but I thought all that came to the refectory savoured to me like manna yt fell from heaven ... and when I had been here three or four months I grew so fatt yt those of ye house and others who saw me enter were amazed at it my very cloaths wch were too big in ye begining grew too straite for me. (*A3*, 143–4)

Several documents report that the physique of other nuns changed after entry; they grew fatter or taller having been sickly before that. Catherine Eyre, for example, one of the sisters who travelled to Lierre in around 1681 (see Chapter 1) who was 'subiect from a child to tormenting paines from Graualle stopages, and to be consumptive ... and groth beinge no biger then a child of 12 yeares old [was] neuer sicke her whole year of nouiship, grew so vastly, as to have a new mantle made for her Profession, much longer then what she clothed in; she not only became one of the tallest of the Community' (*L13.7*, 272–3). Several members of her family were said to be 'low of stature'. This again suggests the relative healthfulness of the religious diet, as well as indicating possible nutritional deficiencies within family homes.

For the most part nuns do not record the actual taste of food or drink, beyond noting with delight its disagreeableness. Presumably those nuns who were reported to be deafened by the effects of catarrh (see p. 149) also suffered changes in taste. Mary Xaveria mentions 'bitter portions' of medicine, her dry mouth struggling with remedies administered by a French woman (a fake doctor) 'tho never so bitter and ungrateful but my stomach could not long retaine any thing it being so weak and all she gave me so unsavoury' (*A3*, 34, 43). Another physician ordered her to take 'asses milk cordial drinks' (73).

The papers' accounts of illness suggest there was, as we might expect, a continuity of dietary care for invalids both inside and outside the convent. One nun indeed was sent 'a kind of opium' by her brother from England, to alleviate her stomach pain; the nuns admired the fact that it did not affect her understanding, so she remained lucid in her dying moments; other 'physic' disagreed with her (*A2*, 221–2).

Nuns mention giving soups to the sick. On one occasion a mentally ill Sister refusing food was actually fed by the Bishop who held the 'poringer of broth' until she took it.[21] Otherwise the women record the use of julep, 'tisan' and drinks of multiplied flowers; Teresa de Jesus herself mentions orange-flavour water (*Book of Foundations*, III, 133). Winefrid of St Teresa was said to be adept in making up medicines; she 'had a very particular devotion to prolong the life of those that were in their agonys giving them from time to time proper cordialls tho only with a feather' (*A2*, 85), a system mentioned several times in the papers and suggesting a particular sensational link between Taste and Touch.[22]

It is natural in such an environment that medicine and miracle meet. In an effort to reverse the affects of alleged witchcraft on the Mostyn sisters that, among other symptoms made food seem tasteless (see p. 83),[23] physicians and priests mixed 'hallowed things' in the nuns' food including pieces of 'Agnus Dei', wax discs impressed with the figure of a lamb, usually worn rather than eaten to ward off evil influences. During their exorcism in April 1651 the Virgin instructed Margaret that they should eat only 'flesh' until August. Luckily for Margaret this was her favoured food (though generally she feigned dislike, and chose to eat things that disgusted to her: 'so that for the most part her whole dayes diet was onely a couple of egges, which she alwayes did eat with great auersion': *L3.27*, 14–15). The Virgin also told the Mostyn sisters to drink wine in moderation and to avoid cold food, this last detail suggesting she was *au fait* with contemporary

---

[21]   Mary Xaveria of the Angels (Margarite Smith: 1697–1777); she was the nun who excommunicated the bells (p. 151). Having persuaded her to eat on this occasion, the Bishop made her promise to take whatever the Infirmarian gave her. She took care thereafter always to say 'before she toucht it In obedience to my Lord Bishop' (*A2*, 318) which no doubt was both tiresome and touching to those who cared for her.

[22]   For example, in the Lierre annals: *L13.7*, 312. See also Chapter 3 on Touch, p. 88.

[23]   Loss of appetite or taste was naturally seen as a symptom of underlying illness, as in the case of Mary Gertrude of the Annunciation who developed 'a great lothing in her meatt, and what some euer she toke it gaue her no norishmen, but turned to a better soubstance, wch she spett up a gaine, wth a violent paine in her wch tormented her very much, and made her restles a nights, not able to sleepe, nor to take lettle or no norishment, haueing euer a good apitett att other times, made us fear ye worst' (*L13.7*, 144–5).

medical wisdom since physicians recommended that humid and warm food and drink be given to the melancholic who were naturally cold and dry (Ranum, 1989, 295). On another occasion when Margaret was suffering from a ten-day urine blockage, a picture of an English martyr was placed on her breast and his blood was mixed with her wine: 'in a short time, she made an incredible quantity of water, to ye admiration for all' (*L3.29*, 62).[24]

The Carmelite papers also mention other occasions of medicinal cannibalism. After the discovery of the intact body of Mary Margaret of the Angels when many miracles were attributed to her saintly intervention, one man was said to have been cured from a fever when dust was taken from the nun's coffin and mixed with his wine.[25] Although the nuns do not account for the taste of such substances, we cannot imagine that they were anything but physically unpleasant even if their effects were thought to be edifyingly healthful.

The tongue, then, was the medium for such exchange, its porosity like that of skin in general transmitting sensation throughout the mouth and benefit (or damage) throughout the body. This explains the centrality of the tongue in both medical and spiritual diagnosis: according to Erasmus 'Surely the most reliable symptoms of a sick or healthy mind are in the tongue, which is the appearance of the mind' (*Lingua*, 1989 ed., 326). William Gearing claimed '*Physicians take great notice of the tongue, judging thereby of the health or sickness of the body: so our words shew plainly the quality of our souls*' (*A Bridle for the* Tongue, 1663; both sources are cited by Mazzio, 1997, 64–5). Let us turn then to words and the second role of the tongue: 'framing of speech'.

The 'crafty Brocage of the Tongue'[26]

That the tongue could be a performative agent in the transformation of substance was a central tenet of transubstantiation: 'Hoc est enim corpus meum'. Words make things happen: 'after the words of Consecration, the Bread, contrary to the

---

[24]   Presumably this displaced a bladder stone from which Margaret was said to suffer.

[25]   See p. 110 n. 64. Coffin dust (which continued to exude a 'delicious perfume') was kept back for future use, to 'cure distempers' (Hardman, 1939, 159). John Webster's play, *The Duchess of Malfi* makes a similar reference to medicinal use of body parts: in reply to Duchess' question 'Who am I?' Bosola replies: 'Thou art a box of wormseed, at best but a salvatory of green mummy' (4.2.123): that is, mummified flesh. Piero Camporesi describes the medicinal application of human tissue and 'aqua divina', a distillation from corpses, used by Robert Boyle among others (1988, 24–47). See also Sugg, 2006 for the suggestion that medical cannibalism was closely integrated with medical theory and ideas of spiritual virtue in the early modern period, and Neill, 2011, for a brief history of the medicinal use of mummy.

[26]   The phrase is Bulwer's, used to underline his claims about the superiority of gesture to signify truth (1644, 4).

Senses of Seeing, and Feeling, and Tasting, is Christ's very Body, and the Wine his Blood' according to the anonymous *Epistle of a Catholique to His Friend a Protestant* (1659, 1).

Words also have the capacity to inflict damage: 'speaking daggers' in Hamlet's terms. Paul of St Ubald writes of passionate 'injurious words' (1654, Part 2, 227); Rodriguez in Gregorian terms of the tongue's biting wit, wounding like a stone thrown; for de Sales, the malicious backbiting tongue is like a razor in a surgeon's hand, capable of precision and of wounding.[27] Carmelite constitutions stress the importance of maintaining civil discourse to curtail possible conflict within their small communities, outlining punishments for those who malign or 'speak against' others.

Devotional and conduct manuals alike insist on the importance of well-regulated speech, curbing 'the Instrument of many passions, as the tongue', prone to superfluity and intemperance, particularly in the women, and apt to leave damaging impressions in the mind (Baker, 1657, 285, 298–9). Rodriguez advocates 'taciturnity', his precepts being taken up by Anne of the Ascension in her personal notes on the subject. His *Treatise of Modesty and Silence* centralises mortification of the tongue to religious life: 'euen as the heat of the Bath diminishes and vapours forth when the doore is often opened, so also with speaking much, the feruour of our deuotion through our mouthes is lost ... ' (1632, 39). The abject mouth is accordingly compared with an uncovered vessel 'apt to receaue all vncleannes falling into it, and be presently filled vp with dust and durte and euery sordid thing' (49); an undefended city without walls, its gates open to the enemy (50). As with Gregory's statements about unguarded senses which he compared with women at open windows (p. 65), some claims are gendered: over-speaking 'is a great vice in a man, but in a woman verie dangerous' (Granada, *Memoriall*, 1599, 717). If such views in a male context generally reflect Ciceronian ideas of *honestas*, 'the self-restraint of potentially domineering speakers' (Richards, 2003, 2)[28] then they also relate to ideas of uncontrolled speech: Lingua personified as garrulous, unchaste.[29] Potential damage is done not only by substance and length of speech but also by pitch of delivery. Not surprisingly, in the convent papers Christ uses soft words

---

[27]   Gregory, *Moralia*, Book 1, 1; Rodriguez, *Modesty*, 1632, 71, 141; Sales, *Introduction*, 1616, 395, 632.

[28]   I am grateful to Phil Withington for this point, raised in discussion of his paper on wit and incivility in early modern England at the University of Sheffield in February 2010.

[29]   Carla Mazzio considers that 'Nowhere are the associations between discursive and sexual promiscuity more explicitly dramatized' than in Thomas Tomkiss' play *Lingua: Or the Combat of the Tongue and the Fiue Senses for Superiority*, performed in Cambridge, registered in 1607. 'As the one organ that can move in and out of the body, Lingua threatens conventional boundaries of inside and outside; she is unruly, transgressive, expansive and alienating' (1998, 210).

(unless he is angry) and the devil has a harsh, shrill voice, loud and admonishing (*L13.7*, 48, 95).[30]

Prayer was naturally to be either silent or spoken in a gentle, clear voice. Some reading took place in private where it too might have been out loud. Luis de la Puente, for example, provided instruction for both silent then vocal reading since 'mentall praier vseth sometimes to breake out into vocall, speaking to our Lord exterior words arising from the interior feruour & deuotion: and vocall praier vseth to quicken the soule to make it more attentiue to mentall' (*Meditation*, 1619, 23).[31]

As in so many areas, we can trace the effects of domestic as well as devotional conduct manuals on the nuns' self-conscious delivery: 'read distinctly, observing your Stops'; 'use in your utterance Hems nor Stammerings; Sputter not as you speak' (*Accomplished Closet*, 1687, 191, 203). Over-slow speech was considered 'lothsome & tedious', 'that a Cart of Hay might passe almost betwixt one word and another' (Wright, 1630, 109).[32] While some nuns were able to follow such advice – Mary Terease of Jesus, for instance, 'haueing a good voyse it was a pleasure to heer her read in ye reffitory, she read so distinkly & plaine to be understod' (*L13.7*, 177) – others agonised about their speech impediments. Mary Joseph of St Teresa, the long-time compiler of the Antwerp annals whose distinctive narrative voice shapes so much of the convent's history, notes her own 'bashfulness wch made wt ever I did in Comty [community] a very hard task, particularly Quire dutys & reading in ye Refectory on account of a great imperfection in my speech, wch made these things a torment to me' (*A2*, 250).[33]

---

[30]   The devil had clearly not read (or chose to ignore) Della Casa's *Galateo*: 'The voice would be neither hoarse nor shrill. And when you laugh and sporte in any sorte you must not crye out and criche like the Pullye of a well ...' (1576, 86).

[31]   See Cordula van Wyhe, 2008, 200–202: one of the 101 engravings in the 1680s emblem book produced for the Carmelites in the Low Countries, the *Idea Vitae Teresianae*, shows a figure of a kneeling nun kneeling reading aloud.

[32]   Rodriguez cites the saintly authority of Ambrose and Bernard, 'that the voice should not be nice and mincing, not fayned or quauering, nor haue any sound of effeminacy in it, but keeping a certain forme & measure, fauouring of mankind and becoming grauety'; he associates civil discourse with social status, disallowing 'rude blunt and rusticall kind of speech' (*Practice*, 1697, 'Treatise of Silence', 68).

[33]   She attributed improvement to the intercession of St Joseph after repeating whose litanies 'I found my self quite another thing in speaking & reading, but to this day have not lost ye difficulty in performing many exteriour dutys' (*A2*, 250). Mary Gertrude of the Annunciation 'spared noe paines in her indeuers to lerne, espessally her lattan for ye Quier, was hard to her, haueing a lettence in her speech, yet it tis incredible, ye paines and diligence, she yoused to attaine ye perfection of it, tho she was very bashfull and aprehenciue' (*L13.7*, 142). Agnes Maria of St Joseph, a native Dutch speaker, 'by reasone of a lettence she had in her speech, offten times she could not pronounce some words of English plaine, tho she understood it well, & could read it also' (*L13.7*, 167). Anne of the Angels (Anne Bedingfield: 1650–1700) 'was dispencd with ye chiefest rigouer & hardship

Because the nuns in exile were reliant on their local associations, they needed to be able to communicate in several languages. Some, including Anne of the Ascension, were praised for their linguistic aptitude; others were sent out into local households to learn 'Dutch'. Given the friars' subterfuge in (allegedly) mis-translating Teresa de Jesus' letters (p. 111), linguistic knowledge gave crucial interpretative power. Manner of delivery in whatever language marked the distinction of the speaker.

Control of the tongue, like other forms of sensory-related behaviour, was a marker of decorum. Religious people were urged 'to speake in conuenient time', not interrupting others, 'a signe of want of breeding, and little humility' (Rodriguez, *Practice*, 1697, 'Treatise on Silence', 64): 'to speake with a low voice is to be silent'. The face should be kept serene and cheerful, girning avoided, and gesturing restricted (66–7). The nuns' low voices signified their devotional demeanour; clear strong voices were praiseworthy on appropriate occasions, such as in the choir or in devotional readings, when the object of speech was clearly not oneself. While compassion is expressed for those who lost the power of their voices through illness or age, and for those whose speech became disordered through mental agonies,[34] others are chastised for speaking too loudly or disturbing others with their prayers. The Virgin passed a message via Margaret of Jesus that another of the religious did just this, suggesting she adopt a quieter manner. This injunction came at a time in which Margaret was herself struggling with speech, before and during the exorcism that so afflicted her sensory powers when she claimed she could only speak by rote, repeating other people's words, having lost her ability verbally to instigate. This marks one of the lowest points in Margaret's anguish. In the terms of Maurice Merleau-Ponty, if language 'presents or rather *is* the subject's taking up of a position in the world of his [*sic*] meanings' (1996, 102), then 'a breakdown of sound all at once cuts off the voice from a character' (187).[35] The nun's voice, 'amputated from its body' (Connor, 2000, 11), is only restored

---

of ye order. ore any strick oblegation to the devine office by reason of a lettins in her speeck & could not pronoune some words righ' (*L13.7*, 214).

[34]   The nuns knew that Mary Gertrude of the Annunciation was approaching death, although she looked well her 'discure was much disordered, and very difarent from her owne way, by ye disorder of her head' (*L13.7*, 144). Agnes Maria of St Joseph, having struggled with some English pronunciation through her professional life, as she approached death suffered 'a kind of pallsise in her tong yt we could hardly understand what she sayd wch continewed 4 or 5 days' (*L13.7*, 165).

[35]   Merleau-Ponty is here (in the second part of this quotation) discussing badly synchronised or failed sound on film when a character continues to gesticulate: 'the spectacle itself is changed. The face which was so recently alive thickens and freezes, and looks nonplussed, while the interruption of the sound invades the screen as a quasi-stupor' (quoted Connor, 2000, 4, 11).

when the Dumb Devil is chained (see p. 84). When Margaret's voice is lost she appears to herself as less than human.[36]

Of course, not all involuntary loss of speech is the same, though it is usually accompanied by some disconcertion, as when sick nuns are aware of their own 'idle' slippage, or those caring for them are concerned this shows their incapacity to understand or communicate and so be shriven by sacraments as death approaches. Others appear exemplary if silenced: Margaret Teresa of the Immaculate Conception (*c.*1657–1745) 'had got such a habitt of praying [that] the nuns supposed her in a sleep, yet her lips moved in prayer' (*L13.7*, 284).[37] Disconcertingly, Mary Anne of St Winefrid (Anne Mostyn: 1663–1715) continued to move her tongue even after the nuns considered her dead (*L13.7*, 259).

As ever, the important aspect of sensory composure is self-control, 'bridling' the tongue to the pleasures of both taste and speech. Strictures surrounding speech in Carmelite convents serve to protect the peace of the community and to discipline those who might disrupt it. The nuns were required to keep silence (often referred to as Great Silence) between Compline (at bedtime) until Prime next day (usually at six in the morning). In general they were not allowed to speak to one another without permission and when not in community or office they were required to 'remaine apart' in their cells or hermitages: 'There ought neuer to be a place where they assemble to worke together, fearing yt this might giue occasion of breaking silence in being together' (*L3.34*, Chapter 10). 'Light faults' listed in the constitutions include speaking 'idle words' and making a noise or 'disquieting' others, the word being used in the papers simultaneously to suggest both sound disturbance and emotional agitation. Punishment included doing 'worke of humility' (usually menial tasks), being made to be silent or abstaining from food (Chapter 16), the tongue being punished in more ways than one. Practice for such mortification was imbued via the Prioress' instructions, making a nun keep silence while others around her spoke (*L3.35*). The dangers of not respecting silence are realised in a Carmelite account of the ghost of a Benedictine nun, included in a letter of 1650 sent to the Antwerp convent, who was 'to remain in Purgatory a whole year for not hauing esteem'd silence' (*A1*, 230).

'Middle faults' include speaking without leave in Chapter; 'Grievous', 'speaking iniurious to another' or 'saying inordinate words of choller'; 'More grievous' include speaking discourteously or contending with superiors (*L3.34*, Chapters 17–19). Nuns were forbidden to 'treat' of anything but spiritual matters, avoiding communication with their families so as not to 'inter medle wth worldly

---

[36]   'Voice is a certain kind of sound made by an ensouled being. Nothing without a soul is vocal' (*De Anima*; Durrant, 1993, 39).

[37]   Of Edmund Bedingfield it was said 'ye relígous of the ospitall, yt tended him sayd yt hee was ye whole time praying, for his mouth went constantly and his hands was euer found, upon his beads' (*L13.7*, 120).

things' (Chapter 3).[38] They were only allowed to speak with seculars in the presence of a chaperone, and all conversations had to be reported.[39]

Here speech is construed as active and potentially injurious; to listen is to be on the receiving end: 'I am sildum', noted Margaret of Jesus, 'in any occation of speaking or of curiosity but in some degre or other I am subiect unto it' (*L3.35*, loose paper).

Accordingly, the nuns were expected to address one another with restraint and politeness, and those who maintained the peaceable atmosphere of the community were especially commended. Of Alexia of St Winefrid (Catherine Powell: 1622–84) it was observed she was 'so extream silent that on this account the religious used to call her the Mouse'. Having arrived at Antwerp in the entourage of Anne Somerset after her father was killed in an accident labouring on the Monmouth estate of the Marquis of Worcester, she worked in the convent kitchen: 'when any came thither on whatsoeuer account, she presenelty gaue them what they wanted without speaking a word' (*L13.7*, 145).[40]

Speech when it happened was to be suitably directed, and confession appropriately couched. On 28 November 1731 Mary Margaret of the Angels (Penelope Chapman: 1693–1739) wrote in her list of 'good purposes' and intentions (a form of spiritual testimony), 'I resolve silence for my particular examin [and] to be upon my guard of speaking of others faults' (*A2*, 73): 'I am apt to speake

---

[38]   Rodriguez stresses that religious should avoid visits and conversations with family: 'this troubles the tranquillity and regularity of our Life'. His warnings are couched in the language of physical injury; 'For the memory of the Life we led in the world, coming again to strike our imagination, may happen to open old sores'; conversation induces bad habits which 'take impression in our heart' (*Practice*, 1697, 5th Treatise, 383). Of letters he asks 'How long time will it be, before I shall be able to deface these Images which they'll cause in my imagination?' (389). Anne Teresa of Jesus (Catherine Nelson: 1642–1700) was commended for her restraint, only seeing her brother, a Franciscan, when he visited once every two or three years, and even then 'she kept him noe longer yt when she had inguird of his health exspriest her owne contente & sattisfaction, recommend her self to his prayers, she had no moer to say' (*L13.7*, 207).

[39]   Catherine of the Blessed Sacrament is typical if exacting in her behaviour: she 'neuer spoeke to any externe att the gratts, be they siculars ore spirituall person, but she always gaue a faithfull account to her superior of euery word that she could remember had passed ...' (*L13.7*, 20).

[40]   Other nuns were also commended for causing minimal disturbance. Margaret of St Teresa Downs: 'her discurce was religious, and not superfluous, but sollaed plaine, and to ye purpose' (*L13.7*, 131). At Antwerp Mary of the Holy Ghost (Mary White: *c.*1600–1640) 'was neuer heard to speake a word in quire how ill soeuer she was [and] was neuer heard to speak one word more then persisly necessary, to ye lay sisters & in ye Infirmary when she went to visit ye sick if they were gone out, she would not speak a word to ye Infirmarian tell ye sick return'd'. Touchingly, 'some 3 dayes before she dyed she was troubled because she had spoken after Compline tell she was told that it was not silence that night' (*A1*, 205).

peevish and fretfull wch I hope to mend.' In December 1732 she notes her failure to achieve this.

Speech was, then, expected to be highly regulated, the tongue bridled in speaking as in response to Taste, the dual aspects neatly summarised in the metaphors of Francis de Sales: 'As Bees take nothing in their little mouths but honey: so should thy tongue be always sweetned with God, thy lips should always be sugred with his praises' (1616, 586). The wanton tongues of he-goats, he warns, degenerate sweet almond trees to bitterness.

Chapter 5

Still Small Voices: Sounds, Sibilance and Silence in Early Modern Convents

Between the last chapter and this one responsibility shifts from speaker to listener. Words hang in their common medium of air. For a moment the loquacious are lascivious lords, their tongues agitating not only the vibrating bones of the unwitting auditor but potentially their passions: 'our heart breaketh by the eare'. But now the listener is liable: 'Let vs', concludes Francis de Sales, 'then keepe our eares diligently from the aire of foolish words; lest it infect our heart' (1616, 531–2).

The nuns experienced the power of sound (seemingly above all other senses) to alter their composure.[1] Mary Margaret Chapman, the peevish-speaking nun (pp. 145–6) knew what it was to be on the receiving end of sharp words: 'as if an injury was done me' (*A2*, 78). Margaret of Jesus Mostyn used similar language, dramatically comparing her absence from God with having 'suddaine fright', the effects of hearing 'som fatall dismall newes' (*L3.35*, loose paper).[2]

Of course, it is not always possible to filter unexpected sounds, so the convents were architecturally and conceptually constructed to protect the nuns as well as to constrain them; to keep as well as guard their peace. The enclosure walls modulated the sounds to which the women were exposed. Through the turn they heard only disembodied voices, and were themselves largely experienced that way by the

---

[1] Many early modern commentators claim, like Brathwaite, the ear 'hath it a distinct power to sound into the centre of the heart' (1631, 6).

[2] '... most commonly when no prayer at all hath emediately preceded ther will com asartain memory and reflection upon me at an instant and strike me as it were euen through wth ye consideration yt I am in absinces from All: God now this happenes some times by ye accoring of or hearing or reading of any such little pious words or sentences ... it semes euen at an instant as if I was all utterly lost and as half out of my witts much after ye self same maner though yet far more viment degree as when som fatall dismall newes wherof there was no precedent is instantly brought upon me or els as if I war surprised by some suddaine fright for all such notics of All: God wch my soule is wont to haue serues now for no comfort ...' (*L3.35*, loose paper). Another time, caught simply going through the motions during Prime, 'I was suddainly asked one ye part of God Alm but I knew not how nether can I say I heard any thing distinctly these words I understood: *I you doe not doe it for loue of mee what doe you doe heer*. I was soe struken with this yt I could not remain in ye Quire' (*L3.31*, 39). Her sister Ursula of All Saints also knew the force of speech that 'left a very deep impression' (*L3.31*, 36; see p. 31 n. 16). On injurious language see Butler, 1997.

seculars who visited.[3] In the speakhouse the topics and modes of conversation were strictly controlled, the Carmelite constitutions designed to protect the nuns from distraction and direct their listening like their speech to pious purposes. The mundane sounds to which they were exposed were accordingly considered necessary evils (or literally demons); sacred murmurings were welcome if not immediately always known as such. The agent ear was required to distinguish source and meaning; by musical analogy, *'The Eares doe iudge of soundes, notes and harmony'* (Nixon, 1612, 17).[4]

Bagpipes, Bells and Bellows

Of the sounds within the convent, those of the sickroom are most evocatively described.

Afflicted with asthma, propped up in her infirmary bed to avoid suffocation (and allowed to read spiritual books), Mary Frances of St Joseph (Mary Bradshaw: 1716–65) was often 'black in the face'; 'her lungs making a noise exactly like a pare of Bag Pipes' (*A2*, 298). Sounds from the sick were often diagnostically helpful, indicative of changes in condition and marking the progress of contagion.[5] The vivid detail of the nuns' life-writing suggests the very difficult conditions within which the nursing sisters worked and the suffering endured by pre-penicillin patients.

For those brought up with the delicate use of handkerchiefs for whom 'it is an *uncomely* thing by *coughing*, and *hauking*, to raise *phlegm* or *corruption* out of the breast and lungs' (Della Casa, 1663, 17), exposure to the sick-bed was in several ways 'disgustfull'. When she was Infirmarian at Antwerp, Margaret of Jesus

---

[3]   It has been argued that after the Council of Trent enforced enclosure, 'The nuns become an invisible presence, they are transformed into a voice' (Gabriella Zarri; quoted Monson, 1992, 191). Monson's discussion focuses on the nuns' disembodied (singing) voices, the citizens' only contact with them. The nuns' own experience was similar, though it has been far less discussed: faceless contact with familiar or strange voices.

[4]   Nixon explicates the hearing mechanism: 'As the aire carrying the sound into the aire, moueth the Hammer of the Eares, and causeth it to strike vpon the Anuile and so maketh a sound by meanes of the little taber, through whose sound the Spirits of hearing are awakened: euen so, God worketh in his Ministers, who recieue his voice after a diuine manner, and then are they (as it were) Hammers to strike vppon the Anuile of mens hearts, by which sound the spirits of the hearers are stirred vp' (1612, 17).

[5]   Teresa of Jesus Maria (Jane Bedingfield: 1617–42) died suddenly at Antwerp, after another nun heard her cough in the night (*A1*, 294). Angela Maria of St Joseph died soon after the nuns noticed a change in her breathing (*A2*, 328). In the long, cold winter from December 1762 to the following March, many members of the Lierre community came down with 'distemper': Frances Xaveria of the Immaculate Conception (Frances Poole: 1697–1763) 'coughed ceaselessly' until just before her death (*L13.7*, 303). In the same convent Mary Aloysia of the Annunciation (nee Thorp) who died in 1776 was 'seized by what was that winter a universal cold' (*L13.7*, 318).

Mostyn took particular care of a blind, confused nun who was 'allways vometing and spitting, most lothsome filt[h]y matter and stouf, and smelt so strong of ye corruption'.[6] Patients often smelled unpleasant (Chapter 6) and were generally noisy. Those who were lame – and there were many, what with incompetent bone-setting, the effects of childhood injury or rickets, some bent double with age – they walked with crutches or a stick, the sound of their progress along corridors or stairs punctuating the quiet.

So, too, did 'deaf men's discourse'[7] or at least deaf nuns. Several are mentioned in the convents, including Mary Magdalen of Jesus who was noted for her all-round sensory delicacy in her younger days (pp. 133, 167). She was made deaf by a long-term 'rotten conssomsife cold wch caused her to cauffe & spiet a great quantitie of loothsome fleames'.[8] As a nun she 'loued to be spokeng sweetly tow', yet in later life was 'forst for some years by reasone of her deffness' to say her devotions outside the choir area (whether for reasons of her own loudness or failure to hear is not made clear).[9] Her near-contemporary at Lierre, Margaret of St Francis was

---

[6]   Margaret of Jesus was faced with a heavy work load: 'being then a boue 40 religous, and constantly a considrable number, of them in ye infermary'. These included Sara Hikx (*c.*1613–48): 'one Blind, in a deipe cunfousition, allways vometing and spitting, most lothsome filt[h]y matter and stouf, and smelt so strong of ye corruption, yt came from her, yt non of ye religous could beare to be neere her only this deare sister, she cherished and tended her, wth all ye loue care, and charity imaginable, empting her poots, washing those nasty foule cloths & continnually, performing those disgustfull things about her wth so much joye and allacrit as if she had no disgust in it ...' (*L13.7*, 52). The Antwerp annals record that Margaret was often helped in her difficult labour by her 'good angel' (*A1*, 293).

[7]   *Duchess of Malfi*, 2.5.53–5: 'This intemperate noise / Fitly resembles deaf men's discourse, / Who talk aloud, thinking all other men / To have their imperfection.'

[8]   She 'was forst to yous meny cloaths for that purpose, wch she contriued so, as neuer to permet any one to tuch or wash them, but stole time early or latt to doe them her selfe alone, for feare of giueing disgust to any, this & her deffnes was her greatest suffarings, for she loued dearly to here & speake of heuenly things ... '(*L13.7*, 158).

[9]   There is an intriguing reference in the Life of Margaret Teresa of the Immaculate Conception (Margaret Mostyn: 1657/59–1745), a niece of Margaret and Elizabeth Mostyn, who joined the Lierre Carmel as a widow having previously tried life with the Poor Clares at Rouen remaining 'till by going barefoot she lost her hearing' (*L13.7*, 282). Robert Boyle similarly described the case of a young boy 'who by standing at a Window lost his Hearing, that he could not go to Church for many weeks' (in Mullins, 1695, 7; see Cockayne, 2003, 498). Catherine Burton provided a vivid account of her childhood ear-pain: 'but before I got to bed such violent pain seased me, as if one of my teath were tore out of my head, and from thence the humor gathering raged so violently ye whole night yt I took no delight in my soft bed ... they said that if ye impostumes broke inwardly it would immediately kill me and it did little less, for it broke before morning and ye blood and corruption fell in such quantity into my throat, that all thought it would choake me, but yet a greater quantity discharged it self by my eares ... the next day I came a little to my self, but my head was in such disorder and so weak that I could not endure to hear any body speak in ye roome, tho in a low voice ...' (*A3*, 52–3).

also 'holy empotent' through profound deafness, and was communicated with by signs (p. 125). There is no evidence in the nuns' papers that they used ear-trumpets (referred to by Francis Bacon as 'ear-spectacles')[10] or more formal signing systems such as those designed by John Bulwer. Nor is there any indication that they tried to find cures for their deafness.[11]

The most regular aural interruptions of the convent quiet were, of course, from bells, sounding so consistently throughout the day that they are rarely mentioned unless they signal something untoward. Ringing marked regular rhythms: the sequence of canonical hours, the calls to recreation or refectory, to confession or to choir. Special forms of ring were noted, such as the use of ceremonial bells in enclosure processions (*A1*, 234), for funerals ('both the bells together two peels': *A1*, 336), for music mass (*A2*, 90), or at the convent gate (*A2*, 320).

The constitutions stipulated that bells should be obeyed promptly. A nun was to be punished if 'after ye sound of ye bell [she] shall be slowe in preparing her selfe to come to ye quire' (*L3.34*, Chapter 16). It was one of the duties of Lay Sisters to ring the 'pardon' or Angelus bell, requiring the whole community wherever they were to say a prayer in honour of the Annunciation. In her final sickness Anne of the Ascension noticed that the bells had not been rung in their usual fashion, finding when she enquired about it that this was on her doctor's orders so as not to disturb her. Another time, Mary Anne of Jesus, 'rang the Angelus bell, it seems, something longer distance between one Ave Maria than another'. This so troubled the Prioress that the nuns had to distract her (Hardman, 1936, 169).

Some religious map their supernatural experience around bell-call. Margaret of Jesus Mostyn noted: 'When the pardon rung twelue at noone; I chanced to rise up first, and whilest I was saying it, I saw our blessed Lady with her sacred sonne, giuing their benediction to all; and she embrased me, and said because I stood up first at the bell she would giue me her blessed sonne the whole, time of recreation' (*L3.27*, 50). Sometimes obedience to the bell was noted rather in breach than observance. On another occasion, Margaret 'two or three times when the bell rung, having forgotten to say the Aue Maria', the voice of her good angel said it for her (*L3.27*, 30). It was regarded as a sure sign of their moral slippage under demonic influence that the Mostyn sisters did not immediately obey the bell-call, and whenever a bell tolled to

---

[10]   According to Cockayne, ear-trumpets were expensive and their use confined to the wealthy (2003, 496). She also suggests that deafness was particularly disabling for Protestants whose devotion stressed the important of 'hearing the word of God' (Romans 10:17). Although her descriptions of the multi-sensory stimulation of Catholic liturgy (with candles, rosaries, holy water, incense and oil) are generally true enough, her conclusion implies a complete break with Catholic-like practices in the English church after 1547 legislation which effectively 'reduced the involvement of the senses' (496). It may be true, however, that a Catholic experience of deafness was different from a Protestant one.

[11]   Cyclonian, for instance, was thought to ameliorate the effects of deafness. Robert Hooke sought to cure tinnitus by pouring warm honey into his ear; others advocated eating radishes, eels or more drastic measures (Cockayne, 2003, 498).

hope it was a portent of their own death (*L3.31*, Catalogue of Demons). Some nuns succumbed eagerly to the aural rhythm since it absolved them of responsibility, made them time-free and simply responsive to acoustic cues. For others such was the tyranny of tintinnabulation that indeed we might empathise with Mary Xaveria of the Angels (Margaret Smith: 1697–1777) whose mental state 'about the turn of life' led her to excommunicate the bells (*A2*, 316).

The level of preoccupation with bells in the papers, and the detail given to their finely-tuned intervals, suggests just how hypnotically habitual was obedience to their call. Some nuns made particular use of regularity, attaching acts to sounds. When you hear a bell, instructed Luis of Granada, consider how your life is shorter on the strike (1598, 9); when the clock strikes say 'Blessed bee the houre in which my Lord Jesus Christ was borne & died for us' (1614, 30). Mary Frances of St Teresa Birkbeck designated a prayerful purpose, 'to renew in my memory the presence of God every time I hear the quarters or hour strike' (*A2*, 16).

Between times, the nuns represent themselves as absorbed by serious silence. Those who consistently disturb the peace are admonished. Eugenia of Jesus, for instance, was invited to 'decline her unquiet disposition' '& pray quietlye' (*L3.31*, 69). Laughter, or causing others to laugh in quire, was punished (if only as a light fault). In keeping with domestic conduct advice, laughter was regarded as unseemly since it caused passions to rise, especially in women out of doors (de Guevara, 1697, 89–90, 215). Rodriguez placed laughter with 'toys & games of children'; it was infantile to satisfy ears with novelty, and merriment was instantly followed 'with exceptious and angry wordes' (*Treatise of Modesty and Silence*, 1632, 49). 'Silence consists not in not speaking' (55) but in tempering sound both in and out of the body; 'it teach vs how to discourse with God Almighty' (36). Some laughter was acceptable, to express delight at holy happenings. Mostly, however, it was negatively represented in the convent papers, suggesting loss of control of oneself to outside forces. Devils were said to laugh with derision at Edmund Bedingfield and Margaret of Jesus during the exorcism in 1651 (*L3.31*, 81). The demons' generally unseemly sounds were signs of their uncouth behaviour; at other times they gnashed their teeth, snorted and snarled, near Teresa de Jesus making 'a noyse of very great blowes' (*Flaming Hart*, 1642, 446, 447).[12] When the word 'noise' is used in the nuns' papers it has almost exclusively negative connotations.[13]

---

[12] One source describes devils making sounds near Margaret of Jesus like 'bellows' (*L3.31*, 80).

[13] The devil's ugly mouth (Teresa de Jesus, *Life*, I, 204, 206) is in contrast to the beauty of Christ's: 'most lovely and devine' (187). The shrill-voiced and scoffing devils howled at the Mostyn sisters, trailing chains, stamping with hideous noise (*L3.29*, 69; *L13.7*, 80, 112). Devotional manuals likewise use 'noise' in negative contexts. Rodriguez refers to the noise of children for example, and of those who do not listen; he draws on the analogies of Gregory to discuss 'noisy' housemaids (the passions and senses) who create mayhem when their mistress (the mind) is absent (*Modesty*, 1632, Book 1, 19, 55).

Indeed, such is the quiet of the convent that it is only unusually intrusive noises (or reactions to them) that are noted. The soldiers in the regiment of the father of Anne Teresa of Jesus for example: 'stoude in awe of her not dairing to shoot at Publicke rejoyccing because ye Noyes offended her' (*L13.7*, 203). Mary of St Joseph (Mary Vaughan: died 1709) performed 'burdensome Actions' for the Lierre community including carry wood and weeding the garden, though 'not louing much that Noise and Hurry which does naturally attend great Labours and stirring works' (*L13.7*, 238). Building work was inevitably disruptive as when in 1771 at Antwerp 'ye Jack by the Brewery [was] pull'd downe'[14] in the same month as the 'Geografer of his Royal highness' the Governor of the Netherlands came to survey the cloister in the run up to the dissolution of the religious houses in the region. Some intrusions had happy endings, such as that caused by the unexpected arrival of Agnes Roosendael who broke into the convent through the turn, the Portress hearing nearby 'an extraordinary noise and busseling' (see pp. 124–5). The unwelcome entry of thieves in 1770 was less happy (p. 43); they woke the nuns whose yells for assistance made literal Rodriguez's advice (in his case to throw off the temptations of impurity) to shout at those who entered at the door (1697, 220).

Significant weather events also disturbed the convents' peace. In around 1648 a whirlwind at Lierre blew barrels in the air, terrifying the nuns who prayed aloud with their chaplain, attributing the event to demonic interference, the devil departing in a clap of thunder.[15] A paper printed in London in 1675 recorded the 'dreadful inundation which happened in Holland' on Sunday 3 November, lasting in Antwerp until the following Tuesday; at Ghent 'a most dreaful Storm of Wind, accompanied with Thunder and Lightning' set fire to two towers (*A True and Perfect Relation*, 1675). In August 1768 a thunder-bolt struck the convent church in Antwerp during the hour of the nuns' midday rest: 'The Religious were all so thunder-struck and alarmed that they thought neither of flight nor self-preservation' (Hardman, 1936, 121–2).In December 1770 'a violent wind blew down & brok at ye root ye great pare tree' near the Antwerp refectory, and a cherry tree 'in ye Hens Court', lifting tiles from the roof; 'much endamaged our Ladyes Church & made great ravage both in ye Town & Country, ye Hurracan was between 9 and 10 in ye morning'. The following year the convent cellars were flooded 'from ye great rains' and needed to be pumped out 'for putting up ye Butter' (uncatalogued papers, St Helens).[16]

All such furore is in contrast to the accomplished calm of the contemplative ideal which Carmelite constitutions sought to preserve and which was often described in terms of caressing voices.

---

14   A 'jack' is a brick used at the end of a course, heading an architrave (*OED*).

15   John Webster's *Duchess of Malfi* mentions similar conclusions: 'As men conveyed by witches through the air, / On violent whirlwinds' (2.3.51).

16   See Hallett, 2012a for accounts by the English Poor Clares of the gunpowder explosion in Gravelines in 1654, and a Bridgettine description of the Lisbon earthquake in 1755.

'A whistling of gentle air':[17] Sibilance and Silence

Carmelite spirituality is especially imbued with a sense of the heritage of Elijah who was said to have lived on Mount Carmel, the first location of hermits of the Order. Silence, or a particular understanding of the significance of sound, accordingly informs important aspects of cloistered eremeticism.[18] Teresa de Jesus' reference to hearing the 'sweet voice' of Christ 'in the manner of whistling'[19] ('una voz muy suave, como metida en un silbo') exegetically evokes I Kings 19:12 ('et post ignem sibilus aurae tenuis'), thereby placing her experience within an Elian tradition.

She is interested in the salvative effects of sibilance and in silence as *part* of such sound, not necessarily its opposite. Accordingly, she is concerned with what silence allows her nuns to hear, with its permissive attributes, and she makes distinctions between different kinds of hearing and the knowledges they offer, in themselves through self-listening, and from outside by allowing spiritual truths to be heard, sometimes literally. At times voices are loud in her ears, at others a Soul comes to understand 'yea and also to heare, as if a thing were spoken to her, from farre off' (*Flaming Hart*, 1642, 264). As for St Augustine, God's 'eternal word is silence' (*Confessions*, XI. vi. 8; 225).[20]

In general, Teresa de Jesus and her nuns are much occupied with sounds that almost cease, bridging and merging into silences, from or beyond the edge of altered spiritual 'states of quiet' in which in union the Bride and Spouse 'doe there understand one another, really, without speaking' (*Flaming Hart*, 1642, 375).[21] At the height of rapture 'she neither sees, nor heares' (264–5):

---

[17]   I Kings 19:12: 'And after the earthquake, a fire: the Lord is not in the fire, and after the fire a whistling of gentle air' (Douay-Rheims version).

[18]   On Elian heritage and Marian devotion informing the various etymologies of *Carmelus* (*car* [spouse] and *melos* [*laus*: praise]: praise of the bride; song of the beloved, see Edden, 1999.

[19]   Teresa de Jesus was praying before a representation of Christ tied to the column: 'I heard one speake to me, in a most sweet voice; but it was framed, as if it had been, in the manner of whistling. For my part I was all in a fright; and the verie haire of my head stood an [*sic*] end', amazed 'how the onlie hearing of a voice (and that, with the onlie [*sic*] eares of flesh, and bloud; yea and without the articulation or framing of anie one word) was able to produce so powerful an operation in the soule' (*Flaming Hart*, 1642, 613–14).

[20]   Augustine likewise implicitly echoes phrasing from Elijah's experience: 'But how did you speak? Surely not in the way a voice came out of a cloud ... That voice is past and done with; it began and ended. The syllables sounded and have passed away, the second after the first, the third after the second ... until, after all the others the last one came, and after the last silence followed' (XI. vi. 8; 225).

[21]   For Benet of Canfield, such communion is reciprocal; God 'sublimes' her, 'as himselfe saith. *The Word which goeth out of my mouth shall not return empty to me, but whatsoever I will, it shall accomplish and prosper in them to whom I send it* ' (1609, 103).

For there, it seems, that the Soule hath some other kind of eares, wherewith to heare; & that he makes her harken, and not, the while, to thinke of somewhat els, as if one, who could heare well, were not suffered, to stop his eares; and that they cryed out alowd, to him, who would therefore be faine to heare them, whether he would or no … (373)

The Soul in such a situation does not simply relax, at least not in the earlier stages of its education. Teresa writes of her torment as the body and soul struggle, the latter she describes a like a person with a rope around their neck, trying to breathe, a voice crying out (*Life*, I, 124).

In the well-learned Prayer of Quiet, communion by contrast is soundless, intimate. The Bride only needs to move her lips for the Spouse to understand (Chapter XIV); she is often much 'altered' by the effects.[22] Margaret of Jesus describes similar such moments, as when the Virgin remained with her, '& though I heard noe distinct words, yet mee thought she tould mee many thinges' (*L3.31*, 37). Another time words came into her mind 'as if spoken', turning her grief to joy (*L3.35*, loose papers). This, then, is a state of almost silence: lips move, miming sound, and are read in its absence as the deaf augment their understanding; knowledge is conveyed and received 'as if' by listening.

In other writing the women more fully accentuate the role of absolute and sign-less silence, not only for those who engross themselves, actively participating in its possibilities, but also in and of itself as the essence of divinity. Among the papers of Margaret of Jesus, for instance, was a copy of a letter from 'Jan of the hole Crosse', 'the summe' of which 'is that the greatest neede wee haue is to be silen: with our great god. Both with the toung and apetits for the best language to his Diuine Maiesti is the silent loue' (*L3.35*, loose paper): a love we are given to understand that would endure even in a forest at night with no one there to hear it.

There are then, many gradations of silence: near-quiet, complete, one-sided, softly conversational. For the most part accounts are written from the point of view of the listener, rather strikingly so given our contemporary focus on the role of the locutor in speech-acts. In the nuns' writing the ear is also active, not only charting the changing of the 'thing' by language and noting the effect of sound on self-composure, but also participating in its transformative ritual like wedding

---

[22]   On 'cruel and furious quiet' (un quietud cruel y furiosa) in the writing of Diego de Jesus (1570–1621), the first editor of John of the Cross, and its links with the teaching of Dionysius, see Tyler, 2010, 69–70. On noise with no sound in the writing of Paul of St Ubald, see p. 8. Teresa de Jesus wrote of unexpected arousal in which a Soul is woken by God as though by a rushing comet or soundless thunderclap (*Interior Castle*, II, 276). See also Francisco de Osuna for discussion of 'that silence wherein understanding is profoundly quieted' (*Third Spiritual Alphabet*, 21.3; Tyler, 2011, 122); and Francisco de Santo Tomas, *Medula Mystica* on aural communion in which 'there is no sound or voice … the species, or similitudes, under which it is apprehended are not corporeal, but spiritual' (see Peers, *Interior Castle*, 1946 ed., II, 279, note 1).

witnesses marking the words' work. Without an ear the enacting tongue would simply be repeating itself to itself, in self-fulfilling circularity.

The nuns' emphasis on listening therefore complicates assumptions about silence as oppressive, assumptions dependent on the idea that some speakers have definitional dominion or, discursively, that speech defines silence.[23] Foucault writes of Christians (at least in certain periods when confession is the primary compulsion) being 'reduced to silence'; then soundlessness is made conspicuous by collapse, a forever conceding-sand to the encroaching sea of speech.

Of course it has been immensely helpful to determine the relationship between discursive dominance, subaltern speech and ideologies of gender among others, and to indicate in which places for early modern women 'Silence, the closed mouth, is made a sign of chastity' (Stallybrass, 1986, 127).[24] Nuns were no less if differently oppressed by cultural expectations of femininity that took especially powerful form within a culture of cloistered celibacy. Catholic commentators indeed were able to draw on Marian themes to stress the immaculacy of enclosure's orifices. Because of this, and because we can readily recognise the areas where women were prohibited from speaking, both inside and outside the convents, we have been more inclined to study loose lips than porous ears, open in self-censoring ways to waves of celestially silent sound-bites. Nuns after all were adept at spiritually-strategic hearing (and at telling us they were).

Anne of the Ascension's notes on 'taciturnity' stress 'the first and princypall effect of silence is to be more willing to hier others speech then ourselues as more estiming thir thoughts and affections then our own' (*L1.6.J*, 1). For Teresa de Jesus listening, of all the senses, requires complete concentration to avoid contrapuntal confusion. We cannot pray and listen, she insists (*Way of Perfection*, II, 102). Hence, given that hearing even our own words is distracting, mental prayer is superior to vocal, and formless to mental, in inducing meditative poise preceding (or constituting) union (89).

For Teresa, to listen is to multi-task. She describes how the mind engages simultaneously in at least two modes. The Soul in Quiet is 'tyed-vp and bound,

---

[23]   'Silence itself – the things one declines to say, or is forbidden to name, the discretion that is required between different speakers – is less the absolute limit of discourse, the other side from which it is separated by a strict boundary, than an element that functions alongside the things said, with them and in relation to them within over-all strategies. There is no binary division to be made between what one says and what one does not say; we must try to determine the different ways of not saying such things, how those who can and those who cannot speak of them are distributed, which type of discourse is authorized, or which form of discretion is required in either case. There is not one but many silences, and they are an integral part of the strategies that underlie and permeate discourses' (Foucault, 1990).

[24]   See also Beilin, 1987; Hannay, 1985; Hull, 1982; Wiesner, 1983. For all the strength of Luckyj's 2002 account, moving beyond a logocentric binary emphasis, her main interest is in the relationship of silence to speech rather than to sound and it does not allow for the special sensory circumstance of mystics or for differentials between Catholic and Protestant quiet.

and yet in condition of enioying'; she is at once Martha and Mary, both active and contemplative. 'It is iust, as if we were speaking with some one; and that withal, at the self same time, some other person were speaking to vs' (*Flaming Hart*, 1642, 208). 'I only wish I could write with both hands, so as not to forget one thing while I am saying another' (*Way of Perfection*, II, 88).

This, then, is spiritual self-fashioning based on intensely directed listening. It requires utter concentration to arrive precisely not on the other side of silence but in a roar-less seism: the un-binary where sound is not.[25] Teresa's own similitudes for silence fail, as of course she planned; human language just is not up to the task of describing God because it seeks to shape the seamless. In Levinas' terms, the totalising power of their representational aesthetic 'introduces a new finality'. 'To disclose a thing is to clarify it by forms' (1969, 74), and hence to obfuscate, especially for writers seeking to account for aural formlessness: 'This wildernized solitarinesse of this Nothing, is that whereof the Bridegroome speaketh; *I will lead her into the Desart, and there I will speake to her heart*' (Benet of Canfield, 1646, 66). For contemplatives, quest for 'the Infinitenesse of this Nothing' becomes habitual, 'an ever-present disposedness' to Union's dissolution. Canfield, like Teresa, pursues a (pre)linguistic as well as extra-sensory path for the Soul, 'stripping her of all forms and Images ... enabling her to go naked and simplified to contemplate without helpe of formes' (49). Beasts, he says, bellow in the pasture: 'The Remedy wherof is to change each sensibility with Love naked and sequestered from all acquaintance with Sense ... Assuredly knowing God is not sensible, nor can bee comprehended by the Senses, but purely Spirit' (95).

This is a very different language (or non-speech) from that surrounding secular silence often conceived of as hiatus flanked by meaning or rendered significant because it is filled with thought.[26] The suggestion that in the absence of sound our other senses compensate similarly substitutes one kind of auditory aesthetic with another ('those who want one Sense, possess the others with greater Force and Vivacity' according to *The Spectator* in 1711: Cockayne, 2003, 502).[27]

This was one of the dilemmas revealed in a recent and engrossing attempt to convey contemplative quiet: Philip Groening's 2006 *Into Great Silence*, a documentary film showing the lives of Carthusian monks in the Grande Chartreuse of the remote French alps. Here filmic still is made intensely visible, as if surface itself is silence, centralised in ways that suggest that the other senses are at once

---

[25]   George Eliot's Dorothea Casaubon notes: 'If we had a keen vision and feeling of all ordinary life, it would be like hearing the grass grow and the squirrel's heart beat, and we should die of that roar which lies on the other side of silence' (*Middlemarch*, 1964 ed., 191).

[26]   The two-minute silence of the annual British Armistice Day, for example, is a pregnant pause 'paradoxically only understood in relation to a language ... a space filled by discourse' (Gregory, 1994, 225, 7).

[27]   Recent research suggests that while children born deaf are slower than hearing children to react to objects in their peripheral vision, adults who have been without hearing since birth react to objects in that field more quickly (Codina et al, 2010).

intensified and ancillary to sound's absence made present and primary. The lens' concentration on material detail – the texture of celery that becomes crunch and taste as we watch, the rough weave of cloth felt with our eye's finger, the rare sounds and the near-trace of them, the possibility that we heard the rasp of skin on paper, the cool drink of ice-cold water in a clear glass against a condensing window pane through which a snowy landscape stands quite still – are all rendered multi-sensual, our only (simply, wondrous) pleasures pressured by the absence of sound.

Silence here is naturalised as reified. For the monks, presumably it is implacably invisible, an habitual given, whereas for those watching the film it is an emphatic, exhaustingly detailed form-full presence: magnification replaces amplification. For the non-monastic audience this is a silence constructed out of, and temporarily displacing, our own experience; we know it for three hours in contrast to our life's hubbub, whereas for the monks silence is (we are led to suppose) more or less continuum. One monk referred to interlude as non-break: 'Once you accept the fact that when the bell rings, you just don't think about it, you just get up and go and do whatever the bell requires you to do, then every moment that you have is a pretty permanently present moment'. This stasis is not quite the 'timelessness' praised by Philip French's review (*The Observer*, 31 December 2006). We are, though, led to believe that contemplation is ever thus, that we can encounter an ancient past that is, if only for the moment, ours; we are put in touch with a purer temporality as with alpine air.

A similar claim was also made by *The Big Silence*, a BBC TV documentary in October 2010 featuring five secular volunteers who entered into silence at a monastic retreat. The Benedictine monk who organised the experiment said 'If you go back 200 years into a rural society, people would see being quiet as normal.'

There is, then, a relativity and context to silence (of course), a personal and a differential experience of it, even when the same silence is shared. There is also a history and spatiality that is not quite the same as geography (though that too has its effects; early modern nuns in Antwerp might not know the same silence as twenty-first-century monks in the French mountains, or English seculars of different or no faith in Sussex, even if they follow the same meditative schemes).

Groening's apparent visual equation of minimalism with silence likewise overlays our contemporary 'Scandinavian' aesthetic, suggesting sharp line is form-free. It is as if beauty's pared-down pleasure is not only a means to truth but truth itself. Yet simplicity is an art won at a price, requiring symmetry suggesting unheard harmony. Obliterating ugliness in order not to appreciate its need takes effort best spent on contemplative detachment from either or both. Teresa de Jesus' disclaimer of words and of time to write them is still a representational ethic that tries (even as she denies it) to delimit alterity, the Other who eludes and defines her spiritual essence. Groening's envisioning of silence gives it form as much as Teresa herself did; it is as if silence has a material contrast present by denial. For Teresa, it is in silence that spiritual union can ensue and be conveyed by only wordlessness. If I can describe it, says Teresa, it does not, did not, exist; likewise, if I can hear it, I am too aware of listening to know divine presence: silence like union simply is.

'full quires of voices and of musick'

The other 'notes and harmony' the nuns describe are celestial. Their accounts enable them to discuss 'off-stage' events, opening up an extra-auditory reality within their spiritual scheme. Some sounds presage imminent death and signify the arrival of the blessed in a heavenly realm (see above, p. 45 n. 49). Before Anne of the Ascension died

> many other prodigies declareing to the community her approaching decease, as a full quire of voices, singing these words of the offices *Vide Surbam Magnum*, at other times instruments of musick ... and at the Instant of her happy death, one of the Religious being only absent was awaked by a full quire of musick, and being very much afrighted, ran that moment to the Infirmary lamenting and saying 'Our Dear Mother is dead, and you did not call me, as you promised', as in effect it was ... (*A1*, 56)

In 1700 at Lierre remarkable sounds were reported during the funeral of Anne Teresa of Jesus:

> ... as the Corps waer sett before ye dead Celler dore ye Relegous singen ye Benedictus some 4 or 5 of our sisters heard very disstinckly severall from thence sing our Quier Tune with them. thay allso thought yt thay perfectly disstingues perticular voyces of our dead sisters. When the Cerimony was ended wee inquierd if ther waer noe singen in the Church Street or Turne. thay assuerd us ther was noe singen & our mayd prottested ther cam noe body to the Turne for she was ther all the time but a pooer old Women; but she heard as she thought singin out of the ded Celler. so wee may piousely beleiue our deseased sisters her Compnyons sung to wellcome her ... (*L13.7*, 210–11).

As when the intact corpses are said to exactly resemble the deceased nun in life, identification of 'perticular voyces' serves to authenticate the event, makes a singularity natural by placing it in the domestic place in which the nuns lived and died. Spaces are thus sanctified, continuous, sensorarily endorsed as blessed.

The nuns recorded that such sounds, unlike those within and of rapture, were 'distinctly heard with their corporall eares' (*A1*, 285). They testify assertively, several times with the adjective 'distinctly' (as when a silver-sounding bell was heard to strike at the Virgin's feet, marking the successful exorcism of the Mostyn sisters: p. 83).[28] Margaret of Jesus claimed to be 'certaine' the Virgin was present, 'I hear many times her uoice' (*L3.31*, 37). This confidence is in stark contrast to her confusion when the devil was said to have preached to her as Christ crucified, to have rung the doorbell and to have called to her from the other side of the turn, invisible in the voice of Edmund Bedingfield (p. 83 n. 38). Given beliefs about the power of hearing to penetrate the heart (for Teresa de Jesus a sermon was a direct means to commune with God) it is no wonder she was in such a state of sensory consternation. And given the ways in which sounds echo source – at best, when Teresa de Jesus during her heart-piercing rapture was forced to utter groans, 'deare, delightfull kinds of entercourse' (*Flaming Hart*, 1642, 420); at worst when the women were reduced to making moans and cries – it is not surprising that the nuns were confounded when even celestial-seeming sounds proved to be untrustworthy.

---

[28]   Teresa de Jesus noted that genuine locutions are 'so clear that, even if it consists of a long exhortation, the hearer notices the omission of a single syllable ... in locutions which are created fancifully by the imagination the voice will be less clear and the words less distinct' (*Interior Castle*, II, 284).

Chapter 6
Of Smell and Space: 'Evaporating Subjects'[1]

On the first profession day after the death of Margaret of Jesus Mostyn, on the feast day of St Clare, 12 August 1680, at the beginning of the first vespers (very precise details these)

> there came out of ye dead cellar, wch is all ways massen'd up, a strong and pleasing perfume, wch not only filled ye whole cellar, but ye Quiere and paents allso, and so contincoued tell ye seond vesparis was sayd, and it was smelt by ye whole comunity, who ware all transported wth joye, and found them selfs a particular deuotion, not visall haueing neuer experienced ye licke, it being much different from yt wch some times, wee are acustomed to smell, wch wee call our Bd Mothers St Teresa smell, or yt of liles and roses, wch when our deare mother was a liue would very often be about her parsone, perticularly in ye chapter, or att prayer, and most comanly, when she treated of heauenly matters, wch gaue a great adiscion and power to her words and made them haue so great, an influence ouer our harts yt sometimes, thay would euen melt wth deuotion; but this kind of sweets, ware neuer before smelt by all ingenarall, only 2 or 3 sisters att a time, or but one and yt for a short time, whereas this lasted so long, and all ye house ware pertackars of it, & it semed to be somthing lick a hott burning perfume, and allso wee fancied, there came as it war, a smoke out of ye chincks of the dore, perticularly from yt side, wher our deare mothers body lyes, it was so strong and sweet, yt it euen remined us and comfort all yt war present, and wee was all lick filled wth it, wth in us, tho not ungratfull, as other parfumes, are wn in excesse; wee injoyed ye same fauour, one her Anaversary day, and very offten, and in seuerall places, some of them not very sweet of themselves, as ye kichin wash house and other placese, but it continews not so long, and most times, all doth not smelel it, but those yt doth, it moues to great devotion wch makes us hope yt our dear Mother according to her promese, remaines wth us, and will assist and helpe her poore chillderne in this banishment tell she bring us to injoye, Eternall Glory wth her, wch our Lord Jesus Christ of her mercie grant us. Amen. (*L13.7*, 98–9)

So concludes the Lierre annals Life of the nun who was by now already considered to be blessed. This is in many ways a remarkable smell: it emerges from the masoned-up crypt, is enduringly experienced by the whole community

---

[1]   The subtitle is taken from an essay by Letizia Schmid (1996), discussed below, note 4.

not just briefly by one or two of their number; it reminds the nuns of Margaret in her lifetime, of that smell she had about her when piously engaged that made them melt with devotion; it emanates like smoke (suggestive of misty visuality) as it were through chinks in the door; like a hot burning perfume (but not excessive like some) it fills the convent, displacing less-sweet odours, penetrating to the kitchen, the wash-house, other places 'some of them not very sweet of themselves'.[2] Most of all, since the nuns smelling this odour distinguish its 'perticular' qualities, it recalls, even in its difference, the scent of lilies and roses: that of Teresa de Jesus herself. The community is sensorily united: the smell is taken 'within' them. The women are moved and made one in their aspirations, drawn together (four references to 'us' in the final phrases) in the concluding crescendo of the piece: Amen.

Smell is an especially intimate sense. Like Taste it involves taking a substance inside the body; all the community are 'partakers'. Compared to food which is macerated and dissolved, it is the recipients of smell who 'even melt' with devotion. Like so many of the wonderful and 'odiferous' sweet smells experienced by the nuns, this particular experience is related to remembrance.[3] It seems to dissolve boundaries, bearing out wider philosophical claims about the sense which, again like Taste, 'blur[s] the separability of the subject and object' (Borthwick, 2000, 129). This, though, is more complicated than ideas of Derridean dissolution in which inhalation of scent merges the object-odour with the subject.[4] This smell seeps through walls, doors and is shared simultaneously, then over time: our dear Mother, they muse (and it is significant that they do not differentiate between Teresa de Jesus and Margaret in this role), remains with us as she gave her word she would. Sensory memory and immediate experience combine, bearing out a past contractual pledge that is enacted indefinitely in the present. The living

---

[2]   This presumably refers to latrines which the papers show coyness about directly naming. Sometimes they are referred to as 'a more contemptible place' (*L3.13*, 74). On the Poor Clares digging latrines in Gravelines, see Hallett, 2012a, 337 in which the chronicler refers to 'little houses' and 'noysome' smells. The reference to the marvellous odour at Lierre is discussed briefly in Hallett, 2011, with reference to notions of exile.

[3]   Margaret Teresa of the Immaculate Conception (Margaret Mostyn: 1657/59–1745), a niece of the Mostyn sisters, experienced a sweet smell around her while in bed after her clothing ceremony (in March 1694), 'yt the memory of it remain'd all her life'; she commemorated the anniversary annually (*L13.7*, 281).

[4]   Letizia Schmid's essay, from which the subtitle of this chapter is taken, suggests: 'Olfaction highlights the violent fragility of our identity as the space between "I" and "you/me" and "other" is subverted. There is no fixed subjectivity for the other odor is never other as it is always within me ...'; '*I smell lavender* not only signifies myself as an "I" and the lavender smell as an object but also marks the instant I am the lavender smell (and it is me) therefore blurring subject-object distinctions. Paradoxically, our identities are simultaneously confirmed and undermined, fixed subjects that are continually evaporating' (1996, 116). On ideas of 'violence' in Derrida's aporetic ethics, in contrast to Levinas' ethical refusal to totalise and reduce 'the other to the same', see Zlomistic, 2007, 68.

subjects and the inhaled object-dead share the same space now, in the remembered past, and in a utopic future. Moreover, by linking the smell of one dead nun with another, the two (or more) deceased are merged in sensory memory and gain mutual benefit by association, bringing credit also to the aspirant community.

This is more than a ritualised sociality brought about by the burning of incense, for example, which creates an 'intersubjective we-feeling' (Howes, 1991, 134); it is also more than internalising the divine, although it is both of these things too. Here the subject essence (two nuns) is fragmented before inhalation, experienced as one smell, then split as they come together mutually resembling 'in several places'; separated again between individual inhalation and the identification of the origin of the smell, then by a group re-garnering of significance. This is a sequential obliteration of individual identity: of the nuns whose scents resemble each other; of the separate subjects smelling them. Paradoxically, of course, this literary gathering of individual sensibility into collective cognition is itself identity; the description of seemingly personal sensory experience is integral to a communal repertoire of recognition of both oneself and of others come together. The vocabulary to describe the perfume exists before the experience itself so that what appears to be a spontaneous, pre-rational response, linked indelibly to non-subjective memory, for the nuns is a finely attenuated recollection.

Because of their temporal preoccupation (with the contemplative present, in anticipation of an historical and celestial return from national and earthly banishment) the nuns' *experience* of smell though I described its process as sequential, is emphatically non-linear; smell transports them in several simultaneous directions, all of them with one goal in mind. In addition, long-standing claims for a direct link between olfactory stimulus and the limbic brain (the view that smell most of all the senses stirs memory) are complicated by a discipline that holds firm control of mnemonic systems. What appears like impulse is therefore textually, if not personally at source, reconfigured to recognisably orthodox and Carmelite expressive modes: the smell of one dead daughter of Teresa recalls the absent-present Mother of the Order. Moreover, the smell of both women recalls that of the Virgin herself who reassured Margaret in her lifetime by her perfumed presence that she was under her protection: 'the signe was a most odoriforous sweett smelt somewhat like Lillys, with which she was recreated telling her yt Sister Ursula in confirmation yt all was true, should acknowledge afterwards to haue smelt the same smel at the same time ... And this sweet smel continued with them by fitts for many dayes after, the Mother [Prioress] once her selfe participating of it in their presence' (*L3.31*, 74).[5]

Description of a spiritual-sensory sociality (the shared experience of smell) in a Carmelite context thus offers additional dimensions to claims about the nature of

---

[5]   A second Life of Margaret of Jesus, quoting her own words, also refers to the nun's awareness of 'an extremely sweet smell' accompanying the Virgin who dictated what she should write: 'Often time, as I haue said, whilest I am awriting I see our Blessed Lady and haue her sweet smell' (*L3.27*, 49–50).

olfactory cognition. Secular philosophers necessarily have conceptualised smell from a human point of view. Teresian theologians conversely imagine the world through the divine senses (even when they deny their existence): we should, wrote Teresa, show gratitude to God 'for enduring our foul odour' (*Way of Perfection*, II, 95). If we, like she, imaginatively (audaciously) assume a near-transcendent position, as mystics do when they empathise with the divine, then we observe that the object (the human) on whom holy perfume falls does not remain intact when she comes in contact with the benignly-scrutinising holy subject; she liquefies in union or she is no mystic. Even from a human point of view, given the nuns' interpretative values, smell is crucial to conceptualising its source; for the religious, it gives access to a particular kind of 'objective' knowledge, one testified to by several witnesses at once.

If, in terms of Derridean sensory philosophy, metaphor has raised 'the senses from the sensible to the intelligible' (Borthwick, 2000, 128), then it does not adequately account for those for whom similitude is unsympathetic to their quest, for whom language itself has failed. For them object-subject relations are bound to be more complicated and predicated on peaceful rather than violent submission.

The nuns' papers make evident the importance of Smell to their aesthetic and to their experience of the convent as a lived environment. They linguistically associate Smell with Taste, whether because the two are literally linked via nasal passages and palate[6] or simply adjectivally (though the latter is seldom accidental). 'Sweet' is the most common and very frequently used word for pleasing experience in the Lierre annals, for example, whether for sounds, scents, sights or tastes; 'not very sweet' the opposite. While some sensory responses are accounted for as visceral and reflex, descriptions of them are ideologically led, almost always related to values held by the defining power; never neutral or pre-social.

Likewise, modes of memorialising convey conceptual values as well as purely recollected states. Another account of the anniversary smell of Margaret of Jesus likens the scent specifically to the Teresian model, referring to 'a Spanish perfume, which we call our Bd Mother St Thereses smell' (*L3.30.G*, 6). English faith is thus linked with the celestial un-foreign which is literally internalised. This mnemonic-tactile claim also echoes Francisco de Ribera's recollection of the body of Teresa de Jesus which transferred its smell to his hands where, however much he washed, it 'continued ... for a fortnight', a long-lasting sensation experienced too by a nun in Teresa's own convent who had lost her sense of smell until she kissed the dead woman's feet, the scent remaining 'in her Nose' (p. 103). Mary Margaret of the Angels' odour similarly lingered on those who came in contact with her intact body. It too reminded the religious of venerated predecessors (p. 118). Such observations complicate Alain Corbin's claim that since smells are ephemeral they 'defy comparisons through memory' (1986, 7). Somatic sensory chains, not all of

---

[6]   'Whatsoeuer agreeth with the *Taste*, agreeth with the *Sent*, but whatsoeuer hath a good sauour, hath not presently a good *Taste*. *Smelling and Tast are ioyned together, the one to helpe the other*' (Nixon, 1612, 25–6).

them physical, also raise interesting questions about where bodies begin and end, if they are sensed beyond the contours of their skin, inside that of the partaking recipient who recalls another non-present body so that both are transported to the here-and-now. In such cases extra-sensory materiality is imitative and literal, drawing in and on another's substance; a body begins presencing in the form of an absent Other, in a state that is not precisely physical.[7] The self is transmutable and borders may indeed be friable.

The transitory Carmelite thus inhabits the 'beyond' of an extended Other self, one which is defined by sameness (or association even through denial) within a community of non-individuated subjectivity. Accounts of such sensory schemes reveal the nuns' imperative to divest themselves of determining power (male Carmelite authority), to inhabit 'the phantasmic space of possession' (Bhabha, 1994, 44). When the women through their sensory descriptions (particularly of Smell and Touch) assert their rights to occupy a stable, infinitely repeatable, extra-bodily location, they make a claim to be the true upholders of an unchanging, unchallengeable and female tradition, and they reveal facets of a post-colonised identity where 'to exist is to be called into being in relation to an otherness'. In this 'the very place of identification is a space of splitting' and always requires 'the transformation of the subject in assuming the image' (44). In other words, the Antwerp and Lierre Carmelites engage in a complex transformation process whereby their bodily states, at times their personal memories, are reconfigured to reflect the iconised Teresian template. The early modern religious is transformed by the chronicling nun (and eventually because of her exposure to such material she comes to do this for herself in her own personal narrative) to replicate Teresian typologies that justify a line of semi-opaque saintliness to secure the contemporary reputation of the female Order.

Such a process challenges secularised constructions of Time and Space. At the moment of invocation of the body of Teresa de Jesus (or of its sensory trace) as a descriptive comparator, it is translated to the here-and-now, and makes the sensing nun's body itself translate to the eternal sphere by association. The two bodies co-exist rather than have a sequential relationship, and they do so in the sensory presence of the living nun who detects their lingering smells. If identification is a place of splitting it is, then, a fracture into identical parts. This has spatial ramifications since the heavenly and earthly selves combine; and the Carmelite body corporate is given eternal status by proximity.

Paradoxically, fortuitously, such a process may counteract the seemingly inevitable condition of female autobiographical testimony. By establishing a process of choral avowal, the nuns construct a singularity that resists fragmentation, perhaps thereby defying Rita Felski's claim concerning a dissipated female self-hood where 'the act of Confession cannot uncover a miraculously intact female subject' (1998, 91). The nuns' narrative process of reiteration, designed to

---

[7]　'A boundary is not that at which something stops but ... from which *something begins its presencing*' (Heidegger, quoted by Bhabha 1994, 1).

orchestrate somatic and textual resemblances, seeks to dispel a tradition (and an alleged link of women with sensory dependence) that otherwise disperses female subjective power.

Early modern Carmelite identity revealed in these papers is not, then, determined by either sensory or literary originality. If the self mimics its own previous self in order to be coherent, it also mimics an Other who is at the heart of typological and imitative practice. Sensory history like '[t]he history of the afterlife is thus a social history, dealing with relationships between one group and the other' (Clark, 2007, 205). When the scented trace is itself ethereal, then sensory and social histories come together in challenging ways.[8] Experience of smell, like that of ghosts, extends the temporality of the convent in extra-dimensional ways: past and present meet just as the living nun meets a dead one on the steps to the dead-cellar; in the case of the perfume of Margaret of Jesus, there is also a whiff of imagined future. On the one hand, then, there is an emphatic repetition of wonder at temporal and spatial coincidence (events happening on anniversaries, women dying in the same chair as others had, nuns meeting ghostly sisters in their own familiar spaces) and on the other a dislocation, afforded by sensory stimulation. For those in exile, this experience of 'uncanny' is especially poignant, indeed runs counter to the usual direction of *unheimlich* since through it they 'home'. They are reaffirmed in their relationship with space in which the everyday and the marvellous co-habit, assimilating the other-worldly into their explanation of earthly existence, and *vice versa*; they are temporarily transported only to return to their own replenished environment.

Extra-sensory experience also extends the convent space therefore and affects the relationship of those within it (to each other and to the location). Scents are incorporated by those who breathe its air so individuals become the space they inhabit and it them. Sensory experience is quasi-sacramental and here specifically Carmelite. Whereas liturgical use of incense marks a literal closeness to the body of Christ, this arrival of odour, spontaneously and in the absence of ritual re-enactment, marks a continual presence of which the nuns are reminded on important occasions. It becomes a way of remembering and a means to recall, physically inscribing the process, the effect and the significance. The whole space, even its most domestic corners, becomes sacred.

In an effort to re-establish olfactory history, said to have been much neglected in analysis of medieval and early modern culture dominated by an interest in sight (a neglect often attributed to the influence of Freud),[9] Holly Dugan

---

[8]   'For ghosts to *be* ghosts, they must be correctly identified, not just as persons but as phenomena' (Clark, 2007, 204). It follows that supernatural smell (or other senses) needs to be identified not only as an experience but as significant and as emanating from a particular extra-bodily source.

[9]   Freud's *Civilisation and Its Discontents* (1929) argues that olfactory sensitivity is archaic, a sign of fixation on anal sexuality. Freud therefore claims there is a direct relationship between the development of 'civilization' and the eradication of smell (see

discusses 'the politics of smell' in theatrical performance identifying, among others, the 'odiferous' liturgical and civic dramatisation of *Mary Magdalene*. The Magdalene's emblem, her scented oil, she suggests, 'works as a hinge' between the two aspects of her legend, central to her transformation from prostitute to saint in which an audience could participate through scent (2008, 235; 2011, 36–41). For our illustrative purposes, the figure of Mary Magdalen of Jesus with her delicate susceptibilities does something similar, mediating between an earthly and a devotional sensibility.[10] It is tempting to think her professional name may have been chosen for its iconographic connotations since we are told that before entering the convent 'ye handsome Mrs Leuession' was admired both for her virtue and her beauty: 'as other Ladys ware wont in those times to carre glasses of essence about them, she carred one of holy watter to wch she euer had a great reuerence & devotion' (*L13.7*, 152).[11] This special sign of grace is the more remarkable since 'she had a great contrary in ill smelles, or any durty fowle things. Yet by her good will she would haue done all ye meanest druggery of ye house ... & when she had fowle pottes to empty or any thing to doe yt was desgustfull or lothsome as will offten happen amongest sicke [when she was Infirmarian] she was so officeius & deligent in all such accations & semed in her kindome' (155).

The nuns' experience of smell (or rather how they account for it) links their constantly-convergent sensory-spiritual worlds. It also provides a structure to the ensuing discussion, of earthly and of celestial smells.

Jenner, 2000, 129). See also Corbin, 1986 who suggests that olfactory sensations are not related to intelligence and are considered relatively useless to a 'civilized society' (6). Annick Le Guerer notes much earlier philosophical roots for suspicion of Smell, in Augustine's question 'Are you not ashamed to believe that the nose is a means to find God?', and in the claims of Aristotle and Plato that Smell is less pure, less noble, than Sight or Hearing (2002, 4).

[10]   She was indeed reported to be especially sensitive in all respects: 'she loued to be spokeng sweetly tow, & not contradicted ... She was also very dellicate & nise in her dyet, both for ye goodnes & clenlynes of it (*L13.7*, 154; see above, pp. 53 n. 70, 133).

[11]   On the use of portable perfume, see Dugan, 2011, 111. The nuns clearly later followed advice like that outlined by Brathwaite, to focus on the smell of the Saviour's ornaments rather than worldly perfume. He cites the example of Democritus who was sustained for nine days only by the smell of hot bread, pledging 'Let the Courtier *smell* of perfumes, the sleeke-fac'd Lady of her paintings, I will follow the *smell* of my Sauiours ointments ... my *Taste,* shall be to taste how sweet the Lord is; my *Touch* the apprehension of his loue; my *sight,* the contemplation of his glory; my *eare,* to accent his praise; my *smell,* to repose in the faire and pleasant pastures of his word' (1620, 59–60). Teresa de Jesus noted her own love of perfume as a young woman (p. 101), later reflecting that when she smelt any beautiful scent in religion she no longer preferred it since it was so removed from her now normal experience (*Spiritual Relations*, I, 309).

Nuns' Noses as 'instruments of vigilance'[12]

The women note everyday odours and echo early modern views that link good air with health and associate foul smell with contagion. Not surprisingly, given views of belching and of farting in polite society, and despite medical views that health required lost equilibrium to be restored by this gaseous transfer of air between inside and out, the nuns do not report either the sound or smells of such effusions. Nor, more oddly, do they mention the smell of food.[13] They do associate clean atmosphere with well-being, mentioning those whom Antwerp's climate does not suit: the Lierre annals record 'there came a religous wth us from Anwarp, to trye if ye chang of ayre, could recouer her, being fare gon in a consumcion' (*L13.7*, 113). A priest, Father Cary, was 'so indisposed' wrote Margaret of Jesus in a letter of 1677, 'I am much afraid the air of Antwerp does not agree with him' (*L3.38G*; Hallett, 2007b, 170). A few months later she reported that Edmund Bedingfield had taken the spa waters to restore his health, lamenting too the lack of 'good meat' in Lierre. The women are conversant, then, with the main precepts of healthy living.[14]

The Italian convent physician Bernadino Ramazzini (1633–1714) in his study of occupational disease and the hazards of certain employments (including that of religion), advised grave-diggers to carry cotton-wool impregnated with vinegar, noting that women who lived near candle-makers stalls complained of 'hysterical passions because of the bad odor' (*De Morbis Artificum*, 64, 180; cited Corbin, 1986). Women, and especially their wombs, were held to be especially prone to the effect of odours (Jenner, 2000, 132).

The Carmelites record the use of vinegar to ward off illness or to revitalise, its effects working either through the skin or nose. As a child, Catherine Burton's body was rubbed with vinegar in the places from which blistering plasters had been removed, an experience described as martyrdom with probably good reason (p. 116). Burton also mentions smelling salts. The dying Anne of the Ascension

---

[12]   Alain Corbin refers to 'the sense of smell as an instrument of vigilance' (1986, 7).

[13]   On the idea that the smell of food alone could provide nourishment, see Palmer, 1993, 63, and note 11, above.

[14]   Clear air was said by Robert Burton to alleviate the effects of melancholy (1621, Part 2, 66). The nuns of the Blessed Institute of the Virgin Mary, founded by Mary Ward (1585–1645) showed similar awareness. During the siege of York in 1644 they returned to their former habitation at Hewarth on the outskirts of the city to find it in 'an ill condition', the lead off the roof, iron gone from the windows and doors, 'full of stinck and vermine'; 'In the garden they had buryed divers of their Soldiers, the whole ayre so infected as in the whole Village there was not three well ... .' Nonetheless, Mary Ward was contented, 'satisfyed as if all senses had found their satisfaction ...' (2008 ed., 71). Mark Jenner notes that in 1631 in the same city the mayor and aldermen recommended the use of sponges soaked in camphor or vinegar to ward of plague's infection, ordering the perfuming of affected houses with rosemary and other fumigants (2000, 132). Nuns at St Monica's in Louvain used pitch to eradicate foul smells.

was revived by being given vinegar to smell at which she expressed 'both grief and displeasure' (Hardman, 1936, 169). Burning perfume was used in the convent sick-room: when Anne of the Ascension, against the advice of the community, visited nuns who were suffering from small-pox, the Infirmarian recorded that several nuns 'ismelt a uery strong sweet smel: thinking it had ben sum raer parfuem which I had burnt in the roem' (*L1.5.D*, 1). This suggests that 'aromatherapy' was a common practice to disperse unpleasant odour, to ward off contagion, raise the spirits and also perhaps to induce drowsiness.[15] Given the stench of the sickroom, the use of perfume was understandable; the nuns record the smell of foul linens, of razed and burning bone, of putrefaction. When Mary Margaret of St Peter (Petronilla van Myel: 1737–76) was ill, the 'disagreeable smell' (attributed to drawing out her humours by blistering and by her general condition) was such that in order to mask it the nuns put roses in her bed (*L13.7*, 319).

Smell is also mentioned in a diagnostic context, though often imprecisely, marking change of condition rather than cause and often linking it to miracle rather than to chemistry.[16] During the months before she died, for example, the nuns remarked on a persistent odour around Mary of St Joseph, the recycling seamstress (pp. 92 n. 18, 93, 152):

> euen the whole community, for halfe a year before she died, as often as they came near unto her, smelt a strong sweet smell like Musk, but rather more agreable, this they also perceiued as sensibly during the time of her last sickness; All she wore in the same half year sauoured of the same smell, two or three times after her death it was perceiued to proceed from her seat in the quire. a full year also after her happy departure, there was found a cap of Hers about the House, which she had worn, and which being by accident put by and misplaced without being washed with the rest of her Linnen, this very cap smelt most sweetly and strongly of the same smell ... (*L13.7*, 241)

---

[15] On the medical use of aroma as narcotic, see Camporesi, 1988, 24. As ever, the nuns' denial of human cause (burning oil or using preserving balsam in embalming) provides insight into normal practices. Robert Burton suggests producing 'artificial air', making it hot and moist by seasoning it with perfume, proposing the smoke of juniper for melancholic people (1621, Part 2, 66). Francis de Sales notes 'The sweet smell of the Mandragora taken farre off, and but for a short time, is most pleasant: but they that smell to it very neare and a long time, become altogether drowsie, faint, and languishing ...' (1616, 345). *The Accomplished Ladies Rich Closet*, which gives 'modest instructions' for making musk-balls to lay in clothing and perfumes and for removing ill-scent from the nostrils ('Snuff up or inject with a Sirringe, White wine, wherein Ginger, Cloves and Calamine have been boiled, and provoke your self to sneeze with the Powder of *Piritum* ...') also gives advice on burning perfume 'against Infectious Air' including spices such as cinnamon, nutmeg and bay-leaves as well as amber-grease, rose-water and civet (1687, 52, 60, 63–5).

[16] A nun who had lost her sense of smell and was 'exceeding sad' had it restored when she kissed the body of Teresa de Jesus (p. 164). Interestingly the loss of this sensation is associated with melancholy by Robert Burton and by others.

Probably the most vivid account of the physical ill-effects of inhalation appears in the unfortunate death of Teresa Joseph Maria of the Heart of Jesus (Catherine Howard: 1722–75):

> her last sickness & death was occasiond by an accident from the fumes of sulpher, going on ascension Eve into the garden, with a chasing dish in one hand and brimstone in the other she threw the sulpher on ye hot coles under a tree to destroy by the fume the catterpillers which were that year in great abudance, and altho she used this dangerous experiment with precausion, the smoke enterd her mouth & fill upon her breast; of which tho in that moment she did not find any bad effect, nor thought she any more of it till a shortness of breath & faintings insued, for which no cause could be assignd; she then reflected on the sulpher; her sufferings were terible, the Doctors declared, that her stomack was drawn & shrivelld up, like a peece of parchment curled by the fire ... (*A2*, 307–8)

Other catastrophes are also attributed to air-infection. Given the nuns' medical knowledge, and given their description of the state of the convent dead-cellar with its 'slimy, wet' remains, it is surprising that Frances of St Ignatius (Margaret Downs: 1598–1650) did not follow health and safety protocols like those suggested by Ramazzini for workers in graveyards: 'she was one day particularly inspired to make very clean & put in order ye Cellars and especially the dead Cellar saying perhaps it may be for my self ... she immediately was seased with and violent feaver wch rendered her uncapable of any thing ...' (*A1*, 206).

A witness to the discovery of the intact body of Mary Margaret of the Angels in 1716 noted the conditions of the Antwerp dead-cellar as windowless, damp and moist all year round, flooding when it rained heavily: 'From the total absence of ventilation the air was so foul and heavy that its inhalation for any length of time was dangerous to health' (Hardman, 1939, 148). It is possible of course, that Sister Frances' excursion was timed on a day when there was unexpectedly no unpleasantness there, a sure sign of impending miracle. When three preserved bodies were found in 1727 at Newburgh, for instance, an account in the Antwerp annals records that Carmelite friars, an apothecary and surgeon attested that there was no smell whatsoever from the bodies, so they judged this to be the work of God (*A1*, 309).

Indeed, a lack of smell is often interpreted as a sign of divine intervention in natural process. After the death of Mary Xaveria, notwithstanding accounts of her harrowing deathbed suffering from gangrene so she 'began to corrupt before she was dead, yet there was not ye least offensive smell when her coffin was thus opened' (*A3*, 444). Similarly, at Lierre around two and a half years after the death of Margaret of Jesus (so 18 or so months after the miraculous smell permeated the convent) the dead-cellar was opened after a flood. The nuns expected the foul water to bring 'an unsauery smaell, and cause much filth; but on ye contrary, when it was opened, it rather smealt sweet, and wholsome, and not ye least corruption in it', a fact sworn to by 'seuearall parsons of quality' including Margaret's brother,

Edward Mostyn who was at that time visiting the convent *(L13.7*, 97). As in other similar cases, an absence of expected sensory proof signals an extra-sensory knowledge.

In contrast to independently witnessed supernatural experiences of sight, smell is often shared and many witnesses come forward to attest to its nature. When Mary Margaret of the Angels' body was found, 'spicy perfume' suddenly filled the room after an English priest put his hand into the incision left by surgeons. Several seculars 'cried out that they had never in all their lives smelt anything so delicious'. The chaplain of the English Carmelites at Hoogstraet also smelt it, but Percy Plowden, the Antwerp spiritual director, did not, concluding this was a sign of his own unworthiness (Hardman, 1939, 159). The witnesses stress that the body had not been balsamically embalmed. The pleasing perfume extended to the dust from the coffin (kept back for medicinal use: p. 110 n. 64) which was not, like that which had not been in contact, earthy and musty.

Putrefaction was well understood in the early modern period, and of course the nuns themselves witnessed and gorily described its results when they uncover 'rotten moist bones' in their searches for uncorrupted bodies in the convent crypt. They knew for themselves the effects of theories expounded by Johann Becher (1635–82) who rather fetchingly described decomposition as continual internal movement that was in conflict with cohesion of the parts, identifying the stages of decay through the progress of smells (Corbin, 1986, 16–19).[17]

Given the frequent reality of death in the convent, with its odour 'the most tangible perception of entropy, of that inexorable and irreversible loss of energy released by a decomposing body in the form of a gas' (Barbara and Perliss, 2006, 25), it is understandable that the nuns attribute their experience of sweet smells in the corpse's proximity to miraculous portent. Such odours are both edifying invasive (a form of nasal cannibalism if, as the nuns accepted, smells carry quantities as well as qualities of the substance they came from) and activate cognition by direct route to the brain.[18] For all sorts of reasons, then, it is little wonder that smell had (or was said to have had) dramatic effects: perhaps because those who experienced it believed it would; because the smells the nuns encountered were startlingly, humanly intimate; and because they sparked off an understanding of spaces beyond their immediate environment.

---

[17]　Corbin also mentions the work of Marie-Genevieve Charlotte Thiroux d'Arconville (1720–1805). Her experiments on the preservation of meat led her to observations about the decomposition of 300 substances, contained in a lengthy study of the subject published in 1766. Corbin rather marvellously notes that 'confined to the virtuous life by the stigmata of smallpox, she seems to have found compensation in the pleasure derived from science' (1986, 19).

[18]　Galen concluded that the organ of smell was not the nose but the brain, with odours passing through the nasal passages via olfactory projections to the brain itself: 'In smell alone the brain was the primary organ of perception' (Palmer, 1993, 63, who gives an account of the ideas of Galen, Vesalius and the seventeenth-century Conrad Victor Schneider).

Invisible Architecture

In their book of that title, Barbara and Perliss suggest that we experience places through our sense of smell, that 'odors are not only profoundly inherent components of place, but at times are actually essential to defining them' (2006, 13). The materials used to create the space, they suggest, infuse it, along with the activities occurring there over time, influenced by orientation, humidity, saturation, timing and the nature of the odours themselves (14).[19] If we think of the domestic as well as sacred uses made of convent space, then we might envisage a rich conglomeration of odours. Experience of these might be partly different for Lay Sisters and choir nuns, depending on their duties or which parts of the building they frequented: scents of food, of cooking and processing of beer, of yeast, cheese, butter, vegetable matter; of washrooms, kitchens and latrines; menstruation; sweat; dust; floor-coverings; mops; bedclothes; wet wool, dry wool; incense; candles; smoke, some of it from outside the convent boundaries; smells carried in by visitors and servants bringing foods and going to and from the markets; from the nearby river; from the sickroom and the crypt.

Bodily smells thus cohabit with celestial essences. Odours that are considered to be miraculous affect not only the experience of smell itself therefore, they also disrupt the spatial components and understanding of the building as a structure which is reconfigured as well as formed by odour. The fixedness of enclosure is accordingly rendered much more fluid than the building form might signify. New smells might temporarily dislocate the nun who smelt them, but she soon assimilated them into her understanding of her environment. Smells might, then, intrude, transport, alarm – as when the Lierre nuns found themselves caught in a whirlwind amidst 'a horred stinck of gunpouder and brimston, yt all thought thay should haue bine choked' (*L13.7*, 54) – but in the end they are understood within the nuns' normalised sensory-supernatural scheme.

Teresian accounts of Smell naturally inform Carmelite experience and understanding of *clausura*. For Teresa de Jesus, of all the senses this one had the literal and accordingly the metaphorical capacity to dissolve boundaries between body, mind and soul. 'The breasts are better than wine, for they give off fragrance of sweet odours', the text from the Song of Songs 1:2 on which she bases her exegesis in Chapter 4 of *Conceptions of the Love of God*. She explores the ways in which the Soul 'feels within itself such great sweetness' of God's presence: 'Both the inward and the outward man seem to receive comfort, just as if into the marrow of the bones had been poured the sweetest of ointments, resembling a fragrant perfume, or as if we had suddenly entered a room where there was a perfume coming not from one place, but from many, so that we cannot tell what or where the perfume is, we only know that it pervades our whole being' (II, 383).

---

[19]   Mark Jenner also notes that 'olfactory quality of airs was a standard feature of topographical description' (2000, 131).

In *Interior Castle*, her most spatially metaphorical treatise, Teresa describes the 'dilation or enlargement' of the Soul in which between Mansions or progressive states 'there is no closed door' (II, 244, 287). She repeats such images throughout her work, drawing on the *Canticles*: 'there is nothing to hinder the soul and her Spouse from remaining alone together, when the soul desires to enter within herself, to shut the door behind her so as to keep out all that is worldly and to dwell in that Paradise with her God' (*Way of Perfection*, II, 120). Her nuns in their convents are seeking to create a literal and emblematic 'Heaven upon earth' (*Interior Castle*, II, 248), and by repeatedly emphasising the material presence of blessed predecessors in the Antwerp and Lierre communities they stress the sensory continuities that bind together their own paradisal spaces. The reality (or at least the community history which the chroniclers chart) and the simile combine in their descriptions of interiority modelled on Teresian homiletic imagery. The convent, their continued body, is thus a space in which they can enact spiritual union.

Teresa de Jesus described by way of comparison the house of the Duchess of Alba where she was obliged to stay during one of her pastoral journeys, entering a *camarín*, the private apartment, the whole impression of which is like 'the empyrean Heaven which we must have in the depths of our souls' (*Interior Castle*, II, 289). Probably her most memorable image is that of the ugly-made-beautiful silk-worm which gradually weaves a cocoon 'to build the house in which it is going to die', by analogy the Prayer of Union (253–5). This state of active suspension in which one withdraws from sensory occupation she elsewhere compares to a hive: the bees entering to make honey, 'and all without any effort of ours' (*Way of Perfection*, II, 116). Sweetness, then, fills the spaces, secures them as sanctified within a free enclosure.

Such dilative imagery counters the nuns' lived experience of confinement, enabling an imaginative expansion for those who claimed to feel 'opprest' or 'immortified' by the small spaces in which they now lived (p. 19). Their sensory re-habituation, incorporating non-worldly perceptions, might offer some solace for those used to earthly before interior mansions.

It is clear that early modern Carmelites conceptually accommodate many spaces within their understanding, overlaying them by sensory as well as spiritual practice. Notwithstanding their perpetual poise, they are open to the unexpected, unwonted arrival of grace, accommodating it readily to their own interior. 'Quite unexpectedly', Teresa wrote, the soul even in vocal prayer and not thinking of interior things, seems 'to catch fire': 'It is as though there suddenly assailed it a fragrance so powerful that it diffused itself through all the senses or something of that kind (I do not say it is a fragrance; I merely make the comparison) ... ' (*Interior Castle*, II, 278)

Chapter 7

Eagle-eyed Nuns: Envisioning Vision in Contemplative Communities

our Rd Mother with her eagell esey did preudentye diue into the depth of thoe suttell and paruers intentions. (*L1.5.H*)[1]

This statement about Anne of the Ascension's perspicacity in penetrating the devious motives of the Carmelite friars in the long-running constitutional dispute suggests (metaphorically at least) the two directions of sight that will shape this chapter: looking out and looking in. Both aspects cohere in long-standing notions of specular reflection so central to contemplative self-scrutinising philosophies.

If the invention of the glass mirror in early modern Europe gave rise to a new form of self-consciousness (and this idea has been challenged on a number of fronts),[2] then we might think that the convent's mirror-less environment not only produced a different kind of self-realising but also advertised itself as doing so. Following mention of the nuns' hair cutting on entry to the convent, the Constitutions stipulated that, 'they ought neuer to haue looking glasses nor any curious [decorated] thinge, but all contempt of themselues' (*L3.34*, Chapter 8). The injunction underlines a devotional stress on interiority, a complicated one at that, requiring intense self-review and imitative renewal, exemplified in Teresa de Jesus' account of her soul in recollection:

> ... it seemed to me, that it was like some cleare, and pure Looking-Glasse, without hauing anie thing, either on the back, or on the sides; or yet, either aboue, or below, which was not all, extreamly cleare. And in the very Center thereof, Christ our Lord was represented to me ... I saw him clearly, in all the parts, and portions of my Soule, as in a Looking-Glasse ... (*Flaming Hart*, 1642, 641–2)

---

[1]   The quotation comes just before reference to the idea that if the nuns gave the friars 'one finger they would take the whole body' (see p. 110).

[2]   Debora Shuger investigated the implications of Georges Gusdorf's 1956 proposal that, following the invention of mirrors, a new self-consciousness emerged in the Renaissance period, leading to new autobiographical genres: 'This pervasive fascination with mirroring would seem to suggest that the mirror both registered and elicited a new awareness of individual identity – what do I look like – and a new reflexive self-consciousness: the specular gaze or Cartesian subjectivity where the perceiving "I" separates from and beholds – as in a mirror – as objectified "me"' (1999, 22). On the making of mirrors in Holland, including some made of ice, see Descartes, *Optics*, 1965 ed., 65.

She was led to understand, she continues, that a soul in mortal sin makes this glass covered and very dark so that, even though the Lord is ever-present 'he is not so represented as to be seen by vs'; how much more so in heresy when the glass is 'directly broken' (642). 'But yet supposing it to be the Diuinitie, in the form of some bright Diamond, which were bigger, then the whole world, or els, of some Looking-Glasse ... all that which we doe is seen in this Diamond ...' (646).[3]

Looking inwards, then, entailed a sequence of subject identifications with both the self and the divine and interiorised not-self. We fail, Teresa wrote elsewhere, if 'we do not see ourselves in this mirror into which we are gazing and in which our image is engraved' (*Interior Castle*, II, 337).[4]

The Constitutions also instruct 'That there neuer be eyther in their habitts or on their beds any coloured thing'. This governance is informed both by a concern to avoid material pleasures from personalising appearance and surroundings and by Galenic ideas about the relationship between colour and passionate arousal. Thomas Wright, for instance, repeats a contemporary commonplace that red inflames the blood (1630, 46–7). Rodriguez revisits philosophers' ideas that the eye receives *species* of colours: '*That which is within, hinders what is without from entering.* If 'twere red, all that we saw wou'd appear red: As we find by experience when we look throu' certain red Glasses; and if 'twere green, all things we look'd upon, wou'd to us appear also green' (*Practice of Christian and Religious Perfection*, 1697, Fifth Treatise, 24–5).[5]

Notwithstanding the nuns' ability to create highly-decorated craft-work for the richly coloured chapel, embroidering vestments for the holy images there and for altar cloths, the convent itself was kept plainly un-enticing to the eye: the visual contrast between community and sacred spaces brought home to the nuns the effects of each. We might infer that such conditions also affected the nuns' mystical visions (or at least their rhetorical exemplariness in describing them). When they mention colour in this context or in oracular dreams, they generally refer to white or sensations of light. Sometimes one kind of seeing leads to another with the same qualities, as when Margaret of Jesus recalled herself as a young

---

[3]   This appears to be a reflection on spiritual maturity of the same kind as I Corinthians 13:12: 'We see now through a glass in a dark manner: but then face to face. Now I know in part: but then I shall know even as I am known.' Teresa de Jesus refers to I Corinthians elsewhere, in her *Spiritual Relations*, LVIII (I, 363). She often interprets her visionary experience through the writing of St Paul.

[4]   This mutual reflection undergoes a further twist in Teresa's poem 'Alma, buscarte has en Mi' in which Christ addresses the Soul: 'Thyself engraven on My breast, / an image vividly impressed'; 'Go not abroad My face to see, / Roaming about from spot to spot, / *For thou must see for Me in thee*' (*Poems*, III, 287).

[5]   On medieval theories of colour and their links to specific emotions, some of which continued through the early modern period, see Woolgar, 2006, 155–74; Milner, 2011, 28 who draws attention to the seasonally variant colours of vestments (116). See Descartes' *Optics* on how colour works (67).

woman looking out of a window at an apple tree then experiencing a prophetic vision of a green apple.[6]

A convent stripped of colour was thought to be a place conducive to contemplative calm. Within it, the nuns were required to restrict the movement of their eyes, focusing only on what was necessary to their pious purpose. Accordingly, Mary of the Blessed Sacrament (Catherine Marie Sonnius: 1649–99) records in typical mode her own meditational exercise in a sequence followed under confessorial direction: 'I purposed with Gods assistance, to Mortify my Senses, the Chief Causes of Sin & imperfection, particularly my Eyes as being the Enterance to all Evill' (*A1*, 504; and see pp. 66–7). Disciplinary procedures underpinned the effort to turn the eye inwards, the Prioress taking responsibility for mortifying sight, binding the eyes of those who were curious enough to look at items she had left deliberately around the convent (p. 66). She also showed the nuns letters they had been sent and then removed them unread to confound their reliance upon sight and, by association, on communication with outside. The beyond they were to have in mind was both personally interior and transcendent; what daily sights there were within the cloister were to be functionally relevant to this quest. As ever with sensory disavowal, in order to divest themselves of visual dependency, the nuns were required to concentrate, initially to be 'all eyes'. Rodriguez, in the version of his text translated by Tobie Matthew in 1631, quotes Revelations 4:8: '*That they were full of eyes both within and without, and round about*. Eyes in the feet, eyes in the hands, eyes in the eares, eyes in the lippes and eyes in the very eyes themselues ... [that] there may be no little thing, which may offend the pure eyes of God' (20–21).

To discipline the eye is to find a means to pure revelation, whether figurative or literal.[7] The eye in such texts is said to have the capacity to discern, to discriminate, to place. It is able to deny the arrival of unexpected stimuli which even the most disciplined of other senses cannot: smells drift, sounds carry, eyes of all the sensory orifices can be closed to intrusion or determinedly focused:

> The eye wanders, selects, approaches things, presses after them, while the ear for its part, is affected and accosted. The eye can seek, the ear can only *wait*. Seeing 'places' things; hearing is placed. ... one cannot stand 'in' the Word, in the sense of 'in luce esse' ... (Blumenberg, 1993, 48)[8]

---

[6]   See Bruce Smith (2004) on green (the colour of youth and rashness and of cool, moist anaemia to which the young were said to be prone) being seen, heard, smelt, tasted and touched.

[7]   See Biernoff, 2002, 114–20 on 'cloistered gaze', 'custody of the eyes' and introspection.

[8]   See Judovitz, 2006 for discussion of the 'primacy of light' and its relationship to 'the logic of hearing' in the work of Georges de la Tour (1593–1652), an article which quotes Blumenberg in support of the idea that La Tour redefines vision as address, in analogy to hearing (145).

The nuns' attention to directing sight appears to affect their experience of seeing (or at least their descriptiveness of it), intensifying the detail of their visual perception. The women mention various qualities of light (as when a nun whose eyes grew dim asked for a candle: *A2*, 40)[9] and of colour-perception (as when a nun whose eyesight had diminished could still distinguish colours and go about the house: *L13.7*, 139). They also refer to the beauty of particular nuns' eyes, though only in death not life, and they mention several other cases of women with diminishing sight or complete blindness, some emblematically Cartesian and cross-sensory in finding their way with a stick.[10] Spectacles are mentioned, and Mary Margaret of the Angels (Chapman) who 'went double' when walking had her eyes 'canock'd' by a 'famous master', paid for by Antwerp women citizens (*A2*, 88). Other commonly-available eye remedies are not mentioned as such.[11]

As with other senses, fallibilities can allow insights to emerge that would otherwise apparently be lost. Some 'truths' take their power from failure to see, as when Anne of St Joseph (Anne Chamberlain: *c.*1623–1709), aspiring to become a choir sister 'applied her self to learn Latten but declared that every time she opened a Book for that end she could not see a letter'. She concluded that this was a sign God instead intended her to continue as a Lay Sister. Other invisible things were central to the convent spatial and ceremonial structure, like the Host in the monstrance before which the nuns prostrated every time they passed the chapel. There is continual interplay in the papers between such visible and invisible mysteries; between 'eye-witnesses' to miraculous happenings and secret, self-revealing truths.

Certainly as we have noted in the previous chapters, despite the mistrust surrounding the other senses, they were often used to supplement, augment, even to replace sight. Sister Winefrid touched with her finger the blood she saw running down the wall near the body of Mary Margaret of the Angels that was later

---

[9]   They mention, as we might expect, the use of candles for practical purposes (one nun mortifying herself by using only one candle over a very prolonged period) and on liturgical occasions, differentiating between types of taper; wax candles (presumably more expensive than tallow) were mentioned for ceremonial use, in funerals or on tombs.

[10]   Descartes wrote that blind people 'see with their hands' or by means of a stick: 'nothing has to issue from the bodies and pass along his stick to his hand; and the resistance or movement of the bodies, which is the sole cause of the sensations he has of them, is nothing like the ideas he forms of them' ('Optics' in *Discourse and Essays*, 1985 ed., I, 153).

[11]   When the nuns made 'little actions' or plays during recreation, Catherine of the Blessed Sacrament (for whom Anne of the Ascension had made the scapular: p. 73) by then the oldest nun in the community 'was forced to use [on] thess Occasions offten spectacles' (*L13.7*, 17). On other remedies for eyes see for example *The Eye Clear'd* (1644), a recipe for eye-bright 'to restore the poreblind, and make the squint-eye to looke forthright', and *Advertisement at the Golden Head* (1675) for remedies and cures, claiming to give sight to the 'stone-blind' within a few days. Nuns were expected to be able-bodied to be accepted for entry to the Order; it emerged that one woman entered blind in one eye, apparently not realising she should have declared it (see p. 93 n. 21).

discovered to be intact. She did not initially trust what she saw and was afraid she would be 'chid' for her claims. Only years later, when many witnesses examined the intact body, its scent remaining on their hands, did she disclose what she had seen (p. 108). In the account of the autopsy itself, sight is by no means privileged; touch and smell seem to have equal interpretive value. Readers are invited to become 'eye-witnesses' by viewing the corpse, yet only after its miraculous nature has first been confirmed by divines whose own multi-sensory perceptions have been endorsed by medical authority: none dare presume independent attribution of holy cause.

Given the alleged epistemological and cultural centrality of the eyes, their scrutinising role in the convents was understandable, as was the nuns' anxiety about precisely what was seen and hence their tendency to bear out visual evidence with other sensory impressions. The women seem to be very aware of the capacity of the eye to move them extremely (one nun received her vocation on seeing a picture of Teresa de Jesus, for example: *A1*, 55) and therefore of their need to maintain guard: this was especially important for women according to early modern secular and religious commentators.

In a period of continuing scepticism and church interrogation of mystic claims, the nuns take great pains to differentiate between types of seeing, making connections and distinctions between what is seen and imaged, and between imaginary and visionary revelation. We can appreciate the careful positioning behind Mary Xaveria's clarification of the nature of her visions when she revisits statements made earlier in her life-writing:

> What I said concerning my seeing these Angels is not meant to be meant yt I saw them with eyes of my Body, for I never saw any thing of this kind in that manner, but with ye eyes of my soul, and it appeareth now much more clear to me tho these things happen'd many yeares ago then any thing I have seen with ye eyes of my body. I had never read nor heard yt there was any other way of seeing things (if I may speak so) then with our corporeal eyes til I came to Religion and heard our Blessed Mother St Teresa speak of it ... yet I remained as certain before yt I had seen them ... I thought he [my Director] would not understand me when I should say I had seen things other ways then with my eyes ... (*A3*, 66–7)

She not only emphasises her own personal orthodoxy, aligning her experience with Teresian precepts, but she also explicates visual possibilities and discusses their relationship to memory. Her pre-taught and apparently intuitive mysticism sits alongside her learned behaviour which does not necessarily supersede it.

It is important to consider the ideas behind such visions as potentially physical and psychical, and how beliefs about them related to seen objects in the convent, in order to appreciate the levels of visuality within the nuns' extensive repertoire (and accordingly the range of doubts they raised).

The Role of Images and Pictures in Convent Life

When Teresa de Jesus wrote of her wish to have an image before her bodily eyes since she could not have it engraven in her soul (*Vida*, 138) she implies a hierarchy in which interior imagining is superior, outward sight in service for its pursuit. On arrival in a new convent during their founding journeys through Spain, Teresa's Carmelites improvised by pasting a piece of paper with a picture of Christ onto a wooden crucifix (*Book of Foundations*, III, 66); Teresa spent some of their meagre funds on two paintings, one to go behind the altar (71).[12] Hers is an aesthetic driven by pious purpose. In her *Vida* she describes her own affective response to a representation, weeping and feeling her heart was breaking when looking at a picture of Christ wounded (*Flaming Hart*, 1642, Chapter IX). Later in more confident stages of prayer (and in order to get to sleep at night) she made mental pictures of Christ suffering, so vivid she wished she could wipe the grievous sweat from his face. Of Christ the man, however, she claimed only to be able to think, never forming a picture 'like one who is blind'.

Her imaginative systems follow Gregorian traditions, laid down in a three-fold rationale for the use of images or pictures. According to Bonaventure these were only introduced to help ignorant people, those who are 'sluggish of feelings' for whom merely hearing about Christ's sacrifice was insufficient: 'Our feeling is more excited by things it sees than by things it hears ... because of the unreliability of memory, in that things that are only heard fade into oblivion more easily than those that are seen' (cited Hamburger, 2006, 15). Although Teresa encouraged her nuns to aspire to imageless devotion within a system of mental prayer, when this was not possible she instructed them to make use of pictures or sculptures to stir their faith; artistic images could inspire imaginative states or on occasion directly stir visionary experience.

Religious writers make allowances for 'humane working' towards formless devotion. Benet of Canfield describes this as a process of 'uncloathing of the spirit': 'stripping her of all forms and Images of all things as well created and uncreated', so she goes forth naked in contemplation. Unclothing cannot be accomplished via forms, though paradoxically metaphor-full descriptions can advance understanding. In a parallel similitude he suggests that a devout person can polish himself, smoothing away images in a process of Purgation then Illumination. Canfield figuratively enacts the process he describes, working through then out of forms. In early stages, then, as he does here, a devout person can make use of images, whether sculptural or mental, the first of these succeeding to the second en route to 'abundance of light' (1646, 46–55).

For Teresians within such a tradition, imaginative presence was to be stirred by sensory perception in the form of statues, for instance, then cognitively processed. The devout could experience a higher level of prayerfulness without sensory

---

[12]   Teresa noted elsewhere: 'I had thought it a sign of poverty to have no pictures other than paper ones' (*Spiritual Relations*, I, 349).

stimulus or intellectual form of any kind; in Canfield's Franciscan-affective terms, Christ is felt, better than imagined, to be crucified (206). Teresa likened this kind of spiritual perception to awareness of an unseen Other beside one in the dark.

The Antwerp and Lierre Carmelites describe themselves as engaging with each stage of the seeing-imaginative-formless progression. *Kleines Andachtsbild* (a term arising in south-west Germany to refer originally to a group of small sculptural forms, and now more generally used to indicate objects used to promote devotional response) were clearly used within the Carmels, most generally referred to as being in the community rather than in private cells where pictures are more commonly mentioned. Importantly, such an image was portable, 'Not an object intended for viewing at a disinterested distance, it asks to be handled and touched' (Hamburger, 1997, 3). These sort of images are mentioned in the convent papers particularly at moments of crisis. A statue of the Our Lady of Sichem (a shrine in the region) was dropped down the stairs by a nun (one version of the story names her as Ursula of All Saints Mostyn) who rushed to fetch it during a whirlwind. That it did not break was considered miraculous. An image of the Virgin of Cluse, a chapel near Lierre which the nuns often mention, was carried by a Dominican in whose keeping it was into Ursula's bedroom when she was ill; he noted it was much lighter to lift after her recovery was wrought.[13]

Other statues seem to have been located in fixed positions. Margaret of Jesus mentions 'porsterning befor our Bd Ladys lettle image' (*L3.35*); she commits herself 'to knelle befor all ye images of our Bd Lady wth my armes acrose ye time of a salue dayly' (*L3.35*). Her detailed accounts helpfully illustrate a personal geography of images in specific convent spaces, each with individual visual-devotional components. 'Thees deuotions I desire to do this lent' (written to request permission from her Confessor for extra-liturgical acts) included visiting the Blessed Sacrament once a day 'saying some deuotions for the conuertione of sinners' and prostrating before Our Lady in the choir 'ye spaces of 7 Aues'; 'to hould my armes across dayly ye spaces of 5 paters and 5 Aues befor ye great Pecter ye Crussefex in ye refectory'; 'to say a te deum upon Barkness [bare knees] befor our Bd Mothers image dayly'; on Saturdays to rise at four in the morning or after Mattins 'to crep upon my bare knees from ye Image in ye quier to ye image in ye garden'. She also wished to do five acts of mortification each day, including self-flagellation, in imitation of Christ's passion (*L3.35*, loose paper).[14]

---

[13]   Many miracles are associated with images. For example, a sign was given to Anne of the Ascension about where to erect a convent: '[Our Lady appeared] and shewd her the place where she wod haue the Convent to be, and as they were takeing down some of the old houses, there was found mured up in the walls, a very handsome stone image of our Bd Lady, aboue a yard high, with little Jesus in her arms ...' (*A1*, 36–7).

[14]   See Bowden, 2011 on bequests of pictures to the Lierre Carmel, including £20 for a painting of the life of the Virgin, and Edmund Bedingfield's gift of 'a great picture of the Nativtye' (493); Vander Motten and Daemen-de Gelder (2010) on networks of illustrators including George Gage (c.1582–1638), 'fides Achates' of Toble Matthew, connected with

　　While the nuns describe their devotional reaction to visual stimuli, they do not account for the physical mechanisms involved in sight. Their only real mention of eyes as organs comes when they refer (fairly frequently) to nuns who die with them open, remaining without their 'eye-strings' broken. Their interest as ever is in effect and significance rather than process.

　　Behind the nuns' insistence that they see only with the eyes of the mind, however, is tacit reference to a system of seeing that was much debated in this period by medics, theologians and philosophers, all in their way concerned with the physical nature and implications of material transfer. Descartes, for instance, considered that although the picture transmitted to the brain resembled the object from which it proceeded, the resemblance itself was not the means to see: 'just as the movements of the nerves which respond to the ears cause it to hear sounds, and those of the nerves of the tongue cause it to taste flavours, and generally those of the nerves of the entire body cause it to feel some tickling ... yet in all this, there need be no resemblance between the ideas that the mind conceives and the movements which cause these ideas' (*Optics*, 1965 ed., 101). Devotional writers translated such ideas into contemplative terms. Benet of Canfield, who couches his description of Union in highly erotic language (even for a culture well-used to such tones), gave a quasi-somatic explanation of spiritual effect:

> For, as the Sunne darts his rayes into any transparent Body, as water, glasse, or crystal, from thence provoking towards himself a certain reflex Light. So, God who descends his Beames and sight into the soule, doth also rebound from her a mutuall aspect towards himselfe ... For, as in Bodily sight an object sends forth the forme or species to the eye, which being instantly reflected upon the eye-sight or seeing-power so toucht, closes therewith, and knitting it selfe thereto, flyes with it to the object it selfe, from which the form was sent forth, and so the sight of the same object is drawn out; So it is in spirituall sight ... (1646, 102–3)

God-like light, he says, shines into the Soul which re-shines it, is 'oned therewith'.

　　Given the extreme delicacy of such discussion, especially (but not only) amidst on-going suspicion of female mysticism, it is no wonder that theologians struggled to define the action of exchange behind such encounters. They offer a range of possibilities: of entirely non-sensory and formless union; of semi-somatic transfer; of somatic-spiritual similitude the convincing nature of which stirs intellectual then affective piety; of identification or surrogacy in which the contemplative imagines herself in the position of the seen object (the Virgin in a Pietà for instance, or as an ecstatic Bride).[15]

Thomas Howard, Earl of Arundel (1585–1646) and with Lionel Wake. For correspondence between Matthew and Rubens, see Mathew and Calthrop, 1907, 117, 177.

[15]　See Hamburger, 1998, 124 on Bernadine balance between conceptual, affective, interpretive and emotional identification in which 'The nuns literally envisage themselves as the Bride of the Canticle.'

Some aspects of the imaginary and of visions suggest there was a potentially synaesthetic component to envisioning. Lucy of the Holy Ghost felt the softness of the Christ-child's hands when she held him in her arms (p. 115). Similar sensation we might consider to be also physically possible through acts of intense meditation. A pious person mentally imaging or actually looking at a Pietà, for instance, with the dead Christ in the arms of the Virgin, is invited to identify with the sorrowing mother to the extent of feeling the weight of death in both meanings. As in so many instances, experience is not only multi-sensory but virtually, imaginatively, physically cross-sensory. Such an ideal response might perhaps be explained in terms of mirror-touch, exemplified in a rather different context by Daria Martin's 2012 film-based exhibition, *Sensorium Tests*. In this a synaesthete is filmed responding as she watches objects and bodies being touched. 'In the presence of real violence' (and for a contemplative, being in the presence of pain, grief or pleasure, we might think), 'mirror-touch synaesthetes may feel themselves slapped, punched or stabbed, and experience similar shocks when watching television or a film' (Dillon, 2012). A perfecting, finely-attuned pious person might not only intellectually appreciate the pain of Christ or the Virgin that she see or imagines, but experience its touch, its feel. Synaesthetic presencing moves, then, beyond memory's failing described by Jerome Plautus' in *The Happiness of a Religious State*: 'We find in the passion of grief, and ioy, and feare, and the rest; which are most violent, when the cause is present.' He gives the example of 'A Mother [who] is more violently transported with grief, when she sees the dead corpse of her sonne lye before her, then when she heares of her death ... Wherefore as grief, and anger, and other passions are sooner and more violently stirred by the presence of their proper objects ...' (1632, 91). Again this suggests the range and complexity of subject positions involved in prayerful envisioning.

Teresa likewise distinguishes between different imaginative pre-, post- or non-sensory states. Many of these have spatial-visual components. In the prayer of recollection, she writes, a Soul can shut herself away: 'hidden there within itself, it can think about the Passion and picture the Son, and offer Him to the Father, without wearying the mind by going to seek Him on Mount Calvary, or in the Garden, or at the Column' (*Way of Perfection*, II, 115). Mental rehearsal of holy spaces, or physically erecting Stations of the Cross, which Catherine Burton had done in her youth, walking or crawling along its route, had its place, therefore, but interior imaging was superior (though itself subject to suspicion, given the relative autonomy it gave the devout person, hence the need to provide instruction on its shape and limits, and to document experience). For Teresa, 'Those who are able to shut themselves up in this way within this little Heaven of the soul, wherein dwells the Maker of Heaven and earth, and who have formed the habit of looking at nothing and staying in no place which will distract their outward senses, may be sure they are walking on an excellent road ...' (115).

It is clear then that images (exterior and interior) worked in several ways, inciting devotion via the eyes, whether literal or figuratively through imagined visualising. To say the convents were undecorated is not to say they did not elicit powerful visual response, therefore; rather that stimuli were strategically positioned and vision strategically managed to direct devotional response.

There are also many references to pictures in the Antwerp and Lierre Carmels. As Margaret of Jesus' Lenten devotions suggest, 'ye great Pectur' of the crucifix (presumably large for less intimate regard, to be visible to an assembly in the Refectory) had its place alongside more diminutive statuary in her scheme. Some pictures (clearly small, presumably mass produced)[16] were given as gifts on special occasions, to either groups or to individuals. When a new community was enclosed, each nun received a holy picture (*A1*, 64), for example; Mary Xaveria presented a novice with a picture of St Francis Xavier on her profession day (*A2*, 8). A representation of St Teresa 'hung at the beds head' of Anne of the Angels (Anne Bedingfield: 1650–1700) until it was moved to the Prioress' 'closet' because the young nun 'would lye awake houers, prayen & making asperations to this pictuer, often setting right up in her bed to kise it' (*L13.7*, 212–16).

There is, then, evidence in the papers of the particular use to which the nuns put their pictures. Margaret of Jesus used visual as well as aural cues for her devotions, looking at a picture in order to recall her pious promises (*L3.31*, 5). One woman was found dead with an image next to her heart (p. 126 n.107), others with their eyes fixed upon a picture (*L13.7*, 17). An ailing nun favoured a representation of the *Ecce Homo* so it was taken to her bedside (p. 123). Such details suggest the intensity of visual desire at crucial moments.

There was naturally a correlation between the pictures seen and visions experienced. Teresa de Jesus had noted this. The Virgin, she recalled, 'looked to me rather like the picture which the Countess gave me ...' (*Spiritual Relations*, I, 346).[17] An Antwerp nun recalled a childhood vision during illness of a man in black, all the while her mother prayed to Blessed Aloysius for her return to health. Afterwards, in the manner of an early modern identikit, she showed the child various pictures, one of which (Aloysius himself) the girl pointed to saying 'O that is he yt cured me' (*A1*, 430).

More troublingly, at Lierre Margaret of Jesus reported to her Confessor that, aware of 'the abhominable condition my soul', 'I went imediatly befor a Picteur of Ecce homo and did repeat those Acts wh yt Rce haue comanded mee, with

---

[16] There is no evidence in the papers of the nuns being artists. Some fairly raw pen-and-ink drawings in the annals are likely to have been produced in-house since the books did not go outside the communities. Several of these are reproduced by Hardman, 1939, including portraits of Mary Xaveria and Mary Margaret of the Angels after death. On nuns as artists and the visual culture of a medieval convent, see Hamburger, 1997.

[17] She continues: 'though the vision passed too quickly for me to decide this because immediately my faculties became completely suspended' (*Spiritual Relations*, 346). Peers identifies the donor and states that the picture remains at St Joseph's convent in Avila, as if both facts bear out the truth of Teresa's claim. There never seems to be any scepticism on the part of the early modern nuns about cause and effect: why their visions, dreams or nightmares look like the pictures they have seen.

the greatest contradiction I euer did them. And suddainly there seemed present our Bd Lord our Bd Lady our Bd Mother & St Augutin in the same maner I haue formerly imagened but much more clear & euident and did seeme to inforce mee to resolue uppon putting away ye ill affection'. 'I remayned' she wrote, not without reason, 'with much fear & trembling & a resolution to helpe my selfe' (*L3.31*, 39). Imagine then the distressing impact on Margaret when the same familiar image turned uncanny in demonic hands: 'Yea some times when she called uppon our Bd Lady to helpe her after comunion yt crucifix or ecce homo would appear & tell her yt she offended him greuiously ...' No wonder 'she seldome durst stay longer in the quire but presently rane out' (46).

On many such occasions, either stirred by pictures or by visions relating to them, the nuns claim to have eidetic recall of the visual experience, behaving when they think about it as if it was actually present. Although Teresa de Jesus denies the materiality of the impact ('if the soul retains no image of them and the faculties are unable to understand them, how can they be remembered?': *Interior Castle*, II, 288) she does not deny the effect ('so deeply impressed upon the memory that they can never again be forgotten'). This eideticism is itself sometimes commemorated visually, extending the influence of the personal event to a wider audience, for example in a portrait of Anne of Jesus envisioning Christ in the Host during communion at the Feast of the Circumcision in 1578, or of Mary of the Incarnation seeing heaven (Hardman, 1932, 90, 192). All such representations fix (expanding or curtailing, depending on one's starting point) the visionary possibilities of the picture's observers. They also make communally available (for this is their ostensible motivation) the intensity of the personal moment. As when Teresa de Jesus was moved simply by reading of St Augustine hearing a voice in the garden, transference of effect across media does not diminish its impact so long as the current observer enters into the spirit of the reproduction, de-intellectualising her response and empathising with the original recipient of grace. As with specular interiority, identification of self in other (or recognition of the grace of another beyond one's own capacity) requires diminution of ego and subjective relocation of an intricate kind. Commemorative pious portraits both depict and enact recollection (in both senses: mnemonic and contemplative). Portraiture is therefore justified since though it records an intense and apparently original personal experience, it does so ostensibly in order to offer that experience to other nuns. It also embeds memory of an individual within corporate consciousness; singular and group recollection are thus blurred, the script of aspirational experience being visualised within the shared confines of community. This is radical and enlarging (since it opens the scope of an individual mysticism that male clerics sought to contain, enabling a spaceless, timeless encounter). It is also limiting (constraining the range of depiction and ensuring future repetition takes place in the same terms). Orthodoxy is at once tested and confirmed.

Such devotional imperatives presumably underlie the motivation for portraiture more generally within the convent. Some of it was 'private', only shared between the nuns and other faithful, some of it more widely disseminated when such images were reproduced. Clothing portraits (see pp. 97, 99) advertised the status of the woman who entered and by association that of the Order, as well as stressed by inference the pious austerity that was to follow, the extent of willing sacrifices made. Posthumous portraiture similarly promotes the reputation of the deceased and of the convent. The Antwerp annals note that Anne of the Ascension was painted three times after her death, with copies being printed in Newburg (*A1*, 37). Anne herself had a strong commemorating instinct, commissioning a picture of Anne of St Bartholomew to whom she was especially close, and another of herself: 'She made a painter draw a picture just in ye manner our Bd Lord had appeard to her, wch euer since we call our Dear Mother's picture, and wch we still hold in great veneration' (*A1*, 52, 53). The chain of authority and of mystic history, embedded in the chronicles at literary level, is thus made visual too.

Some portraits offer their own interpretation and extend it to the observer. That of Anne of St Bartholomew at the Spanish Carmel in Antwerp (reproduced by Anne Hardman, 1936, facing p. 152) has a lengthy inscription in Spanish giving an account of the nun's life, underneath a picture of the nun holding a small crucifix, her eyes seemingly resting in mid-space just above the cross. The captions stresses that this was one 'whom St Teresa chose, with special divine inspiration, as her perpetual companion, until she died in Mother Anne's arms'.[18] The words on a scroll from the nun's mouth ('Love seeks the Cross to fulfil its desires') are taken from her own poem for the day of the Exaltation of the Holy Cross. She thus exemplifies the posture and hieratically enables affectivity. The observer takes in the scene and joins in its desire, as the scroll above it reads, from Psalm 119:64: 'Misericordia tua, Domine, plena est terra; justificationes tua doce me'; 'The earth, O Lord, is full of thy mercy: teach me thy justifications.'

The portrait of Mary Xaveria taken from a sketch after her death has similar biographical commentary below the image (Hardman, 1939, frontispiece).[19] The posture of the two women is similar; both have their arms crossed over their chests, holding a crucifix that occasions the positions of their eyes but not their

---

[18]   I am grateful to Rosie Valerio for her translation of this and other passages in Spanish. These words echo details of the venerable line of Carmelite succession found elsewhere: see p. 111.

[19]   The account of this painting resonates with cross-sensory significance: 'Whilst she lay exposed in ye Quire dress'd up in her habit … one of the religious putting her hand to her side, thought she perceived a perceptable warmth … and tho' no body could reasonably doubt but yt she was certainly dead, yet to satisfy ye desire of ye religious, ye surgeon who attended her was sent for to view ye body … her countenance … was now become so sweet and breathd such an aire of sanctity yt one present cryed out it was a pitty they had not taken her picture, upon this proposal a painter was sent for who took her features craion, and afterwards drew her picture; notwithstanding [that she] … began to corrupt before she was dead, yet there was not ye least offensive smell when her coffin was thus opened. Her features being taken and ye Religious haveing satisfyed their devotion in kissing her feet, and touching her body with their beads, pictures & c: ye coffin was nailed up and deposited again in ye vault' (*A3*, 442; Hallett, 2007a, 160).

physical focus. They adopt a physical posture for prayer outlined by several commentators.[20] The observer might thus imitate the physical gestures depicted while simultaneously recognising the exemplary piety of the sitter, looking as it were with parallax view. Although the image is static (even while it records the transformation of those involved in the event represented, and potentially effects change in the onlooker), the observer mentally aligns, seeing the person depicted first as object, then as subject, eventually (ideally) *becoming* them in fixing the eye not *on* but *through* their gaze.

While some portraits were for use within the convent, then, other works seem to have been kept outside, having a function like that of letters or of secular likenesses, to keep the women in the minds of their families, perhaps to stir piety or in hope of new vocations. Sometimes correspondence between the actual person and that depicted was perceived to be especially acute. Edward Mostyn noticed changes in his portrait of his sister, Margaret of Jesus, the day after her death, although he did not at that time know she had died: 'rising in ye morning, hee found ye picture taken doune, and sett ye other side of ye rome, ouer againes ye dore, yt all wch came must see it; and to his thinking it semed to cast a more resplendent sweetnes then ordinary, att wch hee was much amased, and called seuerall in ye house who obsarued ye same change in ye picture, saying it loked heauenly, but could not tell, what judment to make of it, not dreaming of her death, this being in England thay had not so much as heard of her being sick' (*L13.7*, 55).

One portrait of a nun is especially striking, given the typical stance held by the nuns in their pious portraits. It is an engraving by John Faber Jr. after Gabriel Mathias (*c*.1754–56) of the 'Abbess Howard' now in the London National Portrait Gallery, reproduced on the cover of this book.[21] The style of this portrait resembles that of many secular representations. It is as if she is only accidentally

---

20   A Teresian friar, Juan de Jesus Maria (1564–1615), for example, in his 1598 text *Disciplina Claustralis* suggests that the devout should kneel 'with hands folded together under the scapular resting on the leather belt. Alternatively, the arms can be crossed over the breast or the fingers may be intertwined; depending upon the individual's comfort and devotion' (translated by Cordula Van Whye, 2008, 192).

21   I am extremely grateful to Erika Ingham and Elizabeth Taylor at the NPG for their advice and research on this portrait. Although the archivists cannot find a trace in the NPG records of the original painting on which the portrait is based, they deduce it was produced between 1736 and 1756, and the mezzotint made *c*.1753–56. The NPG and the British Museum both base their attribution on a series of catalogues which reject the claim in Henry Bromley's *Catalogue of Engraved British Portraits* (1793, 310) that this is Mary of the Holy Cross whom I identify as Mary Howard (1653–1735), a Poor Clare from Rouen. On the authority of Chaloner Smith, *British Mezzotint Portraits* (1883) the work is given as 'Howard, Abbess of the English Nuns at Antwerp'. Within the likely dates, therefore, if such details are indeed correctly connected to the Carmelites, there are two possible candidates: Mary Joseph Howard, author of the annals, Prioress 1735–50, and her sister, Teresa of Jesus Howard, Prioress 1750–63. If Evans' 1836 catalogue (No. 5559) is correct to identify the sitter as 'Mary Howard', the likelihood is the former. On these nuns, see pp. 61, 64, 112, 142; 92, 94 n. 26, 125, respectively.

in a religious habit the folds of which move outwards. Although her hair is covered, the wimple is relatively wide to expose her face. If 'early modern viewers expected psychological indicators appropriate to the sitter's class, profession or gender' (Filipczak, 2004, 71), revealing self-control in upright posture, hands still for women (akimbo for men: 83, 88), then the Howard portrait suggests more animation than that typically associated with religious women. She looks at the viewer rather than at a devotional object; her head is turned, not prayerfully down. Her right hand is held up to her scapular and wimple, her left rests on a book; with her weighty-looking clothing also suggesting slight movement, she is as near to active as is femininely, piously, possible.

So much, then, for the nuns looking outward or being looked at, seeing images and assimilating their effects to devotional purpose. In the last stages of this chapter I will turn inward, to consider the nuns' conception of imagining on which such pictures naturally had an influence.

'Picturing within ourselves'[22]

Teresa de Jesus, as we might expect, spends considerable effort in explaining the difference between different kinds of sight and their relative value within a meditative scheme. She also delineates degrees of empathetic intensity arising from them.

In *Way of Perfection*, she describes a woman (thought to be herself, third-personed) who sought to strengthen her faith at communion 'by thinking that it was exactly as if she saw the Lord entering her house, with her own bodily eyes'. 'She imagined herself at His feet and wept with the Magdalen exactly as if she had seen Him with her bodily eyes in the Pharisee's house.' We cannot suppose, she continues, 'that this is the work of the imagination as it is when we think of the Lord on the Cross, or of other incidents of the Passion, and picture within ourselves how these things happened. This is something which is happening now; it is absolutely true; and we have no need to go and seek Him somewhere a long way off' (II, 147). Visual imagining, accompanied by appropriate empathising, therefore compresses time and space. And yet its vividness is less acute than if it were actually, physically real, she continues: 'If you grieve at not seeing Him with the eyes of the body, remember that that would not be good for us, for it is one thing to see Him glorified and quite another to see Him as He was when He lived in the world. So weak is our nature that nobody could endure this sight' (148).

Pictures have their place, then: 'When the person is absent and we are made to feel his loss by our great aridity.' But when he is present, she asks, would it not be foolish to carry on conversing with the portrait not the person? (149). When you are adept, well-practiced in remaining with the Lord, 'try to shut the bodily eyes and to open the eyes of the soul and to look into your own hearts' (150). Having

---

22   Teresa de Jesus, *Way of Perfection*, II, 147.

made use of physical pictures, therefore, then learnt to image mentally, advanced contemplatives were encouraged by their teachers to move even further, to an imageless state. This formless meditation is also advocated by John of the Cross (*Ascent of Mount Carmel*, 1906 ed., 115).

Teresa's nuns naturally follow the range of these approaches, depending on their contemplative stage or their personal state at a given time. Some express themselves unable to rehearse mentally and resort to vocal prayer; some describe habitual recourse to familiar mental images. Margaret of Jesus, for instance, described herself on occasion as picturing scenes in her mind, focusing on the gospel of the Prodigal Son after Mass, a mind's eye painting. Like many of the Carmelite mystics she engages in a process of *ekphrasis*: the description of a work of art or, in these cases, recollection of an event, narratives of which describe 'an experiential whole' (Carruthers, 2006, 290–91). While few of the women had received a formal education that directly exposed them to such precepts, as in so many areas of their lives the nuns' religious training imbued them with its systems. Similar such influence is also evident in the nuns' accounts of their revelations. They shape their descriptions around well-established narrative forms, distinguishing different kinds of locution and making sense of them not as fleeting (though they often say they lasted only a moment) but as part of a longer story of self-realisation.

Their visionary experience falls (as we might expect) into the three-fold scheme outlined by Augustine and by other divines including Teresa de Jesus herself. Augustine's commentary on Genesis describes bodily vision (*visio corporalis*) in which objects were seen with external sight, spiritual vision (*visio spiritualis*) involving imaginative, bodiless form and mental vision (*visio intellectualis*) which was imageless (a succinct account of which is given by Clark, 2007, 204, who suggests the precarious nature of judgements relating to this in the sixteenth and seventeenth centuries). Teresa de Jesus gives similar lists, noting that imaginary visions were said to be especially prone to demonic interference and therefore were most open to doubt. An 'image' she says might arrive suddenly as a revelation, 'but it must not be supposed that one looks as it as at a painting'. She navigates the tricky waters by describing the vision as if it is a picture in order to deny that it is so: 'The brilliance of this vision is like that of infused light or of a sun covered with some material of the transparency of a diamond, if such a thing could be woven.' It exceeds our imagination (*Interior Castle*, II, 315). Thus, as she does when she accounts for other sense-less states, she describes the effect as if it were physical while advocating de-imaging. Since she makes her metaphors operate at once on several levels, it is as if each of the cognitive triplex of the *visio* were simultaneously experienced even in denial.

In her *Spiritual Relations* Teresa describes a sequence of visual-related inspiration, again weaving together different types of sight-inspired piety. In an account from Seville in 1575 she recounts how she found a letter in which St Paul was quoted then, later, she read a book which included another of his sayings. The effect on her is cumulative, thought-based. While pondering, remembering an earlier time when the Lord was present with her, he then spoke to her, she reports, appearing 'in an intellectual vision, in the depths of my being, as though He were beside my heart'. Later at Matins she received another intellectual vision 'so clear that it seemed almost imaginary' in which he 'laid Himself in my arms in the way depicted in the "Fifth Anguish" of Our Lady', that is of Mary with her dead son in her arms. The vision made her afraid, 'so clear was it and so close to me as to make me wonder if it was an illusion': 'This vision has remained in my memory right until now. What I have said about our Lord lasted for more than a month. It has now left me' (I, 363–4).

Some of Teresa's Carmelite successors at Antwerp and Lierre account for their visions in similar ways, indeed the papers are full of examples of ocular mystical experience; happenings are normalised even if they are nonetheless notable for their associated blessings. In her childhood Margaret of Jesus 'visibly saw' her good angel who carried her down stairs and through dark entries because she was afraid of the dark. One Maundy Thursday, she was found in her family chapel having climbed up on a chair in order to see the Host: 'sayd she I would faine see my little Jesus, yt is there, wch she did visiblely behould, att her first Communion, and then was inspiered to a religious course of life' (*L13.7*, 41). Of Monica of St Lawrence it was written: 'When she was a child she often saw little creatures danceing about her, who seemed to offer her something to drink out of curious christall glasses but she still saw one biger then the rest, cloathed in blew and white, who drove them away from her, which afterwards she took to be her holy Angel. One Christmas night going to Mass she saw (out of a window) in the air a tender young virgin with the sacred Infant Jesus naked in her arms' and this sealed her resolve to become a nun (*A1*, 388).

Otherwise, like Mary Xaveria, like Teresa de Jesus before her, the nuns tend to deny the physical nature of their visions. This gives them the great advantage of appearing to be beyond reproach, especially when they claim to be reluctant even to describe their experience or transfer it thereby to the material realm. On St Paul's day in 1558 or 1559 Teresa 'saw a complete representation' of Christ's humanity 'just as in a picture of His resurrection body', describing it to her spiritual advisor only on his 'very insistent request'. Teresa describes herself as 'annihilated' by the process of writing, as if the action replicated the spiritual effect of really having seen with her eyes. This is a characteristically canny move on Teresa's part, anticipating inquisitorial scrutiny: 'I never saw it, or any other vision, with the eyes of the body, but only the eyes of the soul.' Physical vision is the lowest form of sight, most open to delusions of the devil, she claims, correcting her inexperienced self (*Vida*, 179–80). And so she goes on, differentiating kinds of real: it is ridiculous to think the Christ I saw is an image, any more than a living person is like a portrait. Comparisons never hold up; this was a living image in the face of which, indeed *in* which, as she was merely describing it, she is utterly dissolved.

Eyes are a source of both certainty (when Teresa sees devils ill-treating a corpse at a burial and knows with sadness that the man led a wicked life: *Life*, I, 276) and

doubt (when she is anxious that such scenes might mean sinners are beyond God's
redemption, an impossibility, hence she feels she has been deluded). Formlessness
is safer and more compelling to the sceptical or the perplexed faithful.

Teresa helpfully outlines the process whereby sight connects to insight. When
the Soul looks on God, she considers 'I do not think it can be a vision at all. It
must rather be that some striking idea creates a picture in the imagination', an
image much more remote, colder, than the sacred presence, and one that will be
forgotten as quickly as a dream (*Interior Castle*, II, 316). Real presence is by
contrast unforgettable. A test of the strength of mystical visions is indeed their
longevity, in which they defy the effects of material memory.

Some of Teresa's successors express themselves similarly bewildered about
the status of their revelations. They describe their effects, unsure whether sights
are real or imagined, whether they are themselves to blame for ensuing despair.
For Margaret of Jesus, 'ye comone Enimie of manking, would often transforme
him selfe, into an Angelle of light,[23] by yt menes to create in her, meny fears and
aprehentions, yt all was elusions and cheits of ye Diuele, wch gaue her excessue
greif, and affliction, for according to her owne nature, she was very tememerous
and fearfull, and her great humelitie, also made her, thinke it impossible, yt God
Allmt should show him selfe, frequentlie and propistious, to so vile and poore
a creature, this made her oft think all was but temtation, and her owne fancyes'
(*L13.7*, 57).

Vision, then, and especially within a culture so focused on the spiritual
supernatural and in the midst of reforming church controversy, 'was anything but
objectively established or secure in its supposed relationship to "external fact"'
(Clark, 2007, 1); it was ambiguously regarded 'even in an already [allegedly]
ocularcentric age' (5). Often in the convents sight was only trusted when it was borne
out by other senses or subsequent incidents; this is as true of visionary (un)certainty
as is it is of so-called real events. Before she came to Antwerp, Anne of the
Ascension, for example, reported having seen 'a great light, and in that light a
house', recognising it as the same place when she arrived at the convent (Hardman,
1936, 152). Jane of the Cross (Jane Rutter: 1704/10–81) told that 'she had seen all
the nuns of this convent some time before she left England, either in a dream or
she knew not how, but when she came to this house [she] perfectly rememberd all
their faces. One of the religious happend to be absent whom she mist, but meeting
her afterwards, knew her also ...' (*A1*, 321). After the death of Mary Xaveria,
an Antwerp citizen saw the nun standing at the foot of her bed 'her face partly
shaded ... on one side a resplendent starr which dazelled her eyes' (*A3*); Helen
of the Cross saw a deceased nun from her bed too, and 'look'd about her to find
from whence the light could come and perceived the little wooden cross on which

---

[23]   See II Corinthians 11:14. This view was frequently reiterated in Carmelite papers
as well as in other sources (see above, p. 82). Teresa de Jesus wrote: 'we should not cease
to be watchful against the devil's wiles lest he deceive us in the guise of an angel of light'
(*Interior Castle*, II, 211; and see Boguet, 1929 ed., 5, 17; *Malleus Maleficarum*, 122–4).

is painted a Christ invision'd with a bright glory like to the sun at midday and which continued so long that her eyes was weaken'd' (see above, p. 42). Physical sight, even that embedded in a dream or vision seldom stands on its own strength and is only confirmed when what was earlier predicted is apparently proven. At Lierre in January 1680, Anna Maria of St Joseph (Petronella van Dyck: 1650–*c.*1724) in her sickness 'saw clearly' a vision of Margaret of Jesus who had died the previous year: 'with her own countenance, but unspeakably glorious'. Anna's remarkable recovery, attributed to Margaret's intervention, is attested to by several nuns who signed a document describing it (*L3.36*). Yet it was the 'sweet smell' like burning perfume that actively (re)confirmed to the community at large the fact of Margaret's blessedness.

Sight in these documents may be the preliminary sense, the one on which intuitive nuns first draw for proof, but it is seldom the primary one; other senses bear out, indeed clarify, confirm, critically replace ocular evidence. The nuns express doubt about the status of vision in order to reinforce the veracity of their accounts; uncertainty is dispelled by subsequent events or additional signs. Readers in turn witness the nuns' progress from sensory doubt to certainty. The women are ever conformist in their reportage, yet quietly radical in creating its effects. By expressing scepticism that they go on to allay through multi-sensory cross-reference, and by questioning the truth of their own eyes, the nuns rhetorically enforce the strength of their spiritual sensorium. They cast doubt on their body's proof and even as they do so convince their readers and themselves of hidden sacred truths.

The nuns attending Anna Maria in her fever thought she was delirious and speaking 'idle'. They pulled the curtains closed round her bed, and only believed her claims about her vision after she was restored to health: 'Sister', she said to the Infirmarian and the other nuns in her room, 'do you not see a great light?'

Chapter 8

Sensate Certainty:[1] A Conclusion of Sorts

We might conclude where spiritual autobiography is often said to begin: with doubt.[2]

> *Sense* thinks the lightning borne before the thunder:
> What tels vs then they both together are?

So the poetic voice of John Davies' *Nosce Teipsum* (1599, 18) poses the dilemma that many philosophers have claimed to be at the heart of perceptual understanding: that our senses can be mistaken. Some, like Emmanuel Kant, give sharp riposte: '*The senses do not deceive*'; 'Error is thus a burden only to the understanding' (2006, 37).

Views of perception expose the relationship between ideas and their foundations. Davies' question is not after all just about cognitive (un)certainty and the connectivity of body, mind and meaning. It is also a question about our relationship with thought itself, one whose answer would depend on the paradigm adopted:

> If, for example, a person elevated himself [*sic*] above sense perception in order to philosophize and someone else for the same reason doubted sense perception, both would perhaps arrive at the same place, but the movements would be different, and the movement, of course, was what he was asking about in particular (Kierkegaard, *Johannes Climacus*, 1985, 150; a text to which I will return later in this discussion).

Teresa de Jesus responds in a very different way to questions like Davies' and to those of speculative philosophers, thereby revealing her approach to truth as well as her idea of what it is. Descartes wrote, using his stand-in persona Eudoxus who debates with Polyander (Everyman), 'I find it strange that men are so credulous as to base their knowledge on the certitude of the senses' (*Search for Truth*, 1984 ed., 407). Elsewhere he ponders the views of scholastic philosophers that 'there is nothing in the intellect which has not previously been in the senses' when it is certain, he says, that ideas of God and of the soul have never been there: 'It seems to me that trying to use one's imagination in order to understand these

---

[1]   The body is 'the locus of sensory perception ... the provider of all that we can be sure about, of what Hegel calls *sinnliche Gewissheit*, sensate certainty' (Rindisbacher, 1992, 3).

[2]   'Si fallor, sum': if I doubt, I exist (Augustine, *De Civitate Dei*, Book XI, 26).

ideas is like trying to use one's eyes in order to hear sounds or smell odours ... neither our imagination nor our senses could ever assure us of anything without the intervention of our intellect' (*Discourse on Method*, 1985 ed., I, 129).[3]

Teresa's *apatheia* (disengagement), in the manner but not the style of Greek sceptics, is both process and end. Lightning and thunder are to her only relevant (and figurative) because they point to underlying cause: a person is not even thinking (of God) when she is awakened 'as though by a rushing comet or a thunderclap'. Indeed, no sound is heard but the soul 'begins to tremble and complain ...' (*Interior Castle*, II, 276). Truth arrives in, and is authenticated by, sudden effect. A revelation of Christ's humanity similarly comes 'so quickly that we might liken the action to a flash of lightning' (315). Of course her references are metaphorical; they illustrate the irrelevance of the senses to spiritual knowledge.

Speed for her is of the essence. Teresa's approaches are 'event-led', instinctive, thought-less (except in the ensuing reflection). 'In the year 1575, during the month of April, when I was at work on the Beas foundation', one day at a meal, she wrote, giving detail sufficient to authenticate her account, 'I saw this vision, which lasted but the usual brief space of time – that of a lightning-flash. I thought Our Lord Jesus Christ was near me'; 'I was left with a feeling of complete certainty that this was the voice of God' (*Spiritual Relations*, I, 354).

In his treatise on melancholy, Robert Burton accounts for such swift shifts and the changed 'subjective experience of time' in medical-humoural terms, suggesting that suddenness posed danger. '[T]his thunder and lightning of perturbation', he writes

> causeth such violence and speedy alterations in our Microcosm, and many times subverts the good estate and temperature of it. For as the body works upon the mind, by his bad humours, troubling the spirits, sending gross fumes into the brain, and so disturbing the soul, and all the faculties of it ... so, on the other side, the mind most effectually works upon the body, producing by his passions and perturbations, miraculous alterations ... (1.2.3.1; cited Wood, 2010, 24)

For Teresa de Jesus and her Carmelites, while they express their physical 'alteration' in similar terms (pp. 29–33), the illuminative moment renders physical explanation auxiliary and excludes doubt, prompting a spontaneous leap in understanding; there is no consciousness in immediacy. What is more, the quickness of revelation (she repeats, and her nuns repeat: this lasted only a moment) collapses time, negates its relentless passage as irrelevant to wider meaning.[4] As for Søren Kierkegaard, 'An event introduces a rupture in the continuity of history'; it 'signifies what is still underway' but whose meaning is not yet secured (Fratoni, 2009, 183;

---

[3]   On perception of 'eternal truths' see *Principles of Philosophy*, 1985, I, 209–10. On his response to the Council of Trent's views on transubstantiation and the contradictions of sense-perception and surface contact, see *Objections and Replies*, 1984, II, 175–6.

[4]   On Time in the convents, see also Hallett, 2012c.

Kangas, 2007, 39). For Teresa de Jesus hiatus is indeed continuity; it is as if the truth was there from the beginning and the sense-bound self is only now able to catch up with it. Moreover, it is something whose genesis is present in the event itself; manifestations display their origin, first cause. Teresa de Jesus' theories of temporality, like Augustine's and again like Kierkegaard's later views, 'reopen the question of transcendence by means of the question of beginning' (Kangas, 2007, 3). Her approach is evidently un-dialectic; she is interested in self-annihilation in the face of the moment not in the face of an inductive opposition, eager to be spiritually assimilated into another's ambit which is already interiorly present in the self. As such she is not interested in either divorce or dilation of body/mind, and the dilemmas raised by later Cartesian methodologies do not figure in her philosophical ponderings. If in her disengagement she needed to reply to Davies' kind of question, she might then answer as he did, though for different reasons, that intellect and spirit cohabit: 'why do I the *Soule* and *Sense* deuide?' (1599, 19).

Teresa's Carmelite nuns essentially follow her views (with some updates based on place and pressure), even if most of them are less self-consciously systematic thinkers. For these women, real thunder and lightning also reveal underlying spiritual truths: God and his holy associates protect them from danger; the devil raising a thunderstorm 'like the day of judgement' with a stink of brimstone is seen off in a final thunderclap (p. 152); St Francis Xavier in a black cassock protects his namesake, Mary Xaveria, during a tempest on her voyage to Antwerp (*A3*, 122).[5] Sight, sound and smell thus bear out articles of faith that precede them, structure them, and sensory perception is guided by results; God allows the devil to misbehave in order to prove he allows it: he is there at the beginning to make meaning. Their bewilderment is caused by fearfulness not doubt.

Such contemplative theosophy is not intellectually self-centred therefore or concerned in the end with the precise location of cognitive powers. Its adherents have only a temporary interest in the role of an individual mind and body to overcome socialised *habitus* and replace it with a differently habituated poise. Personal narratives chart 'The effect of the [spiritual] traumatic event ... a dephasing of consciousness from its own temporality: the temporal "now" is no longer lived as an integral moment, relating to past-present and future-present, but placed out of time and out of being' (Kangas, 2007, 53). Such 'trauma' is for the Carmelite nuns brought about by acute introspection in which they face what they perceive as devotional aridity, working through purgation to illumination; once they are in a state of recollection, or even unexpectedly when they are not, it is happily brought about by spiritual wonder.

Having briefly mentioned his views, it is worth focusing for a moment on Søren Kierkegaard's discussion of speculative-spiritual approaches to sensory (and other) meaning. There are distinct and interesting overlaps with Teresian proposals. Kierkegaard's *Johannes Climacus or De Omnibus Dubitandum Est*

---

[5]   Likewise, caught at sea in a tempest of thunder and lightning on his way to the continent, Edmund Bedingfield was said to have been protected by the Virgin (*L13.7*, 104).

takes its pseudonym and title from a sixth-century abbot of St Catherine of Alexandria on Mount Sinai, the author of *Ladder of Paradise* which was translated into Latin through the Middle Ages and into Spanish in 1532. His subtitle ('everything must be doubted') epitomises the Cartesian method which the text explores by means of Kierkegaard's characteristic 'melancholy irony'. Johannes is depicted as living in seclusion with an 'inclosed nature'; his head is bowed 'not because he was listening to his [romantic] beloved's voice but because he was listening to the secret whisperings of thoughts' (1985, 118). He is thus framed within familiar contemplative *Canticle* environs yet preoccupied with speculative perusal: 'to him coherent thinking was a *scala paradisi*'. The text shows the consequences of following scepticism to its logical conclusion. When Johannes with his 30 steps arrives at higher thought, he experiences 'an indescribable joy, a passionate pleasure'. Gradually his inductive process unravels. He comes to understand that philosophy begins instead with wonder which is 'plainly an immediate category and involves no reflection upon itself. Doubt, on the other hand, is a reflection-category' (145).[6] Understanding arises in the end (as it does for Teresians) where understanding is not. 'In immediacy there is no relation, for as soon as there is relation, immediacy is cancelled' (167). Johannes faces crises of Cartesian-inspired duality; the moment he makes a statement about reality, contradictions arise: 'what I say is ideality' (language) and hence duplexity: consciousness and relation. In recognising a self who is conscious of both narrative and perception, a further self-fragmentation unfolds. Hence: 'when I say *I* am conscious of *this sensory impression*, I am expressing a triad' (168–9).

Teresa de Jesus' likewise accounts for such a process. She recognises that language cannot explain or sustain spiritual enquiry, that her own narrative 'idealities' are just that: metaphors for a divine-based truth. Her own triadic self-presentation thus answers fundamental questions at the heart of contemplative philosophy about the relationship between human and holy and the ways in which somatic sensibility mediates understanding of spiritual knowledge. In her consciousness of being reflective about the unthinkable, of describing the ineffable, she accordingly adumbrates a sensory self for whom personal history is only important as a means to chart epiphany (marking the before and after of profession, the moment of complete embrace of devotional discipline) and for whom meaning is through unthinking wonder. On the one hand, then, she creates the possibility of a time-free selfhood, available in the 'instant'; on the other she is aware of temporal dislocation caused by use of language. She is also conscious

---

[6]   Kangas argues that for Kierkegaard faith coincides with (is caused by) personal release: 'letting go of one's self-understanding as foundation, letting go of the conception of being (and of God) as what grounds and secures the self's being' (2007, 197). Fratoni suggests that he thereby relates Kierkegaard to the work of the Dominican 'Meister' Eckhart (von Hochheim: *c.*1260–*c,*1327) with his own focus on 'releasement' (*Gelassenheit*) (2009, 184). Eckhart's ideas are often said to have been an influence on Teresa's spirituality; and see above p. 74.

that her self-fashioning takes the shape it does because of the cultural conditions within which she works. She is very aware of her own paradox, considering the eternal while watching her words in front of scrutinising authorities. The Carmelite contemplative is thus linked with long-standing theologies of self that span periods (or make them irrelevant if one takes a still larger view); the early modern Carmelite is (by definition) historically bounded, her spiritual selfhood nuanced by contemporary histories and politics.

The Teresian Historical Moment and its Consequences[7]

Through the course of discussion I have suggested that we can trace the effect of reformist theologies on the ways that the Carmelite nuns at Antwerp and Lierre present their sensory narratives. We can identify important points of contact between the women and well-known proponents of philosophical debate (see above, p. 70). The nuns' writing makes it clear that they were interested in the same sorts of religious questions as Descartes (the relationship of the thinking person to her God) and that they approached these to obtain mainly spiritual answers. The nuns' connection with Jesuit advisors exposed them to philosophical controversies even through their teachers' tacit denial of Cartesian methods and through the ways they phrased their own conjecture to defend themselves against it. The references were two-way: Descartes had received a Jesuit education and echoed, sometimes parodied, their systems in his writing. The Jesuits had condemned Cartesianism, especially after their disputations at Paris and Leuven in 1640 and 1662; Descartes' writings were placed on the Index of prohibited books in 1663.[8] As ever, in order to mount their own campaign, Jesuit directors grappled with Cartesian precepts and built oppositional techniques into their own texts to offer counter-discourse. Their influence in turn shaped some of the nuns' own concerns when they presented accounts of their visionary-sensory experiences that their directors edited for use within, and in some cases outside, the convents.

This is particularly evident in the nuns' writing from the later period, especially in the editorial apparatus that surrounds them. The Life of Mary Xaveria, for example, was prepared at the request of the then-Prioress in around 1723 by Thomas Hunter, himself a Jesuit and previously Professor of logic and philosophy at Liège (see above, p. 32). It makes ready in its method the case for consideration of the nun's blessed status. Just as Percy Plowden constructed his case for the veneration of Mary Margaret of the Angels by citing eye-witness testimony to her autopsy and alleged miracles, so Hunter's pre-text expresses all the concern of

---

[7]   'To the best of [Climacus'] knowledge, the Greeks taught that philosophy begins with wonder (*Foundring*). A principle such as that cannot give rise to any historical consequence whatsoever' (Kierkegaard, 1985, 145).

[8]   On Descartes and the Jesuits, see Ariew, 2003.

an author with his sights on sceptics within his own reforming church and from Protestants keen to find evidence of Catholic extreme:

> I present the Publick with a Book which will be differently received according to the different dispositions of those into whose hands it will chance to fall: the mentioneing of visions, revelations and supernatural favours will raise the curiosity of some and prove a jest to others, and in all probability with relish with very few, in an age so little inclined to belive any thing of this nature. (*A3*, i)

Those who experience visions, revelations and supernatural favours are often considered to be deceived, he continues, using an allusion that often appears in these papers, as if their imagination or fancy was heightened 'by by some exteriour cause, or by an innate propension towards that wch appears extraordinary or singular: if we reflect besides on ye artifices of ye enemy who as ye Apostle says, 2: Cor: 11.14 *transfigures himself into an Angell of light* to seduce unwary souls, we shall still find greater danger of delusion in these uncommon paths'.[9] Accordingly, Masters of Mystical Science instruct that all visions, exterior or interior, imaginary or intellectual, are to be suspected as dangerous, never to be relied on. 'What happened to St Teresa in this kind is very notorious' (*A3*, i, vi). Hunter draws on gendered typologies:

> ... nothing in this kind should be made publick wch is not grounded upon sufficient testimonies to secure the Reader from being imposed upon; tho' this caution is alwayes necessary, yet more particular regard must be had to it when we treat any thing of this nature with relation to weamen, there are not wanting those and in great number, who exaggerate so much in them the weakness of nature, and the force of imagination and fancy that they value themselves upon discrediting every thing in this kind ... (i–ii)

Hunter incorporates into his account not only Mary Xaveria's own words but also testimony from her contemporaries (see p. 37 n. 29), a system of verification that anticipates, and thereby dispels, detractive criticism. Protestant writers use the same sort of technique of course. The 1646 tract *A Declaration of a Strange and Wonderfull Monster*, for instance, which describes the birth of a headless child to a Popish gentlewomen in Lancashire ('No parts in *England* hath had so many Witches, none fuller of Papists') claims to include testimonials from ministers, neighbours and a member of parliament. Other Protestant polemicists railed about the tricks and impostures of Popish priests who pass off 'the Blessed Virgins slippers and many Images of her Son, likewise an *Agnus Dei*, made of Virgins wax, that hath by virtue of our Diabolicall Coniurations hath power to preserve from fire and water' as another London-printed text expressed it in 1642 (*Grand Plutoes Remonstrance*, 3).

---

9   On other references to this possibility, see p. 82.

Edmund Bedingfield, who himself used pieces of *Agnus Dei* in his attempt to cure the Mostyn sisters of their alleged possession, similarly sought to verify his interpretation of bewitchment. His account and those of others in the convent make it clear that exorcism was sharply scrutinised by competing churches and subject to extensive cultural criticism. Shakespeare's *King Lear*, in the depiction of Edgar's 'Old Tom', for example, parodies those who claim to be possessed. Anti-Catholic polemic often suggested that priestly exorcism was a form of subterfuge, representing the exorcist as a 'conjurer' whose sleight of hand tricked the undiscerning audience.[10] Although Margaret (on the authority of the Virgin herself) instructed Bedingfield to make her case publicly known, to erect commemorative monuments and inaugurate anniversary processions (very much in the ways in which both Catholic and Protestant clerics elsewhere celebrated their respective success in casting out demons), the papers relating to her case were concealed within the Lierre community, locked up in the chest-of-the-three-keys. This suggests that a process of self-censorship operated to avoid unwanted publicity that had surrounded similar such cases in other convents, some of which indeed turned out to have been fraudulently conceived.[11] We can, then, identify an historical imperative within the nuns' texts to present their views as self-authenticating and beyond doubt especially that arising from gendered preconceptions, and we can see that their writing was in implicit dialogue with writers from other sects and with 'rationalists' who had their own reformist or speculative axes to grind in shaping sensory (among other) philosophies.

The Teresian Political Present

We can also trace a wider national politics at play in the nuns' writing, a politics that had deeply personal ramifications affecting the ways in which they presented their own sensory spirituality. The senses, indeed, were a key place in which competing 'truths' were played out as if essentially manifested, their various evidences mustered in support of opposing reformist arguments. On the front page of a treatise on 'notorious errors' of 'infidell' Protestants (attributed to Thomas Wright, printed in Antwerp in 1600), for instance, it reads: 'O Lord open the eyes of these men that they may see' (II Kings 6:20). Claims of sensory fault are also at the heart of Protestant satire on transubstantiation and the 'unreasoning' Papist who 'wants the use of his Senses ... he hath Eyes and sees not. For he cannot ...

---

[10]   Greenblatt, 1988 and Brownlow, 1993 both claim that Shakespeare was influenced by reading Samuel Harsnett's 1603 diatribe against exorcism, *A Declaration of Egregious Popish Impostures* ... (see Hallett, 2007b, 15). For discussion of Shakespeare's complex relationship with Catholicism, see Gillian Woods, forthcoming.

[11]   For example, huge adverse publicity was attracted by claims of demonic possession at an Ursuline convent in Loudun in the 1630s (de Certeau, 1970, 213–26), as well as by other contemporary cases (Hallett, 2007b, 17).

distinguish between Colour, Taste and Substance of Flesh and a Wafer' (*Character of a Papist*, 1673).

I have suggested that the nuns in exile sought to shape a restoration, not only by furthering royalist causes but also by inscribing Teresian somatic-spiritual influence, among other ways via a relic of Teresa sent to Mary of Modena in 1688 (p. 113).[12] Ideas of Teresian (and wider) tactility were behind this gifting just as ideas of an incarnational and 'Englishing' ethic motivated Tobie Matthew's dedicatory address to his translation of Teresa's *Flaming Hart* in 1642, prepared for the Antwerp women. He claimed that the then queen, Henrietta Maria, carried 'an extraordinary devotion' to Teresa de Jesus and to 'her holy Religious woemen of her Angelicall Order, whereof the English Nation ... hath a Monastery in Antwerpe' (3). He invites her to head 'that whole Troope, which may addresse it selfe to the imitation of her Heriocall actions ... which the God of Heaven, thought fit to infuse, with his enamoured hart, and omnipotent hand, into that most happy Soule'.

A similar nationalistic, paradoxically pan-European, and somatic-literary effort is pursued by the Discalced Carmelite friar Simon Stock (Thomas Doughty: 1574–1652) who worked as a missionary in England and sought to establish an English novitiate to train friars to work there. His 1619 text *The Practise How to Finde Ease, Rest, Repose, Content and Happines*, presented as *Written by a Religious Man of the Congregation of St Elias the Prophet, and the Order of our Blessed Lady of Mount Carmell* situates the senses and Teresa herself within a treatise on Boethian natural order in the commonwealth of which 'So strait is the bond of *Amitie* between all liuing things, in their kinde.' This is a particular sort of contingency in which he presents a series of sensory recompenses that contrast with Protestant 'carnall liberties and sensuall life under false pretexts' (6). How unlike the civil self-control of Catholic devotional discipline: '*this Epicurian Doctrine of Protestants, and libertie of their Gospell*' (10). He cites what he claims are the views of Luther, Calvin and Zvingli, attacking 'Lasciviousness under pretext of Religion'. Protestant England in particular thus emerges as dissolute.

Doughty presents an alternative vision of a body-politic at ease with itself, healthful in unity of faith. Teresa de Jesus is specifically and strategically mentioned. In the last chapter of his long text he lists the conditions for a restored utopia, qualities already present in those who represent it; this is the celestial city, the new Jerusalem of the Book of Revelations: here '*Corporall eyes* shall be delighted with the sight of the glorious Body of the Sonne of *God*' (462); 'their Eares shall be delighted with the melody of *Angels & Saints*'; 'their *Sense* of Smelling shall be delighted with the delicate smells, which proceed from the Body of our *Sauiour*' and of the martyrs and saints; 'If the bodie of our Blessed Mother *Teresa* [she was canonised three years later] ... yield so sweet a Smell here vpon Earth, as that it exceedeth the delight of all flowers, as is testified by sufficient witnesses: Imagin, if thou canst, how exceeding sweet shall be the Smell of the

---

[12]   For the wider involvement of the English convents in Restoration politics, see Walker, 2000; 2004.

body of our *Sauiour* ...' (462–4); 'their *Touch*, and whole Bodie, shalbe deligted with delitious Rayment' (468).

In reconceptualising the very space of contention, the kingdom from which Catholics are exiled, Doughty answers with directed delight what he construes as heretic epicurean indiscrimination, rhetorically incorporating Teresian sensory trace into the body of state. He presents through his imagery a renationalised religion, creating a baroque paean to Catholic continuity of faith that textually incorporates a process of integration and disputation: Biblical references appear in the page margins and contemporary references are included in the text. His system of remembrance ('their *Memoriei* shall be pleased, with a forgetfulnesse of all Disgustes and Discontents': 468) is calculated to counter alleged Protestant profligacies and put his readers in touch with an alternative imaginative past and future. Rather as Catholic commentators presented like-for-like sensory riposte (devotional for earthly), so Doughty constructs a poetic based on apocalyptic sensuality, one with Teresa firmly and dynamically central.

Body-politics: 'we Women understand them not'

As well as affording a perspective on early modern nationalism and religion, this investigation of perception in convents inevitably casts light on representations of women's relationship to the senses and on early modern constructions of femininity. Teresa de Jesus urged her nuns 'to be strong men', avoiding 'effeminate' affectionate expressions between themselves, instead saving them for Christ. She justified her use of figural speech 'as we women are not learned *or fine-witted*'; 'Do not let us suppose that the interior of the soul is empty; God grant that only women may be so thoughtless as to suppose that' (*Way of Perfection*, II, 35; 117).

Teresa-like claims for female foolishness are echoed in the words of Margaret Cavendish part cited in the sub-heading above: 'And as the matter of Governments, we Women understand them not, yet if we did, we are excluded from meddling therewith, and almost from being subject thereto ...' (*Sociable Letters*, 61). She maintained she had only limited access to the talk of philosophers, and that she did not understand Descartes when they met 'for he spake no English, and I understand no other language' (*Philosophical and Physical Opinions*, 1665, sig. B3v; cited Battigelli, 1998b, 40, note 1). Scholars generally locate Cavendish's education in seminal scientific discourse of the salons and letters of her husband and brother-in-law.[13] Certainly Cavendish's reception at the Royal Society in

---

[13]   Sarasohn notes that Cavendish was sometimes present at Newcastle's 'intellectual salon' in Paris, 'but she disclaimed any direct interaction with the philosophers, who spoke in French and Latin, while she claimed to know only English' (2010, 4). Despite her recognition that 'Cavendish wrote gendered natural philosophy' she seems to consider that she 'reflected', rather than resisted, reshaped or indeed exploited 'traits associated with women and men in the seventeenth century' (3).

1667, and her depiction by Samuel Pepys among others ('The whole story of this Lady is a romance ...') suggests the power of patriarchy to (seek to) undermine female endeavour.[14] Cavendish's stylistic method is similar to that of Teresa de Jesus. Her 'rambling volumes appear to record the spontaneous stream of her thoughts' (Battigelli, 1998b, 40); a self-fashioning 'survival strategy'.[15] Although she may position herself as an 'honorary man', she does so by reaffirming aspects of emphatic femininity that enables this to happen. In fact, like the Teresians, she constructs a complicated response to received typologies of gender. It is clear, therefore, from the networks into and out of the convents, including those within the Cavendish circle embracing Bacon and Hobbes (p. 70), that these women played a part in a debate that has generally been construed as primarily male.

As we have seen, early modern Carmelites engage in their narratives with ideas of historiography which at once appear to enforce and yet to thwart patriarchal attempts to forestall their putative power. Mary Frances Birkbeck began the Antwerp annals with an apology to her male spiritual director that is reminiscent of Teresa's own in her *Vida*: 'tho it be done in a poor and silly manner yet I hope the goodness and substance of the matter will in time move some friendly pious hand to put it into a more advantagious light, least the poorness of the style and want of meathod may lessen its intended effect'. Like Teresa, she cannily builds in a self-authenticating process: 'if your Rec finds any thing Contrary to true Doctrine or edification I beg you will please to scratch it out, as you read it, which will give more authority to what remains' (*A1*, vi–vii); we read *ergo* it is orthodox.

Such considered positioning reveals aspects of colonised as well as gendered resistance. In apparently deferring to male authority while claiming a direct link to Teresa's authority that is both somatic and textual, the nuns are able to occupy a kind of liminal 'third space'. In Bhabha's terms, this a transitive phase, 'a passage' which disrupts 'our sense of the historical identity of culture as a homogenizing, unifying force, authenticated by the originary Past' (1994, 37), kept alive in this case by the patristic tradition that the nuns reclaim, rewrite and reinvest. It is evident that the cultural positions occupied by these women within both

---

[14]   Sarasohn suggests that 'Boyle's dismissal of "ladies" may have inspired Cavendish's plan to ridicule the society ...' (2010, 32). She gives an account of the visit (25–33; quoting Pepys, 29, 31). See also Peter Dear (2007) on Cavendish's visit, her 'self-perceived subject position' and her *Observations Upon Experimental Philosophy* as a riposte to Robert Hooke's *Micrographia*.

[15]   See Semler, 2012, 327 on Cavendish's 'caginess and staginess' in relation to her use of other philosophers. She turned 'slipperiness' in her works to her own advantage; her 'authorial, assertive self-construction was based partly on her insistence that she had not read other authors' (Clairhout and Jung, 2011, 732). Webster notes of Cavendish's connection of women's 'useless experiments' in cooking with experimental philosophy that this is 'a savvy attempt to get the best of both worlds when it comes to positioning herself as an upper-class, female philosopher ... she grants herself the authority to critique these same experiments' despite being otherwise 'an honorary man' (2011, 725–6).

church and state directly influenced their textual strategies. If it is problematic to simplify the Nun as an emblematically colonised figure and the consciously-resisting religious as subaltern, then the writing of the Carmelite community in seventeenth-century Antwerp nonetheless displays features of resistance to an imperialising imperative. This is particularly evident in the nuns' composition of their own 'celebratory romance of the past' (Bhabha, 1994, 9), one which stakes claims for female authority. The women deviate in their writing from prescribed and patriarchal 'fixed tablets', creating a distinctive historicised narrative based on, and performing as it does so, a chain of sensorily-infused 'repeatable materiality' (Foucault, 1972, 102; 105), one which somatically exposes 'the difference of the same' (Bhabha, 1994, 22): of bodies, of texts, one with another.

Here mimicry is textually as well as bodily central. Bhabha draws on Naipaul's *The Mimic Men* (1967) in which the 'colonised' reveal desire to be 'authentic' by mimicking their would-be oppressors (1994, 85–92). As well as aping and reshaping male symbolic form, the Antwerp nuns themselves took a gendered stance within this scheme, embracing Teresa de Jesus' rhetoric of exaggerated femininity and, like Cavendish in a different context, thereby assuming positions of mimic *women*.

A Sensory Summary

This study of Carmelite expressiveness has uncovered a range of meanings attached to the sensory moment and to sensory history. Philosophical, theological, social, cultural and political impetuses can be seen to have shaped the nuns' understanding of their own personal experience during a period of intense debate about the nature of human-ness and its relationship (if any) with the divine. Such material, because it is so prolific and so detailed, invites study from a number of angles. It has the advantage of being time-framed, space-framed and composed by authors who are intent on self-scrutiny. While clearly not all aspects of the nuns' sensory explanations are uniquely Teresian, their expressiveness is often peculiarly so, and bears the marks of specifically Carmelite pressures and modes of perspicuity. It also reveals facets of wider cultural beliefs about the senses, not all of them of course deriving from an exclusively Catholic perspective though they are sometimes (not by any means always) nuanced by its tenets of belief.

In order to widen the exploration, and test still further the particularity of Carmelite experience, other similar groups might be likely subjects for future research. Papers from the domestic environs from which the nuns originated (and since they are often aristocratic households, such documents exist) might be investigated to see whether those who remained behind in England express their sensory experience in similar or different ways from family members who later lived in cloistered exile. Material from different religious Orders, of other denominations or faiths, may also offer contrasting or complementary gender, class or ethnic case-studies.[16] Papers from other contemplative religions, most especially those for whom detachment is central might be helpfully instructive, as would writings from more 'active' Orders, exposed on a more regular basis to both convent and non-cloistered life. Expatriate communities, migrants or travellers have also produced written testimony about their sensory encounter with, traversing and incorporating, 'difference'.[17] Individuals in sensory-defined groups (such as deaf or blind writers) may offer other sustained self-narratives that chart their sensory histories and raise issues to challenge hegemonic claims.

On the basis of this study of two convents, then, with their proximity to the cultural and literary worlds of other 'convents of pleasure' including those of Margaret Cavendish, we might investigate anew the relationships between canonical literary senses and histories, to review afresh the 'social energy' that accrued from, as well as into, convents, thereby collapsing cultural notions of 'centre' and 'periphery'. For those individuals and groups, like the Carmelites whose narratives span centuries of continuity, such research is likely to throw up challenges to historicising gestures of periodisation. For others we might trace moments of sensory realignment in the many histories of the body that are (or are not) attached to religious reformations. There are indeed many possibilities:

Here *Senses Apprehension* end doth take,
As when a Stone is into water cast ... (Davies, 1599, 47)

---

[16]   Matthew Milner offers a powerful account of the senses in fifteenth century and in post-Protestant-Reformation England, showing continuities and differences between Catholic and Protestant sensation (2011, 13–52). He alleges that: 'Reformed thought emphasized the distinction between the inner and outer self, between the transcendence of the divine and the sensible realties of human existence. This denied long established beliefs that shaped medieval religious sensing' (343). Such claims are complicated by Catholic continuities that were themselves reformist and which challenge ideas of periodicity and hiatus, and by reference to texts by mystics and by women in both denominations.

[17]   See for example Philip Major's edited collection of essays on *Literatures of Exile* (2010) which demonstrates the un-insularity of English intellectual life. Nuns and women have yet to be fully included in such histories.

Bibliography

Primary Sources

Manuscript Material

Antwerp archive: formerly at Lanherne Carmelite Convent, Cornwall, now St Helens Carmelite Convent, Merseyside

A1: Antwerp Annals, Volume 1

A2: Antwerp Annals, Volume 2

A3: The Life of Mary Xaveria of the Angels (Catherine Burton)

A4: The Life of Mary Margaret of the Angels (Margaret Wake)

Lierre archive: formerly at Darlington Carmelite Convent, County Durham

L1.1: Letters to and from Anne of the Ascension (Anne Worsley)

L1.5: Anne of the Ascension: prayers and appreciations

L1.6: Anne of the Ascension: papers by and relating to this nun

L3.5: 'How a Prioress is to exercise the religious in mortifications'

L3.27: Edmund Bedingfield's Life of Margaret of Jesus (Margaret Mostyn)

L3.39: Ursula of All Saints' account of Margaret of Jesus

L3.30: Life of Ursula of All Saints (Elizabeth Mostyn) and accounts of Margaret of Jesus by various nuns

L3.31: Life of Margaret of Jesus, Ursula of All Saints and an account of the Mostyn exorcism

L3.34: Constitutions and the Rule of St Albert; ghost story and other papers associated with Margaret of Jesus

L3.35: Margaret of Jesus' spiritual confessions

L4.39: Life of Margaret of St Teresa (Margaret Downes)

L4.41: A note on the eyes of Mary Margaret of the Angels (Margaret Wake)

L5.52: Plans of the convent

L13.7: Lierre Annals (recording deaths from 1652–1776)

L13.8: Lierre Annals (recording deaths from 1779–1877)

Printed and Reference

An Abridgement of the Life of S. Francis Xavrius of the Society of Iesus, New Apostle of India and Japony, Together with Some Few of the Innumerable Authentical Miracles Wrought by Him of Late Years [by W.B.] (St Omers: Thomas Gevbels, 1667)

The Accomplished Ladies Rich Closet of Rarities; Or, The Ingenious Gentlewoman and Servant-Maids Delightfull Companion ... (London: Nicholas Boddington & Joseph Blare, 1687)

Advertisement: At the Golden Head in King's-gate-street, near Red-Lyon-Square in Holborn is to be had Extraordinary Remedies for the following Distempers and Reasonable Rates ... (London, 1675)

Alacantara, Peter, *A Golden Treatise of Mentall Praier With Diuerse Spirituall Rules and Directions, No Lesse Profitable Then Necessarie For All Sorts of People,* trans. Giles Willoughby (Brussels: widow of Hubert Antone, 1632)

Ana de San Bartolome, *Autobiography and Other Writings*, ed. and trans. Darcy Donahue (Chicago & London: University of Chicago Press, 2008)

Aristotle, *De Anima* in R. McKeon ed. *The Basic Works of Aristotle* (New York: Random House, 1941)

Augustine, St, *Confessions*, trans. Henry Chadwick (Oxford: Oxford University Press, 1992, rep. 2008)

Bacon, Francis, *The New Organon, Or True Direction Concerning the Interpretation of Nature* (1620)

——, *Silva Silvarum: Or a Natural History* (London: JH for William Lee, 1626)

Baker, Augustine, *Sancta Sophia, or Directions for the Prayer of Contemplation & C, Extracted Out of More Then XL Treatises Written by the Late Ven. Father F. Augustine Baker, a Monke of the English Congregation of the Holy Order of S. Benedict, and Methodically Digested by the R.F. Serenvs Cressy of the Same Order and Congregation* (Douai: John Patte and Thomas Fievet, 1657)

Benet of Canfield, *The Rule of Perfection* (Rouen: Cardin Hamillion, 1609)

——, *The Bright Starre, Leading to & Centring In Christ our Perfection* (London: MS, 1646)

Boguet, Henri, *An Examen of Witches Drawn from Various Trials of Many of this Sect in the District of Saint Oyan de Joux Commonly Known as Saint Claude in the County of Burgundy Including the Procedure Necessary to a Judge in Trials for Witchcraft*, trans. E. Allen Ashwin, ed. Montague Summers (London: John Rodker, 1929)

Bonhours, Dominique, *The Life of St Francis Xavier of the Society of Jesus, Apostle of the Indies and of Japan*, trans. John Dryden (London: Jacob Tonson, 1688)

Boyle, Robert, *Some Considerations Touching the Usefulnesse of Experimentall Naturall Philosophy* (London, 1663)

——, *Experiments, and Observations, About the Mechanical Production of Tast* (London: E. Flesher, 1675)

Brathwaite, Richard, *Essaies Vpon the Fiue Senses* (London: E. Griffin, 1620)

——, *The English Gentlewoman, Drawne Out of the Full Body Expressing What Habillments Doe Best Attire Her, What Ornaments Doe Best Adorne Her, What Complements Doe Best Accomplish Her* (London: B. Alsop and T. Fawcet, 1631)

——, *The English Gentleman, and The English Gentlewoman: Both in One Volume* (3rd edition: London: John Dawson, 1641)

Bromley, Henry, *A Catalogue of Engraved British Portraits, from Egbert the Great to the Present Time* ... (London, 1793)

Brown, Levinus, *The Manner of Performing the Novena, or, The Nine Days devotion to St Francis Xaverius of the Society of Jesus and Apostle of India, As Also the Devotion of Nine Fridays to the Same Saint* (St Omer, sn, 1690)

Browne, Thomas, *Religio Medici* (London, 1642)

Bruto, Giovanni Michele, *The Necessarie, Fit and Conuenient Education of a Yong Gentlewoman, Written Both in French and Italian and Translated into English by W.P.* (London: Adam Islip, 1598)

Bulwer, John, *Chirologia, Or The Naturall Language of the Hand* (London: Thomas Harper, 1644)

Burton, Robert, *The Anatomy of Melancholy*, [1621] ed. Holbrook Jackson (New York: Review Books, 2001)

Cavendish, Margaret, *Philosophical and Physical Opinions* (London, 1655)

——, *Philosophical Letters* (London, 1664)

——, *The Description of a New World, Called the Blazing World* [1666] in *Paper Bodies: A Margaret Cavendish Reader*, ed. Sylvia Bowerbank and Sara Mendelson (Letchworth: Broadview, 2000), 151–251

——, *Observations Upon Experimental Philosophy* [1666] (Cambridge: Cambridge University Press, 2001)

——, *Life of the thrice noble, high and puissant prince William Cavendish, Duke, Marquess and Earl of Newcastle* (London, 1667)

——, *Grounds of Natural Philosophy* (London, 1668)

——, *The Convent of Pleasure* [1688], in *Paper Bodies: A Margaret Cavendish Reader*, ed. Sylvia Bowerbank and Sara Mendelson (Letchworth: Broadview, 2000), 97–135

——, *Sociable Letters*, ed. James Fitzmaurice (Letchworth: Broadview, 2004)

Chapman, George, *Ouids Baquet of Sence, A Coronet for his Mistress Philosophie, and His Amorous Zodiake* (London: James Roberts, 1595)

——, *Ouids Baquet of Sence, A Coronet for his Mistress Philosophie, and His Amorous Zodiake* (London: B. Alsop & T. Fawcet, 1639)

The Character of a Papist (London, 1673)

Cloud of Unknowing, ed. Clifton Wolters (Harmondsworth: Penguin, 1961, rep. 1976)

Coleridge, H.J., ed., *An English Carmelite: The Life of Catharine Burton, Mother Mary Xaveria of the Angels, of the English Teresian Convent at Antwerp*, (London: Burns, Oates & Washbourne, 1876)

——, ed., *The Life and Letters of St Teresa* (2nd edition; London: Burns & Oates, 1893)

Courtin, Antione de, *The Rules of Civility, or Certain Ways of Deportment Observed in France, Amongst All Persons of Quality, Upon Several Occasions* (London: John Martyn, 1671)

Crooke, Helkiah, *Mikrokosmographia: A Description of the Body of Man* (London: 1615)

Davies, John, *Nosce Teipsum* (London: Richard Field, 1599)

——, *Nosce Teipsum: A Work for None But Angels & Men, That is To Be Able to Look Into, and To Know Ourselves* ... (London: MS for Thomas Jenner, 1653)

Daza, Antonio, *The Historie, Life and Miracle, Extasies and Revelations of the Blessed Virgin, Sister Ioane of the Crosse of the Third Order of Our Holy Father S. Francis* (St Omers: C. Boscard, 1625)

Declaration of a Strange and Wonderfull Monster: Born in Kirkham Parish in Lancashire (the Childe of Mrs. Haughton, a Popish Gentlewoman) ... (London, 1646)

Della Casa, Giovanni, *Galateo of Maister Iohn Della Casa, Archbeshop of Beneuenta, or Rather, A Treatise of the Manners and Behauiours, it Behoueth a Man to Vse and Eschewe in His Familiar Conuersation*, trans. Robert Peterson (London: Henry Middleton, 1576)

——, *Galateo Espagnol, or The Spanish Gallant Instructing Thee in That Which Thou Must Doe and Take Heed of in Thy Usuall Cariage, To Be Well Esteemed, and Loved of the People*, trans. and ed. Lucas Gracian Dantisco, based on Giovanni Della Casa, *Galateo* (London: E. Griffin, 1640)

——, *The Refin'd Courtier, or A Correction of Several Indecencies Crept into Civil Conversation*, trans. Nathaniel Waker (London: R. Royston, 1663)

Descartes, René, *Rules for the Direction of the Mind; The World and Treatise on Man; Discourse and Essays; Principles of Philosophy; Comments on a Certain Broadsheet; Description of the Human Body; The Passions of the Soul* in *The Philosophical Writings of Descartes, Volume I*, trans. John Cottingham, Robert Stoothoff and Dugald Murdoch (Cambridge: Cambridge University Press, 1985, rep. 2006)

——, *Meditations on First Philosophy; Objections and Replies; The Search for Truth* in *The Philosophical Writings of Descartes, Volume II*, trans. John Cottingham, Robert Stoothoff and Dugald Murdoch (Cambridge: Cambridge University Press, 1984, rep. 1999)

——, *Discourse on Method, Optics, Geometry and Meteorology*, trans. Paul J. Olscamp (Indianapolis & Cambridge: Hackett Publishing, 1965, rep. 2001)

——, *Descartes: Philosophical Letters*, trans. and ed. Anthony Kenny (Minneapolis: University of Minnesota Press, 1970)

Doughty, Thomas, *The Practise How to Finde Ease, Rest, Repose, Content and Happines. Written by a Religious Man of the Congregation of St Elias the Prophet and the Order of Our Blessed Lady of Mount Carmell, Restored by the Blessed Mother Teresa* (Rouen: Jacques Fouet, 1619)

Drayton, Michael, Idea [1619], in *Daniel's Delia and Drayton's Idea*, ed. Arundell Esdaile, (London: Chatto and Windus, 1908)

Dryden, John, trans. Dominique Bonhours, *The Life of St Francis Xavier of the Society of Jesus, Apostle of the Indies and of Japan* (London: Jacob Tonson, 1688)

Eliot, George, *Middlemarch* (Harmondsworth: Penguin, 1964)

EEBO: Early English Books Online

An Epistle of a Catholique to his Friend a Protestant Touching the Doctrine of Reall Presence, Or the Answer to a Question Propounded in These Tearms What Should Move You, Contrary to the Plain Testimony of Your Senses (SI, sn, 1659)

Erasmus, Desiderius, *The Ciuilite of Childehode, With the Discipline and Instrucion of Children*, trans. Thomas Paynell (London: John Tisdale, 1560)

——, *Lingua* in *Collected Works of Erasmus*, ed Elaine Fantham and Erika Rummel (Toronto: University of Toronto, 1989)

Evans, Edward, *Catalogue of a collection of engraved portraits ... comprising nearly twenty thousand portraits of persons connected with the history and literature of this country, from the earliest period to the present time* (London, 1836)

The Eye Cleard, Or, A Preservative for the Sight Being a Quaint Composition Without Fenell or Bright-Eye to Restore the Poreblind ... (London: G. Bishop, 1644)

Falconer, John *The Mirrour of Created Perfection, Or The Life of the Most Blessed Virgin Mary Mother of God* (St Omer: English College Press, 1632)

Francis Xavier: Torsellino, Orazio, *The Admirable Life of S. Francis Xavier* (St Omer: English College Press, 1632)

——, *An Abridgement of the Life of S. Francis Xavrius of the Society of Iesus, New Apostle of India and Japony, Together with Some Few of the Innumerable Authentical Miracles Wrought by Him of Late Years* [by W.B.] (St Omers: Thomas Gevbels, 1667)

——, *An Instruction to Performe With Fruit the Devotion of Ten Fridays in Honour of S. Francis Xaverius Apostle of the Indies* (St Omer: sn, 1670)

——, Bonhours, Dominique, *The Life of St Francis Xavier of the Society of Jesus, Apostle of the Indies and of Japan*, translated John Dryden (London: Jacob Tonson, 1688)

——, Brown, Levinus, *The Manner of Performing the Novena, or, The Nine Days devotion to St Francis Xaverius of the Society of Jesus and Apostle of India, As Also the Devotion of Nine Fridays to the Same Saint* (St Omer, sn, 1690)

Galen, *Galen: Selected Works*, trans. P.N. Singer (Oxford: Oxford University Press, 1997)

Grand Plutoes Remonstrance, or, The Devill Horn-mad at Roundheads and Brownists ... 2. His Copulation with a Holy Sister ... (London, 1642)

Gregory, St, *Morals on the Book of Job*, ed. James Bliss, and Charles Marriott (Oxford: J.H. Parker, 1844)

Guevara, Antonio de, *The Government of a Wife, or, Wholsom and Pleasant Advice for Married Men in a Letter to a Friend, Written in Portuguese by Don Francisco Manuel [Mello]* (London: Jacob Tonson, 1697)

Hamilton, Adam, *The Chronicle of the English Augustinian Canonesses Regular of the Lateran, at St Monica's in Louvain (Now at St Augustine's Priory, Newton Abbot, Devon) 1548 to 1625* (Edinburgh and London: Sands & Co., 1904)

Harsnett, Samuel, *A Declaration of Egregious Popish Impostures Practised by Edmunds, alias Weston, a Jesuit, and Divers Romish Priests His Wicked Associates* (London: James Roberts, 1603)

Hawkins, Francis, *Youths Behavior Or Decency in Conversation Amongst Men* (London: W. Wilson, 1651)

Herbert, Edward, *On Truth, as it is Distinguished from Revelation, the Probable, the Possible and the False* (Paris, 1624; London, 1633, trans. 1639)

Hilton, Walter, *The Scale (or Ladder) of Perfection* (London: T.R., 1659)

Hobbes, Thomas, *Leviathan*, ed. K.R. Minogue (London and New York: Dent & Dutton, 1973)

——, *A Minute or First Draft of the Optics*, in *The English Works of Thomas Hobbes*, ed. William Molesworth, 11 volumes, Volume VII (London, 1839–45)

John of Avila, *The Audi Filia, Or a Rich Cabinet Full of Spirituall Iewells*, trans. Tobie Matthew (St Omer: English College Press, 1620)

——, *The Cure of Discomfort, Conteyned in the Spirituall Epostles of Doctour I de Auila, Most Renowned Preacher of Spaine, Most Profitable For Allm, and Particularly For Persons in Distress* (Rouen and St Omer: John le Coustourier, 1623)

——, *Certain Selected Spirituall Epistles Written by That Most Reuerend Holy Man Doctor I de Auila, a Most Renowned Preacher of Spaine Most profitable for All Sortes of People, Whoe Seeke Their Saluation* (Rouen: the Widow of Nicolas Courant, 1631)

John of the Cross, *The Ascent Of Mount Carmel*, trans. David Lewis (London and Aylesbury, 1906, rep. 1928)

Jorden, Edward, *A Briefe Discourse of a Disease called the Suffocation of the Mother. Written Uppon Occasion Which Hath Beene of Late Taken Thereby, to Suspect Possession of an Evill Spirit, or Some Such like Supernaturall Power ...* (London: John Windat, 1603)

Journal of Meditations for Every Day of the Year [by N.B.] (Sl: sn, 1687)

Julian of Norwich, *XVI Revelations of Divine Love Shewed to a Devout Servant of Ouyr Lord Called Mother Juliana, an Anchorete of Norwich Who Lived in the Dayes of King Edward the Third, ed. By RFS Cressy* (London: sn, 1670)

——, *A Book of Showings of the Anchoress Julian of Norwich*, ed. E. Colledge and J. Walsh, 2 volumes (Toronto: University of Toronto Press, 1978)

Kant, Immanuel, *Anthropology from a Pragmatic Point of View*, trans. Robert B. Louden (Cambridge: Cambridge University Press, 2006)

Kempis, Thomas A., *The Imitation of Christ*, trans. Leo Sherley-Price (Melbourne, London, Baltimore: Penguin, 1952, rep. 1954)

Kenworthy-Browne, Christina, ed., *Mary Ward (1585–1645): 'A Briefe Relation', with Autobiographical Fragments and a Selection of Letters* (Woodbridge, Suffolk: Boydell Press for the Catholic Record Society, 2008)

Kierkegaard, Søren, *Johannes Climacus or De Omnibus Dubitandum Est*, ed. and trans. Howard V. Hongand and Edna H. Hong (Princeton NJ: Princeton University Press, 1985), 113–72

——, *The Sickness Unto Death: A Christian Psychological Exposition for Edification and Awakening by Anti-Climacus*, trans. Alastair Hannay (Harmondsworth: Penguin, 1989)

Knatchbull, Lucy, *The Life of Lady Lucy Knatchbull by Sir Tobie Matthew*, ed. David Knowles (London: Sheed & Ward, 1931)

Lavatar, Ludwig, *Of Ghostes and Spirites Walkyng By Nyght and of Strange Noyses, Crackes and Sundry Forewarnyngs Which Commonly Happen Before the Death of Menne, Great Slaughters, and Alterations of Kyngdomes*, trans. Robert Harrison (London, 1572)

Louis Lémery, *A treatise of all sorts of foods, both animal and vegetable: also of drinkables: Giving an account how to chuse the best sort of all kinds; of the good and bad effects they produce; the principles they abound with; the time, age and constitution they are adapted to. Wherein their nature and use is explain'd according to the sentiments of the most eminent physicians and naturalists ancient and modern. The whole divided into one hundred seventy-six chapters. With remarks upon each. Written originally in French, by the Learned M.L. Lemery, physician to the King, and member of the Royal Academy. Translated by D. Hay, M.D. To which is added, an introduction treating of foods in general: a table of the chapters, and an alphabetical index. A work of universal use to all who are inclin'd to know the good or bad qualities of what they eat or drink* (London: Printed for W. Payne, opposite Durham-Yard, in the Strand, MDCCXLV. [1745]

Lessius, Leonard, *Hygiasticon: Or, The Right Course of Preserving Life and Health Unto Extream Old Age Together With Soundnesse and Integritie of the Senses, Judgement and Memorie* (Cambridge: R. Daniel and T. Buck, 1634)

Lodge, Thomas, *A Treatise of the Plague* (London, 1603)

Luis de Granada, *Of Prayer and Meditation Contayning Foure-teene Meditations for the Seauen Dayes of the Weeke, Both for Mornings and Euenings, Treating of the Principall Matters and Holy Miseries of our Fayth*, trans. Richard Hopkins (London: Thomas Gosson and Richard Smith, 1596)

——, *Granados Spirituall and Heuenlie Exercises: Deuided into Seuen Pithie and Briefe Meditations, for Euery Day in the Weeke One*, trans. Francis Meres (London: James Roberts, 1598)

——, *The Sinners Guyde, A Worke Contayning the Whole Regiment of a Christian Life, Deuided into Two Bookes, Wherein Sinners are reclaimed from the by-path of Vice and Destruction, and Brought Vnto the High-way of Euerlasting Happinesse*, trans. Francis Meres (London: James Roberts, 1598)

——, *A Spiritual Doctrine, Conteining a Rule to Liue Wel, With Diuers Praiers and Meditations*, trans. Richard Gibbons (Louvain: Laurence Kellan, 1599)

——, *A Memoriall of a Christian Life, Wherein are Treated al Such Things as Appertaine vnto a Christian to do from the Beginning of his Co[n]uersion, vntil the end of his Perfection*, trans. Richard Hopkins (Rouen: George Loyselet, 1599)

——, *The Flowers of Lodowicke of Granado*, trans. Thomas Lodge (London: Thomas Heyes, 1601)

——, *A Paradise of Prayers, Containing the Purity of Deuotion and Meditation, Gathered Out Of All the Spirituall Exercises of Lewes of Granado*, trans. Thomas Lodge (London: R. Field, 1614)

Luis de la Puente, *Meditations Vpon the Mysteries of Oyr Holie Faith With the Practise of Mental Prayer Touching the Same* (St Omers: Boscard, 1619)

——, *Meditations Vpon the Mysteries of Our Faith Corresponding to the Three Wayes, Purgatiue, Illuminatiue and Vnitiue* (St Omer: English College Press, 1624)

Macrobius, *Commentary on the Dream of Scipio*, ed. and trans. W.H. Stahl (New York, 1952, rep. 1990)

The Manner of Receiving the Poor Clares of St Clare to Clothing: and the Ceremonies of their Professing in that Religious Order (Dublin: J. Barlow, 1795)

Mathew, Arnold Harris, and Annette Calthrop, *The Life of Sir Tobie Matthew: Bacon's Alter Ego* (London: Elkin Mathews, 1907)

Matthew, Tobie, trans. *The Confessions of the incomparable doctour S. Augustine, translated into English. Togeather with a large preface, which it will much import to be read ouer first; that so the book it selfe may both profit, and please, the reader, more* (St Omer, 1620; 2nd ed. Paris, 1638)

——, *Of the Love of our Only Lord and Savior, Jesus Christ. Both that which he beareth to Vs; and that also which we are obliged to beare to Him. Declared By the principall Mysteries of the Life, and Death of our Lord; as they are deliuered to us in Holy Scripture* (Antwerp, 1622)

The Malleus Maleficarum of Heinrich Kramer and James Sprenger [1487], ed. and trans. Montague Summers (New York: Dover Publications, 1971)

Meditations Collected and Ordered for the Vse of the English Colledge of Lisbon (Lisbon: Paul Crasbeeck, 1649)

Mello, Francisco Manuel de, *The Government of a Wife, or Wholsom and Pleasant Advice for Married Men in a Letter to a Friend* (London: Jacob Tonson, 1697)

Meres, Francis, *Palladis Tamia: Wits Treasury Being the Second Part of Wits Common Wealth* (London: P. Short, 1598)

Molina, Antonio de, *A Treatise on Mental Prayer* (St Omer: English College Press, 1617)

——, *Spiritual Exercises, Very Profitable for Actiue Persons Desirous of Their Salvation* (Mechlin: Henry Iaey, 1623)

More, Gertrude, *The Holy Practises of a Devine Lover, or, The Sainctly Ideots Deuotions* (Paris: Lewis de la Fosse, 1657)

——, *Confessio Amantis: The Spiritual Exercises of the Most Vertvovs and Religious D. Gertrude More of the Holy Order of S. Bennet and the English Congregation of Our Ladies of Comfort in Cambray* (Paris: Lewis de la Fosse, 1658)

——, *The Spiritual Exercises of the Most Vertvovs and Religious D. Gertrude More of the Holy Order of S. Bennet and the English Congregation of Our Ladies of Comfort in Cambray*, selected and introduced by Arthur F. Marotti, *The Early Modern Englishwoman: A Facsimile Library of Essential Works* (Aldershot and Burlington VT: Ashgate, 2010)

More, Henry, *The Life and Doctrine of Our Savior Iesus Christ, With Short Reflections for the Help of Such as Desire to Use Mentall Prayer* (Ghent: Maximiliaen Graet, 1656)

Mullins, James, *Some Observations Upon the Cylonian Plant: Shewing Its Virtues Against Deafness* (London, 1695)

Nixon, Anthony, *The Dignitie of Man, Both in the Perfections of his Soule and Bodie, Shewing As Well the Faculties in the Disposition of the One: As The Senses and Organs in the Composition of the Other* (London: Edward Allde, 1612)

ODNB: Oxford Dictionary of National Biography

Osuna, Francisco de, *The Third Spiritual Alphabet*, trans. M. Giles (New York: Paulist, 1981)

Paré, Ambroise, 'Introduction a la chirugie', *Oeuvres Completes d'Ambroise Paré* (Paris: Chez Gabriel Buon, 1585)

Paul of St Ubald, *The Soul's Delight* (Antwerp: William Lesteems, 1654)

Pepwell, Henry, *The Cell of Self-Knowledge: Seven Early English Mystical Treatises Printed by Henry Pepwell in 1521* (London: Hard Press, nd)

Plautus, Jerome, *The Happines of a Religious State*, trans. Henry More (Rouen: John Cousturier: 1632)

Procesos de Beatificación y Canonización de Santa Teresa de Jesús, ed. Silverio de Santa Teresa, 3 vols., *Bliblioteca Mistica Carmelitana* (Burgos, 1934–35)

Puccini, Vincenzo, *The Life of the Holy and Venerable Mother Suor Maria Maddalena De Patsi, a Florentine Lady & Religious of the Order of the Carmelites*, trans. Tobie Matthew (St Omer: English College Press, 1619)

——, *The Life of St Mary Magdalene of Pazzi, a Carmelite Nunn, Newly Translated Out of Italian by the Rev F Lezin de sainte Scholastique ...* (London: R. Taylor, 1687)

A Queens Delight: The Art of Preserving, Conserving and Candying, As Also, A Right Knowledge of making Perfumes, and Distilling the Most Excellent Waters (London, 1671)

Rémy, Nicolas, *Demonolatry* (Lyons: Vincentius, 1595)

Reynolds, Edward, *A Treatise of the Passions and Faculties of the Soule of Man* (London, 1640)

Ribera, Francisco de, *A Second Part of the Life of the Holy Mother S. Teresa of Jesus, or the History of Her Foundations Written by Herself, Whereunto Are Annexed her Death, Burial and the Miraculous Incorruption and Fragrancy of her Body, Together with her treatise of the Manner of Visiting the Monasteries of Discalced Nuns* (London: sn, 1669)

Rio, Martín del, *Investigations into Magic*, trans. P.G. Maxwell-Stuart (Manchester: Manchester University Press, 2000)

Ripa, Cesare, *Iconologia* (Rome, 1603)

Rodriguez, Alfonso, *A Treatise of Mentall Prayer, With Another of the Presence of God*, trans. Tobie Matthew (St Omer: English College Press, 1627)

——, *A Short and Sure Way to Heauen, and Present Happines, Taught in a Treatise of our Conformity with the Will of God* (St Omer: the widow of C. Boscard, 1630)

——, *A Christian Mans Guide, Wherein are Contayned Two Treatises, The One Shewing Vs the Perfection of Our Ordinary Workes, The Other the Purity of Intention We Ought To Haue In All Our Actions*, trans Tobie Matthew (St Omer: George Seutinb, 1630)

——, *A Stoope Gallant, Or a Treatise of Humilitie*, trans. Tobie Matthew (Rouen: J. Cousturier, 1631)

——, *The Two First Treatises of the First Part of Christian Perfection*, trans. Tobie Matthew (St Omer: G. Seutin, 1631)

——, *A Treatise of Modesty and Silence* (St Omer: widow of C. Boscard, 1632)

——, *Practice of Christian and Religious Perfection* (London: Thomas Hales, 1697)

Rule of the Holy Virgin S. Clare, Togeather With the Admirable Life of S. Catharine of Bologna, of the Same Order, Both Translated into English, selected and introduced by Claire Walker, *The Early Modern Englishwoman: A Facsimile Library of Essential Works* (Aldershot and Burlington VT: Ashgate, 2006)

Sabran, Lewis, *A Sermon Preach'd in the Chappel of His Excellency the Spanish Ambassador on the Second Sunday of Advent, December 4 1687, On Which was Solemniz'd the Feast of St Francis Xaverius of the Society of Jesus, Apostle of the Indies and Kingdom of Japan* (London: Henry Hills, 1687)

Sales, Francis de, *An Introduction to a Deuout Life, Leading to the Way of Eternitie*, trans. John Yakesley (London: Nicholas Okes, 1616)

——, *A Treatise of the Loue of God* (Douai: Gerard Pinchon, 1630)

——, *Delicious Entertainments of the Soule* (Douai: Gerard Pinchon, 1632)

——, *The Spiritual Director of Devout and Religious Souls* (London: sn, 1704)

Scarisbricke, Edward, *The Life of Lady Warner of Parham in Suffolk, in Religion Call'd Sister Clare of Jesus* (London: Thomas Hales, 1691)

Sidney, Philip, *The Countess of Pembroke's Arcadia (The Old Arcadia)*, ed. Katherine Duncan-Jones (Oxford: Oxford University Press, 1985, rep. 1999)

Teresa de Jesus, *The Lyf of the Mother Teresa of Iesus, Foundresse of the Monasteries of the Descalced or Bare-footed Carmelite Nunnes and Fryers of the First Rule*, translated W.M. (Antwerp: Henry Jaye, 1611)

——, *The Flaming Hart or the Life of the Glorious S. Teresa, Foundresse of the Reformation of the Order of the All-Immaculate Virgin-Mother, our B. Lady of Mount-Carmel*, trans. Tobie Matthew (Antwerp: Iohannes Meursius, 1642)

——, Francisco de Ribera, *A Second Part of the Life of the Holy Mother S. Teresa of Jesus, or the History of Her Foundations Written by Herself, Whereunto Are*

Annexed her Death, Burial and the Miraculous Incorruption and Fragrancy of her Body, Together with her treatise of the Manner of Visiting the Monasteries of Discalced Nuns (London: sn, 1669)

——, *The Life of the Holy Mother S. Teresa, Foundress of the Reformation of the Discalced Carmelites, According to the Primitive Rule, Divided into Two Parts, the Second Containing Her Foundations* (London: Walter Travers, 1671)

——, *The Complete Works of St Teresa, Volume I: The Life; The Spiritual Relations*, ed. E Allison Peers (London and New York: Sheed & Ward, 1944)

——, *The Complete Works of St Teresa, Volume II: Book Called Way of Perfection; Interior Castle; Conceptions of the Love of God; Exclamations of the Soul to God*, ed. E Allison Peers (London and New York: Sheed & Ward, 1946)

——, *The Complete Works of St Teresa, Volume III: Book of the Foundations; Minor Prose Works; Poems*, ed. E. Allison Peers (London and New York: Sheed & Ward, 1946)

——, *The Book of Her Life; Spiritual Testimonies*; *Soliloquies,* in *The Collected Works of St Teresa of Avila*, Volume I, trans. Kieran Kavanaugh and Otilio Rodriguez (Washington DC: Institute of Carmelite Studies, 1976)

Tomkis, Thomas, *The Combat of the Tongue, and the Fiue Senses for Superiority, A Pleasant Comoedie* (London: G. Eld, 1607)

Torsellino, Orazio, *The Admirable Life of S. Francis Xavier* (St Omer: English College Press, 1632)

A True and Perfect Relation of the Late and Dreadful Inundation Which Happened in Holland on Sunday Novemb[er] 3, 1675 at 4 of the Clock Afternoon ... as Also a Brief Account of a Dreadful Storm with Thunder and Lightning on the same day at Antwerp and Gent ... (London: sn, 1675)

Turberville, Henry, *An Abridgement of Christian Doctrine, With Proofs of Scripture for Points Controverted, Catechistally Explain'd By Way of Question and Answer* (Basil: sn, 1680)

Ward, Mary, *Mary Ward (1585–1645): A Briefe Relation ... with Autobiographical Fragments and a Selection of Letters,* ed. Christina Kenworthy-Browne (Woodbridge, Suffolk: Boydell Press for the Catholic Record Society, 2008)

Webster, John, *The Duchess of Malfi* in *English Renaissance Drama: a Norton Anthology,* David Bevington et al, eds., (New York and London: Norton, 2002), 1749–1832

West, Richard, *The Schoole of Vertue, the Second Part: Or, The Young Schollers Paradice Contayning Verie Good Precepts, Wholesome Instructions, the High-way to Good Manners, Dieting of Children, and Brideling Their Appetites* (London: Edward Griffin, 1619)

A Wonderful Relation of a Strange Appearance of the Devil in the Shape of a Lion to a Popish Novice, Not Far from Redborn in Hertfordshire (London, 1680): Wing W3374A

The Whore of Babylon's Pockey Priest or, a True Narrative of the Apprehension of William Geldon alias Bacon a Secular Priest of the Church of Rome Now Prisoner in Newgate .... (London: for Thomas Fox, 1679/80): Wing W2068

Wilson, Thomas, *Arte of Rhetorique* (London, 1553)

Woolley, Hannah, *The Compleat Servant-Maid; or, The Young Maidens Tutor ...* (London, 1664; 1685)

Wright, Thomas, *Certaine Articles or Forcible Reasons Discouering the Palpable Absurdities & Most Notorious Errours of the Protestants Religion* (Antwerp, 1600)

——, *The Passions of the Minde in Generall in Six Bookes* (London: Miles Flesher, 1630)

Yepes, Diego de, *Vida, Virtudes y Milagros de la Bienaventurada Virgen Teresa de Jesús* (Madrid, 1599) rep. *Vida de Santa Teresa de Jesús* (Buenos Aires: Emecé Editores, 1946)

Secondary Sources

Adkins, Lisa, 'Introduction: Feminism, Bourdieu and After', in *Feminism After Bourdieu*, ed. Lisa Adkins and Beverley Skeggs (Oxford: Blackwell, 2004), 3–18

Ahlgren, Gillian T.W., *Teresa of Avila and the Politics of Sanctity* (Ithaca and London: Cornell University Press, 1996)

——, *Entering Teresa of Avila's 'Interior Castle': A Reader's Companion* (New York and Mahwah NJ: Paulist Press, 2005)

Albala, Ken, *Eating Right in the Renaissance* (Berkeley and London: University of California Press, 2002)

Anderson, Misty G., 'Living in a Material World: Margaret Cavendish's *The Convent of Pleasure*' in *Sensible Flesh: On Touch in Early Modern Culture*, ed. Elizabeth D Harvey (Philadelphia: University of Pennsylvania Press, 2003), 187–204

Andreadis, Harriette, *Sappho in Early Modern England: Female Same-Sex Literary Erotics, 1550–1714* (Chicago: Chicago University Press, 2001)

Arblaster, Paul, *Antwerp and the World: Richard Vestegan and the International Culture of Catholic Reformation* (Leuven: Leuven University Press, 2004)

Arenal, Electa and Stacey Schlau, 'Stratagems of the Strong, Stratagems of the Weak: Autobiographical Prose of the Seventeenth-Century Hispanic Convent', *Tulsa Studies in Women's Literature*, 9:1 (Spring 1990), 25–42

Ariew, Roger, 'Descartes and the Jesuits: Doubt, Novelty and the Eucharist', in Mordechaai Feingold ed., *Jesuit Science and the Republic of Letters* (Massachusetts, MIT: 2003), 157–96

Armstrong, Nancy and Leon Tennenhouse, 'The Literature of Conduct, the Conduct of Literature, and the Politics of Desire: An Introduction' in *The Ideology of Conduct: Essays in Literature and the History of Sexuality*, ed. Nancy Armstrong and Leon Tennenhouse (London and New York: Methuen, 1987), 1–24

Barbara, Anna and Anthony Perliss, *Invisible Architecture: Experiencing Places Through the Sense of Smell* (Milan: Skira, 2006)

Battigelli, Anna, *Margaret Cavendish and the Exiles of the Mind* (Kentucky: University Press of Kentucky, 1998) [1998a]

——, 'Political thought/political action: Margaret Cavendish's Hobbesian dilemma', in *Women Writers and the Early Modern British Political Tradition*, ed. Hilda L. Smith (Cambridge: Cambridge University Press, 1998), 40–55 [1998b]

Becker, Marvin B., *Civility and Society in Western Europe, 1300–1600* (Bloomington and Indianapolis: Indiana University Press, 1988)

Beilin, Elaine V., *Redeeming Eve: Women Writers of the English Renaissance* (Princeton, New Jersey: Princeton University Press, 1987)

Beneden, Ben van, 'Introduction', in *Royalist Refugees: William and Margaret Cavendish in the Rubens House, 1648–1660*, ed. Ben van Beneden and Nora de Poorter (Leuven: Rubenshuis & Rubenianum, 2006), 8–12

Benedict, Barbara, *Curiosity: A Cultural History of Early Modern Enquiry* (Chicago: University of Chicago Press, 2001)

Benjamin, Walter, *Illuminations*, trans. H. Zohn (London, 1973)

——, *Charles Baudelaire: A Lyric Poet in the Era of High Capitalism*, trans. Harry Zohn (London; Verso, 1983)

Benthien, Claudia, *Skin: On the Cultural Border Between Self and the World* (New York and Chichester: Columbia University Press, 2002)

Bhabha, Homi K., *The Location of Culture* (Routledge: London and New York, 1994)

Biernoff, Suzannah, *Sight and Embodiment in the Middle Ages* (New York: Palgrave Macmillan, 2002)

Bilinkoff, Jodi, 'Teresa of Jesus and Carmelite Reform, in *Religious Orders of the Catholic Reformation: Essays in Honor of John C. Olin on His Seventy-fifth Birthday*, ed. Richard L. DeMolen (New York: Fordham University Press, 1994), 165–86

——, 'Navigating the Waves (of Devotion): Towards a Gendered Analysis of Early Modern Catholicism' in *Crossing Boundaries: Attending to Early Modern Women*, ed. Jane Donawerth and Adele Seeff (Newark: University of Delaware Press, 2000), 161–72

——, *Related Lives: Confessors and Their Female Penitents, 1450–1750* (Ithaca and New York: Cornell University Press, 2005)

Blumenberg, Hans, 'Light as a Metaphor for Truth: At the Preliminary Stage of Philosophical Concept Formation' (1957), trans. Joel Anderson in *Modernity and the Hegemony of Vision*, ed. David Levin (Berkeley: University of California Press, 1993), 30–62

Boeckl, Christine M., 'Plague Imagery as Metaphor for Heresy in Rubens', *The Miracles of St Francis Xavier*', *The Sixteenth Century Journal*, 27:4 (Winter 1996), 979–95

Bonin, Erin Lang, 'Margaret Cavendish's Dramatic Utopias and the Politics of Gender', *Studies in English Literature*, 40:2 (2000), 339–54

Bora, Renu, 'Outing Texture' in *Novel Gazing: Queer Readings in Fiction*, ed. Eve Kosofsky Sedgwick (Durham NC: Duke University Press, 1997)

Bordo, Susan, *The Flight to Objectivity: Essays on Cartesianism and Culture* (Albany, NY: State University of New York Press, 1987)

Borthwick, Fiona, 'Olfaction and Taste: Invasive Odours and Disappearing Objects', *The Australian Journal of Anthropology*, 11:2, 2000, 127–40

Bound, Fay, *Emotion in Early Modern England, 1660–1760: Performativity and Practice at the Church Courts of York*, DPhil, University of York (May 2000)

Bourdieu, Pierre, *Outline of a Theory of Practice*, trans. Richard Nice (Cambridge: Cambridge University Press, 1977, rep. 1991)

Bowden, Caroline, 'Collecting the Lives of Early Modern Women Religious: Obituary Writing and the Development of Collective Memory and Corporate Identity', *Women's History Review*, 19:1, 2010, 7–20

——, 'Patronage and Practice: Assessing the Significance of the English Convents as Cultural Centres in Flanders in the Seventeenth Century', *English Studies*, 92:5, 2011, 483–95

——, ed., *English Convents in Exile, 1600–1800: Volume I: History Writing:* (London: Pickering & Chatto, 2012)

Boyle, Marjorie O'Rourke, *Senses of Touch: Human Dignity and Deformity from Michelangelo to Calvin* (Leiden: Brill, 1998)

Braddick, Michael, 'Introduction: The Politics of Gesture', in *The Politics of Gesture: Historical Perspectives*, ed. Michael Braddick (Oxford: Oxford University Press, 2009), 9–35

Brown, Judith, 'Everyday Life: Longevity and Nuns in Early Modern Florence' in *Renaissance Culture and the Everyday*, ed. Patricia Fulmerton and Simon Hunt (Philadelphia: University of Pennsylvania Press, 1999), 115–38

Brownlow, F.W., *Shakespeare, Harsnett and the Devils of Denham* (Newark: University of Delaware Press, 1993)

Bryson, Anna, *From Courtesy to Civility: Changing Codes of Conduct in Early Modern England* (Oxford: Clarendon Press, 1998)

Burkitt, Ian, *Social Selves: Theories of the Social Formation of Identity* (London, 1991)

Butler, Judith, *Excitable Speech: a Politics of the Performative* (New York and London: Routledge, 1997)

Bynum, Caroline Walker, *Holy Feast and Holy Fast: The Religious Significance of Food to Medieval Women* (Berkeley & Los Angeles: University of California Press, 1987)

——, *Fragmentation and Redemption: Essays on Gender and the Human Body in Medieval Religion* (New York: Zone Books, 1992)

Cahill, Patricia, 'Take Five: Renaissance Literature and the Study of the Senses', *Literature Compass*, 6:5 (2009), 1014–30

Caldwell, Mark, 'Hamlet and the Senses', Modern Language Quarterly 40.2 (1979), 135–55

Camporesi, Piero, *The Incorruptible Flesh: Bodily Mutation and Mortification in Religion and Folklore*, trans. Tania Croft-Murray and Helen Elsom (Cambridge: Cambridge University Press, 1988)

——, *Bread of Dreams: Food and Fantasy in Early Modern Europe*, trans. David Gentilcore (Cambridge: Polity Press, 1989)

Carrera, Elena, *Teresa of Avila's Autobiography: Authority, Power and the Self in Mid-Sixteenth-Century Spain* (London: Legenda, 2005)

Carruthers, Mary, 'Moving Images in the Mind's Eye' in *The Mind's Eye: Art and Theological Argument in the Middle Ages*, ed. Jeffrey H. Hamburger and Anne-Marie Bouche (Princeton: Princeton University Press, 2006), 287–305

de Certeau, Michel, *La Possession de Loudun* (Paris: Gallimard/ Julliard, 1970)

Chorpenning, Joesph F., 'St Joseph in the Spirituality of Teresa of Avila and of Francis de Sales: Convergences and Divergences' in *The Heirs of St Teresa of Avila: Defenders and Disseminators of the Founding Mother's Legacy*, ed. Christopher C. Wilson (Washington and Rome: Institute of Carmelite Studies, 2006), 123–40

Clairhout, Isabell and Sandro Jung, 'Cavendish's Body of Knowledge', *English Studies*, 92:7 (2011), 729–43

Clark, Stuart, *Thinking with Demons. The Idea of Witchcraft in Early Modern Europe* (Oxford: Oxford University Press, 1997, rep. 1999)

Clark, Stuart, *Vanities of the Eye: Vision in Early Modern European Culture* (Oxford: Oxford University Press, 2007)

Clarke, Danielle, 'The Iconography of the Blush: Marian Literature of the 1630s' in *Voicing Women: Gender and Sexuality in Early Modern Writing,* ed. Kate Chedzoy, Melanie Hansen and Suzanne Trill (Edinburgh: Edinburgh University Press, 1996, rep. 1998), 111–28

Classen, Constance, *Worlds of Sense: Exploring the Senses in History and Across Culture* (London and New York: Routledge, 1993)

——, 'The Witch's Senses: Sensory Ideologies and Transgressive Femininities from the Renaissance to Modernity' in *Empire of the Senses: The Sensual Culture Reader* ed. David Howes (Oxford and New York: Berg, 2005), 70–84

Claydon, Tony, *Europe and the Making of England, 1660–1760* (Cambridge: Cambridge University Press, 2007)

Clucas, Stephen, ed., *A Princely Brave Woman: Essays on Margaret Cavendish, Duchess of Newcastle* (Aldershot and Burlington VT: Ashgate, 2003)

Cockayne, Emily, 'Experiences of the Deaf in Early Modern England', *The Historical Journal*, 46:3 (2003), 493–510

Cockcroft, Robert, *Rhetorical Affect in Early Modern Writing: Renaissance Passions Reconsidered* (Basingstoke: Palgrave Macmillan, 2003)

Codina, Charlotte, David Buckley, Michael Port and Olivier Pascalis, 'Deaf and hearing children: a comparison of peripheral vision development', *Developmental Science*, 14:4, 2010, 725–37

Cohen, Ted, *Thinking of Others: On the Talent for Metaphor* (Princeton: Princeton University Press, 2008)

Connor, Steven, *Dumbstruck: A Cultural History of Ventriloquism* (Oxford: Oxford University Press, 2000)

——, *The Book of Skin* (London: Reaktion Books, 2004)

Coolahan, Marie-Louise, 'Identity Politics and Nuns' Writing', *Women's Writing*, 14:2 (August 2007), 306–20

Copeman, W.S.C., *Doctors and Disease in Tudor Times* (London: Dawson's of Pall Mall, 1960)

Corbin, Alain, *The Foul and the Fragrant: Odor and the French Social Imagination* (Leamington Spa, Hamburg, New York: Berg, 1986)

Craik, Katharine A., *Reading Sensations in Early Modern England* (Basingstoke: Palgrave Macmillan, 2007)

Crane, Mary Thomas, 'Marvell's Amazing Garden', in *Environment and Embodiment in Early Modern England*, ed. Mary Floyd-Wilson and Garrett A. Sullivan Jr. (Basingstoke: Palgrave Macmillan, 2007), 35–54

Cranefield, Paul F., 'On the Origin of the Phrase *Nihil Est in Intellectu Quod Non Prius Fuerit in Sensu*', *Journal of the History of Medicine and Allied Sciences*, 25: 1 (1970), 77–80

Crawford, Julie, 'Sidney's Sapphics and the Role of Interpretive Communities', *English Literary History*, 69.4 (2002), 979–1007

Crus, Anna J., 'Juana and her Sisters: Female Sexuality and Spirituality in Early Modern Spain', in *Recovering Spain's Feminist Tradition*, ed. Lisa Vollendorf (New York: Modern Language Association, 2001), 88–102

Cummings, Robert, 'Recent Studies in English Translation c1590–c1660, Part 2: Translations from Vernacular Languages', *English Literary Renaissance*, 39:1 (2009), 197–227

Daybell, James, 'Introduction: Rethinking Women and Politics in Early Modern England', in *Women and Politics in Early Modern England, 1450–1700*, ed. James Daybell (Aldershot and Burlington VT: Ashgate, 2004), 1–20

——, 'Scripting a Female Voice: Women's Epistolary Rhetoric in Sixteenth-Century Letters of Petition', *Women's Writing*, 13.1 (March 2006): 3–22

Dear, Peter, 'A Philosophical Duchess: Understanding Margaret Cavendish and the Royal Society', in *Science, Literature and Rhetoric in Early Modern England* (Aldershot and Burlington VT: Ashgate, 2007), 125–42

Diefendorf, Barbara D., *From Penitence to Charity: Pious Women and the Catholic Reformation in Paris* (Oxford: Oxford University Press, 2004)

——, 'Barbe Acarie and her Spiritual Daughters: Women's Spiritual Authority in Seventeenth-Century France' in *Female Monasticism in Early Modern Europe*, ed. Cordula van Wyhe (Aldershot and Burlington VT: Ashgate, 2008), 155–72

Dijkhuizen, Jan Frans van, 'Partakers of Pain: Religious Meanings of Pain in Early Modern England', in Jan Frans van Dijkhuizen and Karl AE Enenkel eds, *The Sense of Suffering: Constructions of Physical Pain in Early Modern Culture* (Leiden and Boston: Brill, 2009), 189–220

Dillon, Brian, 'At the MK', *London Review of Books*, 9 February 2012, 28

Dinshaw, Carolyn, *Getting Medieval: Sexualities and Communities, Pre- and Postmodern* (Duke University Press: Durham and London, 1999)

Dolan, Frances E., 'Reading, Work and Catholic Women's Biographies', *English Literary Renaissance*, 33:3 (November 2003), 328–57

——, *Whores of Babylon: Catholicism, Gender and Seventeenth-Century Print Culture* (Notre Dame, IN: University of Notre Dame Press, 1995, rep. 2005)

Duffin, Jacalyn, *Medical Miracles: Doctors, Saints and Healing in the Modern World* (Oxford: Oxford University Press, 2009)

Dugan, Holly, 'Scent of a Woman: Performing the Politics of Smell in Early Modern England', *The Journal of Medieval and Early Modern Studies*, 38:2 (2008), 229–52

——, 'Shakespeare and the Senses', *Literature Compass*, 6:3 (2009), 726–40

——, *The Ephemeral History of Perfume: Scent and Sense in Early Modern England* (Baltimore: The Johns Hopkins University Press, 2011)

Duncan-Jones, Katherine, *Sir Philip Sidney, Courtier Poet* (London: Hamish Hamilton, 1991)

Dunn, Marilyn, 'Spaces Shaped for Spiritual Perfection: Convent Architecture and Nuns in Early Modern Rome' in *Architecture and the Politics of Gender in Early Modern Europe*, ed. Helen Hills (Aldershot and Burlington VT, 2003), 151–76

Durrant, Michael, *Aristotle's 'De Anima' in Focus* (London and New York: Routledge, 1993)

Edden, Valerie, 'The Mantle of Elijah: Carmelite Spirituality in England in the Fourteenth Century', in *The Medieval Mystical Tradition in England, Ireland and Wales*, ed. Marion Glasscoe (Woodbridge: Boydell & Brewer, 1999)

Edwards, Jess, 'Thomas Hobbes, Charles Cotton and the "wonders" of the Derbyshire Peak', *Studies in Travel Writing*, 16:1 (2012), 1–15

Eire, Carlos M.N., *From Madrid to Purgatory: The Art and Craft of Dying in Sixteenth-Century Spain* (Cambridge: Cambridge University Press, 1995, rep. 2002)

Elias, Norbert, *The Civilizing Process: Sociogenetic and Psychogenetic Investigations*, trans. Edmund Jephcott (Oxford: Blackwell, 2000)

Emery, Kent, 'Mysticism and the Coincidence of Opposites in Sixteenth- and Seventeenth-Century France', *Journal of the History of Ideas*, 45:1 (Jan–Mar 1984), 3–23

——, *Renaissance Dialectic and Renaissance Piety: Benet of Canfield's 'Rule of Perfection'* (Binghampton, NY: Medieval and Renaissance Texts and Studies, 1987)

Ennis, Lambert, 'Anthony Nixon: Jacobean Plagiarist and Hack', *The Huntington Library Quarterly*, 3:4 (July 1940), 377–401

Felski, Rita, 'On Confession', (1989); rep. *Women, Autobiography, Theory*, ed. Sidonie Smith and Julia Watson (Madison and London: University of Wisconsin Press, 1998), 83–96

Filipczak, Zirka Z., 'Poses and Passions: Mona Lisa's "Closely Folded" Hands', *Reading the Early Modern Passions: Essays in the Cultural History of Emotion* ed., Gail Kern Paster, Katherine Rowe and Mary Floyd-Wilson (Philadelphia: University of Pennsylvania Press, 2004), 68–88

Findlay, Alison, *Playing Spaces in Early Women's Drama* (Cambridge: Cambridge University Press, 2006)

Fisher, Will, *Materializing Gender in Early Modern English Literature and Culture* (Cambridge: Cambridge University Press, 2006)

Fitzmaurice, James, 'Margaret Cavendish in Antwerp: the Actual and the Imaginary', *In-Between: Essays & Studies in Literary Criticism*, 9:1 and 2 (2000), 29–39

Flather, Amanda, *Gender and Space in Early Modern England* (Woodbridge and Rochester NY: Boydell Press, 2007)

Fletcher, Anthony, *Gender, Sex and Subordination in England, 1500–1800* (New Haven: Yale University Press, 1995)

Floyd-Wilson, Mary and Garrett A. Sullivan Jr., 'Introduction: Inhabiting the Body, Inhabiting the World', in *Environment and Embodiment in Early Modern England*, ed. Mary Floyd-Wilson and Garrett A. Sullivan Jr. (Basingstoke: Palgrave Macmillan, 2007), 1–13

Foucault, Michel, *The History of Sexuality*, trans. Robert Hurley, 2 volumes (New York: Vintage, 1990)

——, *The Archaeology of Knowledge* (Tavistock: London)

Frangenberg, Thomas and Robert Williams, eds, *The Beholder: The Experience of Art in Early Modern Europe* (Aldershot and Burlington VT: Ashgate, 2006)

Fratoni, Mark J., Review of David J. Kangas, *Kierkegaard's Instant: On Beginnings* (Bloomington and Indianapolis: Indiana University Press, 2007), *Janus Head*, 11(1), 2009

French, Philip, Review of *Into Great Silence*, *The Observer*, 31 December 2006

Gilchrist, Roberta, *Gender and Material Culture: The Archaeology of Religious Women* (London and New York: Routledge, 1994)

Goldberg, Jonathan, *Sodometries: Renaissance Texts, Modern Sexualities* (Stanford: Stanford University Press, 1992)

Gouk, Penelope and Helen Hills, 'Towards Histories of Emotions', in *Representing Emotions: New Connections in the Histories of Art, Music and Medicine*, ed. Penelope Gouk and Helen Hills (Aldershot and Burlington VT: Ashgate, 2005), 15–34

Gowing, Laura, *Common Bodies: Women, Touch and Power in Seventeenth-Century England* (New Haven: Yale University Press, 2003)

Greenblatt, Stephen, *Shakespearean Negotiations: The Circulation of Social Energy in Renaissance England* (Oxford: Clarendon Press, 1988)

Gregory, Adrian, *The Silence of Memory. Armistice Day 1919–1946* (Oxford and Providence, USA: Berg, 1994)

Groening, Philip, director, *Into Great Silence* (2007)

Guerer, Annick le, 'Olfaction and Cognition: A Philosophical and Psychoanalytic View', in *Olfaction, Taste and Cognition*, ed. Catherine Rouby (Cambridge: Cambridge University Press, 2002), 3–15

Guilday, Peter, *The English Catholic Refugees on the Continent 1558–1795. Volume I: The English Colleges and Convents in the Catholic Low Countries, 1558–1795* (London: Longmans, Green & Co, 1914)

Habermas, Jurgen, *The Structural Transformation of the Public Sphere: An Inquiry Into a Category of Bourgeois Society*, trans. Thomas Burger (Cambridge: Polity, 1962, rep. 1989)

Hallett, Nicky, '"fayre wordes brake neuer bone": Chaucer's Women', in *A Companion to Chaucer*, ed. Peter Brown (Oxford and Malden, Massachusetts: Blackwell, 2000, rep. 2001), 480–94

——, *Lives of Spirit: English Carmelite Self-Writing of the Early Modern Period* (Aldershot and Burlington VT: Ashgate, 2007) [2007a]

——, *Witchcraft, Exorcism and the Politics of Possession in a Seventeenth-Century Convent: How Sister Ursula was once bewiched and Sister Margaret twice* (Aldershot and Burlington VT: Ashgate, 2007) [2007b]

——, 'Paradise Postponed: the Nationhood of Nuns in the 1670s' in *Religion, Culture and the National Community in the 1670s*, ed. Tony Claydon and Tom Corns (University of Wales Press, 2011), 10–34

——, ed., *English Convents in Exile, 1600–1800: Volume 3: Life Writing I:* (London: Pickering & Chatto, 2012) [2012a]

——, 'Philip Sidney in the Cloister: The Reading Habits of English Nuns in Seventeenth-Century Antwerp, *Journal of Early Modern Cultural Studies*, 12:3 (July 2012), 88–116 [2012b]

——, '"So short a space of time": Early Modern Convent Chronology and Carmelite Spirituality', *Journal of Medieval and Early Modern Studies*, 42:3 (Fall 2012), 539–66 [2012c]

——, 'Shakespeare's Sisters: Anon and the Authors in Early Modern Convents', in *Communities, Culture and Identity: The English Convents in Exile, 1600–1800*, ed. Caroline Bowden and James Kelly (Ashgate, forthcoming)

Hamburger, Jeffrey F., *Nuns As Artists: The Visual Culture of a Medieval Convent* (Berkeley, Los Angeles and London: University of California Press, 1997)

——, *The Visual and the Visionary: Art and Female Spirituality in Late Medieval Germany* (New York: Zone Books, 1998)

——, 'The Place of Theology in Medieval Art History: Problems, Positions, Possibilities' in *The Mind's Eye: Art and Theological Argument in the Middle Ages*, ed. Jeffrey H. Hamburger and Anne-Marie Bouche (Princeton: Princeton University Press, 2006), 11–31

Hampton, Timothy, 'Strange Alteration: Physiology and Psychology from Galen to Rabelais' in *Reading the Early Modern Passions: Essays in the Cultural History of Emotion*, ed. Gail Kern Paster, Katherine Rowe and Mary Floyd-Wilson (Philadelphia: University of Pennsylvania Press, 2004), 272–96

Hannay, Margaret Patterson, ed., *Silent But For the Word: Tudor Women as Patrons, Translators and Writers of Religious Works* (Kent State, Ohio: Kent State University Press, 1985)

Hardman, Anne, *Life of the Venerable Anne of Jesus, Companion of St Teresa of Avila* (London: Sands, 1932)

——, *English Carmelites in Penal Times* (London: Burns, Oates & Washbourne, 1936)

—— *Mother Margaret Mostyn, Discalced Carmelite, 1625–1679* (London: Burns, Oates & Washbourne, 1937)

—— *Two English Carmelites: Mother Mary Xaveria Burton (1668–1714) and Mother Mary Margaret Wake (1617–78)* (London: Burns, Oates & Washbourne, 1939)

Harley, David, 'Mental Illness, Magical Medicine and the Devil in Northern England, 1650–1700', in Roger French and Andrew Wear, eds, *The Medical Revolution of the Seventeenth Century* (Cambridge, New York, Melbourne: Cambridge University Press, 1989), 114–44

Harting, Ursula, 'Inhabitants of Antwerp: *The civilest and best-behaved people that I ever saw*', in *Royalist Refugees: William and Margaret Cavendish in the Rubens House, 1648–1660*, ed. Ben van Beneden and Nora de Poorter (Leuven: Rubenshuis & Rubenianum, 2006), 63–9

Harvey, Barbara, *Living and Dying in England, 1100–1540: The Monastic Experience* (Oxford: Clarendon Press, 1993, rep. 1995)

Harvey, Elizabeth D., 'Introduction: The Sense of All Senses', in *Sensible Flesh: On Touch in Early Modern Culture*, ed. Elizabeth D. Harvey (Philadelphia: University of Pennsylvania Press, 2003), 1–21

Healy, Margaret, 'Anxious and Fatal Contacts: Taming the Contagious Touch', in *Sensible Flesh: On Touch in Early Modern Culture,* ed. Elizabeth D. Harvey (Philadelphia: University of Pennsylvania Press, 2003), 22–38

Heller-Roazen, Daniel, *Fortune's Faces: The 'Roman de la Rose' and the Poetics of Contingency* (Baltimore and London: Johns Hopkins University Press, 2003)

——, *Echolalias: On the Forgetting of Language* (New York: Zone Books, 2005)

——, *The Inner Touch: Archaeology of a Sensation* (New York: Zone Books, 2007)

Hillman, David and Carla Mazzio, 'Introduction: Individual Parts', in *The Body in Parts: Fantasies of Corporeality in Early Modern Europe*, ed. David Hillman and Carla Mazzio (New York and London: Routledge, 1997), x–xxix

Hills, Helen, 'Theorizing the Relationships Between Architecture and Gender in Early Modern Europe', in *Architecture and the Politics of Gender in Early Modern Europe*, ed. Helen Hills (Aldershot and Burlington VT, 2003), 3–22

——, *Invisible City: The Architecture of Devotion in Seventeenth-Century Neapolitan Convents* (Oxford: Oxford University Press, 2004)

——, 'Architecture and Effect: Leon Battista Alberti and Edification' in *Representing Emotions: New Connections in the Histories of Art, Music and*

Medicine, ed. Penelope Gouk and Helen Hills (Aldershot and Burlington VT: Ashgate, 2005), 89–108

——, 'Nuns and Relics: Spiritual Authority in Post-Tridentine Naples' in *Female Monasticism in Early Modern Europe*, ed. Cordula van Wyhe (Aldershot and Burlington VT: Ashgate, 2008), 11–38

Hollander, Anne, *Seeing Through Clothes* (New York: The Viking Press, 1975, rep. 1978)

Howells, Edward, *John of the Cross and Teresa of Avila: Mystical Knowing and Selfhood* (New York: Crossroad Publishing, 2002)

——, 'Relationality and Difference in the Mysticism of Pierre de Berulle', *Harvard Theological Review*, 102, 225–43

Howes, David, ed., *Empire of the Senses: The Sensual Culture Reader* (Oxford and New York: Berg, 2005)

Hull, Suzanne W., *Chaste, Silent & Obedient: English Books for Women, 1475–1640* (San Marino: Huntington Library, 1982, rep. 1988)

Hunter, Michael, *Boyle: Between God and Science* (New Haven and London: Yale University Press, 2009)

Hutton, Sarah, 'In dialogue with Hobbes: Margaret Cavendish's natural philosophy', *Women's Writing*, 4:3 (1997), 421–32

Huxley, Andrew, 'The *Aphorismi* and *A Discourse of Laws*: Bacon, Cavendish and Hobbes 1615–20', *The Historical Journal*, 47:2 (2004), 399–412

Irvine, Craig A., 'The Other Side of Silence: Levinas, Medicine and Literature', *Literature and Medicine*, 24:1 (Spring 2005), 8–18

Israel, Jonathan, *The Dutch Republic. Its Rise, Greatness and Fall, 1477–1806* (Oxford: Clarendon Press, 1995)

Jablonski, Nina G., *Skin: A Natural History* (Berkeley, Los Angeles and London, 2006)

Jackson, Ken and Arthur Marotti, 'The Turn to Religion in Early Modern Studies', *Criticism*, 46:1 (Winter 2004), 167–90

James, Susan, *Passion and Action: The Emotions in Seventeenth-Century Philosophy* (Oxford: Clarendon Press, 1997)

Jardine, Lisa, *Francis Bacon: Discovery and the Art of Discourse* (Cambridge: Cambridge University Press, 1974)

——, *Going Dutch: How England Plundered Holland's Glory* (London: Harper Perennial, 2009)

Jenkins, Eugenia Zuroski, 'Nature to Advantage Drest: Chinoiserie, Aesthetic Form and the Poetry of Subjectivity in Pope and Swift', *Eighteenth-Century Studies*, 43:1 (Fall 2009), 75–88

Jenner, Mark, 'Body, Image, Text in Early Modern Europe: Review essay', *The Society for the Social History of Medicine*, 12:1, 1999, 143–54

—— 'Civilization and Deodorization? Smell in Early Modern English Culture' in *Civil Histories: Essays Presented to Sir Keith Thomas*, ed. Peter Burke, Brian Harrison and Paul Slack (Oxford: Oxford University Press, 2000), 127–44

Jones, Ann Rosalind 'Nets and Bridles: Early Modern Conduct Books and Sixteenth-Century Women's Lyrics' in *The Ideology of Conduct: Essays in Literature and the History of Sexuality*, ed. Nancy Armstrong and Leon Tennenhouse (London and New York: Methuen, 1987), 39–72

Judovitz, Dalia, 'Georges de la Tour: the Enigma of the Visible' in *The Beholder: The Experience of Art in Early Modern Europe*, ed. Thomas Frangenberg and Robert Williams (Aldershot and Burlington VT: Ashgate, 2006), 143–63

Jütte, Robert, *A History of the Senses From Antiquity to Cyberspace* (Cambridge and Malden MA: Polity Press, 2005)

Kangas, David J., *Kierkegaard's Instant: On Beginnings* (Bloomington and Indianapolis: Indiana University Press, 2007)

Kelly, Erna, 'Playing with Religion: Convents, Cloisters, Martyrdom and Vows', *Early Modern Literary Studies*, 4:1 (May 2004), 1–24

Kiernan, Michael, ed., *The Oxford Francis Bacon: XV: The Essayes or Counsels, Civill and Morall* (Oxford: Oxford University Press, 1985, rep. 2000)

Kemp, Martin, 'The Handy Worke of the Incomprehensible Creator' in *Writing on Hands: Memory and Knowledge in Early Modern Europe* (Carlisle, PA: Dickinson College, 2000), 22–7

Kermode, Frank, 'The Banquet of Sense' in Frank Kermode, *Shakespeare, Spenser, Donne: Renaissance Essays* (London: Routledge & Kegan Paul, 1971), 84–115

——, 'Eliot and the Shudder', *London Review of Books*, 32:9 (13 May 2010), 13–16

Krueger, Lester E., 'Tactual perception in historical perspective: David Katz's world of touch' in *Tactual Perception: A Sourcebook*, ed. William Schiff and Emerson Foulke (Cambridge: Cambridge University Press, 1982), 1–54

Kuhns, Elizabeth, *The Habit: A History of the Clothing of Catholic Nuns* (New York and London: Doubleday, 2003)

Lakoff, George and Mark Johnson, *Metaphors We Live By* (Chicago: University of Chicago Press, 1980)

Lamb, Mary Ellen. 'Exhibiting Class and Displaying the Body in Sidney's Countess of Pembroke's *Arcadia*, *Studies in English Literature, 1500–1900*, 37.1 (Winter 1997), 52–72.

Latz, Dorothy L., *Glow-worm Light: Writings of Seventeenth-Century English Recusant Women: from Original Manuscripts (Elizabethan and Renaissance Studies)* (Salzburg: University of Salzburg, 1989)

Lawler, Steph, 'Rules of Engagement: Habitus, Power and Resistance' in *Feminism After Bourdieu*, ed. Lisa Adkins and Beverley Skeggs (Oxford: Blackwell, 2004), 110–28

Lederer, David, *Madness, Religion and the State in Early Modern Europe* (Cambridge: Cambridge University Press, 2006)

Lederman, Susan J., 'The Perception of Texture by Touch', in *Tactual Perception: A Sourcebook*, ed. William Schiff and Emerson Foulke (Cambridge: Cambridge University Press, 1982), 130–67

Lehfeldt, Elizabeth A., 'Spatial Discipline and its Limits: Nuns and the Built Environment in Early Modern Spain' in *Architecture and the Politics of Gender in Early Modern Europe*, ed. Helen Hills (Aldershot and Burlington VT, 2003), 131–50

Lehmann, Gilly, *The British Housewife: Cookery-Books, Cooking and Society in 18th Century Britain* (London: Prospect Books, 2003)

Levinas, Emmanuel, *Totality and Infinity: An Essay on Exteriority*, trans. Alphonso Lingis (Pittsburgh PA: Duquesne University Press, 1969)

Lewalski, Barbara K., 'Milton and Idolatry', *Studies in English Literature, 1500–1900*, 43.1 (2003), 213–32

Lindquist, Sherry C.M., 'Women in the Charterhouse: the Liminality of Cloistered Spaces at the Chartreuse de Champmol in Dijon', in *Architecture and the Politics of Gender in Early Modern Europe*, ed. Helen Hills (Aldershot and Burlington VT, 2003), 177–92

Loxley, James, '"Not Sure of Safety": Hobbes and Exile', in Philip Major, ed., *Literatures of Exile in the English Revolution and its Aftermath, 1640–1690* (Farnham and Burlington VT: Ashgate, 2010), 133–51

Luckyj, Christina, *A Moving Rhetoricke: Gender and Silence in Early Modern England* (Manchester: Manchester University Press, 2002)

Lux-Sterritt, Laurence, *Redefining Female Religious Life: French Ursulines and English Ladies in Seventeenth-Century Catholicism* (Aldershot and Burlington VT: Ashgate, 2005)

——, ed., *English Convents in Exile, 1600–1800: Volume 2: Spirituality* (London: Pickering & Chatto, 2012)

—— and Carmen M. Mangion, eds, *Gender, Catholicism and Spirituality* (Basingstoke: Palgrave Macmillan, 2011)

McCann, Justin and Hugh Connolly, *Memorials of Father Augustine Baker and Other Documents Relating to the English Benedictines* (Leeds: Catholic Record Society, 1933)

MacKendrick, Karmen, 'The Multipliable Body', advance online publication of essay for *Postmedieval: a Journal of Medieval Cultural Studies*, 9 February 2010 [www.palgrave-journals.com/pmed/: accessed 24 March 2010]

McNay, Lois, 'Agency and Experience: Gender as a Lived Relation', in *Feminism After Bourdieu*, ed. Lisa Adkins and Beverley Skeggs (Oxford: Blackwell, 2004), 175–90

Major, Philip ed., *Literatures of Exile in the English Revolution and its Aftermath, 1640–1690* (Farnham and Burlington VT: Ashgate, 2010)

Malcolm, Noel, 'A Summary Bibliography of Hobbes', in *Cambridge Companion to Hobbes*, ed. Tom Sorell (Cambridge: Cambridge University Press, 1996, rep. 1999), 13–44

——, 'Charles Cotton, translator of Hobbes' *De Cive*', *Huntington Library Quarterly*, 61:2 (1999/2000), 259–87

Mansfield, Brocard, 'Father Paul Brown OCD, 1598–1671', *Dublin Historical Review*, 37:2 (March 1984), 54–8

Marotti, Arthur F., 'Alienating Catholics in Early Modern England: Recusant Women, Jesuits and Ideological Fantasies' in *Catholicism and Anti-Catholicism in Early Modern English Texts*, ed. Arthur Marotti (Basingstoke: Macmillan, 1999), 1–34

——, ed., *Gertrude More, The Early Modern Englishwoman: A Facsimile Library of Essential Works*, Series 2, Printed Writings 1641–1670, Part IV, Volume 3 (Aldershot and Burlington VT: Ashgate, 2009)

Martinich, Aloysius, *Hobbes: A Biography* (Cambridge: Cambridge University Press, 1999)

Mason, Mary G., 'The Other Voice: Autobiographies of Women Writers' in James Olney, ed. *Autobiography: Essays Theoretical & Critical* (Princeton University Press, 1980), 207–35

Matthews, Steven, *Theology and Science in the Thought of Francis Bacon* (Farnham and Burlington VT: Ashgate, 2008)

Mazzio, Carla, 'Sins of the Tongue' in *The Body in Parts: Fantasies of Corporeality in Early Modern Europe*, ed. David Hillman and Carla Mazzio (New York and London: Routledge, 1997), 53–80

——, 'Staging the Vernacular: Language and Nation in Thomas Kyd's *The Spanish Tragedy*', *Studies in English Literature, 1500–1900*, 38:2 (Spring 1998), 207–32

——, 'Acting with Tact; Touch and Theater in the Renaissance', in *Sensible Flesh: On Touch in Early Modern Culture*, ed. Elizabeth D. Harvey (Philadelphia: University of Pennsylvania Press, 2003), 159–86

——, 'The Senses Divided: Organs, Objects and Media in Early Modern England', in *Empire of the Senses: The Sensual Culture Reader*, ed. David Howes (Oxford and New York: Berg, 2005), 85–105

Medwick, Cathleen, *Teresa of Avila* (London: Duckworth, 1999)

Mendelson, Sara H., 'The Civility of Women in Seventeenth-Century England', in *Civil Histories: Essays Presented to Sir Keith Thomas*, ed. Peter Burke (Oxford: Oxford University Press, 2000), 111–25

—— 'Concocting the World's Olio: Margaret Cavendish and Continental Influence', *Early Modern Literary Studies*, 4:1 (May 2004), 1–34

Merleau-Ponty, Maurice, *Le Visible et l'Invisible, Suivi de Notes de Travail*, ed. Claude Lefort (Paris: Gallimard, 1964)

——, *Phenomenology of Perception*, trans. Colin Smith (London and New York: Routledge, 1996)

Merton, Thomas, 'Self-Knowledge in Gertrude More and Augustine Baker', in *Mystics and Zen Masters*, ed. Thomas Merton (New York: Dell, 1967), 154–77

Miller, Jacqueline T., 'The Passion Signified: Imitation and the Construction of Emotions in Sidney and Wroth', *Criticism*, 43:4 (2001), 407–21

Milner, Matthew, *The Senses and the English Reformation* (Farnham and Burlington VT: Ashgate, 2011)

Monson, Craig, 'Disembodied Voices: Music in the Nunneries of Bologna in the Midst of the Counter-Reformation' in *The Crannied Wall: Women, Religion and the Arts in Early Modern Europe* (Ann Arbor: The University of Michigan Press, 1992) ed. Craig Monson, 191–209

Morrissey, Mary and Gillian Wright, 'Piety and Sociability in Early Modern Women's Letters', *Women's Writing*, 13.1 (March 2006), 44–59

Mujica, Barbara, 'Beyond Image: The Apophatic-Kataphatic Dialect in Teresa de Avila', *Hispania,* 84:4 (December 2001), 741–48

——, *Teresa de Avila: Lettered Woman* (Nashville: Vanderbilt University Press, 2009)

Muldrew, Craig, *Food, Energy and the Creation of Industriousness: Work and Material Culture in Agrarian England, 1550–1780* (Cambridge and New York: Cambridge University Press, 2010)

Mulherron, Jamie and Helen Wyld, 'Mortlakes Banquet of the Senses', *Apollo*, March 2012: http://www.apollo-magazine.com/features/7665388/mortlakes-banquet-of-thesenses.thtml [accessed 2 January 2013]

Neill, Michael, 'Amphitheaters in the Body: Playing with Hands on the Shakespearean Stage', *Shakespeare Survey 48: Shakespeare and Cultural Exchange*, ed. Stanley Wells (Cambridge: Cambridge University Press, 1995), 23–50

——, 'Physicke from another Body', *London Review of Books*, 1 December 2011, 13–16

Netzloff, Mark, 'The English Colleges and the English Nation: Allen, Persons, Verstegan and Diasporic Nationalism' in *Catholic Culture in Early Modern England*, ed. Corthell, Ronald, Frances E. Dolan, Christopher Highley and Arthur F. Marotti (Notre Dame, IN: University of Notre Dame Press, 2007), 236–60

Nordenfalk, Carl, 'The Five Senses in Late Medieval and Renaissance Art', *Journal of the Warburg and Courtauld Institutes*, 48 (1985), 1–22

Norman, Marion, 'Dame Gertrude More and the English Mystical Tradition', *Recusant History*, 13 (1975/6), 196–211

Orlin, Lena Cowen, 'Three Ways to be Invisible in the Renaissance: Sex, Reputation and Stitchery', in *Renaissance Culture and the Everyday*, ed. Patricia Fulmerton and Simon Hunt (Philadelphia: University of Pennsylvania Press, 1999), 183–203

Pallasmaa, Juhani, *The Eyes of the Skin: Architecture and the Senses* (Chichester: John Wiley & Sons, 2005)

Palmer, Richard, 'In Bad Odour: Smell and its Significance in Medicine From Antiquity to the Seventeenth Century' in *Medicine and the Five Senses*, ed. W.F. Bynum and Roy Porter (Cambridge: Cambridge University Press, 1993), 61–8

Park, Katharine, *Secrets of Women: Gender, Generation and the Origins of Human Dissection* (New York: Zone Books, 2006)

Paster, Gail Kern, *Humoring the Body: Emotions and the Shakespearean Stage* (Chicago and London: University of Chicago Press, 2004)

——, Katherine Rowe and Mary Floyd-Wilson, 'Introduction: Reading Early Modern Passions', in *Reading the Early Modern Passions. Essays in the*

Cultural History of Emotion, ed. Gail Kern Paster, Katherine Rowe and Mary Floyd-Wilson (Philadelphia: University of Pennsylvania Press, 2004), 1–20

Pinkard, Susan, *A Revolution in Taste: the Rise of French Cuisine, 1650–1800* (Cambridge: Cambridge University Press, 2009)

Pohl, Nicole, *Women, Space and Utopia, 1600–1800* (Aldershot and Burlington VT: Ashgate, 2006)

Ranum, Orest, 'The Refuge of Intimacy' in *A History of Private Life: III: Passions of the Renaissance*, ed. Roger Chartier (Cambridge MA and London: The Belknap Press of Harvard University Press, 1989), 207–63

Raylor, Timothy, '"Pleasure Reconciled to Virtue": William Cavendish, Ben Jonson and the Decorative Scheme of Bolsover Castle', *Renaissance Quarterly*, 52:2 (Summer 1999), 402–39

Rees, Emma, *Margaret Cavendish: Gender, Genre, Exile* (Manchester and New York: Manchester University Press, 2003)

Richards, Jennifer, *Rhetoric and Courtliness in Early Modern England* (Cambridge: Cambridge University Press, 2003)

Riddy, Felicity, 'Publication before Print: the Case of Julian of Norwich', in *The Uses of Script and Print, 1300–1700*, ed. Julia Crick and Alexandra Walsham (Cambridge: Cambridge University Press, 2004), 29–49

Rindisbacher, Hans J., *The Smell of Books: A Cultural Historical Study of Olfactory Perception in Books* (Ann Arbor: University of Michigan Press, 1992)

Robson, Mark, *The Sense of Early Modern Writing: Rhetoric, Poetics and Aesthetics* (Manchester and New York: Manchester University Press, 2006)

Roper, Lyndal, *Oedipus and the Devil: Witchcraft, Sexuality and Religion in Early Modern Europe* (London and New York: Routledge, 1994)

Rowe, Erin Kathleen, 'The Spanish Minerva: Imagining Teresa of Avila as Patron Saint in Seventeenth-Century Spain', *The Catholic Historical Review*, 92: 4 (October 2006), 574–96

Rowe, Katherine, 'God's Handy Worke', in *The Body in Parts: Fantasies of Corporeality in Early Modern Europe,* ed. David Hillman and Carla Mazzio (New York and London: Routledge, 1997), 285–312

——, *Dead Hands: Fictions of Agency, Renaissance to Modern* (Stanford: Stanford University Press, 1999)

Sarasohn, Lisa T., 'A Science Turned Upside Down: Feminism and the Natural Philosophy of Margaret Cavendish', *Huntington Library Quarterly*, 47:4 (Autumn 1984), 289–307

——, 'Thomas Hobbes and the Duke of Newcastle: A Study in the Mutuality of Patronage before the Establishment of the Royal Society', *Isis*, 90: 4 (December 1999), 715–37 [1999a]

——, 'Margaret Cavendish and Patronage', *Endeavour*, 23:3 (1999), 130–32 [1999b]

——, *The Natural Philosophy of Margaret Cavendish* (Baltimore: Johns Hopkins University Press, 2010)

——, 'Margaret Cavendish, William Newcastle and Political Marginalization', *English Studies*, 92:7 (2011), 806–17

Sawday, Jonathan, *The Body Emblazoned: Dissection and the Human Body in Renaissance Culture* (New York and London: Routledge, 1995)

Scarry, Elaine, *The Body in Pain: The Making and Unmaking of the World* (New York and Oxford: Oxford University Press, 1985)

Schmid, Letizia, 'The Evaporating Subject' in *Invisible Architecture: Experiencing Places Through the Sense of Smell*, ed. Anna Barbara and Anthony Perliss (Milan: Skira, 2006), 116

Sedgwick, Eve Kosofsky, *Touching Feeling: Affect, Pedagogy, Performativity* (Durham NC and London: Duke University Press, 2003)

Seguin, Colleen M., 'Cures and Controversy in Early Modern Wales: The Struggle to Control St Winifred's' Well', *North American Journal of Welsh Studies*, 3:2 (Summer 2003), 1–17

Semler, L.E., 'Margaret Cavendish's Early Engagement with Descartes and Hobbes: Philosophical Revisitation and Poetic Selection', *Intellectual History Review*, 22:3 (2012), 327–53

Serres, Michel, *The Five Senses: A Philosophy of Mingled Bodies (I)*, trans. Margaret Sankey and Peter Cowley (London and New York: Continuum, 1998)

Shell, Alison, *Catholicism, Controversy and the English Literary Imagination, 1558–1660* (Cambridge: Cambridge University Press, 1999)

——, *Oral Culture and Catholicism in Early Modern England* (Cambridge: Cambridge University Press, 2008)

Sherman, Claire Richter, *Writing on Hands: Memory and Knowledge in Early Modern Europe* (Carlisle, PA: Dickinson College, 2000)

Shuger, Debora, *Habits of Thought in the English Renaissance: Religion, Politics and the Dominant Culture* (Berkeley: University of California Press, 1990)

—— 'The I of the Beholder: Renaissance Mirrors and the Reflexive Mind' in *Renaissance Culture and the Everyday*, ed. Patricia Fulmerton and Simon Hunt (Philadelphia: University of Pennsylvania Press, 1999), 21–41

Siegel, R.E., *Galen on Sense Perception* (New York: S. Karger, 1970)

Siegfried, B.R., 'The City of Chance, or, Margaret Cavendish's Theory of Radical Symmetry', *Early Modern Literary Studies*, 9:1 (May 2004), 1–29

Simpson, James, 'Confessing Literature', *English Language Notes*, 44 (2006), 121–6

Slade, Carole A., *St Teresa of Avila: Author of a Heroic life* (Berkeley, Los Angeles and London: University of California Press, 1995)

——, 'Este gran Dios de las Cavalleries: [This Great God of Chivalric Deeds] St Teresa's Performances of the Novels of Chivalry' in *The Vernacular Spirit: Essays on Medieval Religious Literature*, ed. Renate Blumenfeld-Kosinski, Duncan Robertson and Nancy Bradley Warren (Basingstoke and New York, 2002), 297–316

Smith, Bruce R., 'Hearing Green' in *Reading the Early Modern Passions: Essays in the Cultural History of Emotion*, ed. Gail Kern Paster, Katherine Rowe and Mary Floyd-Wilson (Philadelphia: University of Pennsylvania Press, 2004), 147–68

Smith, Geoffrey, *The Cavaliers in Exile* (Basingstoke: Palgrave Macmillan, 2003)

Smith, Mark M., 'Producing Sense, Consuming Sense, Making Sense: Perils and Prospects of Sensory History', *Journal of Social History* 40:4 (Summer 2007), 841–58 [2007a]

——, *Sensory History* (Oxford and New York: Berg, 2007) [2007b]

Sorell, Tom, ed., *Cambridge Companion to Hobbes* (Cambridge: Cambridge University Press, 1996, rep. 1999)

Spiller, Elizabeth A., 'Speaking for the Dead: King Charles, Anna Weamys and the Commemorations of Sir Philip Sidney's *Arcadia*', *Criticism*, 42.2 (Spring 2000), 229–51

Spinnenweber, Kathleen T, 'The 1611 English Translation of St Teresa's Autobiography: A Possible Carmelite-Jesuit Collaboration', *SKASE: Journal of Translation and Interpretation*, 2:1 (2007): http://www.skase.sk/Volumes/JT102/pdf_doc/1.pdf [accessed 6 January 2010]

Stallybrass, Peter, 'Patriarchal territories: The Body Enclosed', in Margaret W. Ferguson and Maureen Quilligan eds, *Rewriting the Renaissance. The Discourses of Sexual Difference in Early Modern Europe* (Chicago and London: University of Chicago Press, 1981), 123–44

Starobinski, Jean, 'The Natural and Literary History of Bodily Sensation' in *Fragments for a History of the Human Body: Part II*, ed. Michel Feher (New York: Zone, 1989) 351–405

Stewart, Susan, *Poetry and the Fate of the Senses* (Chicago, IL: University of Chicago Press, 2002)

——, 'Remembering the Senses' in *Empire of the Senses: The Sensual Culture Reader*, ed. David Howes (Oxford and New York: Berg, 2005, 59–69

Sugg, Richard, 'Good Physic But Bad Food: Early Modern Attitudes to Medicinal Cannibalism and its Suppliers', *Social History of Medicine*, 19:2, 2006, 225–40

Summers, David, *The Judgement of Sense: Renaissance Naturalism and the Rise of Aesthetics* (Cambridge: Cambridge University Press, 1987)

Summit, Jennifer, 'From Anchorhold to Closet: Julian of Norwich in 1670 and the Immanence of the Past' in *Julian of Norwich's Legacy: Medieval Mysticism and Post-Medieval Reception*, ed. Sarah Salih and Denise N. Baker (Basingstoke and New York: Palgrave Macmillan, 2009), 29–48

Thøfner, Margit, 'How to Look Like a (Female) Saint: The Early Iconography of St Teresa of Avila' in *Female Monasticism in Early Modern Europe*, ed. Cordula van Wyhe (Aldershot and Burlington VT: Ashgate, 2008), 59–80

Tilmouth, Christopher, *Passion's Triumph Over Reason: A History of the Moral Imagination from Spenser to Rochester* (Oxford: Oxford University Press, 2007)

Traub, Valerie, *The Renaissance of Lesbianism in Early Modern England* (Cambridge: Cambridge University Press, 2002)

Travitsky Betty and Anne Lake Prescott, eds., *Female and Male Voices in Early Modern England: An Anthology of Renaissance Writing* (New York: Columbia University Press, 2000)

Tumbleson, Raymond D., *Catholicism in the English Protestant Imagination* (Cambridge: Cambridge University Press, 1998)

Tyler, Peter, *St John of the Cross* (London and New York: Continuum, 2010)

——, *The Return to the Mystical: Ludwig Wittgenstein, Teresa of Avila and the Christian Mystical Tradition* (London and New York: Continuum, 2011)

Vander Motten, J.P. and Katrien Daemen-de Gelder, '"The Times Are Dangerous": An Unnoticed Allusion to William Cavendish's The Variety (1641–42', *American Notes and Queries*, 21:3 (Summer 2008), 35–41

——, 'Sir Toby Matthew and His "Fides Achates" George Gage, 1607–1620', *American Notes and Queries* 23:1 (January/March 2010), 20–31

——, 'A Cloistered Entrepôt: Sir Tobie Matthew and the English Carmel in Antwerp', *English Studies*, 92:5 (2011), 548–61

Vingt, Louise, *The Five Senses: Studies in a Literary Tradition* (Lund, Sweden: Liuber Laromedal, 1975)

Walker, Claire, 'Combining Martha and Mary: Gender and Work in Seventeenth-Century English Cloisters', *Sixteenth Century Journal*, 30: 2 (1999), 397–418

——, 'Prayer, Patronage and Political Conspiracy: English Nuns and the Restoration', *The Historical Journal*, 43:1 (2000), 1–23

——, 'Doe not suppose me a well mortified Nun dead to the world: Letter-Writing in Early Modern Convents' in *Early Modern Women's Letter Writing, 1450–1700*, ed. James Daybell (Basingstoke: (Palgrave Macmillan, 2001), 159–76

——, *Gender and Politics in Early Modern Europe: English Convents in France and the Low Countries* (Basingstoke: Palgrave Macmillan, 2003)

——, 'Loyal and Dutiful Subjects: English Nuns and Stuart Politics', in *Women and Politics in Early Modern England, 1450–1700*, ed. James Daybell (Aldershot and Burlington VT: Ashgate, 2004), 228–42

—— 'Securing Souls or Telling Tales? The Politics of Cloistered Life in an English Convent' in *Female Monasticism in Early Modern Europe*, ed. Cordula van Wyhe (Aldershot and Burlington VT: Ashgate, 2008), 227–44

Walter, John, 'Gesturing at Authority: Deciphering the Gestural Code of Early Modern England', in *The Politics of Gesture: Historical Perspectives*, ed. Michael Braddick (Oxford: Oxford University Press, 2009), 96–143

Ward, Patricia A., 'Madame Guyon and Experiential Theology in America', *Church History*, 67:3 (September 1998), 484–98

Warren, David H., 'The development of haptic perception', in *Tactual Perception: A Sourcebook*, ed. William Schiff and Emerson Foulke (Cambridge: Cambridge University Press, 1982), 82–129

Warren, Nancy Bradley, 'Incarnational (Auto)biography' in *Oxford Twenty-First Century Approaches to Literature*, ed. Paul Strohm (Oxford: Oxford University Press, 2007), 369–85

——, *The Embodied Word: Female Spiritualities, Contested Orthodoxies and English Religious Cultures, 1350–1700* (Notre Dame, IN: University of Notre Dame Press, 2010)

Watson, Nicholas, 'Desire for the Past', *Studies in the Age of Chaucer*, 1999, 59–97

Watson, Nicholas and Jenkins, Jacqueline, eds, *The Writings of Julian of Norwich: A Vision Showed to a Devout Woman and a Revelation of Love* (Pennsylvania: Penn State Press, 2006)

Wear, Andrew, *Knowledge and Practice in English Medicine, 1550–1680* (Cambridge: Cambridge University Press, 2000)

Weber, Alison, *Teresa of Avila and the Rhetoric of Femininity* (Princeton, NJ: Princeton University Press, 1990)

——, 'Spiritual Administration: Gender and Discernment in the Carmelite Reform', *The Sixteenth Century Journal*, 31:1 (Spring 2000), 123–46

——, 'The Partial Feminism of Ana de San Bartolome' in *Recovering Spain's Feminist Tradition*, ed. Lisa Vollendorf (New York: Modern Language Association, 2001), 68–87

——, 'Introduction', *Book for the Hour of Recreation* (Chicago and London: University of Chicago Press, 2002), 1–26

Webster, Erin, 'Margaret Cavendish's Socio-Political Interventions into Descartes' Philosophy', *English Studies*, 92:7 (2011), 711–28

Weddle, Saundra, 'Women in Wolves' Mouths: Nuns' Reputations, Enclosure and Architecture at the Convent of the Le Murate in Florence', in *Architecture and the Politics of Gender in Early Modern Europe*, ed. Helen Hills (Aldershot and Burlington VT, 2003), 115–30

Wekking, Ben, ed. Augustine Baker O.S.B., *The Life and Death of Dame Gertrude More* (Salzburg: Institut fur Anglistik und Amerikanistik, University of Salzburg, 2002)

Weiner, Andrew D., *Sir Philip Sidney and the Poetics of Protestantism: A Study of Contexts* (Minneapolis: University of Minnesota Press, 1978)

Weld-Blundell, Benedict, ed., *The Inner Life and the Writings of Dame Gertrude More*, 2 Volumes, 1658 (London: Wasbourne, 1910)

Westphal, Merold, *Becoming A Self: A Reading of Kierkegaard's 'Concluding Unscientific Postscript'* (West Lafayette IN: Purdue University Press, 1996)

White, Helen C., *English Devotional Literature (Prose), 1600–1640* (Madison: University of Wisconsin Studies, 1931)

White, Roger M., *Talking About God: The Concept of Analogy and the Problem of Religious Language* (Aldershot and Burlington VT: Ashgate, 2010)

Wiesner, Merry E., *Women and Gender in Early Modern Europe* (Cambridge: Cambridge University Press 1993, repr. 1995)

Williams, Rowan, *Teresa of Avila* (London: Continuum, 1991, rep. 2003)

Wilson, Christopher C., 'Taking Teresian Authority to the Front Lines: Ana de San Bartolome and Ana de Jesus in the Art of the Spanish Netherlands' in *The Heirs of St Teresa of Avila: Defenders and Disseminators of the Founding Mother's legacy*, ed. Christopher C Wilson (Washington DC and Rome: ICS Publications, 2006), 72–106

Winston-Allen, Anne, *Convent Chronicles: Women Writing About Women and Reform in the Late Middle Ages* (Pennsylvania: Pennsylvania State University Press, 2004)

Wolfe, Heather, 'Reading Bells and Loose Papers: Reading and Writing Practices of the English Benedictine Nuns of Cambrai and Paris', in *Early Modern Women's Manuscript Writing: Selected Papers from the Trinity/ Trent Colloquium*, ed. Victoria E. Burke and Jonathan Gibson (Aldershot and Burlington VT: Ashgate, 2004), 135–56

——,'Dame Barbara Constable: Catholic Antiquarian, Advisor and Closet Missionary', in *Catholic Culture in Early Modern England,* ed. Ronald Corthell, Frances E. Dolan, Christopher Highley and Arthur F. Marotti (Notre Dame, IN: University of Notre Dame Press, 2007), 158–88

Wood, David Houston, *Time, Narrative and Emotion in Early Modern England* (Farnham and Burlington VT: Ashgate, 2009

Woodhouse, R.S., *Descartes, Spinoza, Leibniz: The Concept of Substance in Seventeenth Century Metaphysics* (London and New York: Routledge, 1993, rep. 2002)

Woods, A.T., and E. Poloakoff, D.M. Lloyd, J. Keunzel, R. Hodson, H. Gonda, J. Batchelor, G.B. Dijksterhuis and A. Thomas, 'Effect of background noise on food perception', *Food Quality and Preference*, 2010

Woods, Gillian, *Shakespeare's Unreformed Fictions* (Oxford: Oxford University Press, forthcoming)

Woolgar, C.M., *The Senses in Late Medieval England* (New Haven and London: Yale University Press, 2006)

Wootton, David, *Bad Medicine: Doctors doing Harm Since Hippocrates* (Oxford: Oxford University Press, 2006, rep. 2007)

Worsley, Lucy and Tom Addyman, 'Riding Houses and Horses: William Cavendish's Architecture for the Art of Horsemanship', *Architectural History*, 45 (2002), 194–229

Wyhe, Cordula van, 'The Idea Vitae Teresianae (1687): The Teresian Mystic Life and Its Visual representation in the Low Countries', in *Female Monasticism in Early Modern Europe*, ed. Cordula van Wyhe (Aldershot and Burlington VT: Ashgate, 2008), 173–210

Wynne-Davies, Marion, 'Suicide at the Elephant and Castle, or did the lady vanish? Alternative endings for early modern women writers', in *Region, Religion and Patronage: Lancastrian Shakespeare*, ed. Richard Dutton, Alison Findlay and Richard Wilson (Manchester and New York: Manchester University Press, 2003), 123–42

Yates, Frances A., *The Art of Memory* (Harmondsworth: Penguin, 1966, rep. 1978)

Zlomislic, Marko, *Jacques Derrida's Aporetic Ethics* (Plymouth: Lexington Books, 2007)

Index